Notes from the Publisher

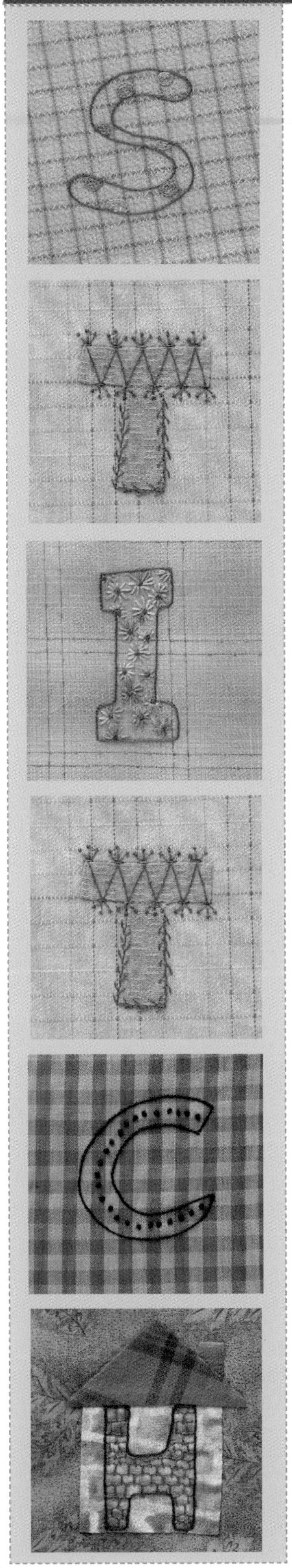

Welcome to a glimpse into the world of international quilting and handwork. At Stitch Publications our wish is for you to be able to explore beyond the boundaries of the country you live in to experience and see what other fiber artists are doing.

In many countries, rather than learning from various books, quilters and crafters study under a single master, spending years progressing from simple techniques to the extremely difficult. Intricate designs are celebrated and sewing, embroidery and quilting by hand is honored, and as such, appliqué, embroidery and quilting by hand is the typical method used to quilt.

This book was written in its original language, Japanese, by a master quilter, Yoko Saito. We have done our best to make the directions for each embroidery project easy to understand, and fairly easy to figure out if you have some level of quilting experience for the "patchwork embroidery" projects, while maintaining the appearance and intent of the original author and publisher.

We hope the beautifully designed handmade items in this book inspire and encourage you to make them for yourself.

- Important Tips Before You Begin -

The embroidery designs and patterns are relatively simple and self-explanatory. For beginners, to those who are most advanced in embroidery skills, there should be no problem doing the embroidery. When it comes to the "patchwork embroidery" projects, such as the quilted bags, wall hangings, etc., the following facts might suggest that intermediate or advanced quilters will be more comfortable working on these projects.

- Techniques -

The techniques used for embroidery and "patchwork embroidery" are detailed from pages 180~189. Each of the individual embroidery patterns are from pages 6~179. In this book, Ms. Saito has designed a number of projects that combine patchwork and embroidery. These quilted projects are somewhat more challenging. The patterns and project instructions are located on pages 191~223. For these, she assumes that the creator is familiar with sewing, quilting and bag-making techniques to some degree and thus relies heavily on the creator's ability to figure out the directions that are not specifically written out. It is advisable to read through and understand each project's direction page from beginning to end, including finding the corresponding patterns on the included pattern sheet before beginning.

- Measurements -

The original designs were created using the metric system for dimensions. In order to assist you, we have included the imperial system measurements in brackets. However, please note that samples that appear in the book were created and tested using the metric system. Thus, you will find that if you use the imperial measurements to make the projects, the items you make will not be exactly the same size as when using the metric measurements.

- Patterns/Templates -

Full pattern information for the embroidery designs will be from pages 6~179 and the pattern will be shown next to the completed sample. Full pattern information for each patchwork embroidery project appears in several different ways: a) in the materials list b) in the illustrations and captions c) in the pattern sheet insert. One must read through all the instructions carefully to understand what size to cut the fabric and related materials, including instructions for each project relating to seam allowances.

Stitch Publications, 2013

120 Original Embroidery Designs

by Yoko Saito

Includes 20 patchwork embroidery projects with instructions.

Stitch
PUBLICATIONS

Introduction

This is the third book in a series in which I have designed original quilt blocks, appliqués and now embroidery patterns. I very much wanted to design patterns that were specifically made to be embroidered on patchwork and quilted items, as opposed to traditional French embroidery or cross stitch where the design is paramount.

I used the simple outline stitch for the majority of the patterns, along with the french knot and straight stitch and others. However, in keeping with this notion of "patchwork embroidery," the selection of the background fabric is equally as essential as the embroidery design itself, where embroidery adds a three dimensional aspect that can't be achieved by fabric alone. The feeling that is evoked comes from the combination of both of these arts. As you go through this book you will see how I carefully chose the background fabrics for each of the embroidery designs.

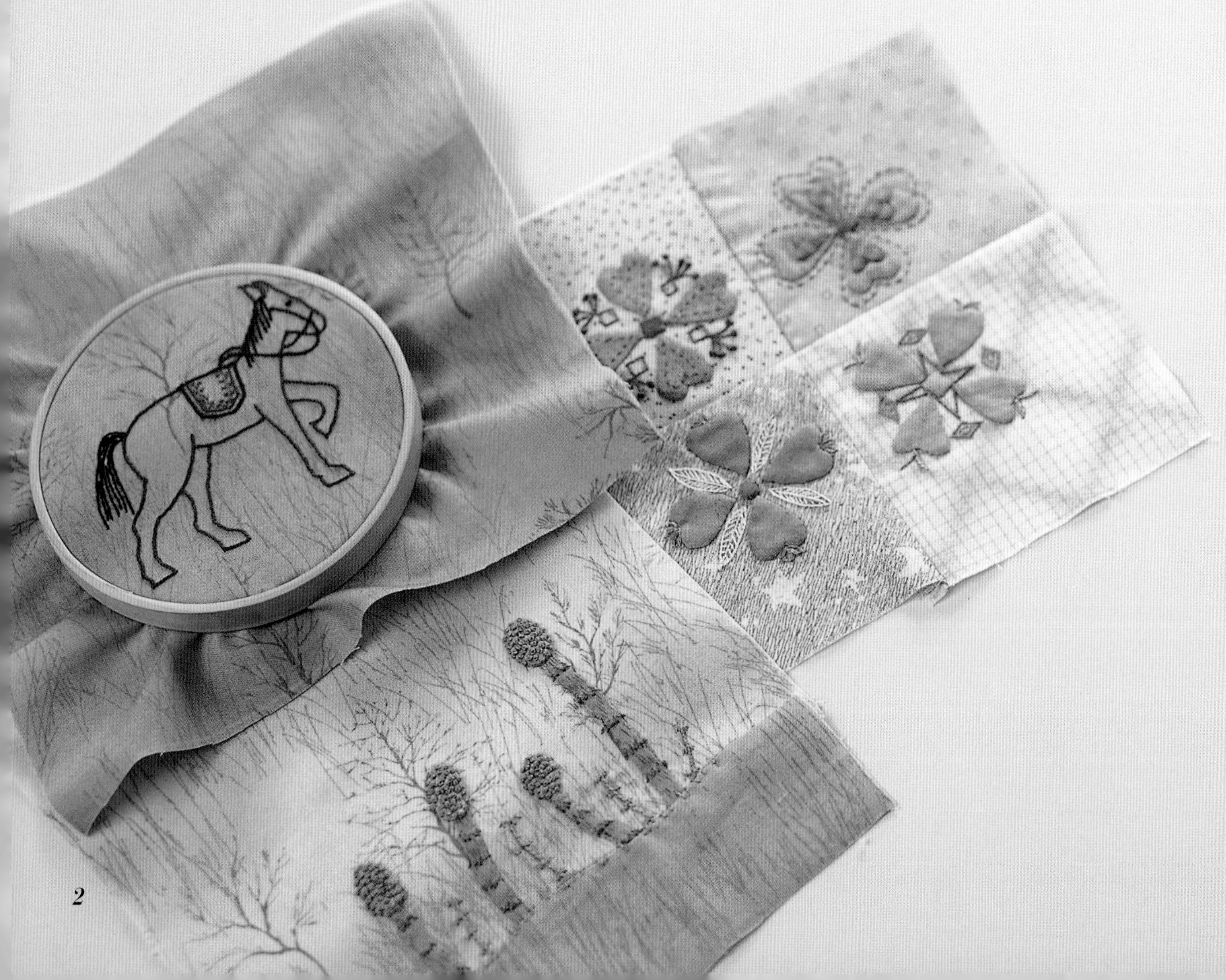

I have designed 120 original embroidery patterns. There are also twenty different patterns including wall hangings, bags, pouches and other assorted quilted projects that show how some of these patterns can be used. Meticulously selecting the yarn-dyed homespuns or print fabrics, along with the embroidery designs and floss colors, to create a finished piece is nothing short of a creative challenge.

"Patchwork embroidery" is the notion of combining both of these arts into one, where each enhances the charm of the other. I hope that each of you will also be inspired by this concept and have fun using embroidery in your own quilts and projects.

Yoko Saito

Contents

1 ~ 18

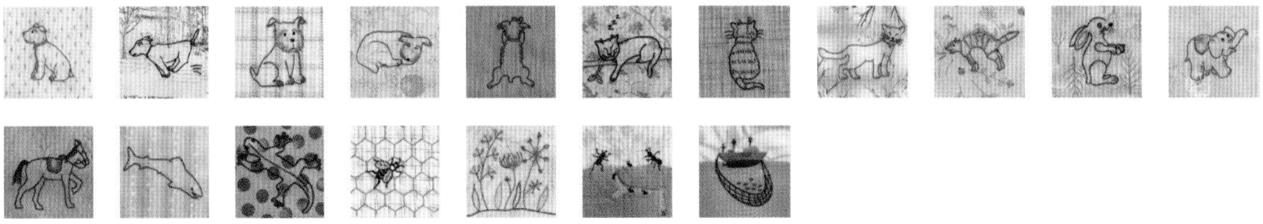

19 ~ 37

38 ~ 41

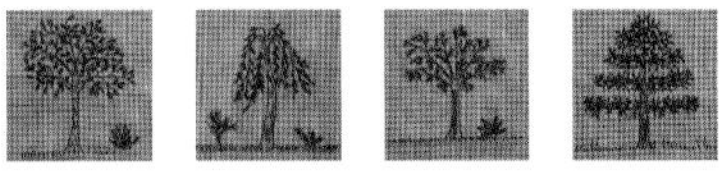

42 ~ 51

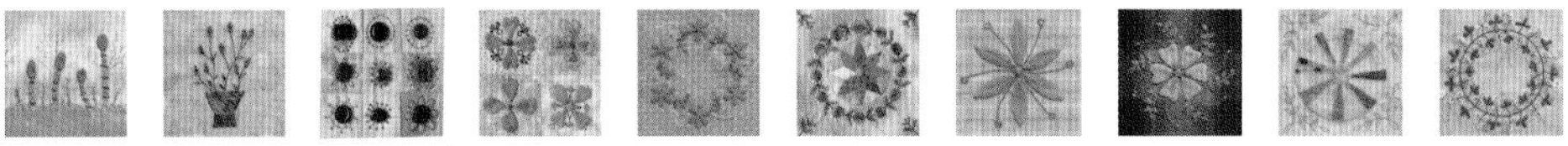

52 ~ 62

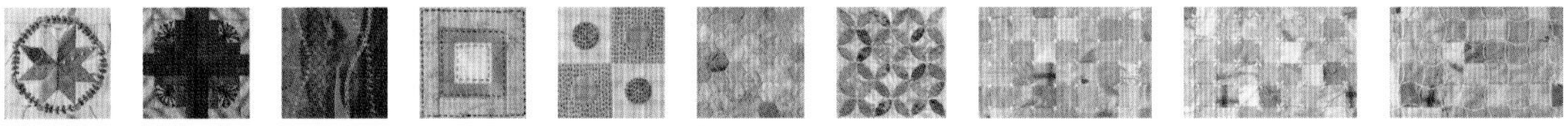

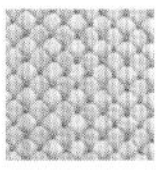

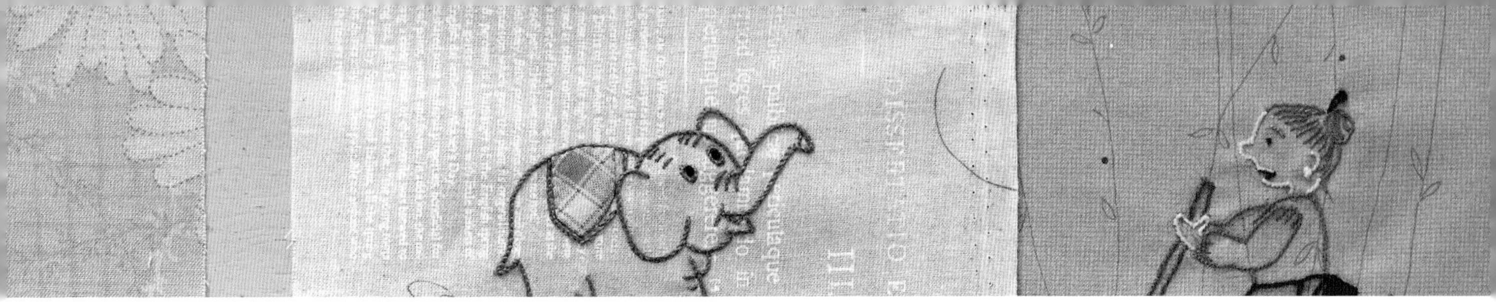

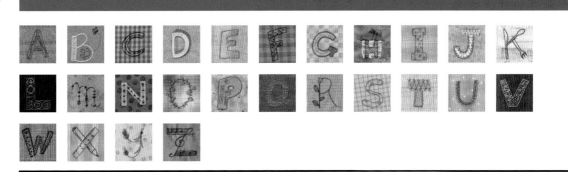

- All embroidery floss used in this book, unless otherwise specified within the pattern, is No. 25.
- All embroidery stitches used are specified for each pattern.
- In designs that have appliqué in addition to the embroidery, the outlines for the appliqués are represented by thin colored lines.
- On page 180, I describe in detail how to use the designs in this book (transferring the designs to fabric, working with appliqué, embroidering the designs). Additionally, on page 181 I have written a guide to embroidery basics.

1 Sit Down

If a dog is a member of your family, you will understand how all of their little habits and cuteness grow on you. I tried to sketch a profile of a dog who is sitting with perfect manners while you praise him for being "such a good boy!" This design is one of nine used in the wall hanging seen on p. 12.

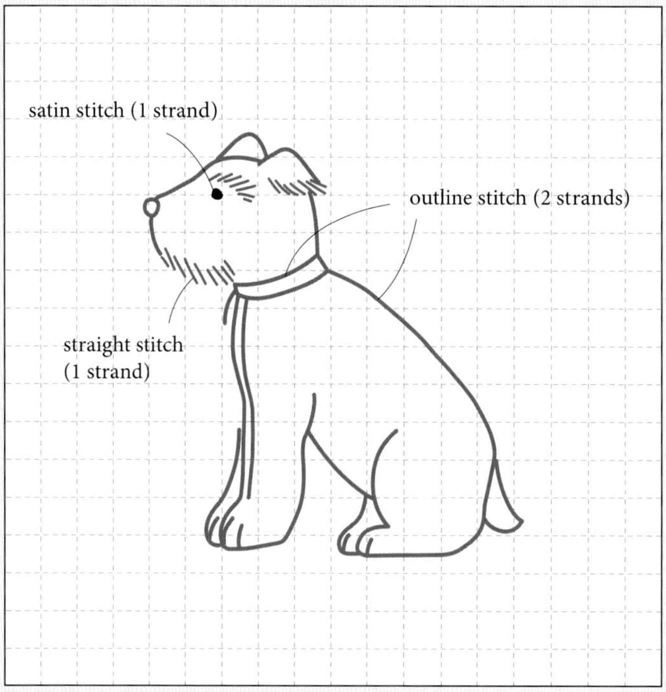
satin stitch (1 strand)
outline stitch (2 strands)
straight stitch
(1 strand)

2 *Scamper*

Embroidered on a background fabric depicting the streets of Paris, I can almost hear the sound of the little dog scampering by. The pattern on the fabric is the perfect scale to give artistic perspective. This design is one of nine used in the wall hanging seen on p. 12.

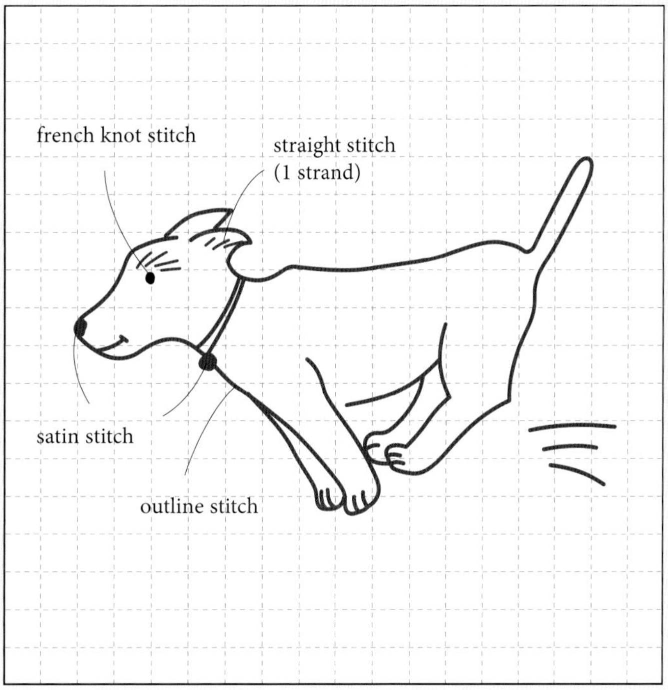
french knot stitch
straight stitch
(1 strand)
satin stitch
outline stitch

◆ use 2 strands of embroidery floss if it is not specified above

3 *Wait!*

I captured the look of impatient longing on the little dog's face when you are getting his dinner and telling him to "wait!" Use a running stitch to outline the face under the whiskers and hair that are done with a straight stitch. This design is one of nine used in the wall hanging seen on p. 12.

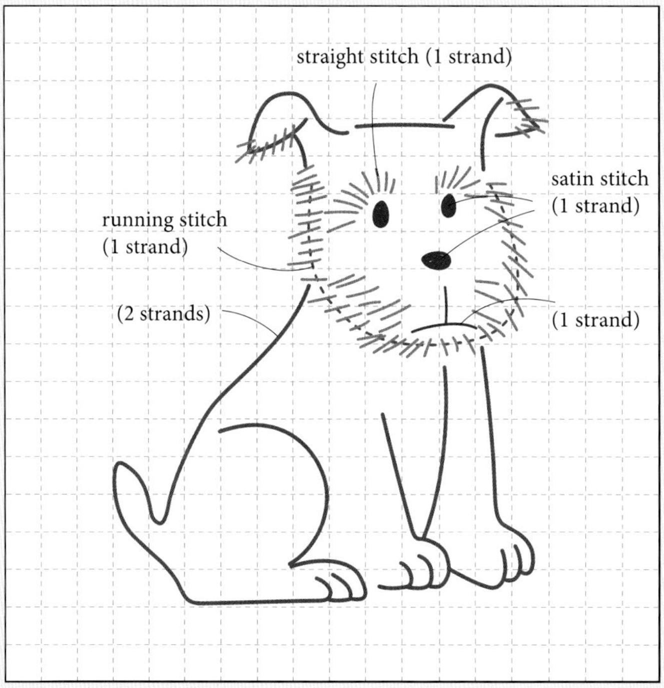
straight stitch (1 strand)
satin stitch
(1 strand)
running stitch
(1 strand)
(2 strands)
(1 strand)

◆ use an outline stitch for any area not specified above

4 Grandpa Dog

A well-loved member of the family for many years, this little dog, who is a grandpa, is curled up and sleeping peacefully. Stitch some white hairs in randomly along with the others around his face and ears to show his age. This design is one of nine used in the wall hanging seen on p. 12.

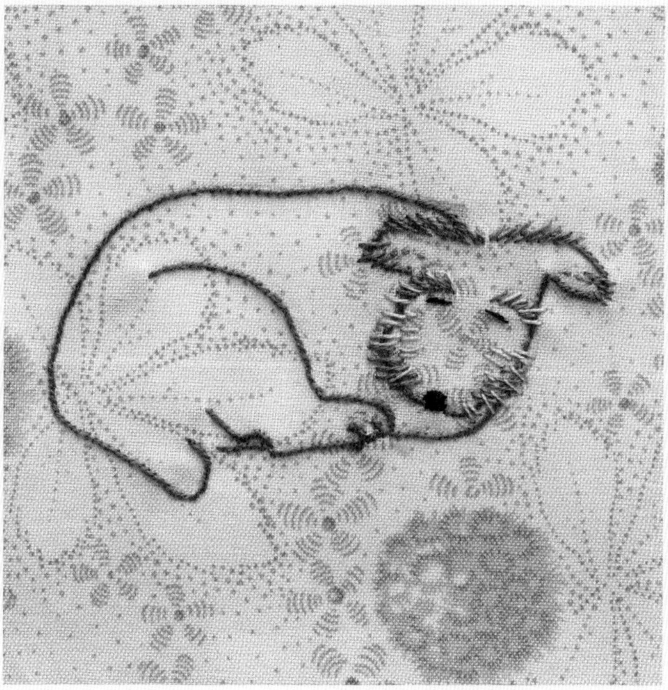

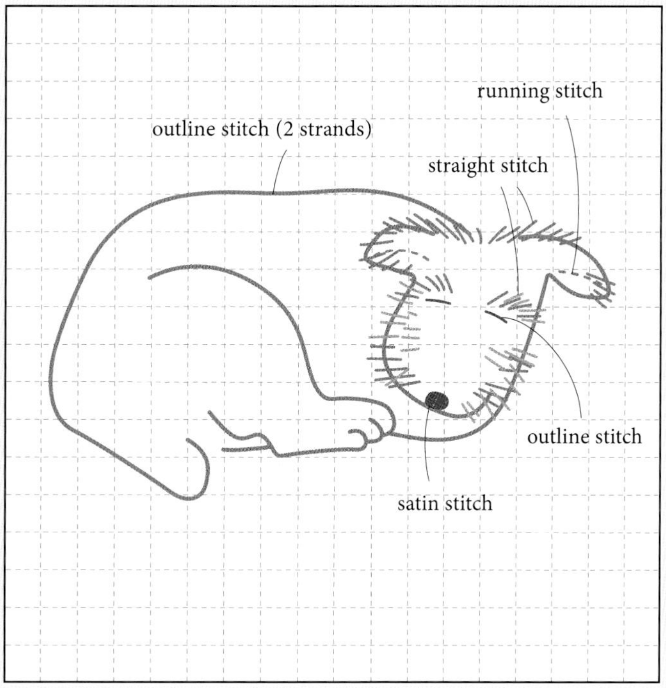
running stitch
outline stitch (2 strands)
straight stitch
outline stitch
satin stitch

◆ use 1 strand of embroidery floss if it is not specified above

5 *Taking a Break*

How cute is it when your dog relaxes completely and stretches out with his hind legs splayed behind him? If you are putting embroideries of dogs and cats next to each other in various poses, it is always interesting to add a different perspective such as this one from above. This design is one of nine used in the wall hanging seen on p. 12.

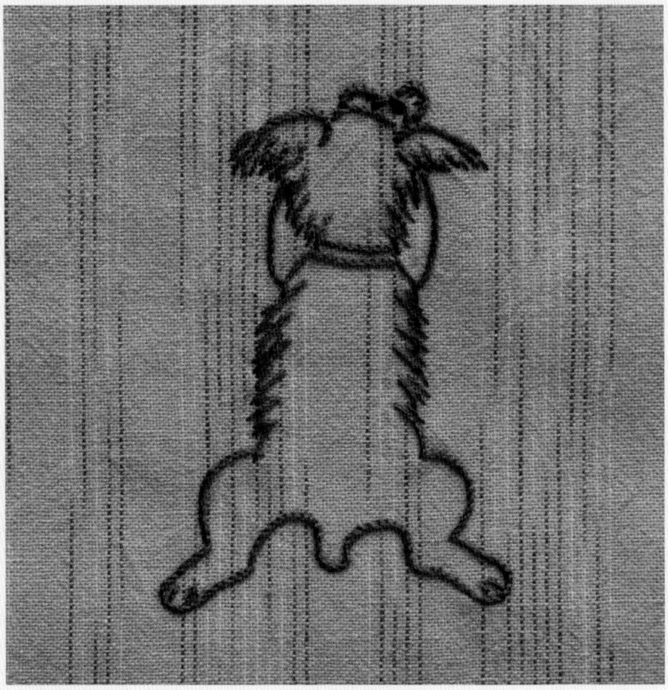

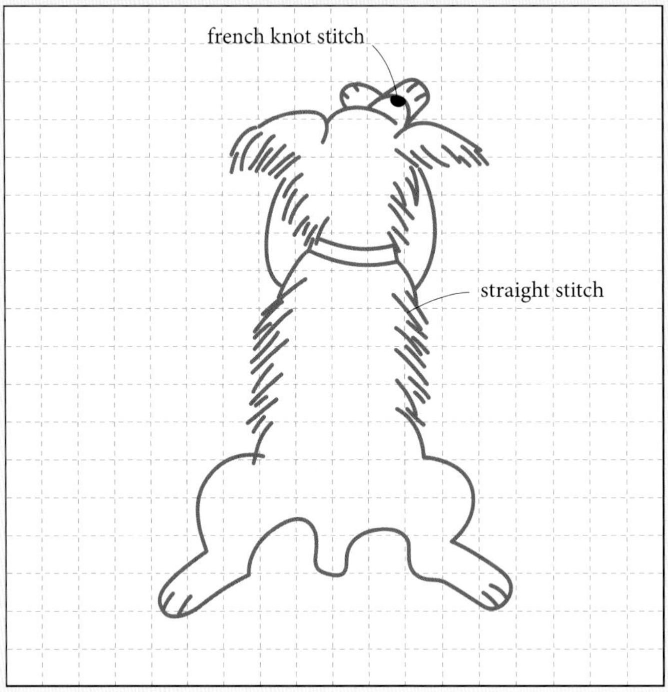

◆ use an outline stitch (2 strands) for any area not specified above

6 *Napping in a Tree*

It seems as though I often see cats in this relaxed position, with their paws and tail hanging down when they sleep. Since she is napping on the limb of a tree, I used fabric with an ivy pattern in the background to give the illusion of leaves. This design is one of nine used in the wall hanging seen on p. 12.

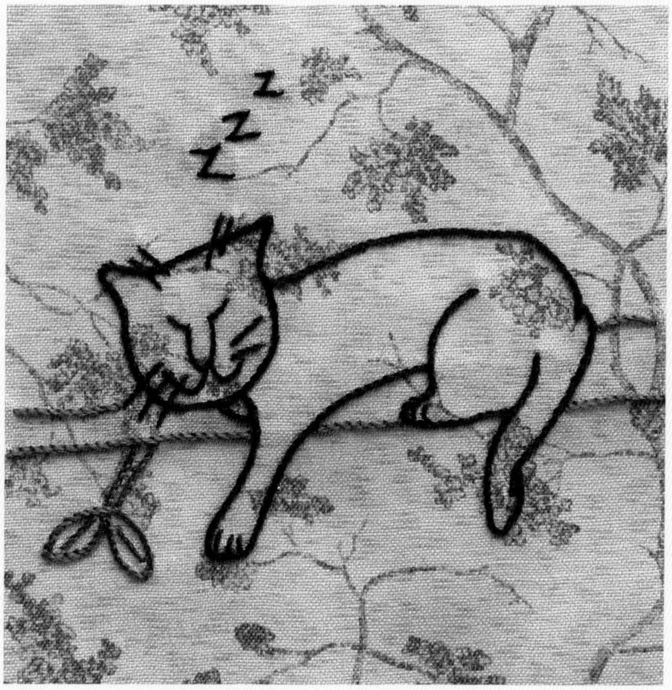

◆ use an outline stitch (2 strands) for any area not specified above

a Wall Hanging

I must admit I am a dog person and so there is one more dog design than there are of cats. In this wall hanging made of nine embroidered blocks, I embroidered what looks like twigs along the seams where the blocks are pieced together. The embroidery adds a nice transition between the nine different background fabrics and showcases them almost like picture frames.

The designs are from patterns **1-9** (pp. 6-11, 14-16). Instructions for the wall hanging are on p. 191.

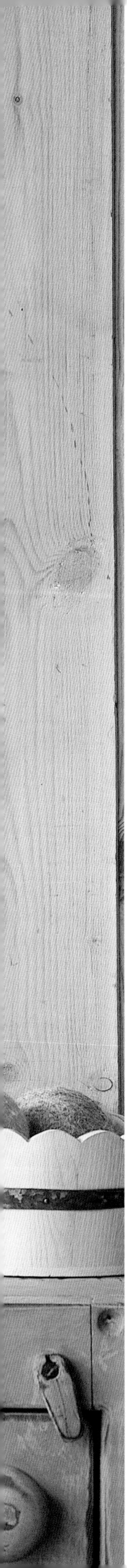

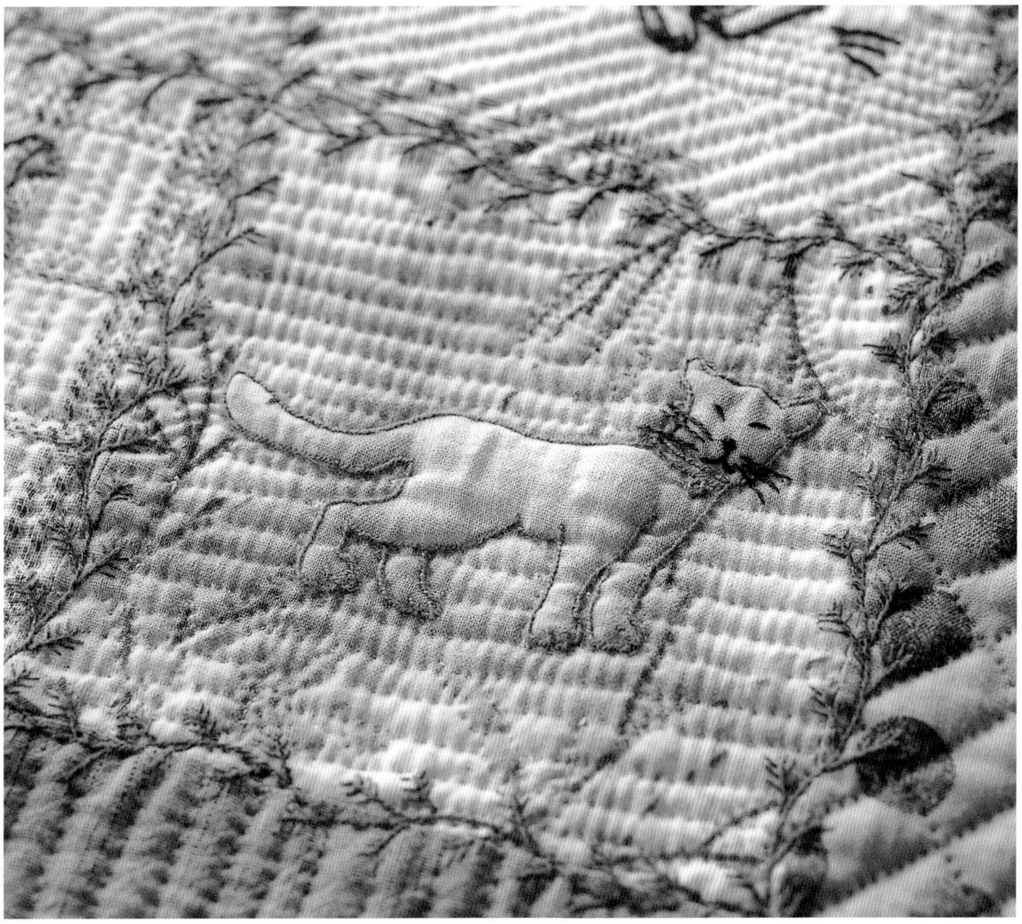

7 *Cat's Back*

I think cats look particularly cute when seen from the back. I did this embroidery all in one color, but it is easy to make it look like your cat or even a tabby cat by changing or adding colors. This design is one of nine used in the wall hanging seen on p. 12.

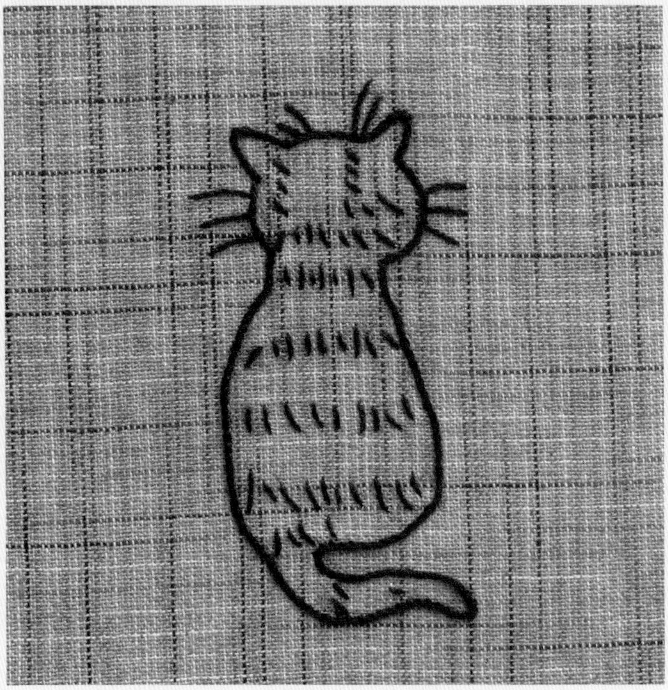

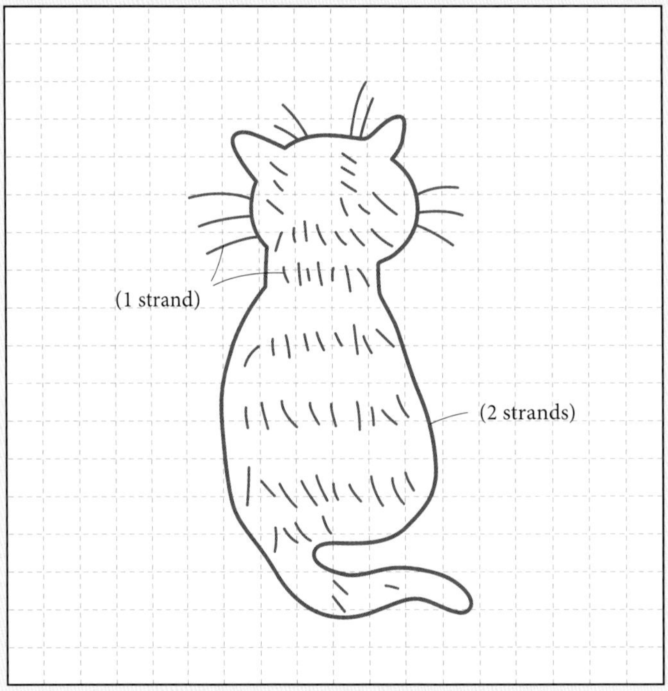

◆ use an outline stitch for the entire design above

8 *Neighbor's Cat*

The neighbor's cat is always in a stylish collar. I chose this background fabric with branches and buds in its pattern as though the cat is walking outside. Use tiny little outline stitches for the outline of the body. This design is one of nine used in the wall hanging seen on p. 12.

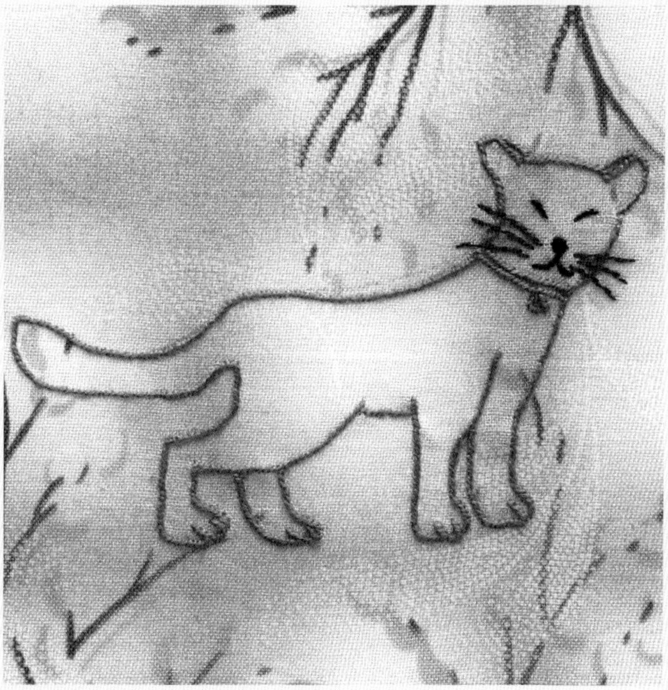

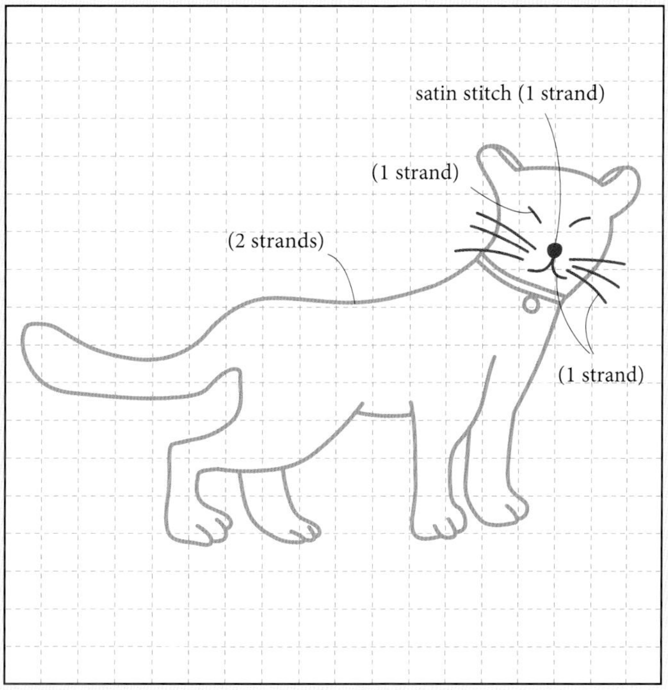

satin stitch (1 strand)
(1 strand)
(2 strands)
(1 strand)

◆ use an outline stitch for any area not specified above

9 Startled Cat

When startled with nowhere to run or stand their ground, cats often arch their backs and cause their fur to stand on end, making themselves appear larger. I used vertical straight stitches for the fur standing up. This design is one of nine used in the wall hanging seen on p. 12.

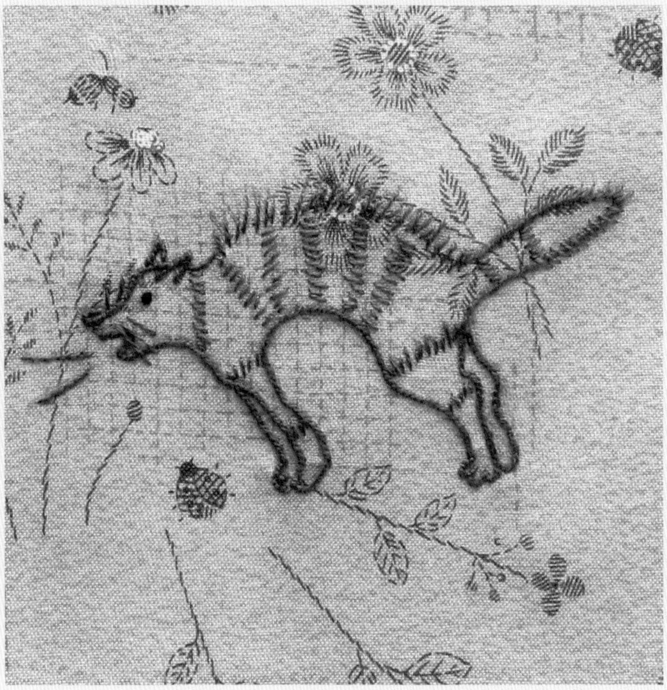

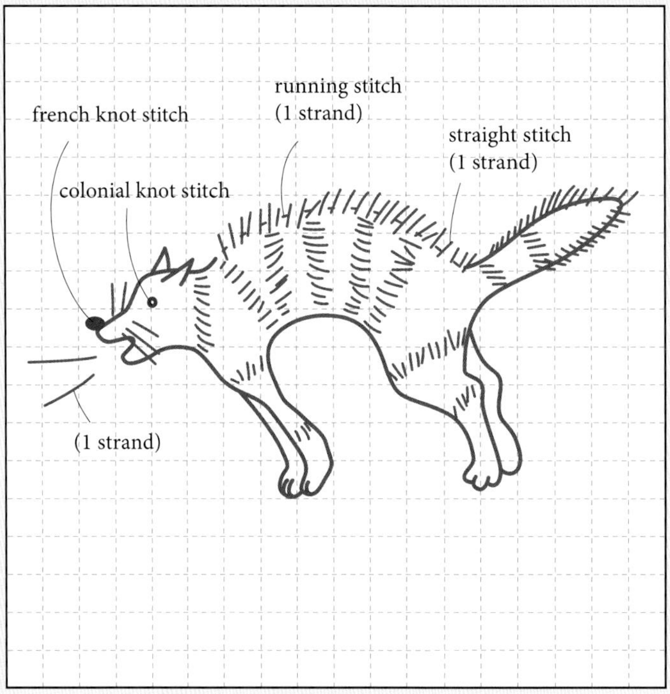
running stitch
(1 strand)
french knot stitch
straight stitch
(1 strand)
colonial knot stitch
(1 strand)

◆ use an outline stitch (2 strands) for any area not specified above

10 *Rabbit in the Forest*

This little rabbit appears relaxed with his ears down and back while holding an acorn. I made the tail appear fluffier with perpendicular straight stitches. The tree pattern in the background fabric adds to the overall feeling of being in the woods.

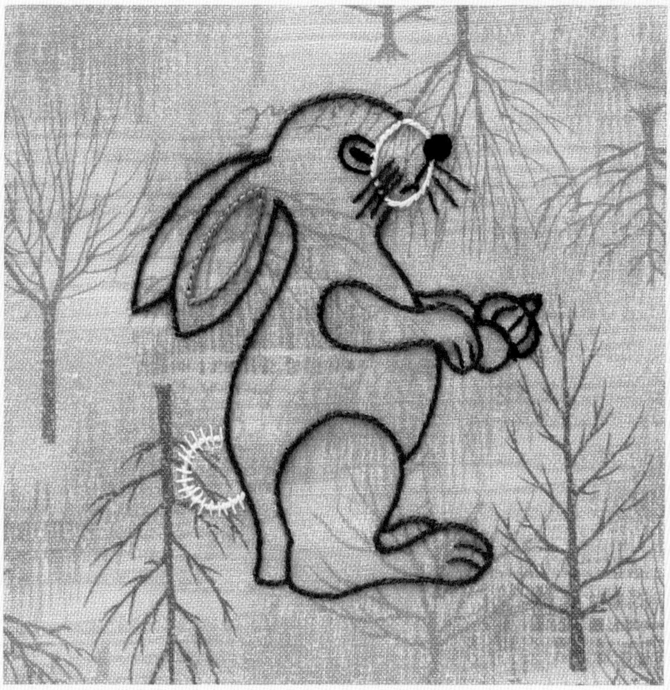

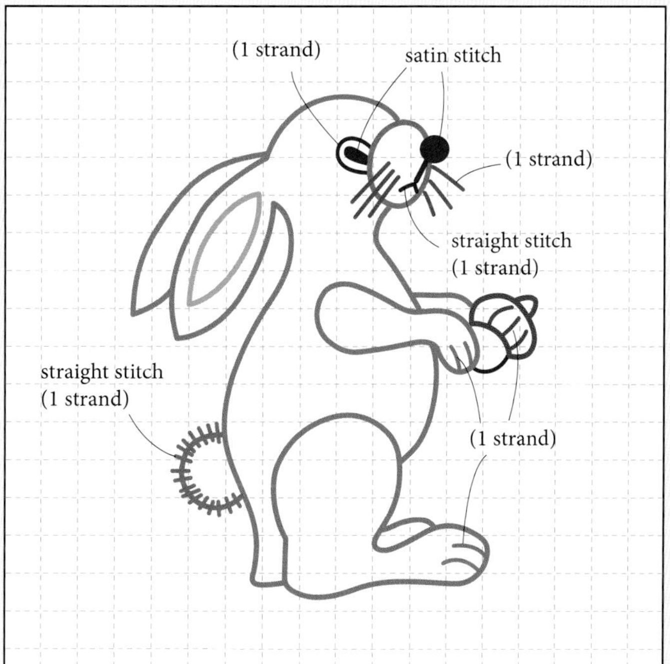

(1 strand)
satin stitch
(1 strand)
straight stitch
(1 strand)
straight stitch
(1 strand)
(1 strand)

◆ use an outline stitch (2 strands) for any area not specified above

11 *Baby Elephant*

I wanted to sketch a baby elephant. I shortened the tail and the legs to make him appear roly-poly. With his head embroidered slightly to the side, it looks like he is happily marching along. I appliquéd a piece of plaid fabric cut on the bias for his back.

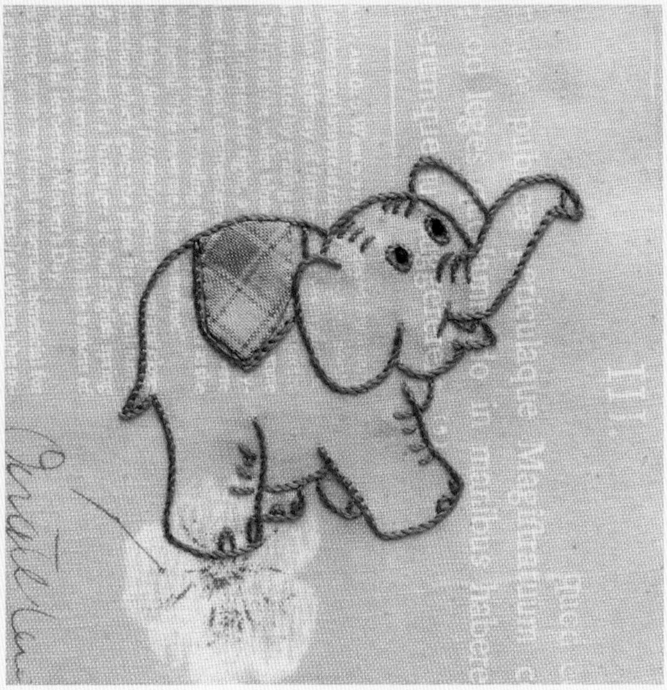

french knot stitch
(1 strand)
(1 strand)

◆ use an outline stitch (2 strands) for any area not specified above

12 *Pony*

I drew a gentle little pony all ready to go on a ride. It is important to get the shape of the legs right as you use tiny little outline stitches. Embellish the saddle with the herringbone stitch and french knots.

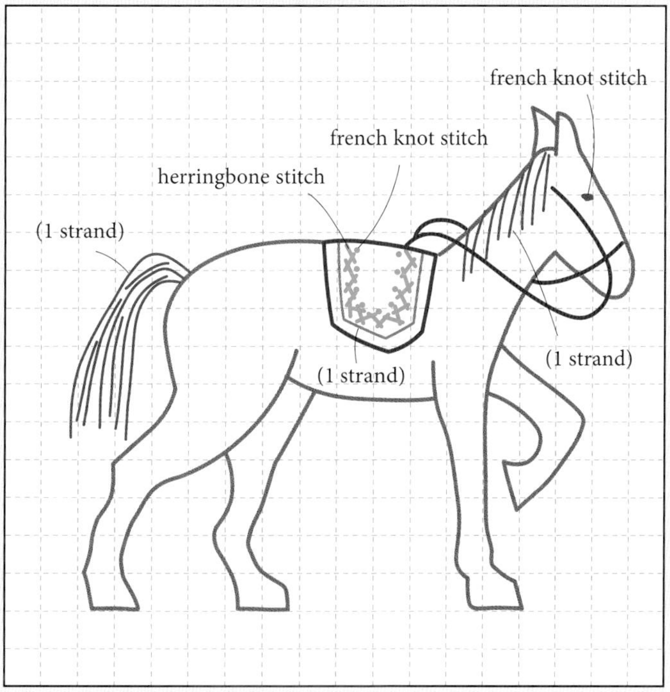

french knot stitch
french knot stitch
herringbone stitch
(1 strand)
(1 strand)
(1 strand)

◆ use an outline stitch (2 strands) for any area not specified above

13 *Shark*

I have heard sharks referred to as the "gangsters of the sea" so I suppose it is all right to give it razor sharp teeth that make it look a little sinister. The white dots on the background fabric appear to be air bubbles in the water.

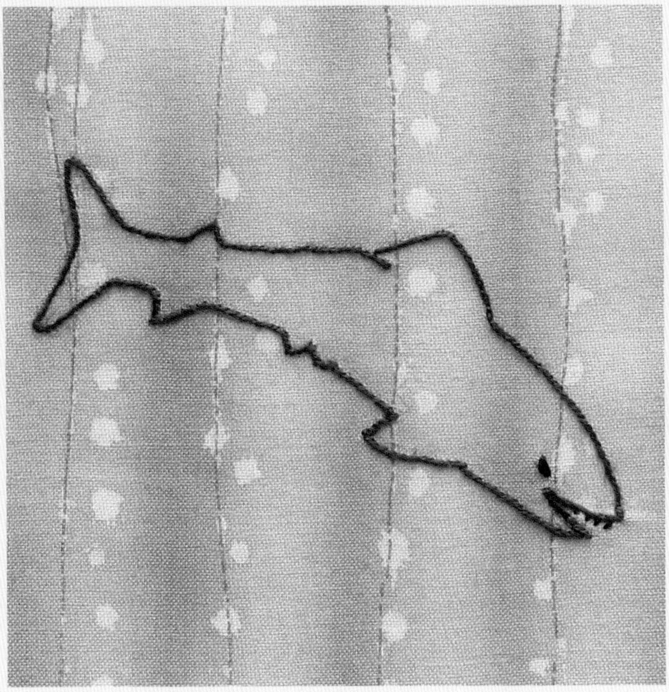

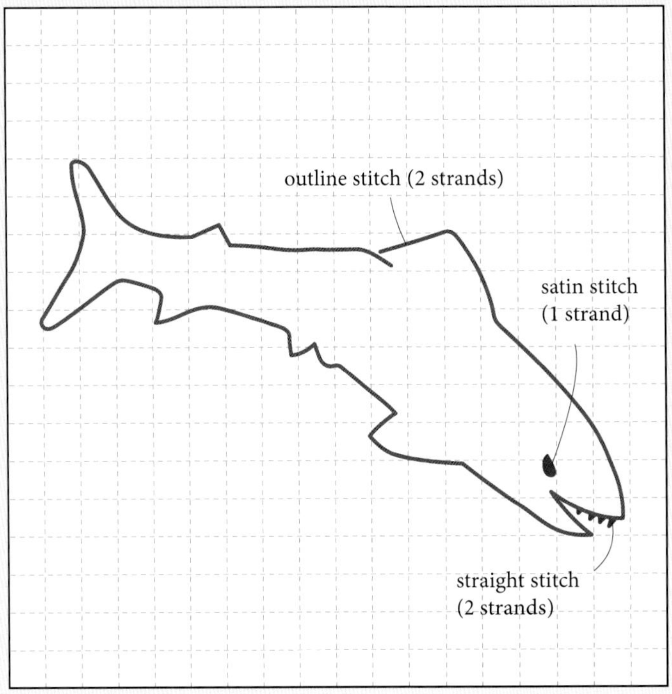

outline stitch (2 strands)
satin stitch
(1 strand)
straight stitch
(2 strands)

14 *Lizard*

I think this lizard design would appeal to most little boys. It is fun to embroider little lizards in the midst of plant pattern fabric or appliqués. By stitching it on this dot fabric, it adds a mysterious quality of not knowing where the little guy is.

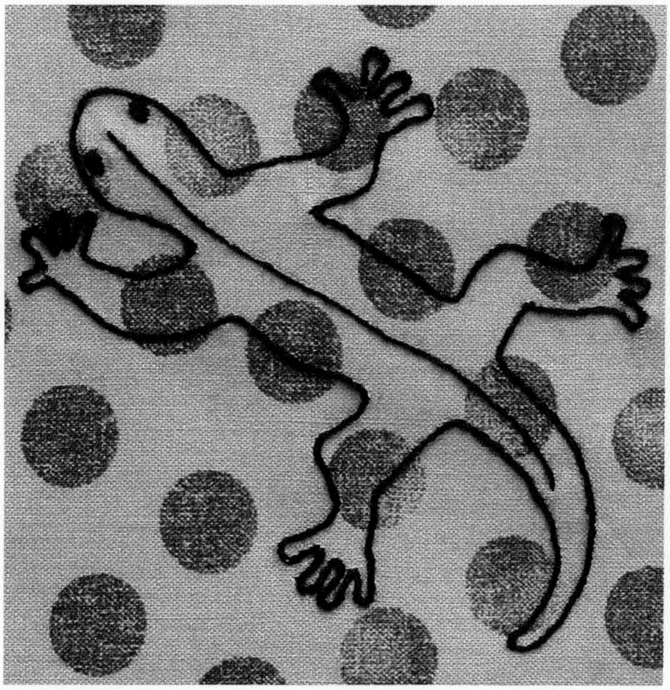

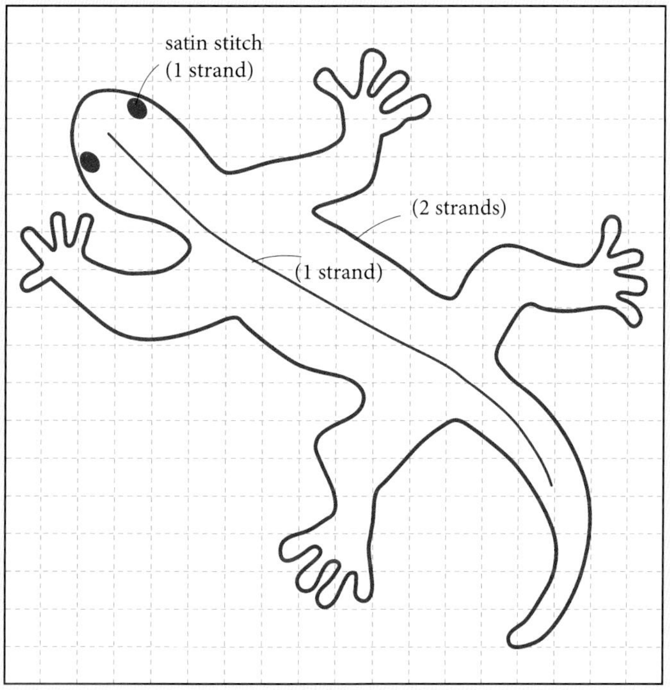
satin stitch
(1 strand)
(2 strands)
(1 strand)

◆ use an outline stitch for any area not specified above

15 *Honeybee*

I love bees. I often create honeybee appliqué designs, but I find that I can be much more detailed when I do embroidery designs from the wings to the stinger. Make the hexagonal honeycomb with an outline stitch. I used this embroidery design for the front of the pouch on pp. 24-25.

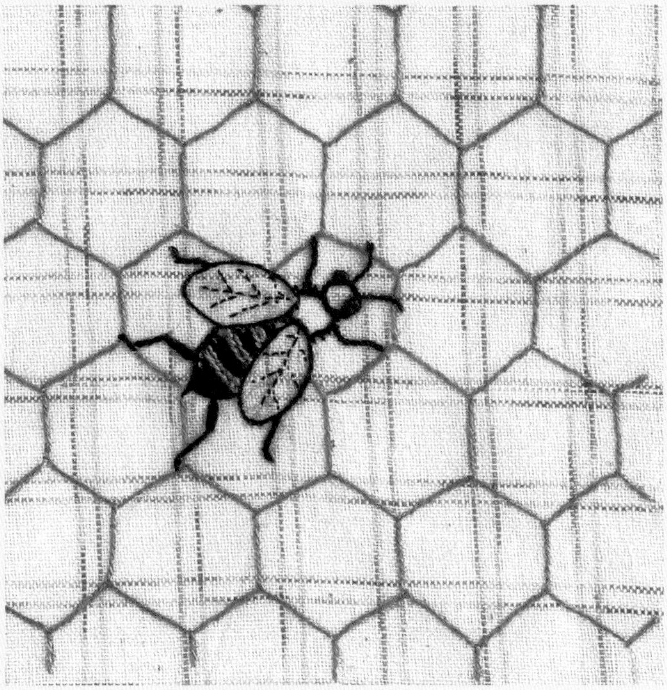

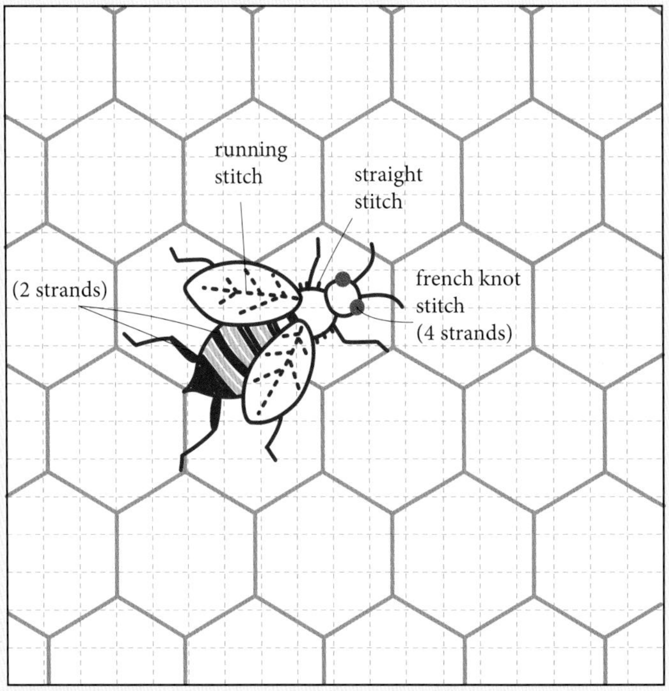
running
stitch
straight
stitch
(2 strands)
french knot
stitch
(4 strands)

◆ use an outline stitch (1 strand) for any area not specified above

16 *Scandinavian Flowers*

These flowers remind me of those I often see in Scandinavia. The lightly printed background fabric adds depth to the embroidery. I used this design for the back of the pouch on pp. 24-25.

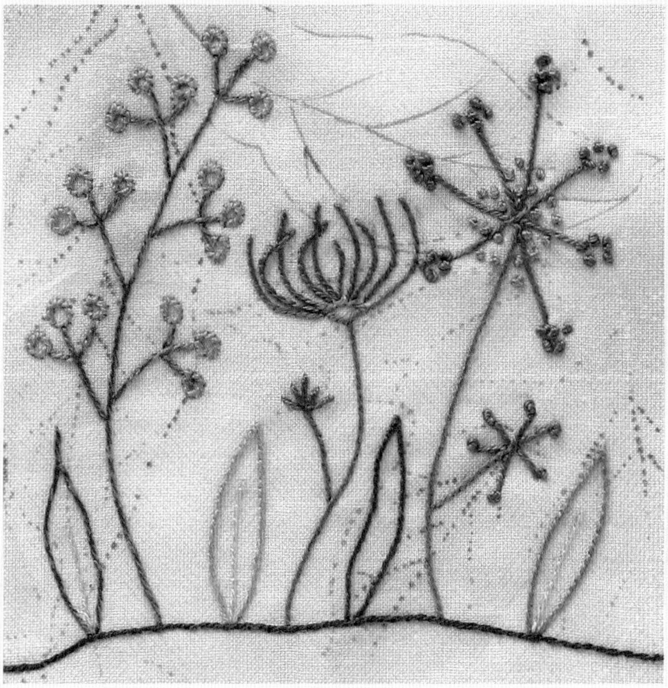

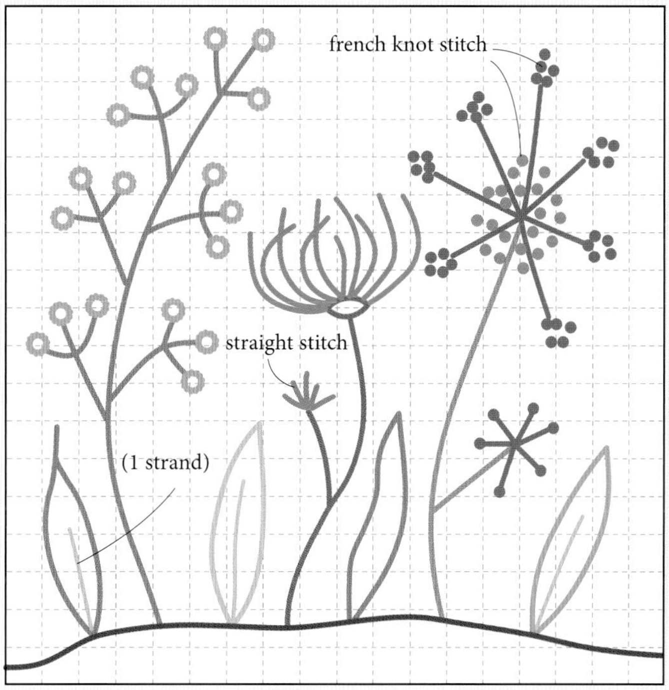
french knot stitch
straight stitch
(1 strand)

◆ use an outline stitch (2 strands) for any area not specified above

b Pouch

I used both the honeybee pattern and the Scandinavian flowers pattern for the front and back of the pouch, although you might choose to only use one of them as well. Despite being a small pouch, it can hold quite a bit because of the trapezoid shape.

The designs are from patterns **15-16** (pp. 22-23).
Instructions for the pouch are on p. 192.

17 *Ant Farm*

Ants are hard-working little creatures who live in colonies. From the smallest ants to the larger adult ants, this design shows them in their underground home as well as outside. Use the reverse appliqué technique to show the tunnel underground. I used this design for the front of the coin purse on p. 30.

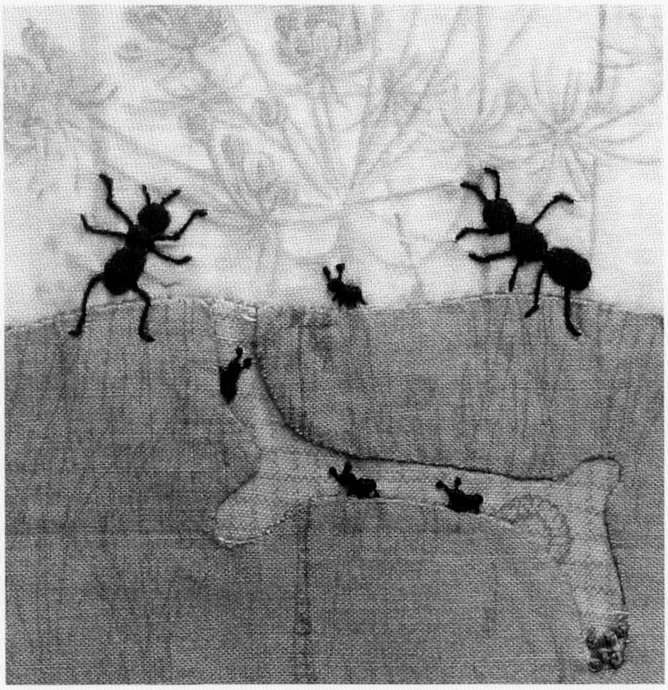

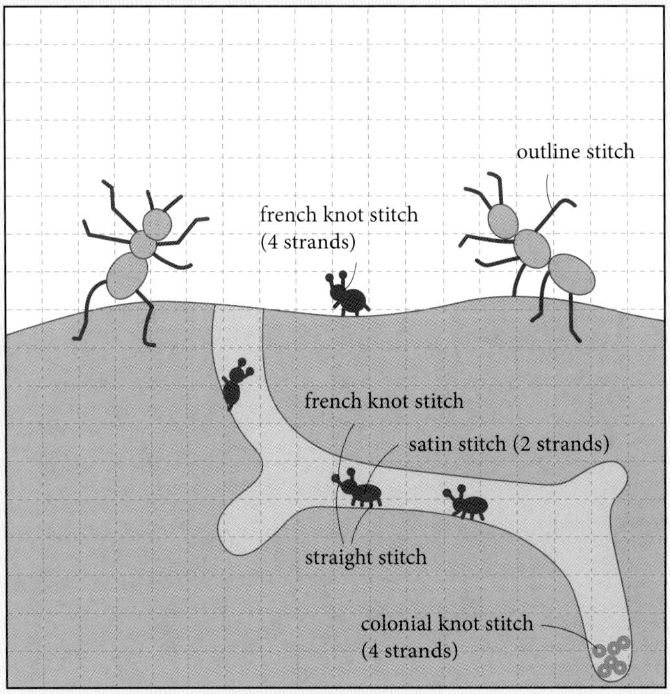
outline stitch
french knot stitch
(4 strands)
french knot stitch
satin stitch (2 strands)
straight stitch
colonial knot stitch
(4 strands)

◆ use 1 strand for any area not specified above

18 *Catch of the Day*

The fishing trawler is out catching a school of fish. Use a fabric that reminds you of the ocean for the water. You can embroider small or large fish in and around the net if you choose. I used this design for the back of the coin purse on p. 30.

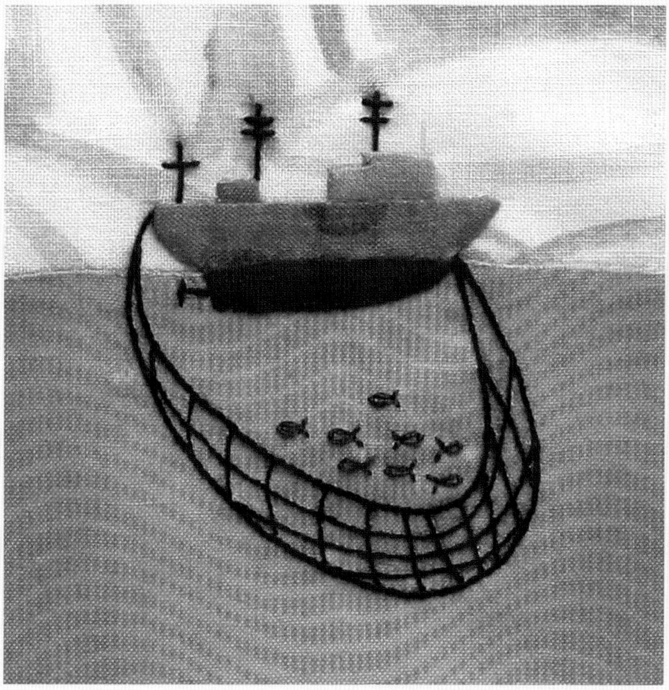

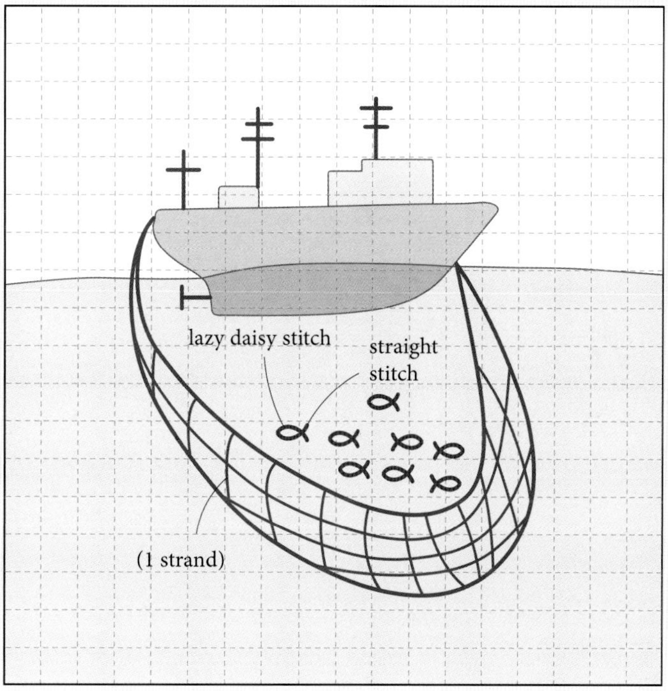
lazy daisy stitch
straight stitch
(1 strand)

◆ use an outline stitch (2 strands) for any area not specified above

19 *Shopping Cart*

This very large and well-built shopping cart is the size that is seen in supermarkets in the United States. There is plenty of room for lots of fresh vegetables and desserts. I've used 3 strands of floss for the basket and metal portions. I used this design for the back of the mini pouch on p. 31.

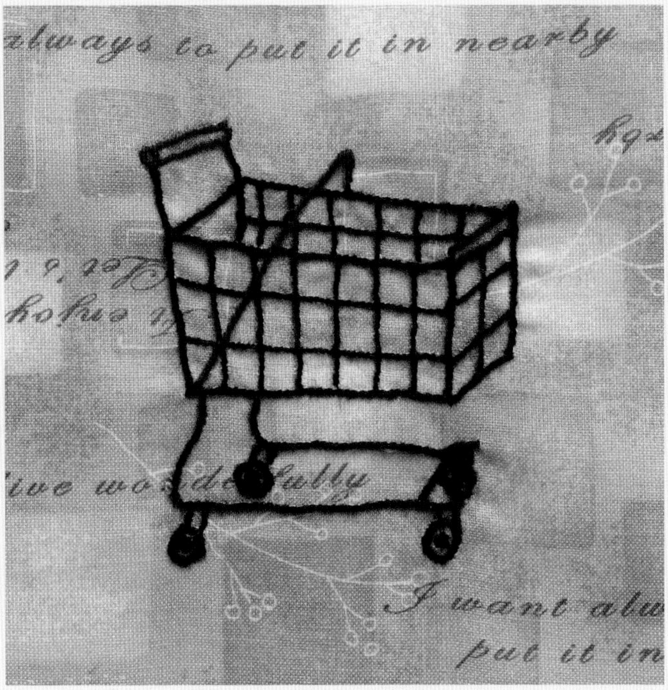

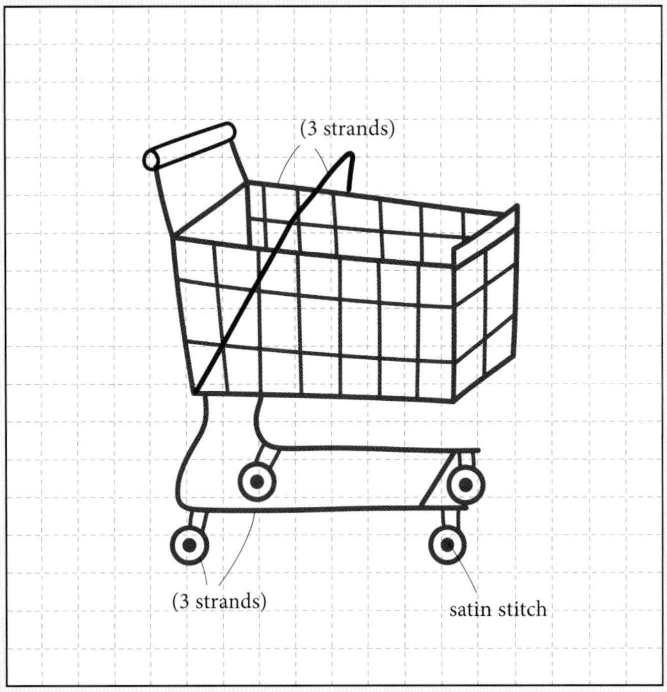

◆ use an outline stitch (2 strands) for any area not specified above

20 *Bicycle*

The classic shape of a bicycle is embroidered on a background fabric depicting a map of Paris. If you use only black floss it reminds one of a black and white film of old. Feel free to change colors for the seat or the light to get a different feeling. I used this design for the front of the mini pouch on p. 31.

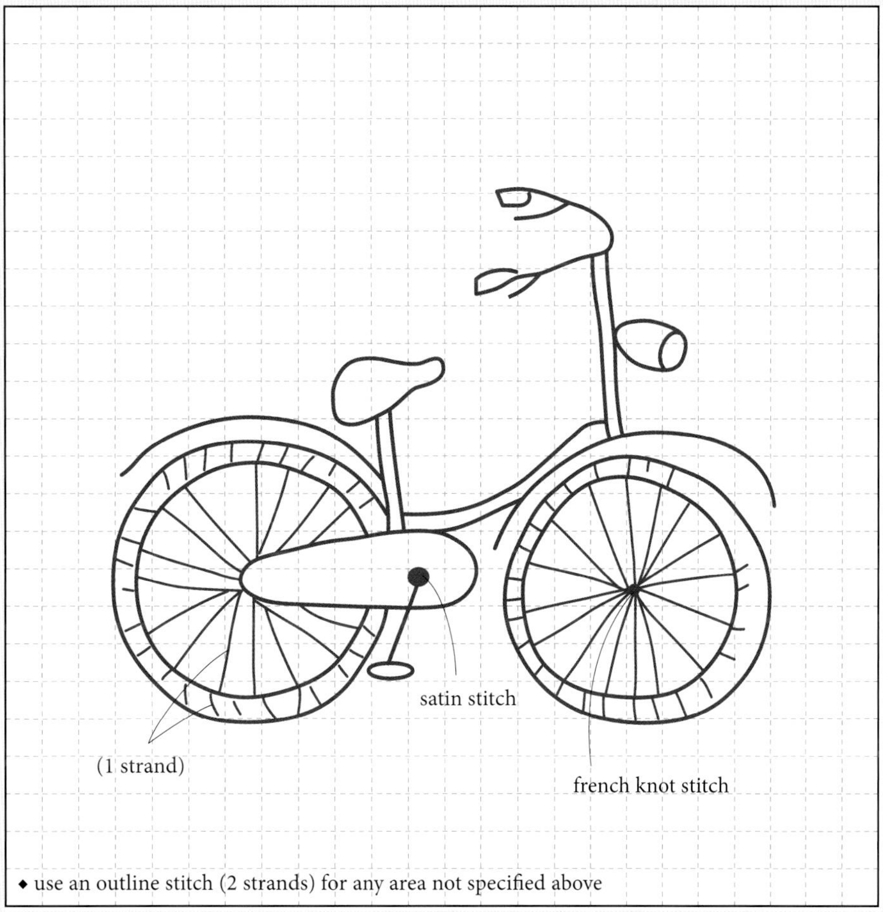

satin stitch
(1 strand)
french knot stitch
◆ use an outline stitch (2 strands) for any area not specified above

C Coin Purse

Easy to open and close with one hand, this wide mouth coin purse is useful to carry with you. Quilt both the front and back pieces to highlight the embroidery.

The designs are from patterns **17-18** (pp. 26-27). Instructions for the coin purse are on p. 194.

d Mini Pouch

This mini quilt can be used for many different purposes. The machine-quilted gusset, with a zipper opening going all the way around, looks cute with a contrasting fabric. Embroider your own favorite designs on either side.

The designs are from patterns **19-20** (pp. 28-29).
Instructions for the pouch are on p. 196.

21 *Landing*

This is one of two airplane designs that I drew. This one is a nostalgic early model plane that appears to be flying far above the world. I used a fabric, that when fussy cut, looks like part of an old map.

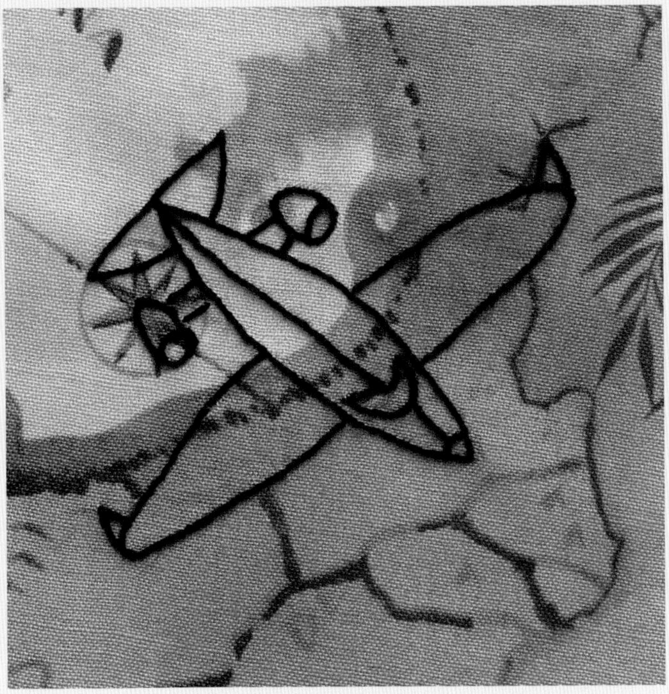

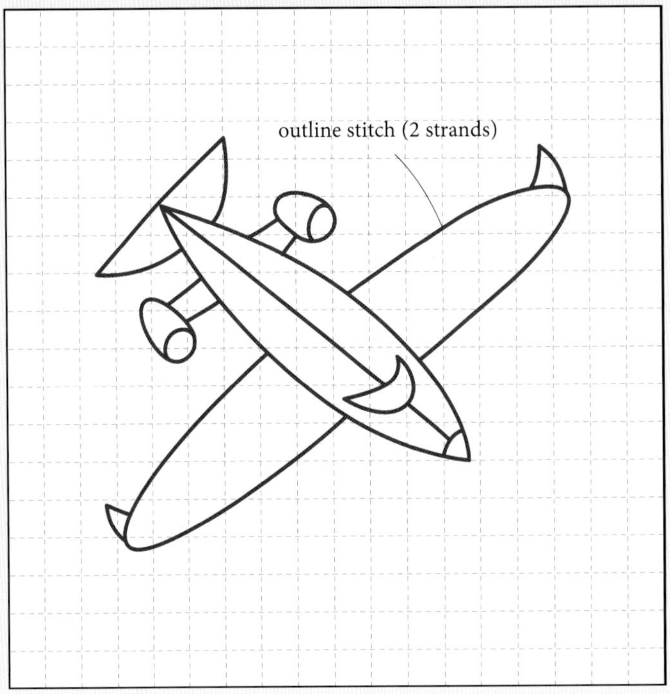

22 *Airplane*

This second airplane design is of a jumbo jet. I fly overseas several times a year, but it is never as much fun as it would be if I could fly in a cute little one like this. The background fabric has a pattern that looks like wind currents and adds to the overall feeling of flying.

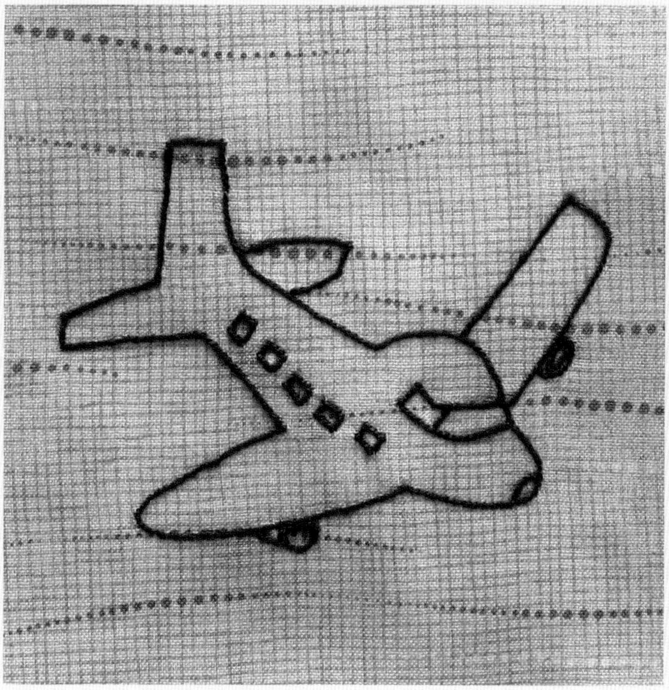

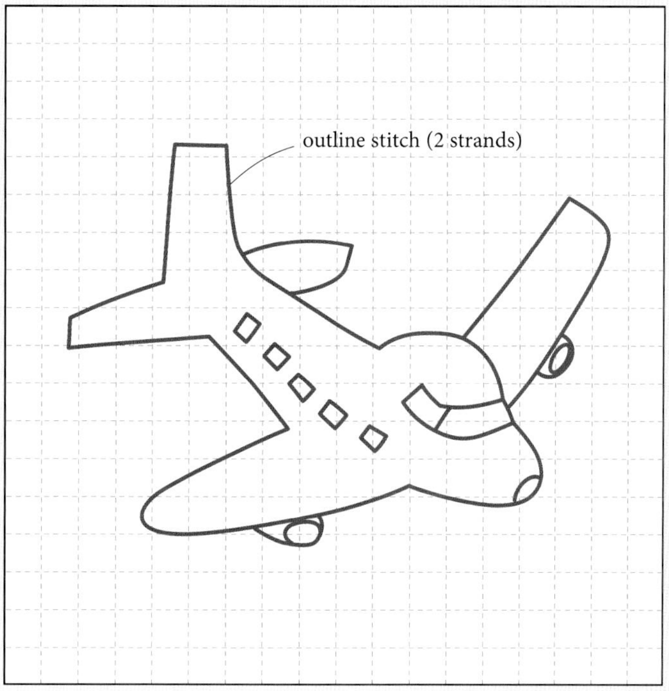

23 *Tumbler*

By appliquéing a piece of fabric that is slightly smaller and within the lines of the embroidery of the tumbler, it makes the glass appear to be thick. The polka dot background fabric makes me think that this drink will be refreshing.

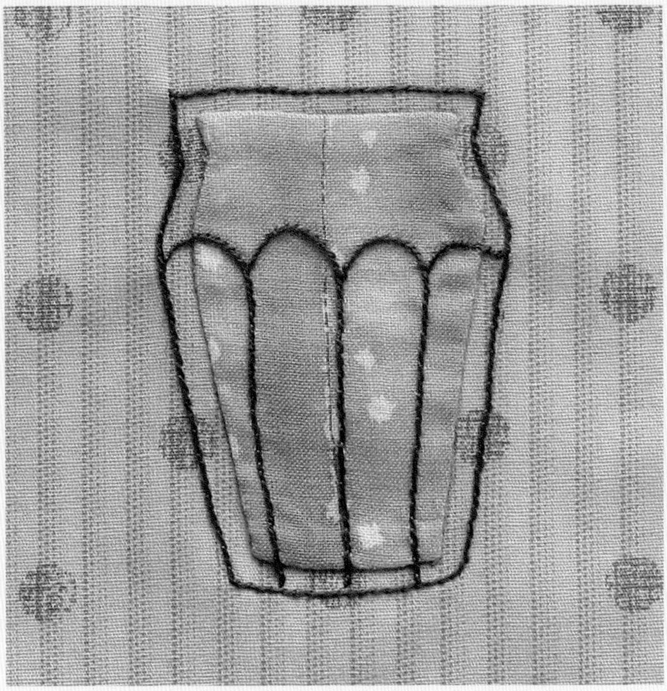

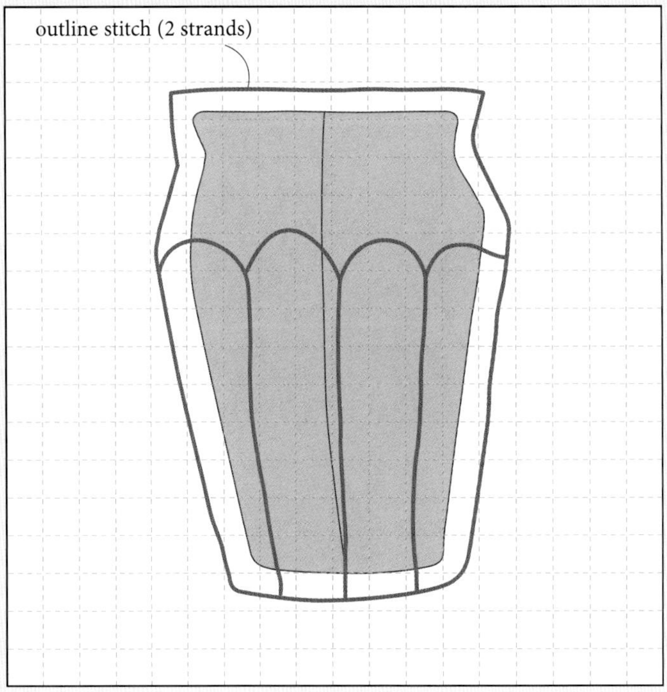

24 *Light Bulb*

This classic design of a light bulb is emphasized against a background fabric that has writing printed on it. Use a piece of fabric to appliqué the bulb. If you want to emphasize it further, stitch around it with an outline stitch.

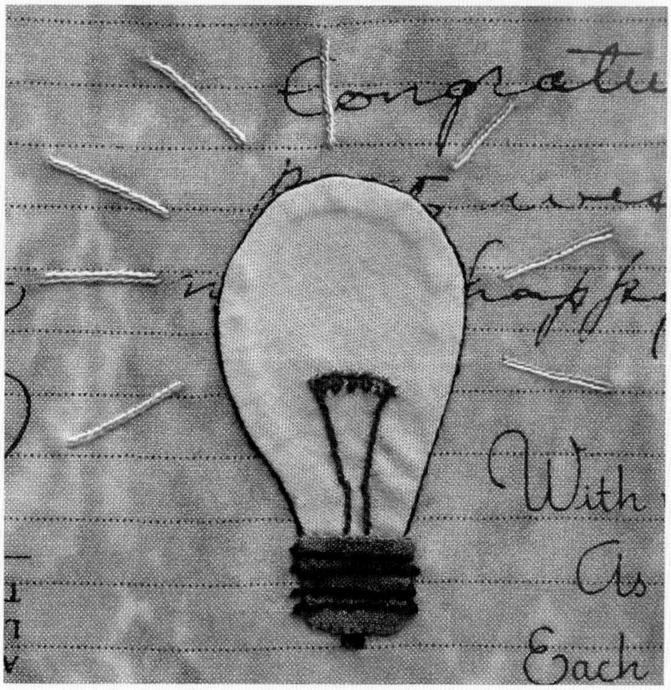

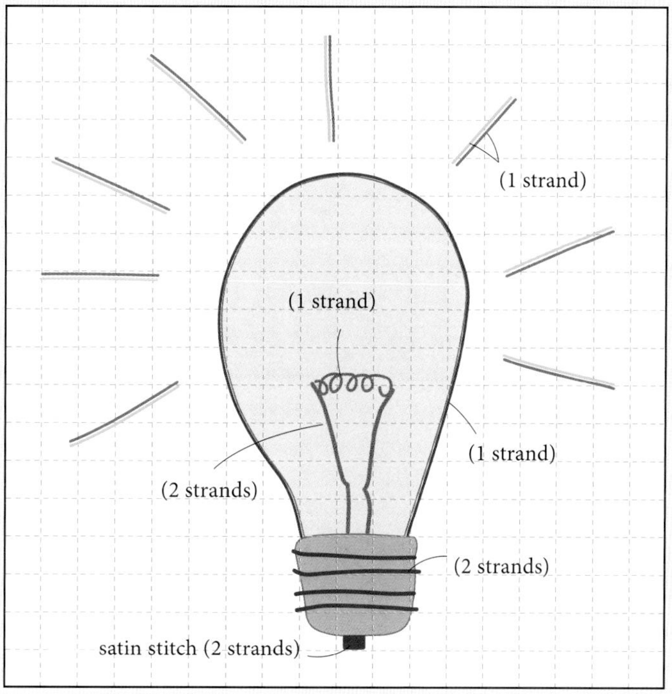
(1 strand)
(1 strand)
(1 strand)
(2 strands)
(2 strands)
satin stitch (2 strands)

◆ use an outline stitch for any area not specified above

25 *Turn It Off!*

All the water faucets at the elementary schools looked exactly like this when I was growing up. It seemed as though they would never quite turn off all the way and you could hear the water plinking as it hit the sink. This is a simple embroidery done in an outline stitch.

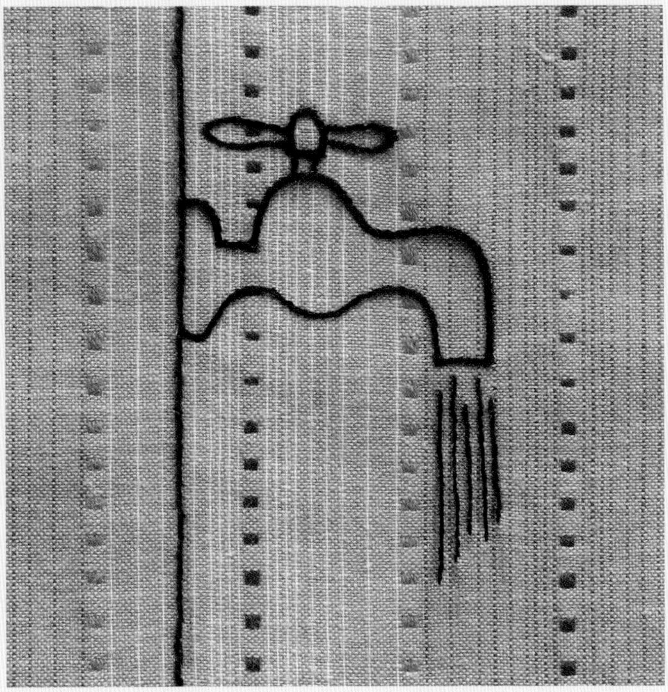

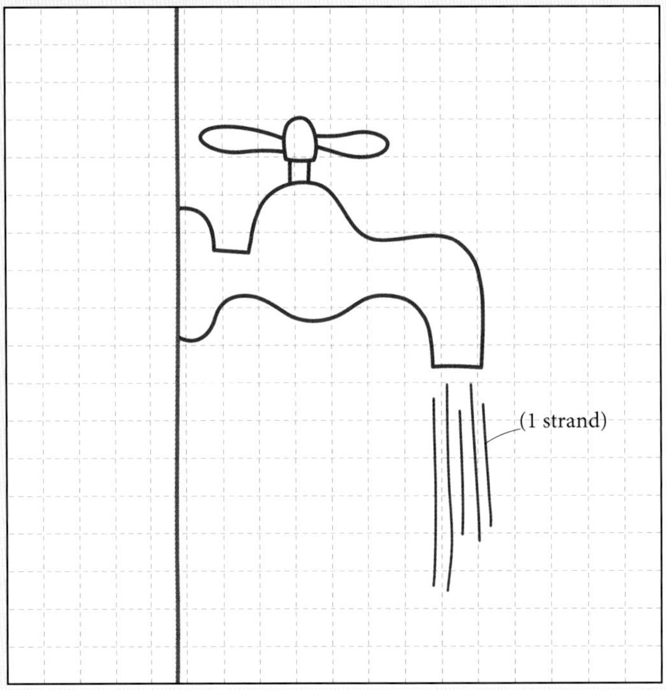

◆ use an outline stitch (2 strands) for any area not specified above

26 Pendulum Clock

The old antique clocks had to be wound every day and would often gong upon the hour. I set the time to be 10:10, but embroider in whatever time you like.

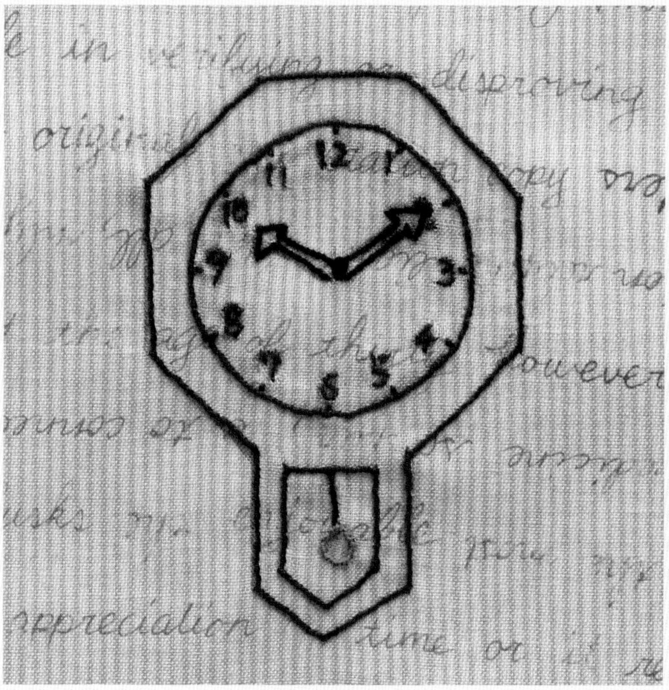

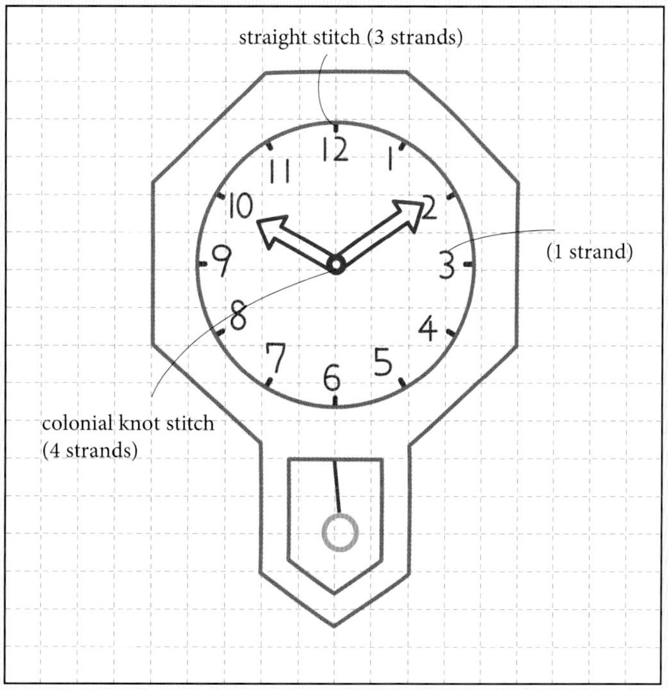

◆ use an outline stitch (2 strands) for any area not specified above

27 *Tape Dispenser*

I drew a design of a tape dispenser that sat on my desk. I chose a dark red floss that makes it look like redwork embroidery. The background fabric reminds me of a newspaper cutting and makes the overall piece particularly interesting.

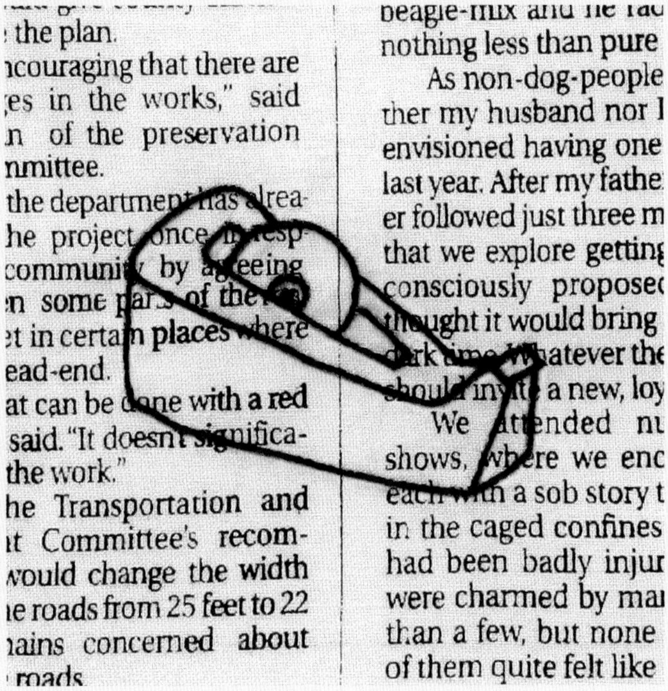

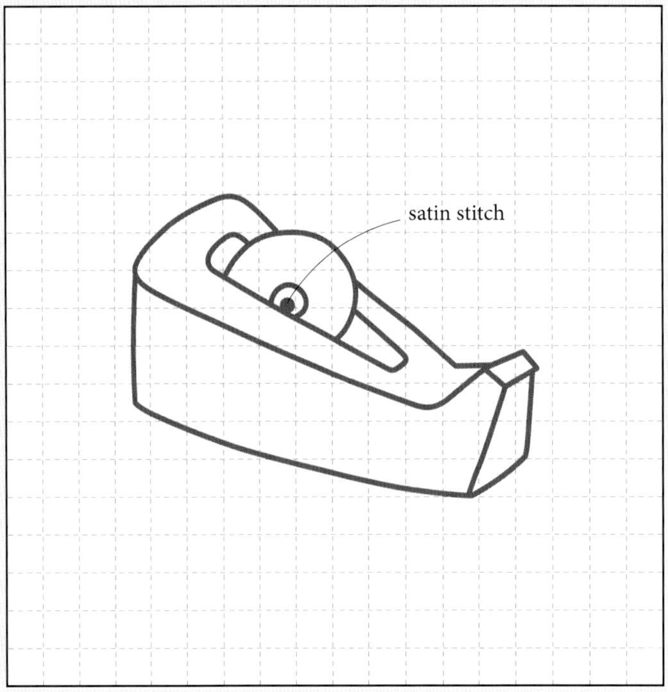

◆ use an outline stitch (2 strands) for any area not specified above

28 *Tennis*

The old wooden tennis racquets had a special appeal. I even drew the gut on the outside edge that came from when they would string them. Both the racquet and tennis ball are done in an outline stitch.

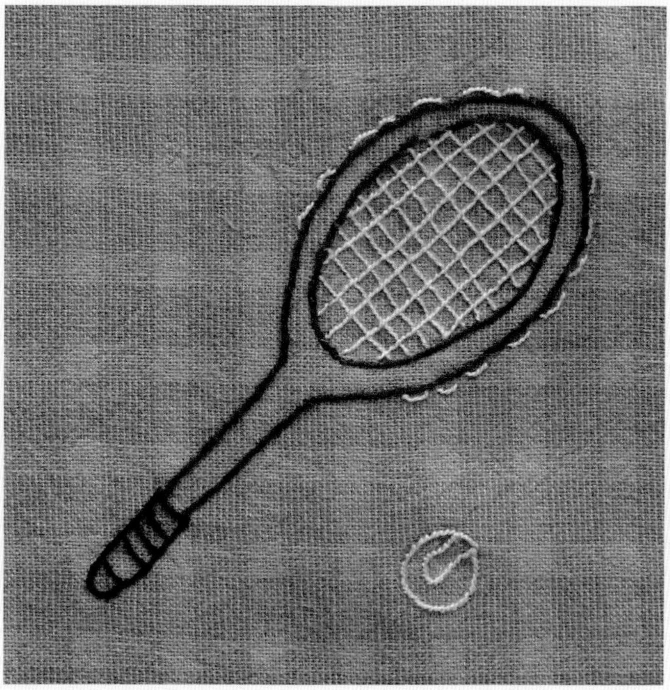

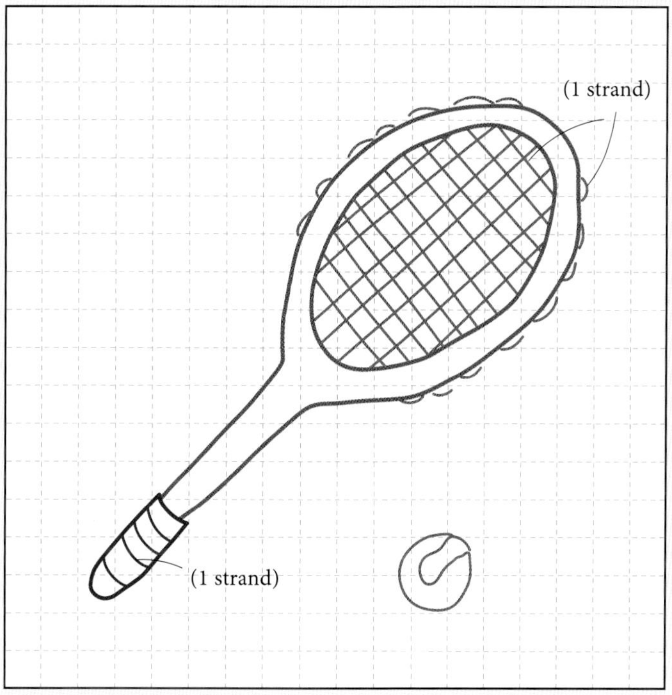

◆ use an outline stitch (2 strands) for any area not specified above

29 *Nantucket Basket*

The classic Nantucket basket can be used as a handbag. Historically, the embellishments were made of whale bone (whale ivory). Embroidery is ideal to be able to add in these details. I used this design for the front of the mini pouch on p. 41.

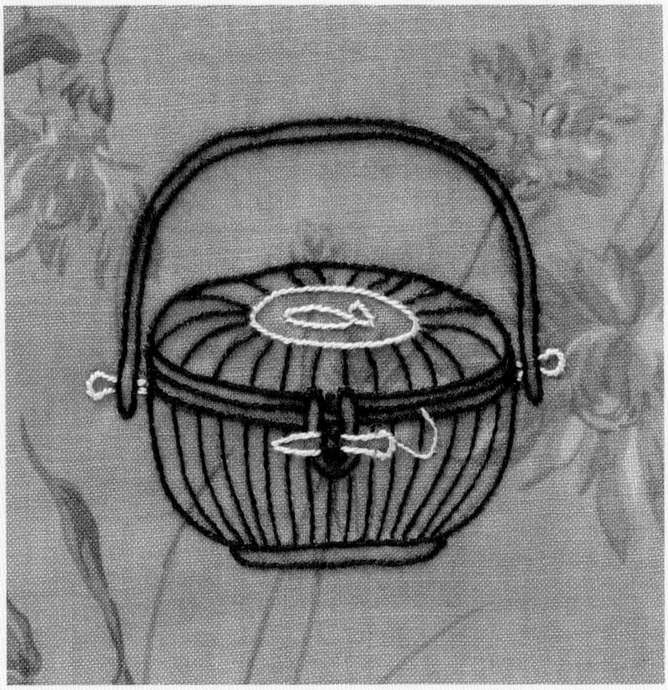

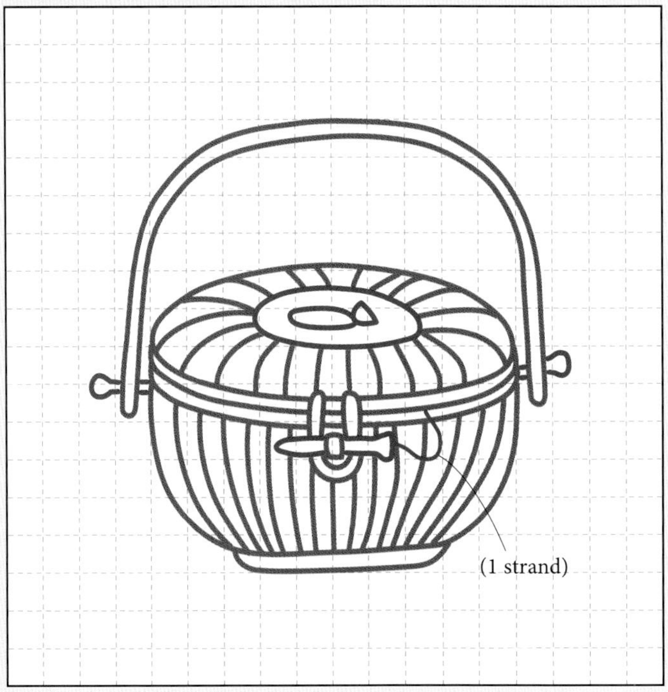

◆ use an outline stitch (2 strands) for any area not specified above

e Mini Pouch

This cute mini pouch fits nicely into the palm of your hand and is perfect to use as a coin purse or for little items. The embroidery will stand out if you quilt around the design. The back of the mini pouch is made from one piece of fabric with the quilting following the patterns in the fabric.

The design is from pattern **29** (p. 40).
Instructions for the pouch are on p. 198.

30 *Green Satchel*

I can imagine myself going out in the fall wearing a tweed jacket and carrying something like this satchel. The gentle curves are created with an outline stitch.

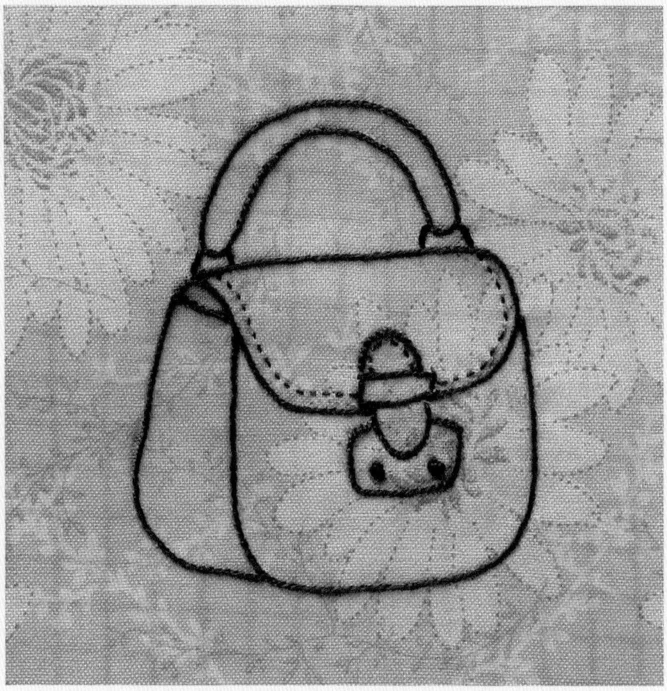

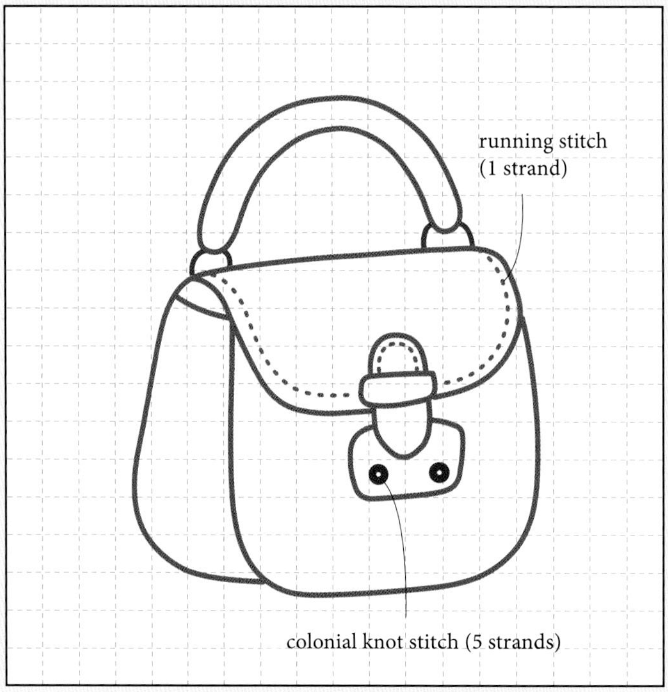

running stitch
(1 strand)
colonial knot stitch (5 strands)

◆ use an outline stitch (2 strands) for any area not specified above

31 *Blue Pumps*

One of the fun things about embroidery and why I like to design patterns so much is that you can easily design simple to complicated things. Even though it is not that comfortable to wear heels this high, these chic pumps with the straps are very cute.

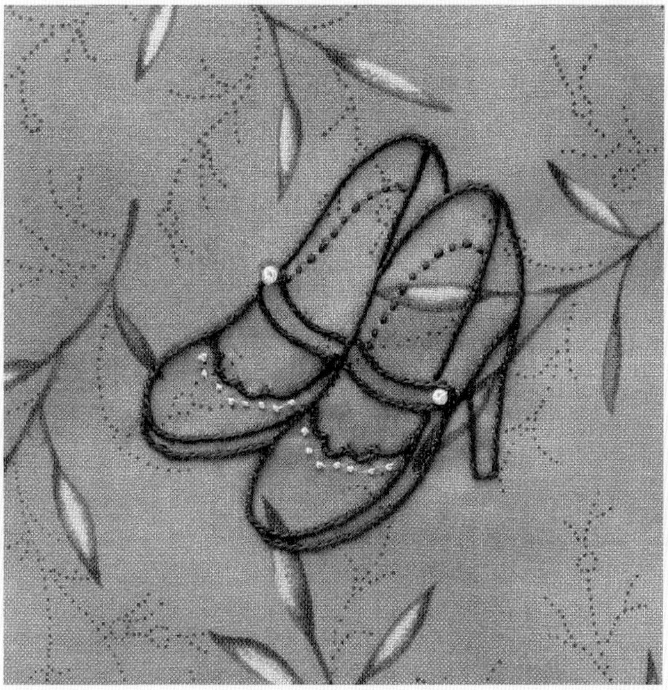

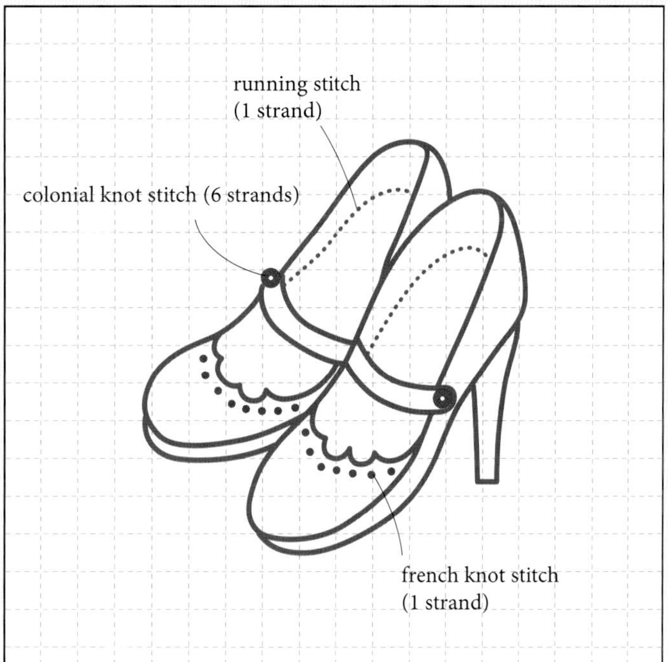
running stitch
(1 strand)
colonial knot stitch (6 strands)
french knot stitch
(1 strand)

◆ use an outline stitch (2 strands) for any area not specified above

32 *Left Hand*

I thought it was a little bit of fun to embroider the outline of the hand in blue floss. This is a very simple design of a small hand, such as a child's, but could be seen as an adult hand if you added a ring or two.

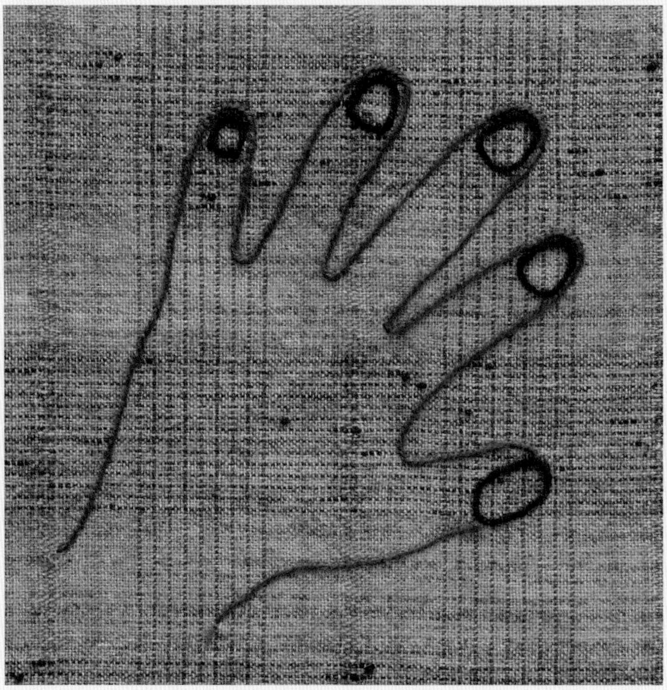

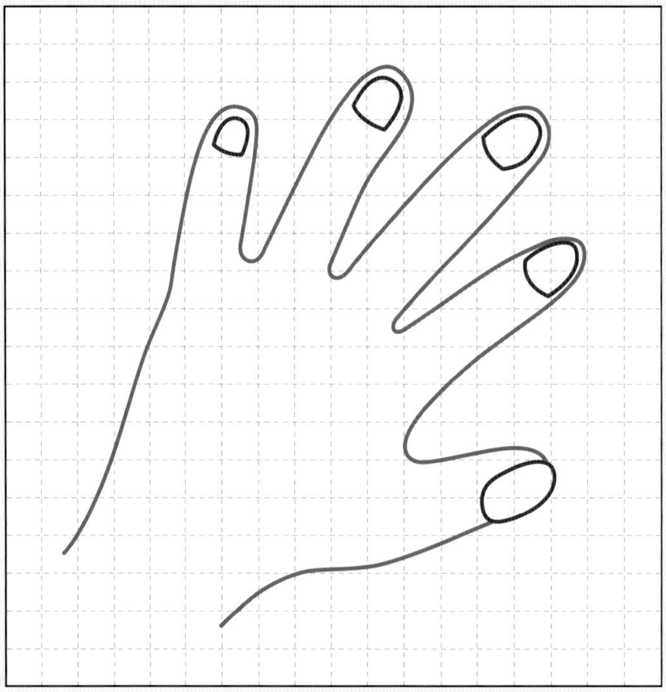

◆ use an outline stitch (2 strands) for any area not specified above

33 *Footprint*

The footprint is about the same size as a newborn baby. You can always make it as large as you want, but it is probably cuter when it is small. The background fabric I used has a pattern that reminds me of a sampler.

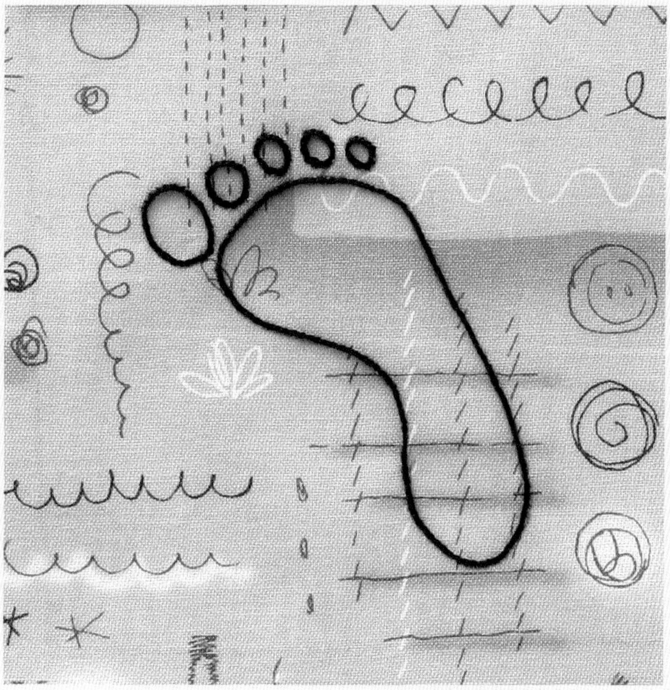

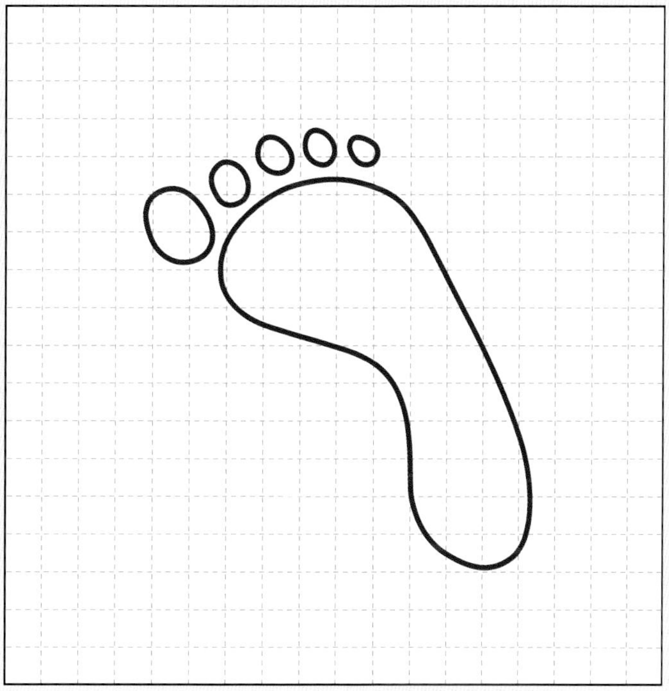

◆ use an outline stitch (2 strands) for any area not specified above

34 *Grandpa*

Grandpa is happily enjoying his retirement years. Use an outline stitch and take tiny stitches. The plaid homespun background fabric looks a little bit like wallpaper.

french knot stitch (1 strand)
(1 strand)
french knot stitch
(1 strand)

◆ use an outline stitch (2 strands) for any area not specified above

35 Grandma

Grandma reminds me of those that you read about in fairy tales. She wears earrings and a stylish hair clip even when she is hard at work cleaning in her apron.

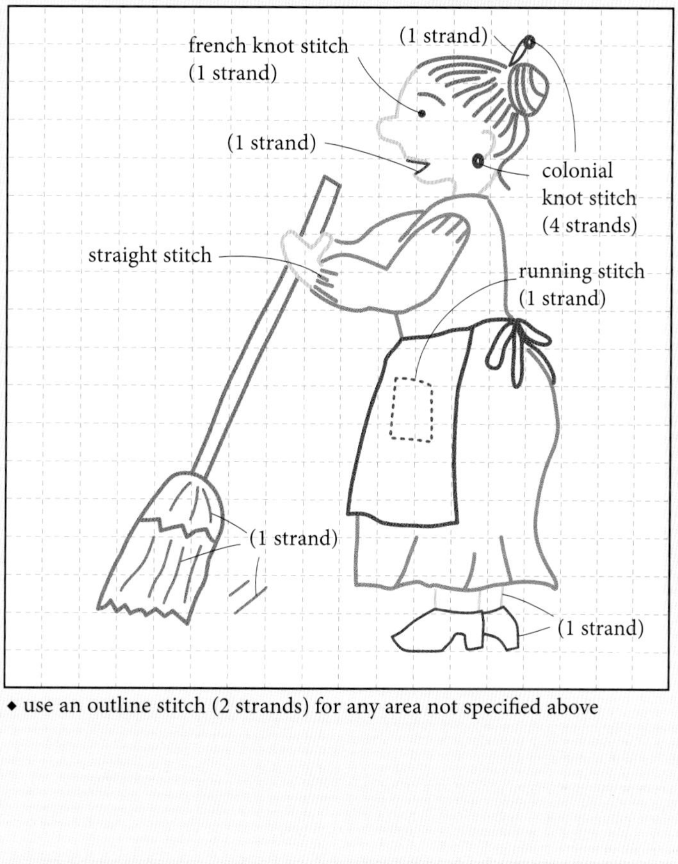

french knot stitch
(1 strand)
(1 strand)
(1 strand)
colonial
knot stitch
(4 strands)
straight stitch
running stitch
(1 strand)
(1 strand)
(1 strand)

◆ use an outline stitch (2 strands) for any area not specified above

36 *Elf*

The shoes, pointy red hat, round nose and the coat with the belt are the epitome of a cheerful little elf. He is extremely happy as he dances. The background fabric with brushed swirling circles adds to the sense of being carefree.

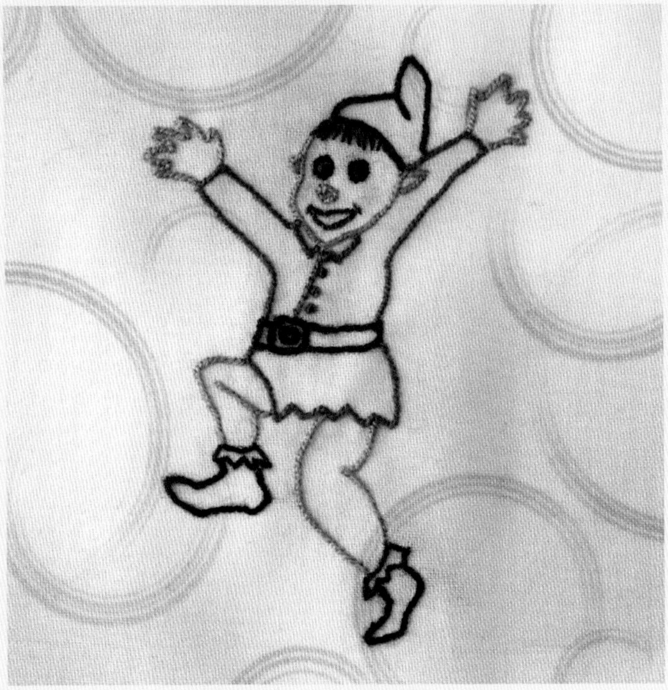

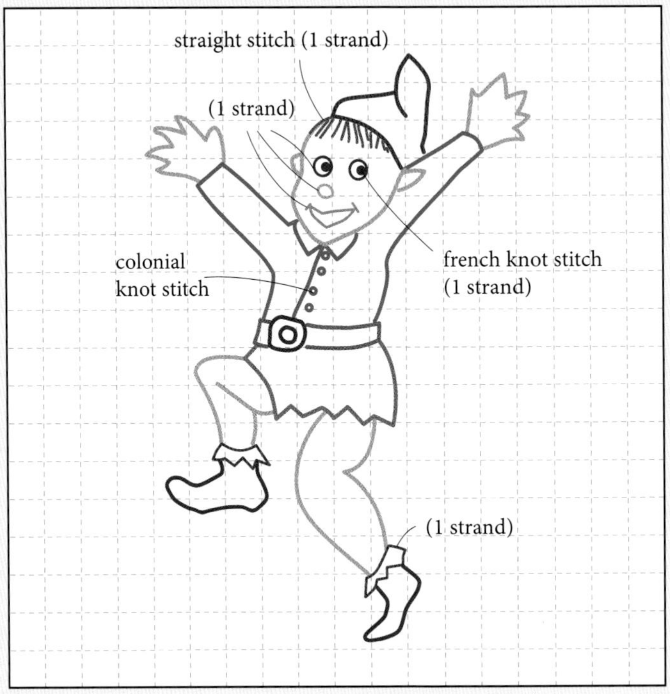
straight stitch (1 strand)
(1 strand)
colonial
knot stitch
french knot stitch
(1 strand)
(1 strand)

◆ use an outline stitch (2 strands) for any area not specified above

37 *Happy Birthday*

A perfect way to frame a message such as "Happy Birthday," "Thank you" or "Good Luck." Framed with little hearts, you can use this as a block in a quilt or maybe even stitched to the front of a card as a gift.

◆ use an outline stitch (2 strands) for any area not specified above

38 Zelkova Tree

I started with a 20 cm square [7⅞"] and drew a tree pattern. The first one is of a stately Zelkova tree with its branches extending out evenly and loaded with leaves. This design is one of four used in the wall hanging on p. 58.

◆ use an outline stitch (2 strands) for any area not specified above

39 *Weeping Willow Tree*

I love the way the Weeping Willow tree grows with its branches swaying gently whenever the wind blows. This is reflected in the soft curving of the embroidery stitches. This design is one of four used in the wall hanging on p. 58.

◆ use an outline stitch (2 strands) for any area not specified above

40 *Ash Tree*

Tall and impressive, the Ash tree is said to be the symbol of the "World Tree" in Norse mythology. This design is one of four used in the wall hanging on p. 58.

◆ use an outline stitch (2 strands) for any area not specified above

41 *Dawn Redwood Tree*

The majestic Metasequoia, also known as the Dawn Redwood, is a beautiful cone-shaped deciduous tree. I used a lazy daisy stitch to give the appearance of many leaves. This design is one of four used in the wall hanging on p. 58.

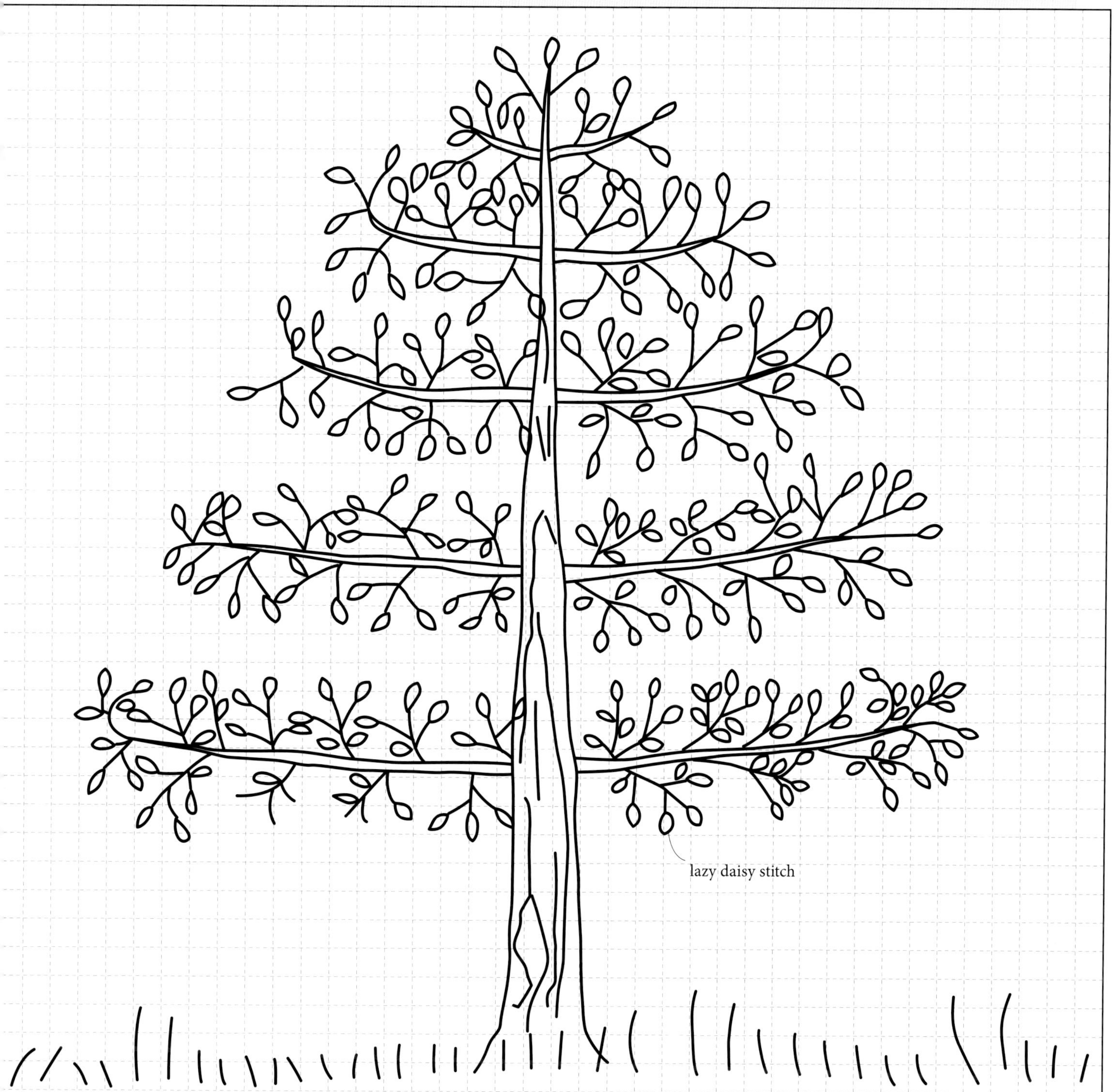

◆ use an outline stitch (2 strands) for any area not specified above

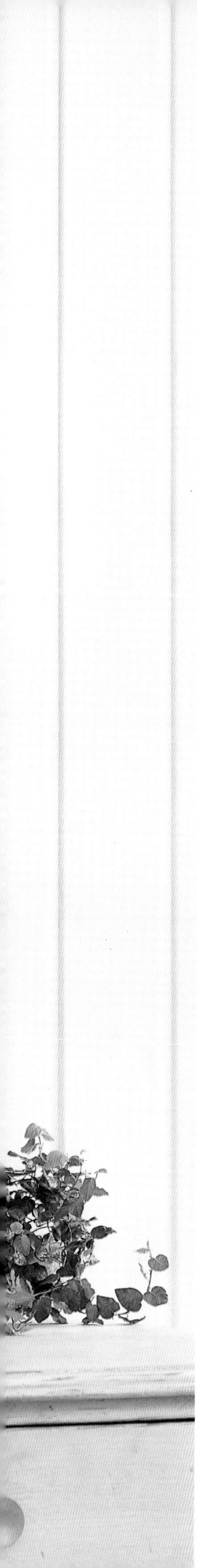

f Wall Hanging

I designed this wall hanging using the four embroidered tree blocks. The quilting in the background of each tree block mimics the wind and adds much more visual interest than with just the embroidery alone.

The designs are from patterns **38-41** (pp. 50-57). Instructions for the wall hanging are on p. 200.

42 *Horsetail*

This interesting plant is known as "horsetail." I've designed the pattern with a combination of both appliqué and embroidery. Stitch the colonial knots very close together to resemble the brushy head of the plant and straight stitches along the stems.

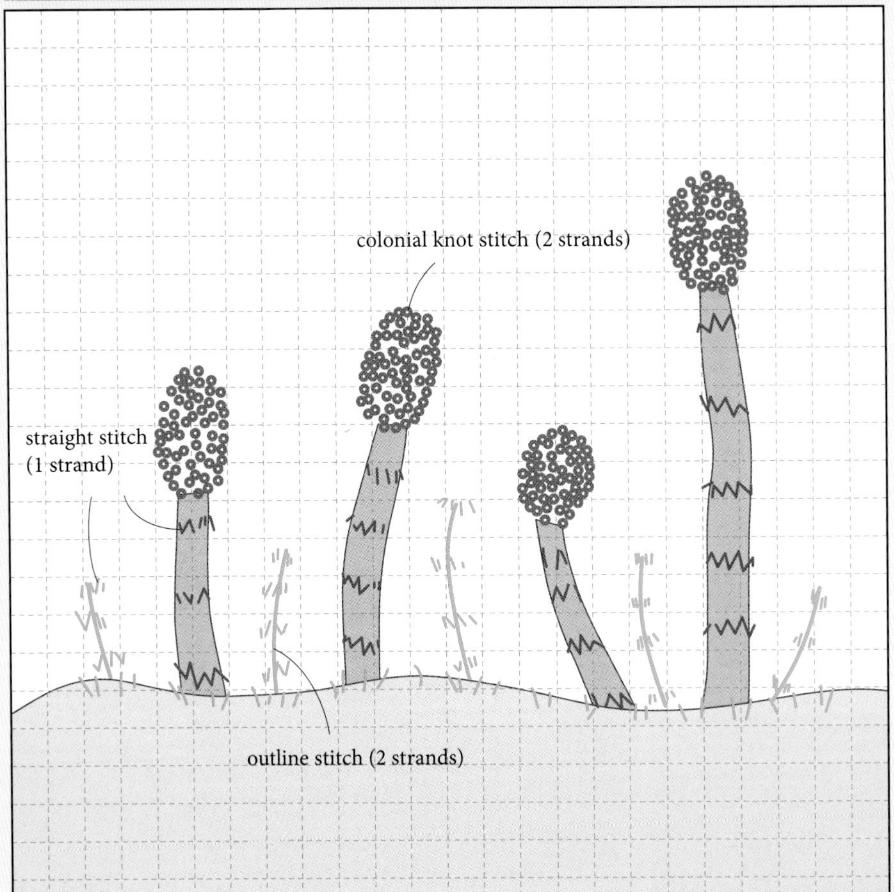
colonial knot stitch (2 strands)
straight stitch
(1 strand)
outline stitch (2 strands)

43 Autumn Flowers

I am reminded of autumn flowers with these small yellow blooms. Use 4 strands of floss to make the yellow flowers with colonial knots. Stitch different numbers of colonial knots in different groupings and positions to balance out the overall design.

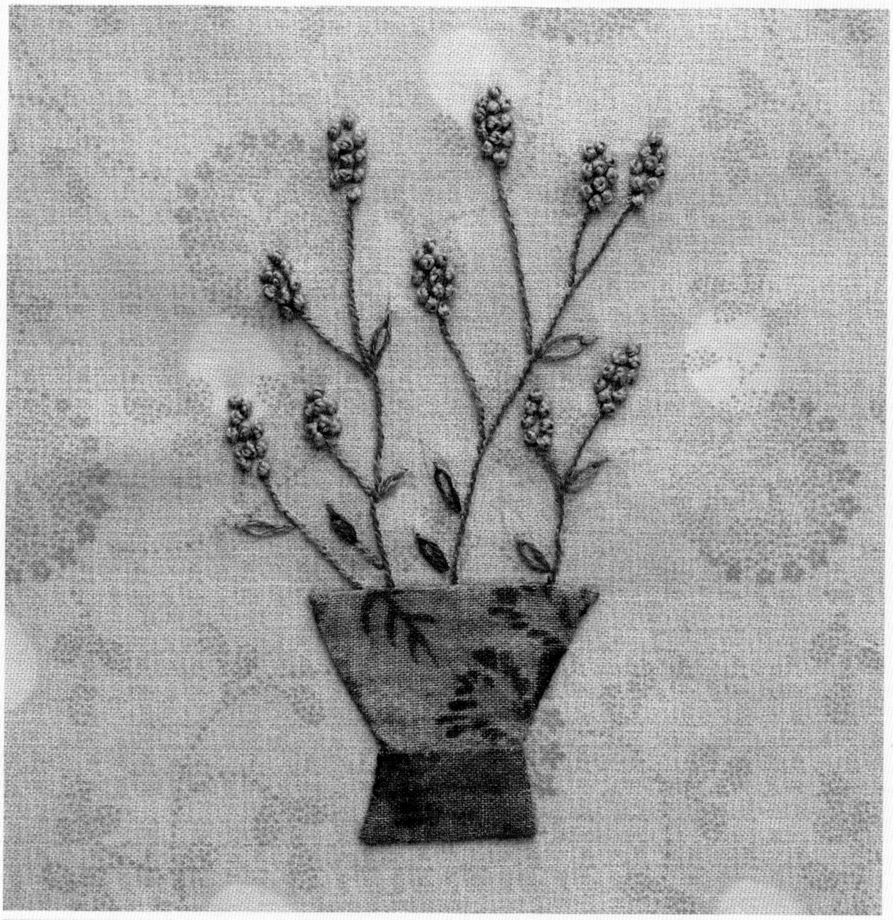

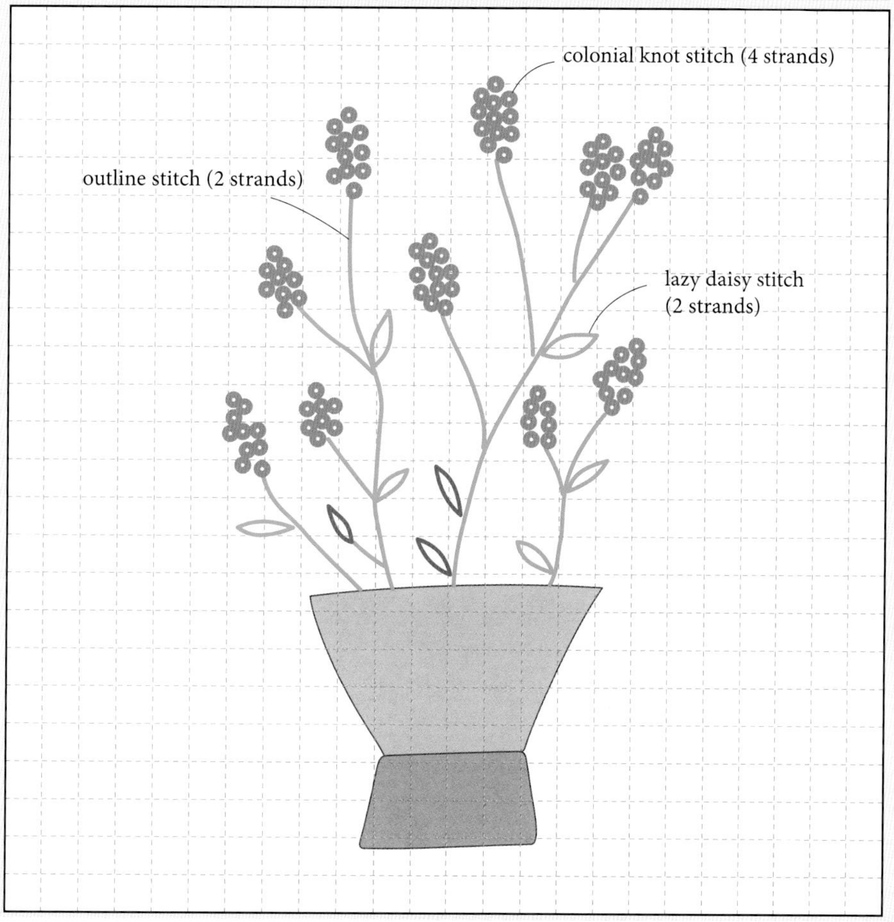
colonial knot stitch (4 strands)
outline stitch (2 strands)
lazy daisy stitch
(2 strands)

44 *Button Sampler*

I thought it would be cute to embellish various buttons by adding embroidery around them using fairly simple stitches. I couldn't stop with one, so ended up making a nine-patch where I also chose to use different background fabrics. Have fun trying this with buttons that you have on hand.

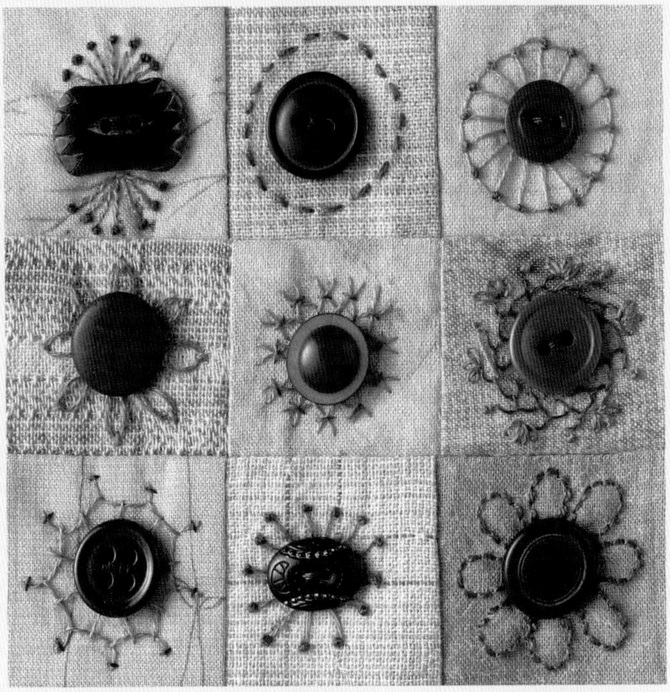

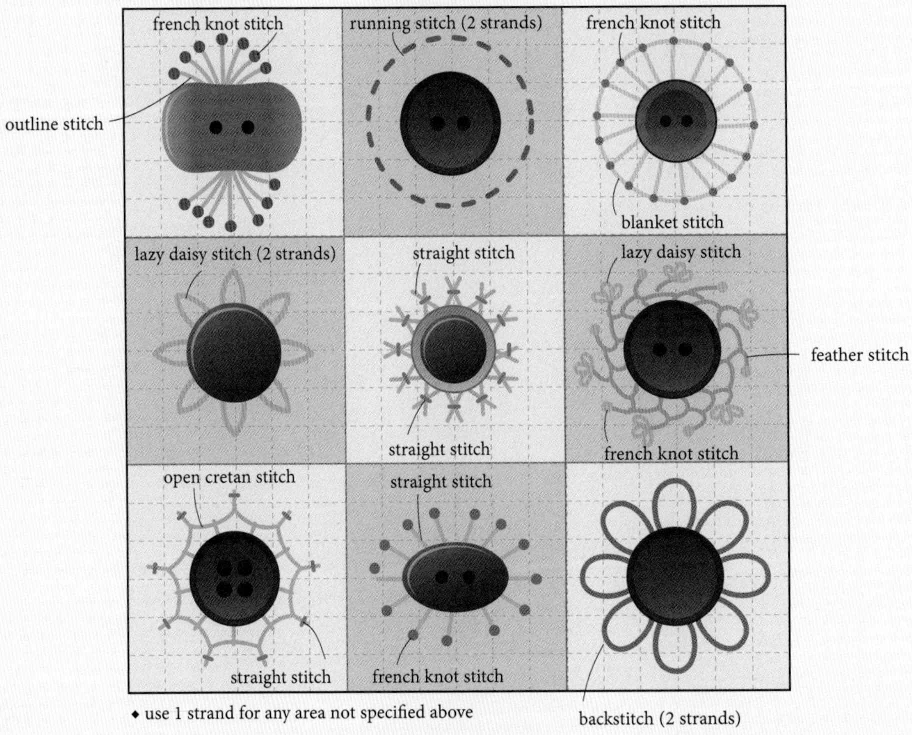

french knot stitch
outline stitch
running stitch (2 strands)
french knot stitch
blanket stitch
lazy daisy stitch (2 strands)
straight stitch
straight stitch
lazy daisy stitch
feather stitch
french knot stitch
open cretan stitch
straight stitch
straight stitch
french knot stitch
backstitch (2 strands)

◆ use 1 strand for any area not specified above

45 Four-Leaf Clover

The lucky four-leaf clover has heart-shaped leaves with perfect symmetry. I used different stitches for each one, but deliberately upset the balance by positioning the lower right-hand one on an angle.

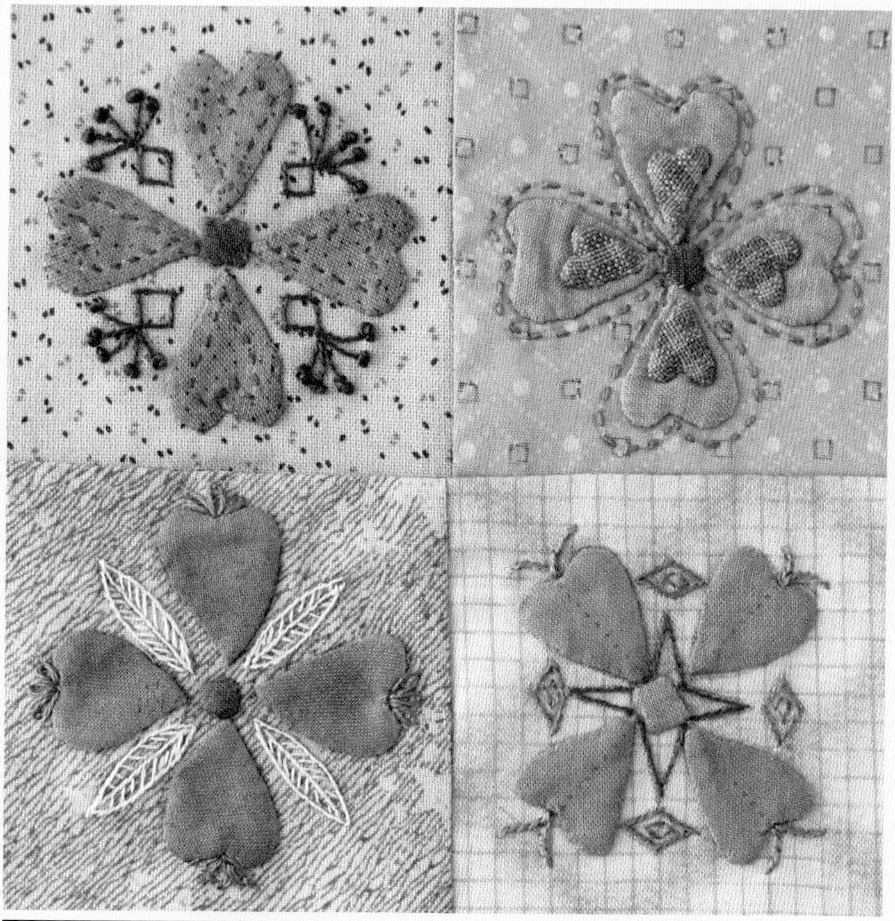

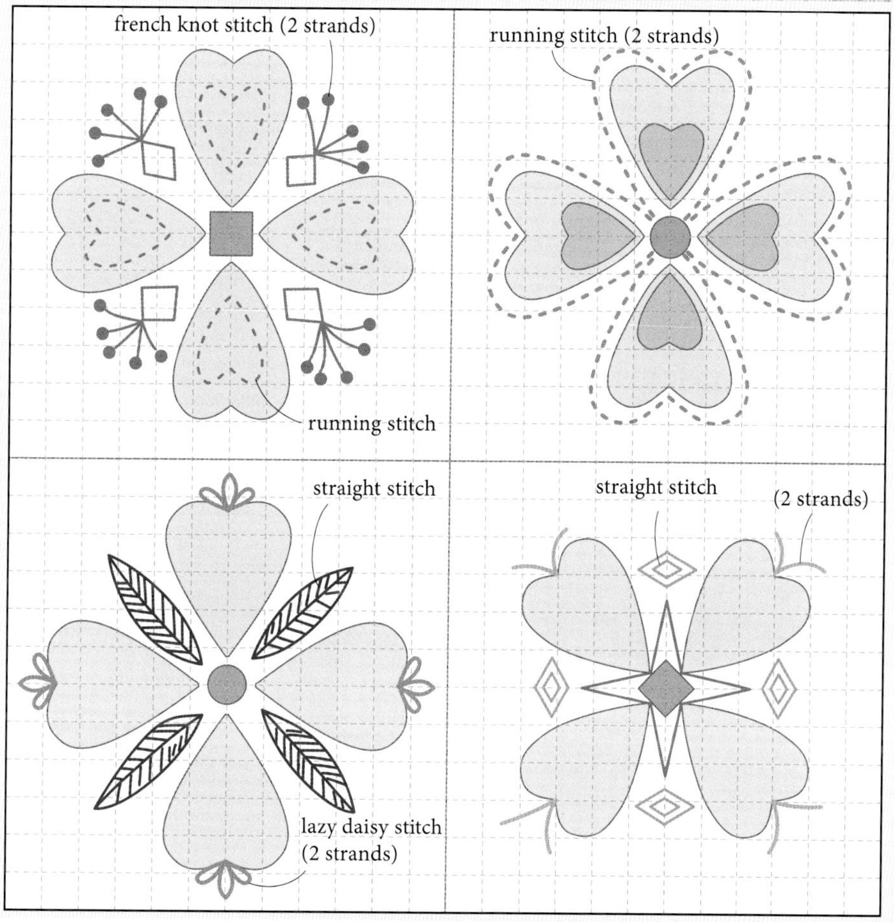

french knot stitch (2 strands)
running stitch
running stitch (2 strands)
straight stitch
lazy daisy stitch (2 strands)
straight stitch
(2 strands)

◆ use an outline stitch (1 strand) for any area not specified above

46 *Floral Wreath*

I combined two different kinds of greenery and the pink flowers in a circle to create a wreath. You can enlarge this 12 cm square [4¾"] pattern, but I would suggest that you increase the number of the motifs rather than just enlarge them.

colonial knot stitch (4 strands)
lazy daisy stitch
(3 strands)
outline stitch (3 strands)
straight stitch (1 strand)
outline stitch (2 strands)

47 Star & Cranberries

Piece a Lemoyne Star for the center and appliqué the little circles all the way around to represent the cranberries. The embroidery is done between the circles to create a wreath as well as in the four corners. This design is used in the keepsake box on p. 66.

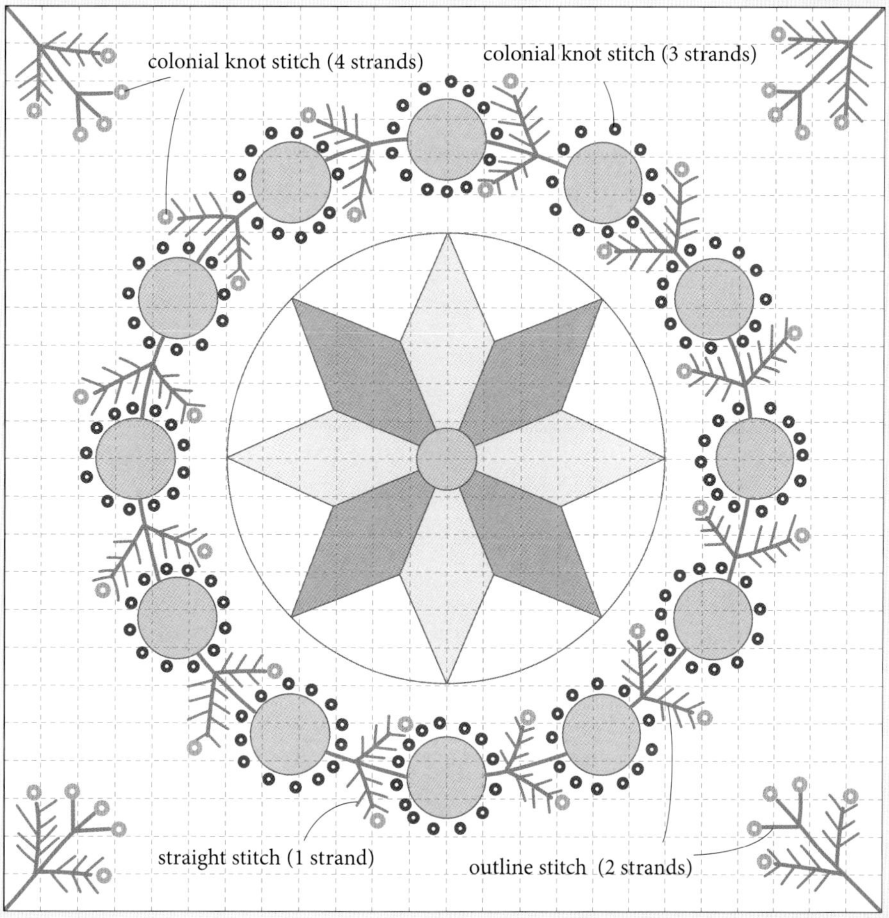
colonial knot stitch (4 strands)
colonial knot stitch (3 strands)
straight stitch (1 strand)
outline stitch (2 strands)

g Keepsake Box

The circular shape of the wreath, as well as the gentle curves framing the appliqué and embroidered design, complement the square structure of the box. The colonial knots add a visually pleasing 3-dimensional effect.

The design is from pattern **47** (p. 65).
Instructions for the box are on p. 202.

48 *Tree Dahlia*

Tree Dahlia's can grow to 20 ft. high and are loaded with beautiful flowers such as this one in pink. I used tiny outline stitches for the embroidery, including the green buds on the ends. The background fabric is a finely woven homespun.

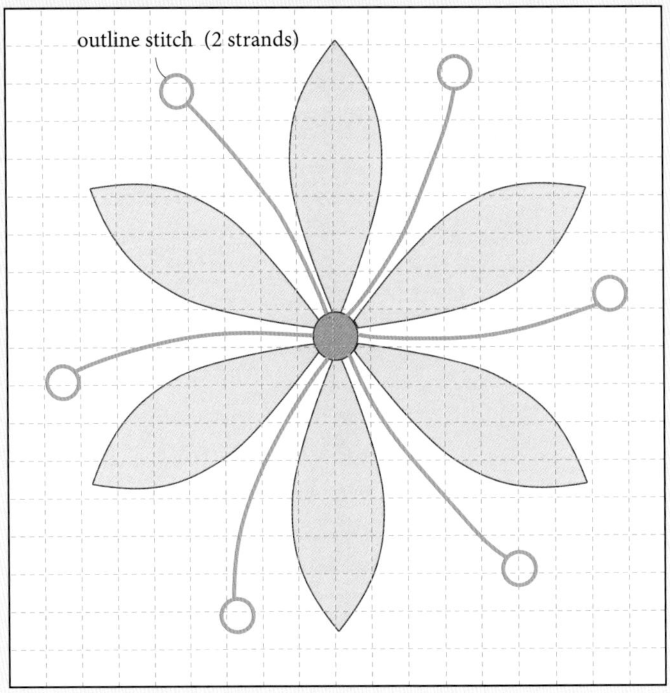

49 *Marigold*

For a unique look and one which is similar to nature, I fussy cut the flower petals so that the centers of them were darker than the outer portions. The curved stems and leaves are done using a lazy daisy stitch (the same as pattern 46, p. 64) and enhance the appliquéd flower.

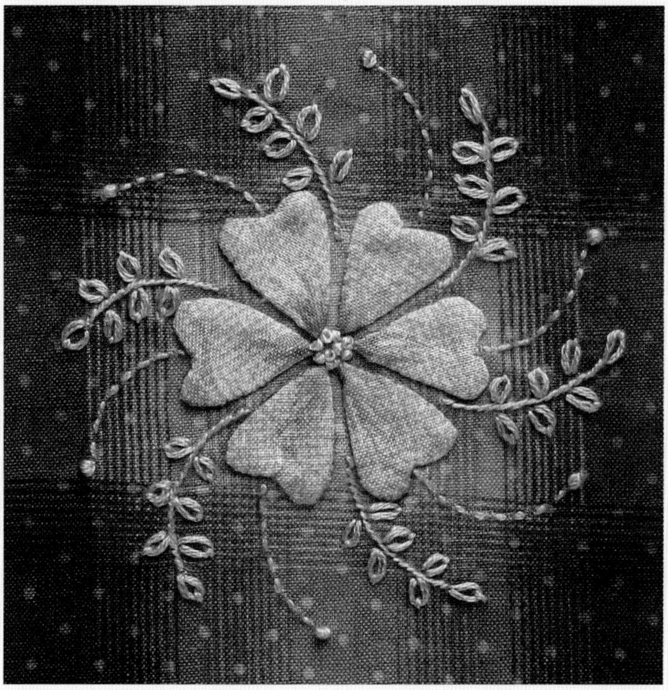

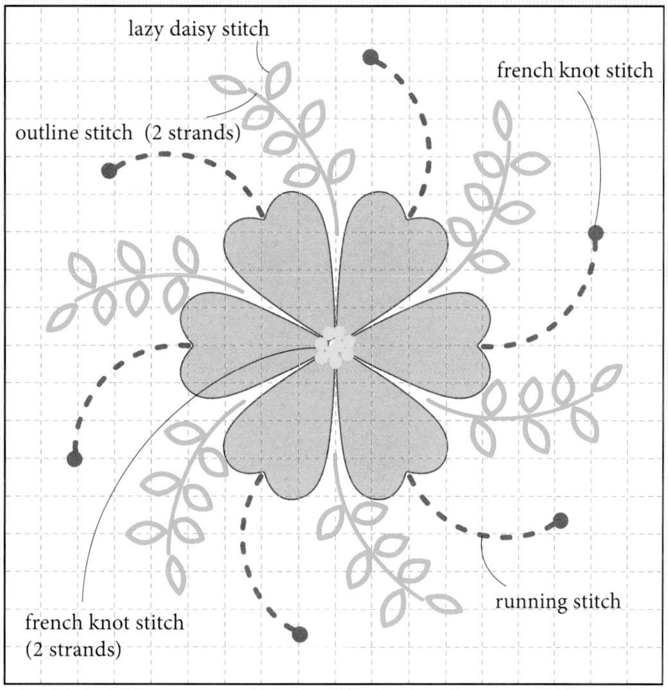
lazy daisy stitch
french knot stitch
outline stitch (2 strands)
running stitch
french knot stitch
(2 strands)

◆ use 3 strands for any area not specified above

50 *Compass Sage*

This was easy to design as well as fun to put together. I made a circle and then divided it up. Although the background of the circle is the same as the background of the block, the individual pieces are cut on the straight of grain and pieced. The seams between the pieces, as well as the outer circle, are embroidered with a herringbone stitch. Soft green sage leaves are embroidered in the four corners.

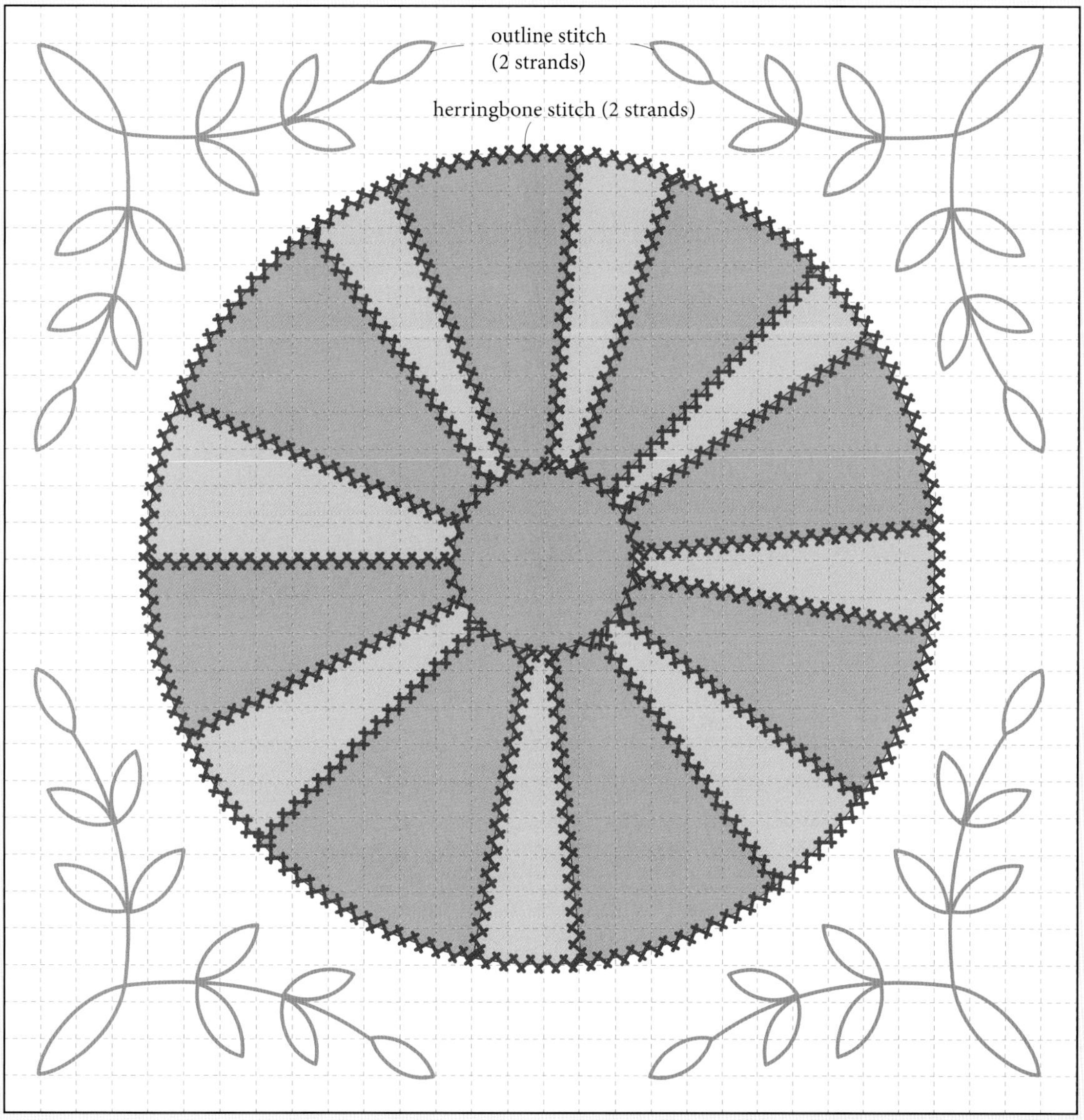

outline stitch
(2 strands)
herringbone stitch (2 strands)

51 *Clover Garland*

Reminiscent of flower chains made of clover, I designed this garland of clover using a combination of appliqué and embroidery. It could easily be used as a continuous border pattern if you straighten out the center line. I added a layer of interest by choosing a background fabric that has a printed clover pattern as well. This design is used in the round keepsake box on p. 74.

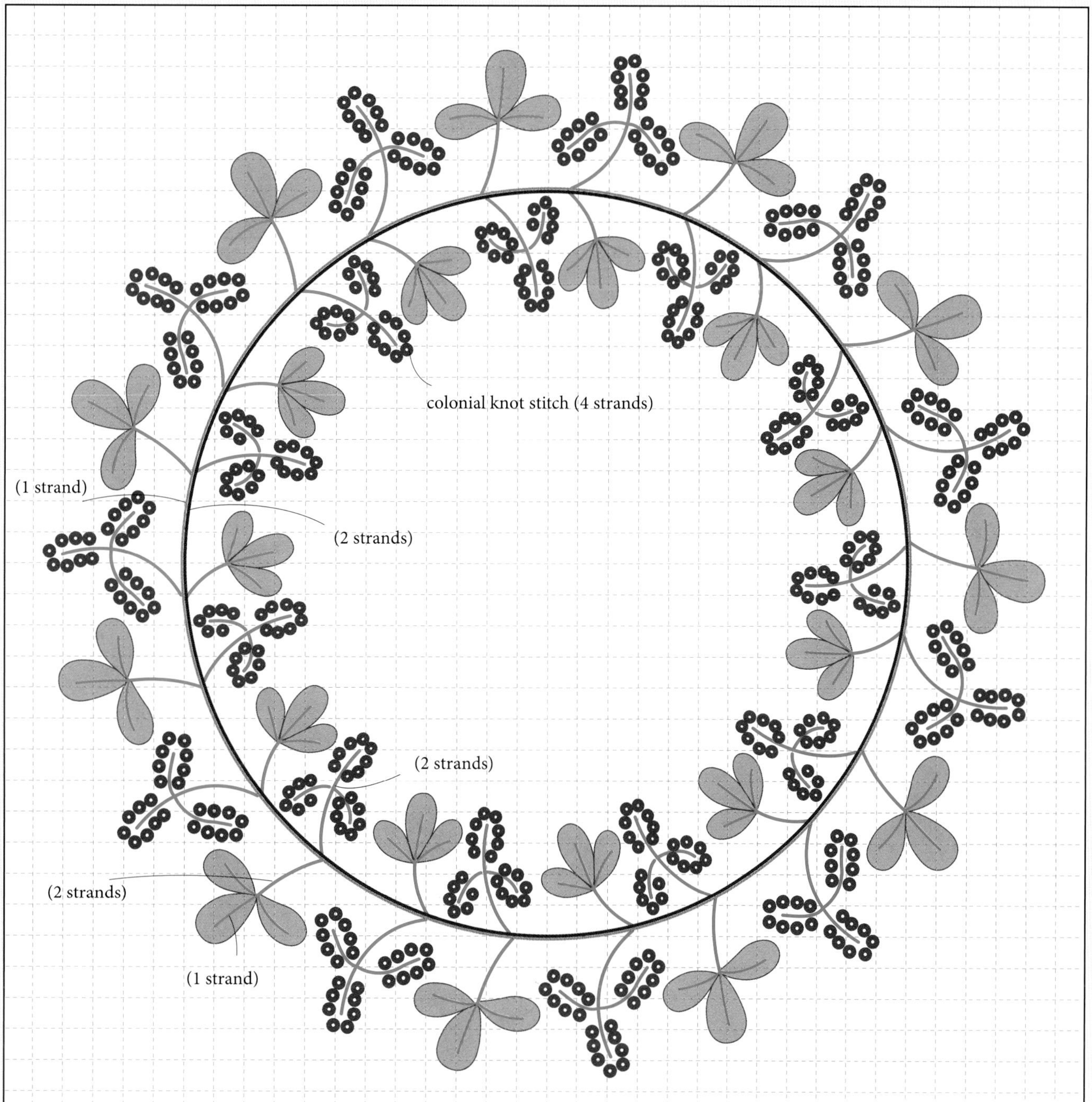

colonial knot stitch (4 strands)
(1 strand)
(2 strands)
(2 strands)
(2 strands)
(1 strand)

◆ use an outline stitch for any area not specified above

h Round Keepsake Box

I wanted to use the clover garland pattern in a project and decided it would be perfect on the top of a lid. The large bead on top and the piping around the edges of the top and bottom of the box make it unique. I chose to use a wood grain-patterned fabric for the vertical side pieces to make it look like fencing.

The design is from pattern **51** (pp. 72-73).
Instructions for the box are on p. 204.

52 *Passion Flower*

In this section of the book, I am introducing patterns that combine both appliqué and embroidery. Piece a Lemoyne Star (pattern 47, p. 65) for the center and embroider both lazy daisy and french knot stitches around in a circular pattern to make it stand out.

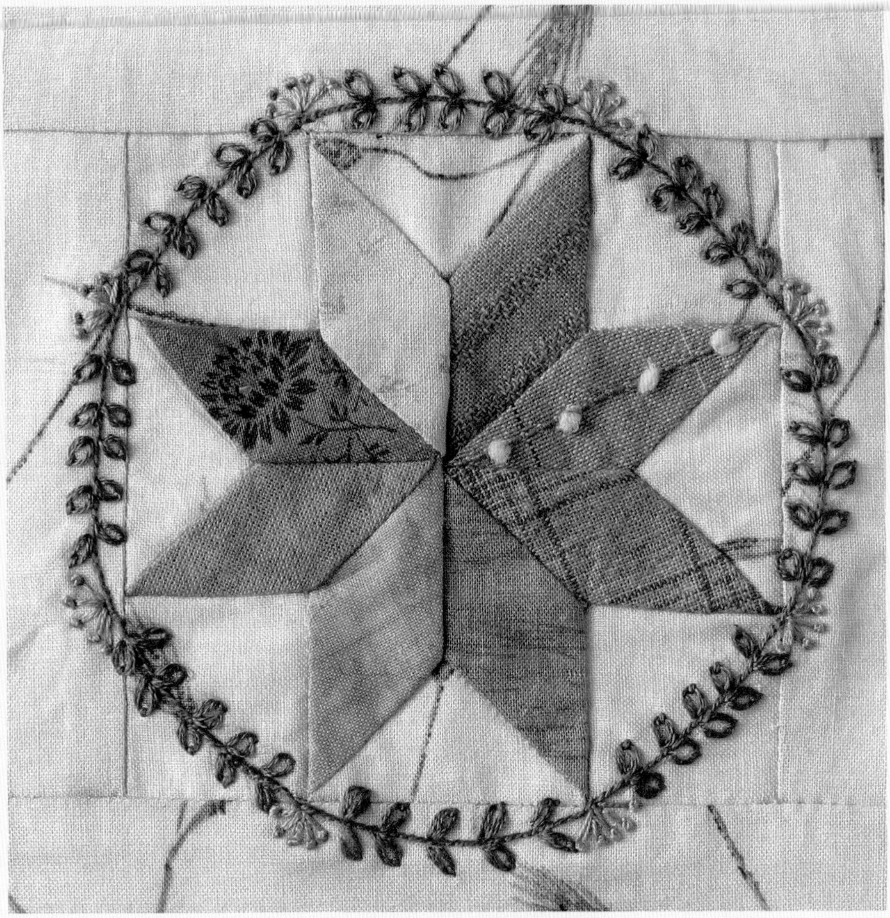

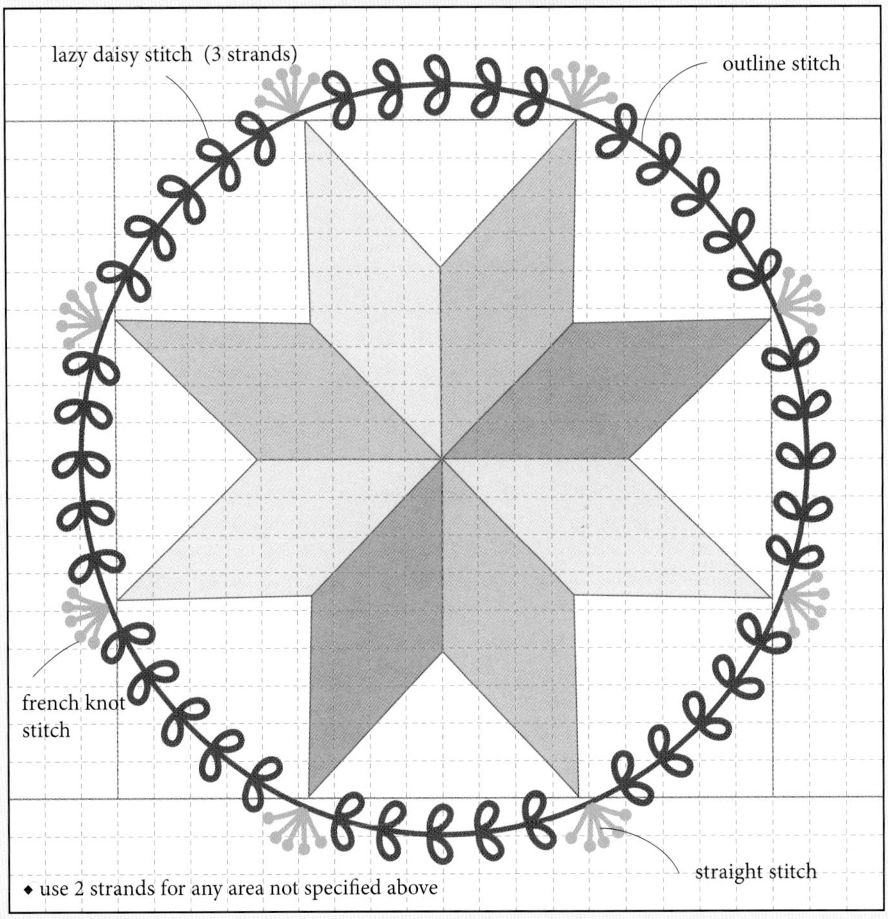

lazy daisy stitch (3 strands)
outline stitch
french knot stitch
straight stitch
◆ use 2 strands for any area not specified above

53 *Dill Log Cabin*

Adding embroidery to pieced blocks can add a sense of softness, such as this dill pattern in the four corners of this log cabin. I "tied" each bundle of herbs with a little bit of red for fun.

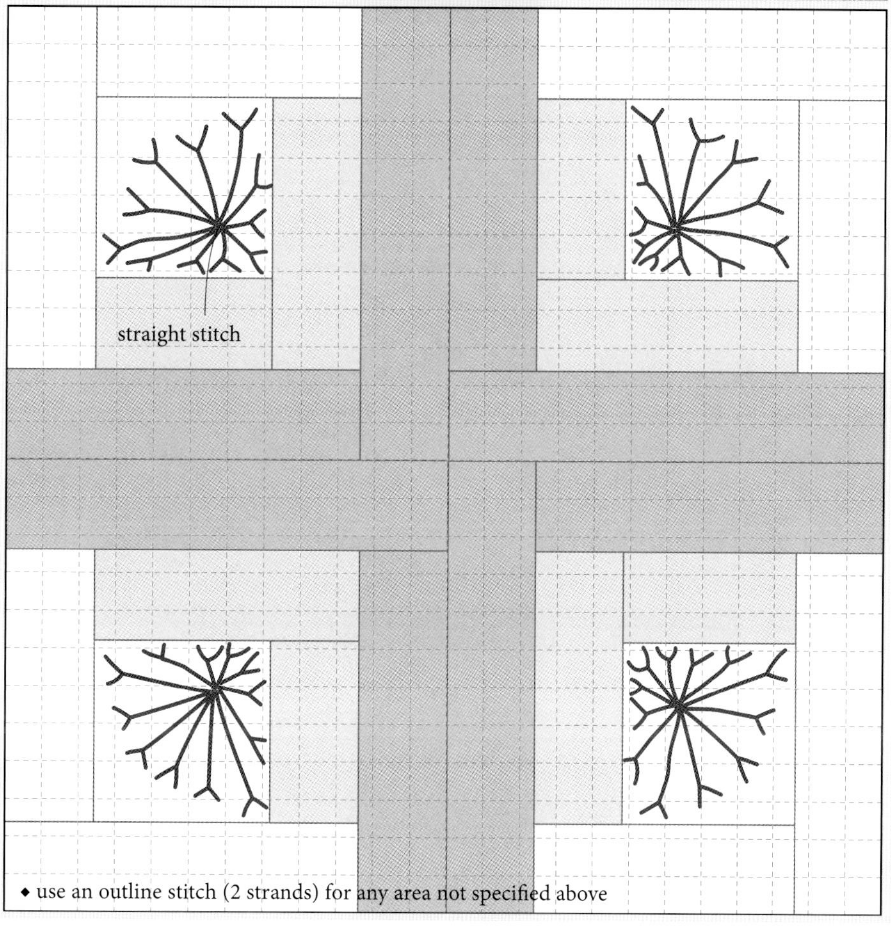
straight stitch
◆ use an outline stitch (2 strands) for any area not specified above

54 *Curves & Curves*

Piece the block using gently curved pieces of fabric. Embroider undulating lines of various stitches on top, being careful not to follow the seam lines. This design is used in the pouch on p. 79.

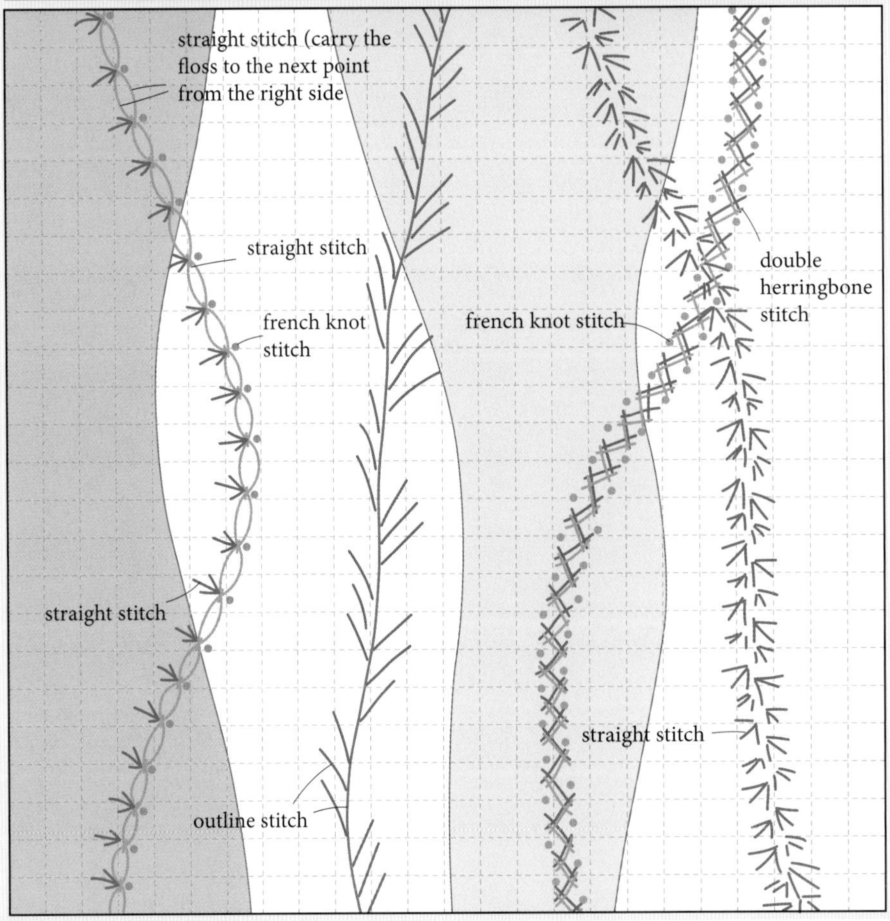

straight stitch (carry the floss to the next point from the right side
straight stitch
french knot stitch
french knot stitch
double herringbone stitch
straight stitch
straight stitch
outline stitch

◆ use 1 strand for any area not specified above

i Coin Purse

I wanted to make a simple little coin purse that didn't have a gusset. I pieced and embroidered the front of the coin purse following pattern 54 (p. 78). The embroidery might look complicated, but is really just a combination of several stitches. The opposing lines of the seams and the embroidery help to visually balance each other.

The design is from pattern **54** (p. 78).
Instructions for the coin purse are on p. 201.

55 *Square Stitch*

I have found that some people think that it is difficult to do embroidery on top of patchwork or pieced blocks, but I have never found this to be true. Combining embroidery with appliqué or piecework can actually make any piece so much more interesting, such as the case in these squares outlined with a running stitch.

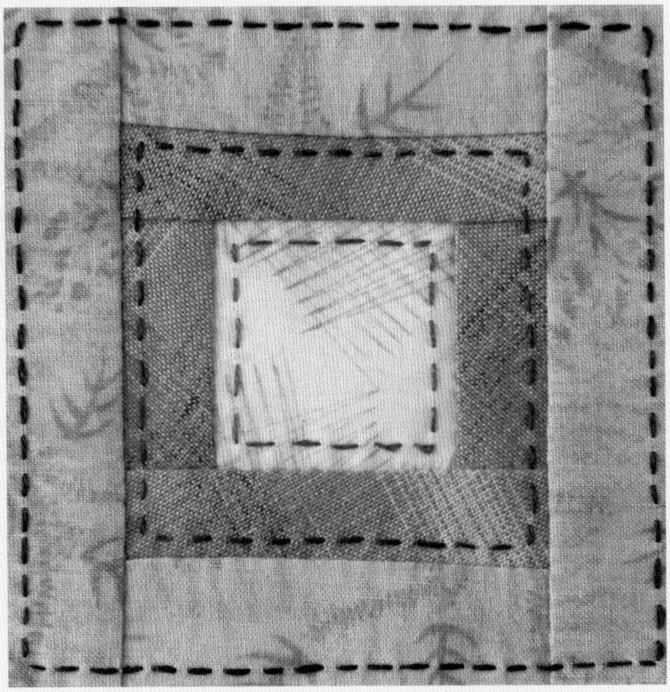

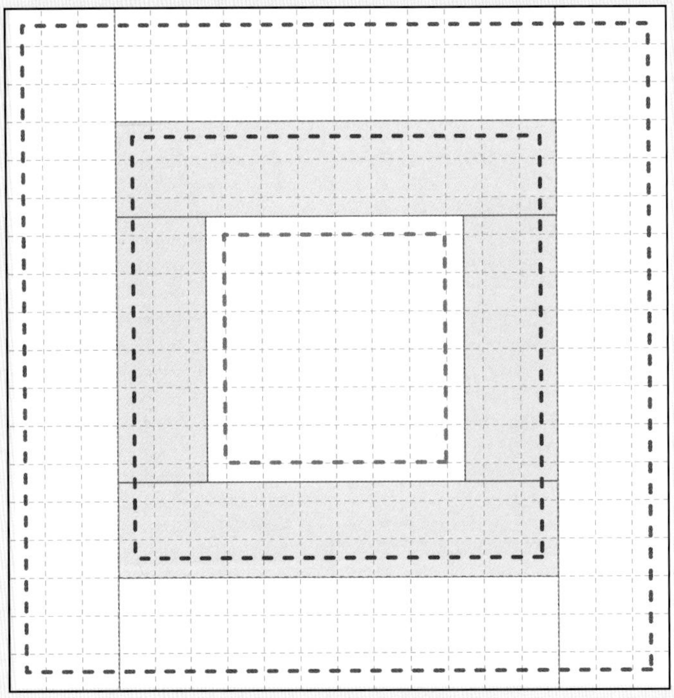

◆ use a running stitch (2 strands) for the area above

56 Circles & Dotted Lines

It can be fun to use embroidery to create your own fabric by doing an all-over pattern. Embroider the background pieces of the four patch with a running stitch before appliquéing the circles on top. Use the same embroidered fabric to appliqué the circles on the other two squares. This design is used in the shoulder bag on p. 82.

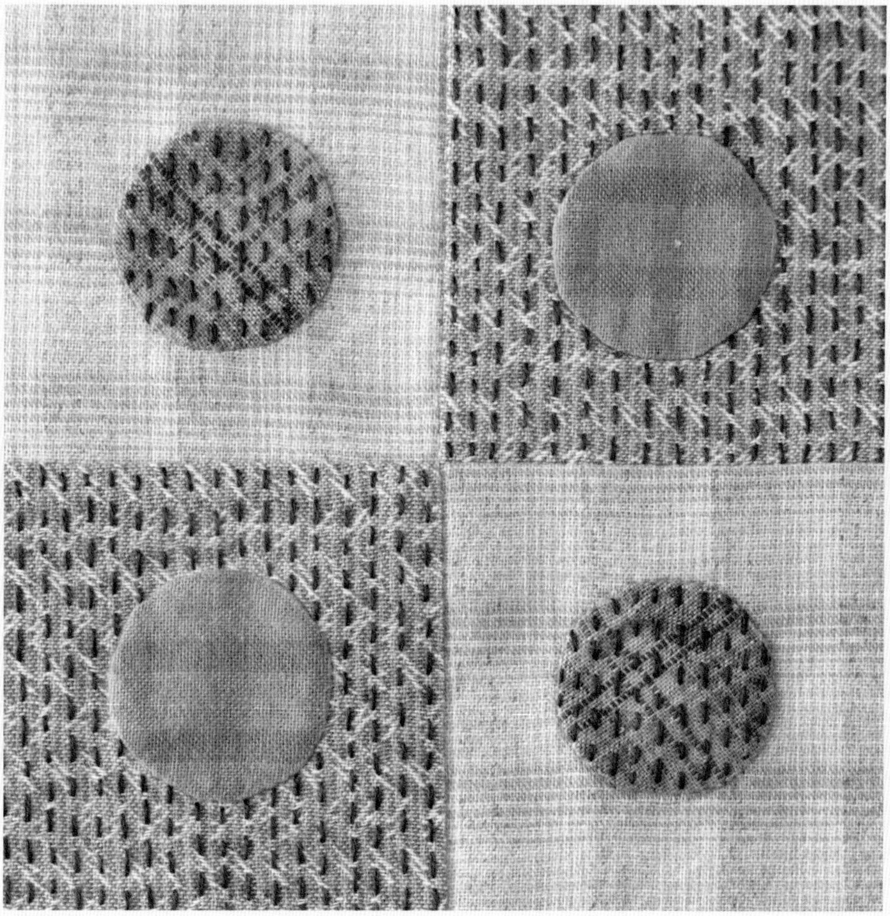

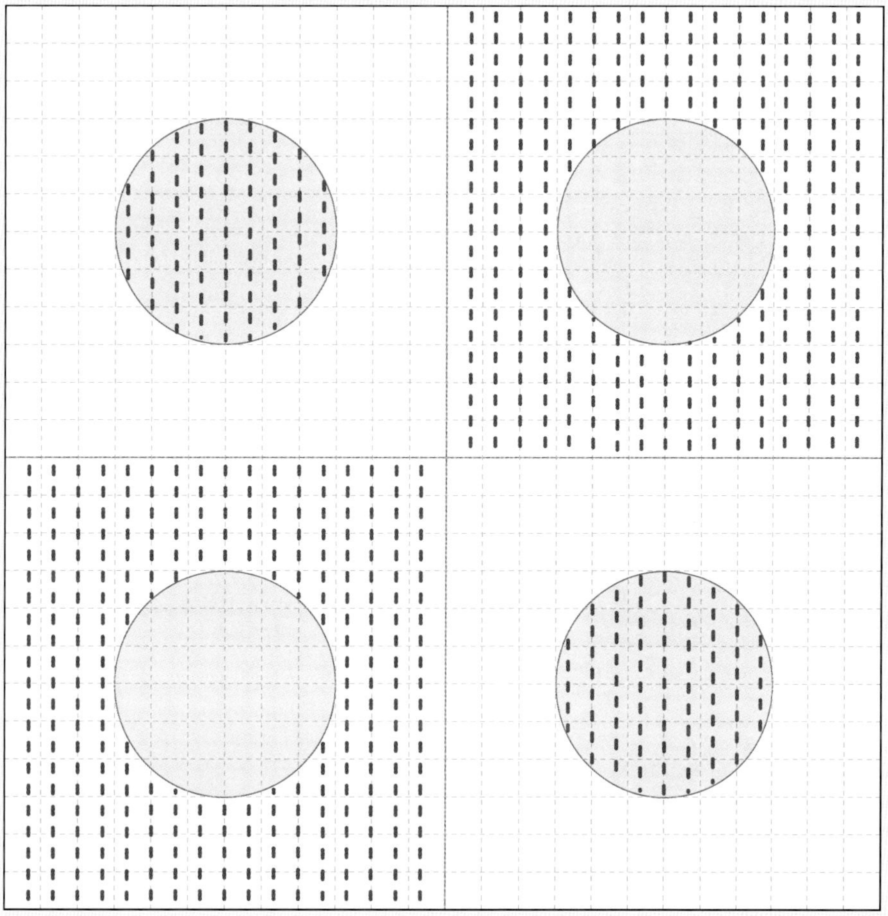

◆ use a running stitch (2 strands) for the entire design

j Shoulder Bag

I used pattern 56 for the flap of the shoulder bag. I chose to quilt lines in the background pieces of the nine-patch that go in the opposite direction to the running stitches in order to add visual texture and interest. This is an easy-to-use, throw-over-your-shoulder, kind of bag for everyday use.

The design is from pattern **56** (p. 81).
Instructions for the bag are on p. 206.

57 *Beehive*

The background is created simply by sewing hexagons together, commonly known as Grandmother's Flower Garden. However, the depth of design really comes from embroidering the same shape and size of hexagons on top and shifted to the right a little bit.

◆ use an outline stitch (1 strand) for the entire design

58 *Bay Leaf Flower*

The appliqué pattern is cute by itself, but it is much more charming with the added flowers and buds stitched into where the bay leaves intersect.

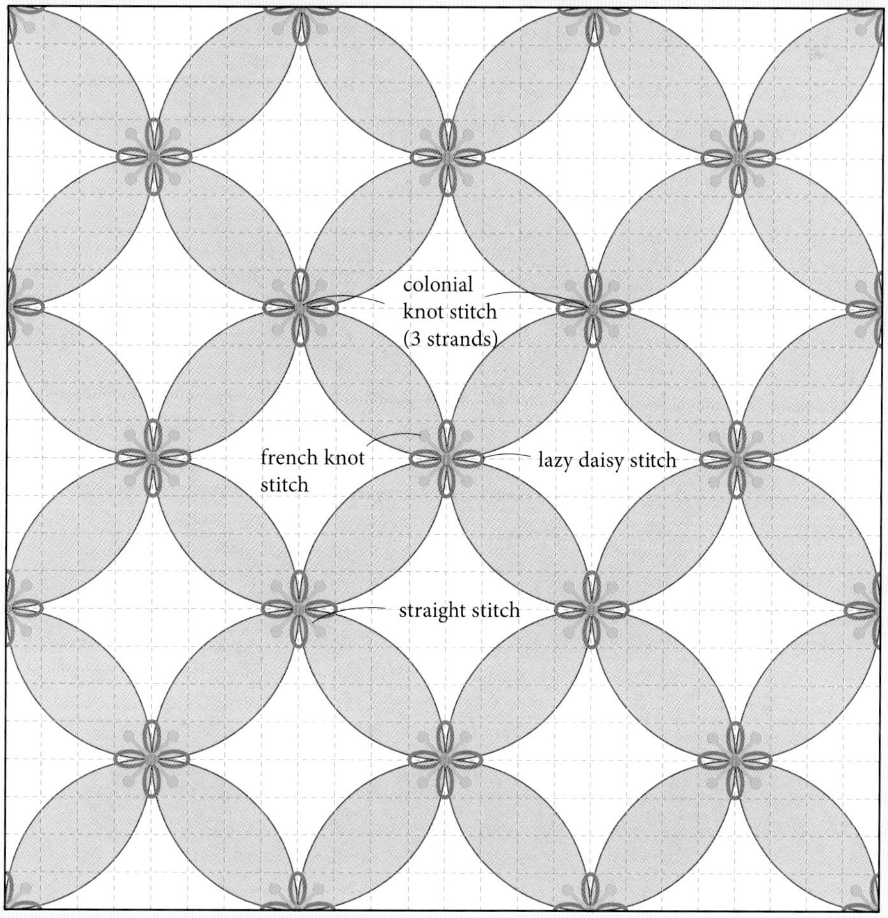

colonial
knot stitch
(3 strands)
french knot
stitch
lazy daisy stitch
straight stitch

◆ use 2 strands for any area not specified to the left

59 *Small Stars*

Create the background by piecing together 2 cm [¾"] squares. Stitch a double cross stitch where each square intersects to make it appear like stars scattered across the fabric. Be sure that the seam allowances on the wrong side are all going in one direction as you embroider.

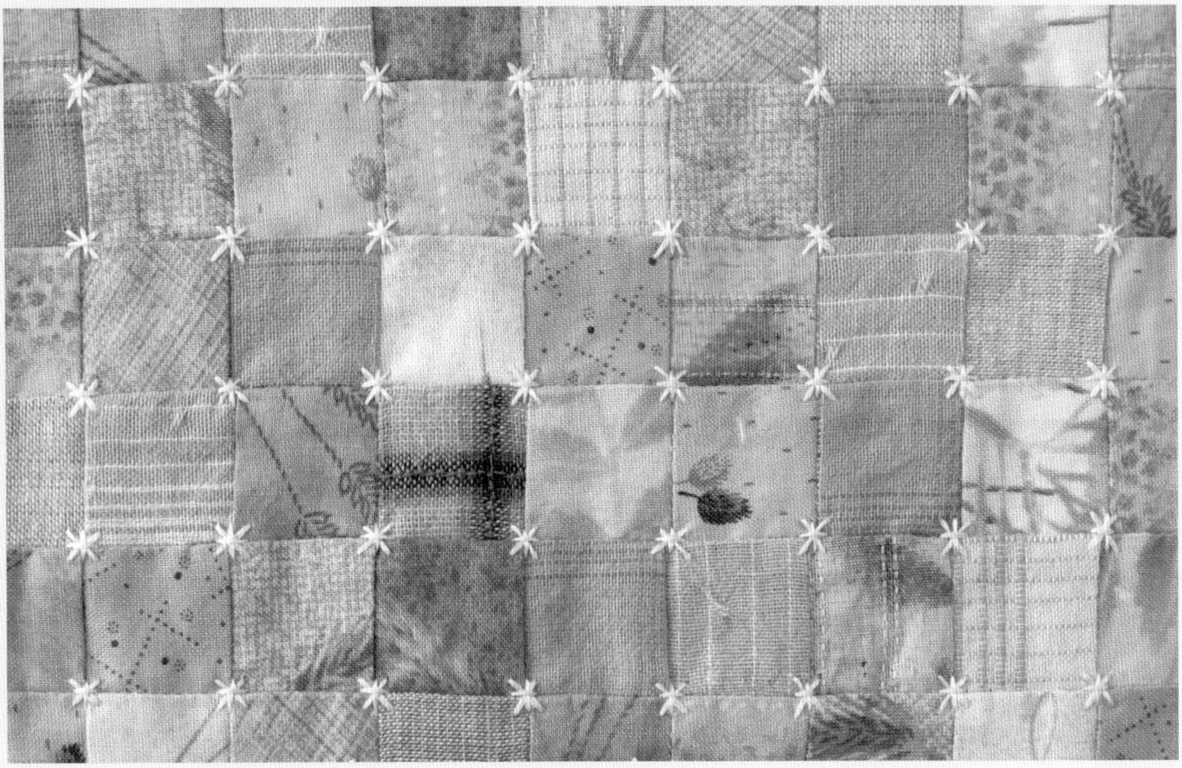

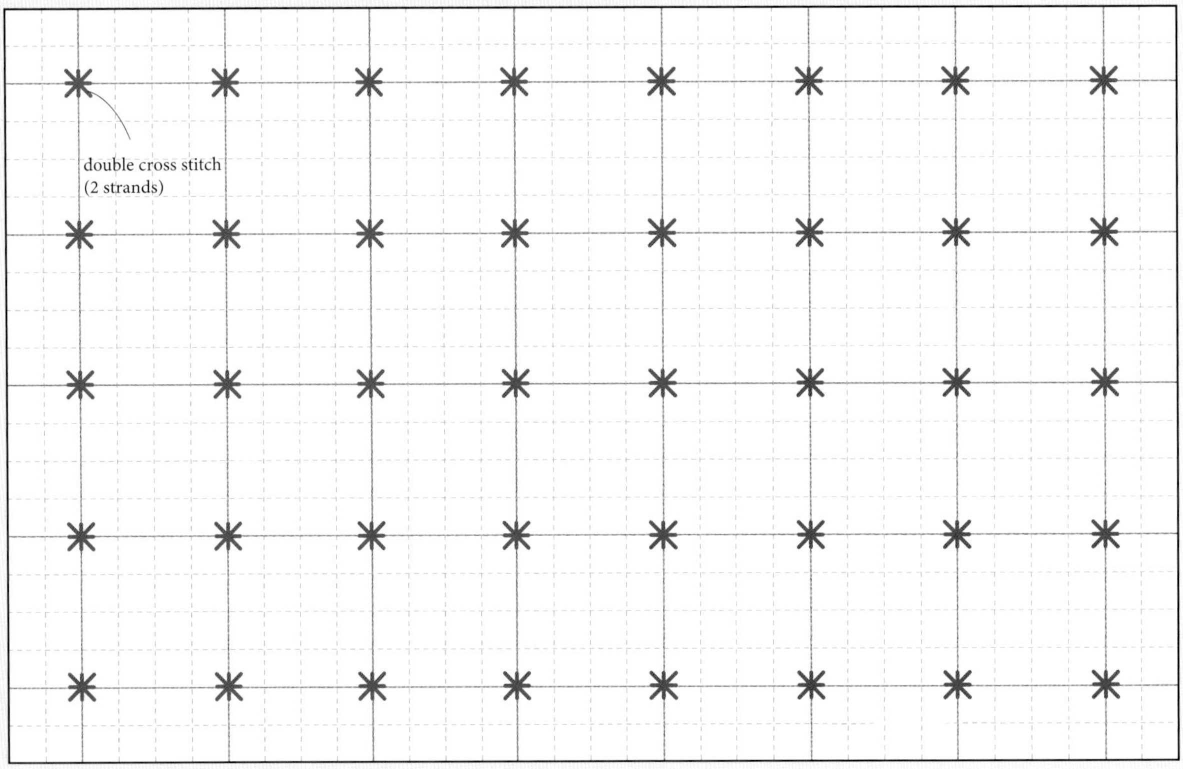

60 *Chamomile*

This is essentially the same as pattern 59, but with different stitches embroidered in the intersection of the pieced squares. I made a field of blooming chamomile flowers by using the lazy daisy and colonial knot stitches.

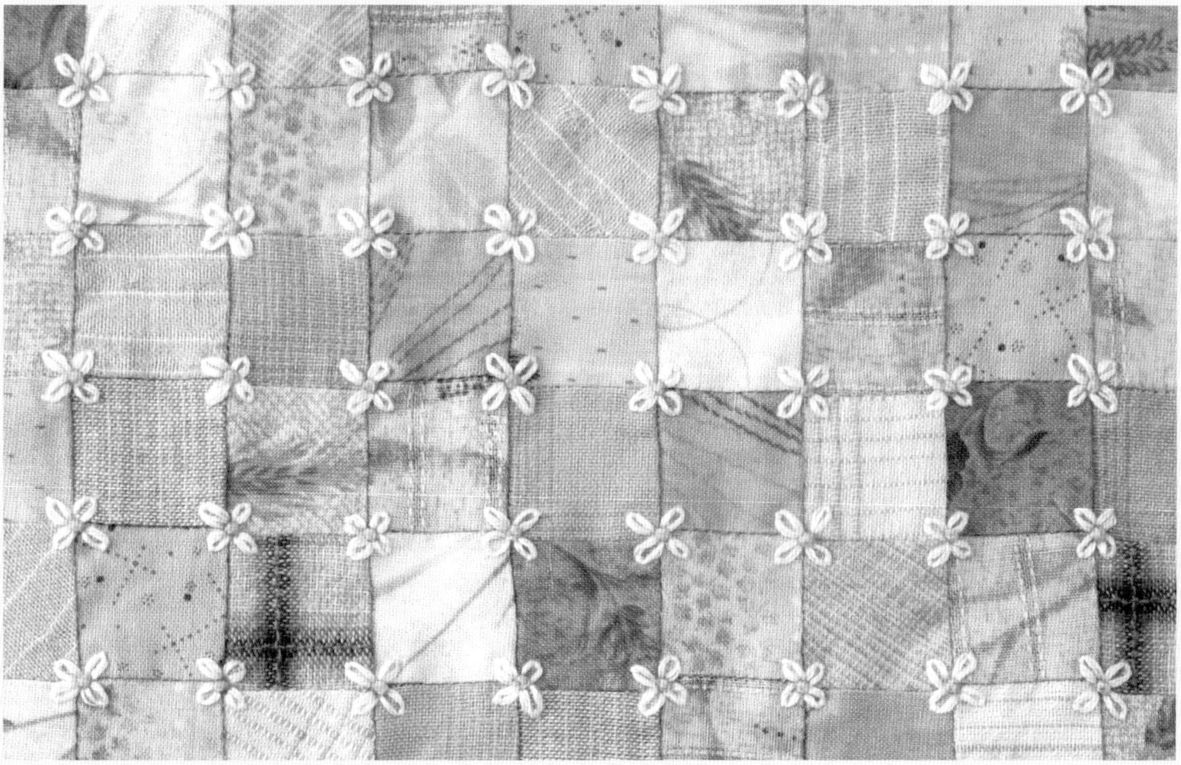

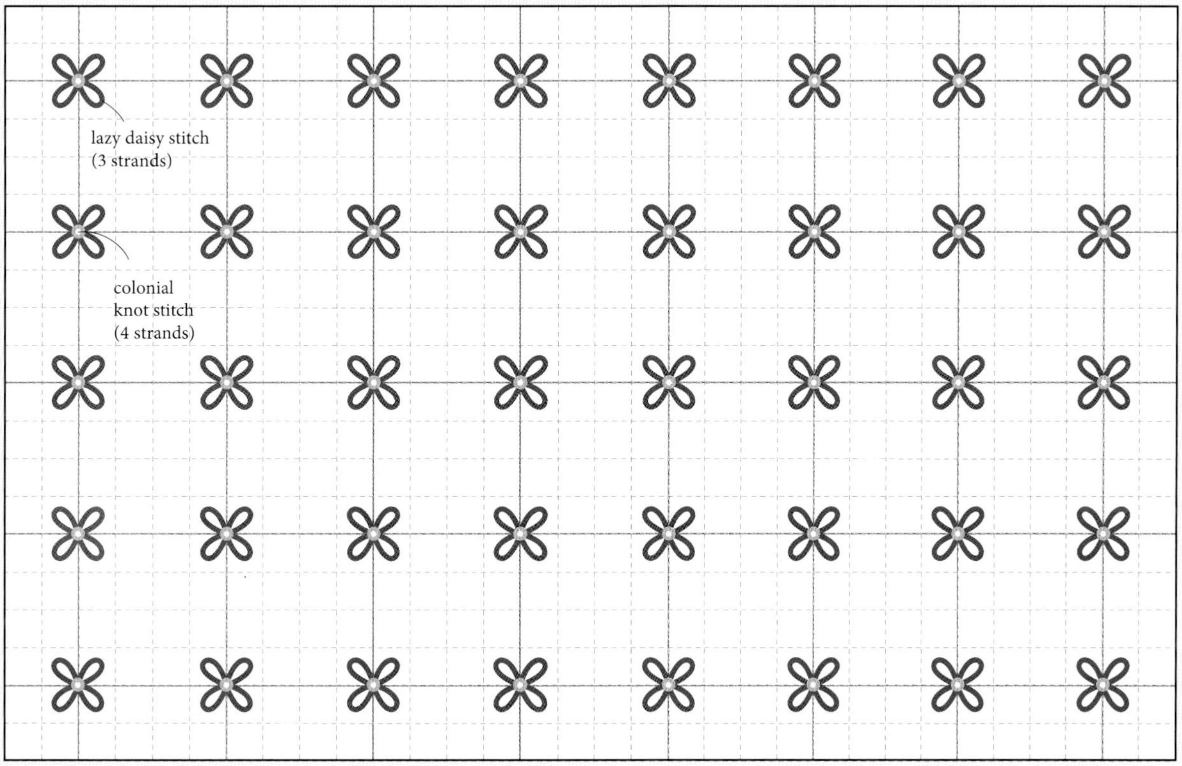
lazy daisy stitch
(3 strands)
colonial
knot stitch
(4 strands)

61 *Square Wave*

Create the background by piecing together 2 cm [¾"] squares. Much like pattern 57, embroider a wavy square shape approximately the same size as the squares on top and shifted to the right a little bit. Because of the continuous pattern, it would be good to use a large area when drawing the embroidery design.

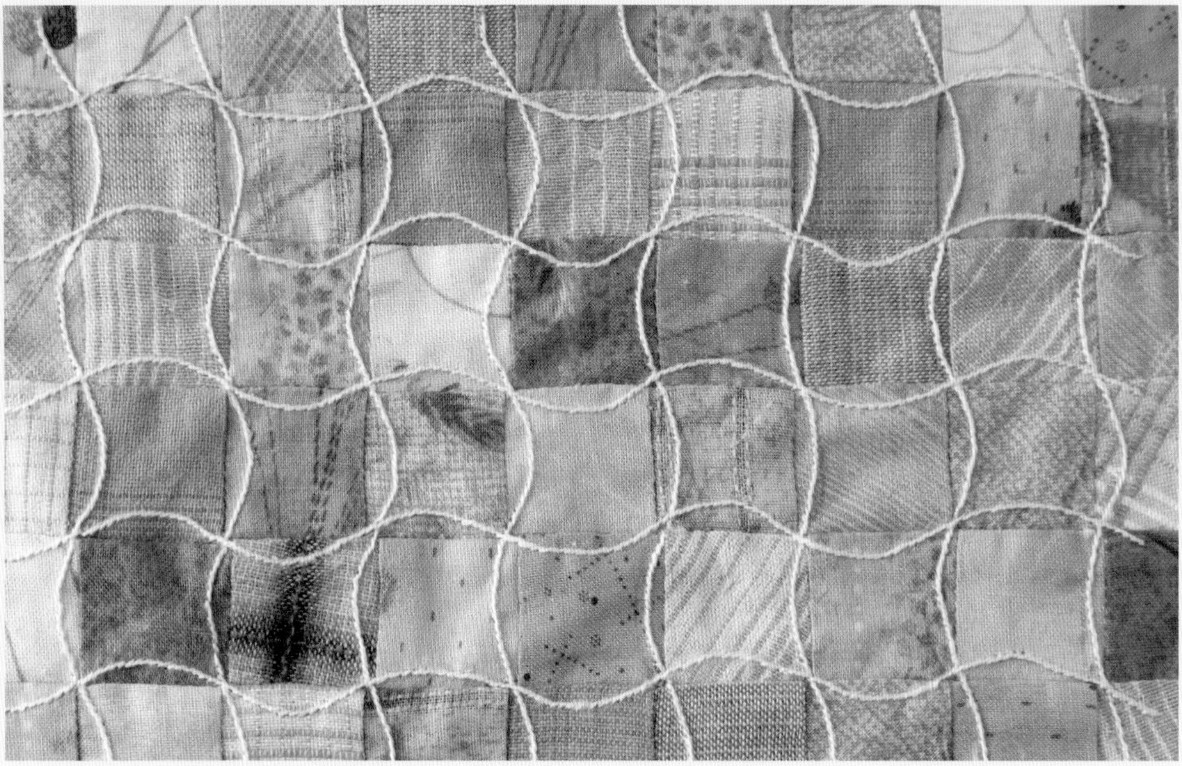

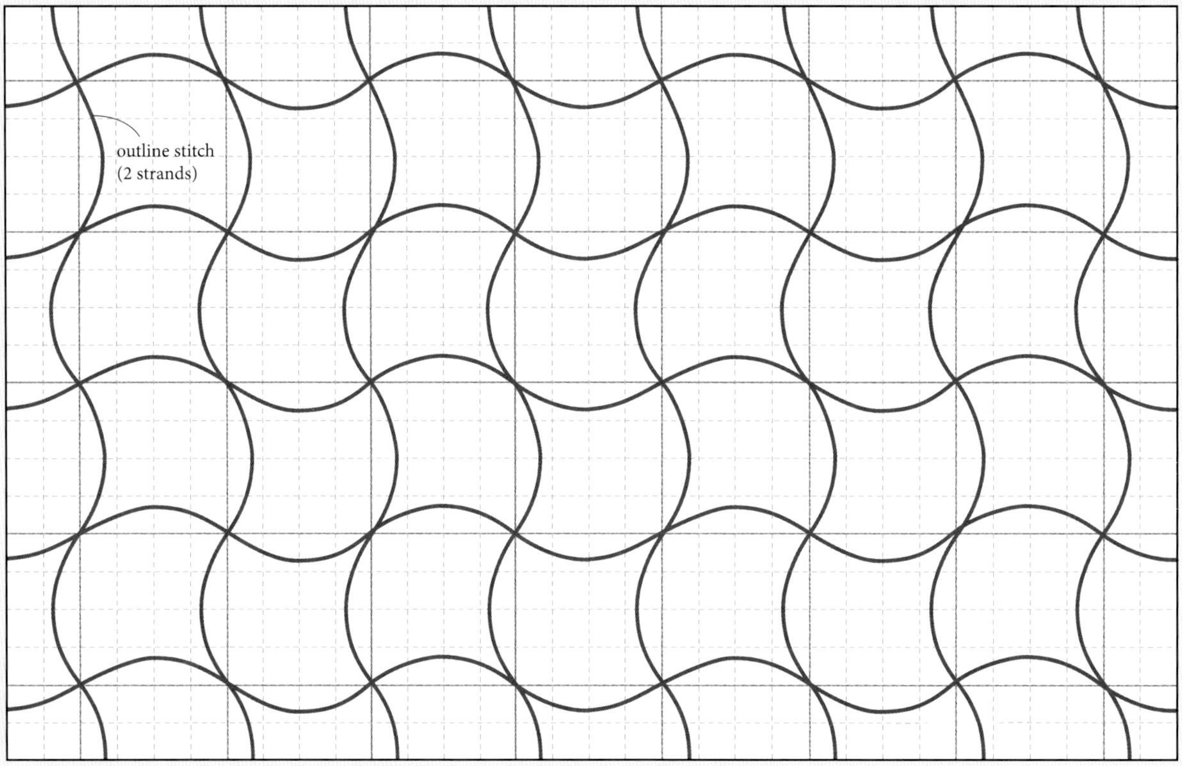

62 *Cross on Cross*

To achieve this design, quilt the entire background fabric in a 1.5 cm [⅝"] grid on a 45 degree angle to begin. Then, with one strand of perle cotton go back and embroider double cross stitches where the quilting lines intersect. This design is used as the all-over pattern for the handbag on p. 90.

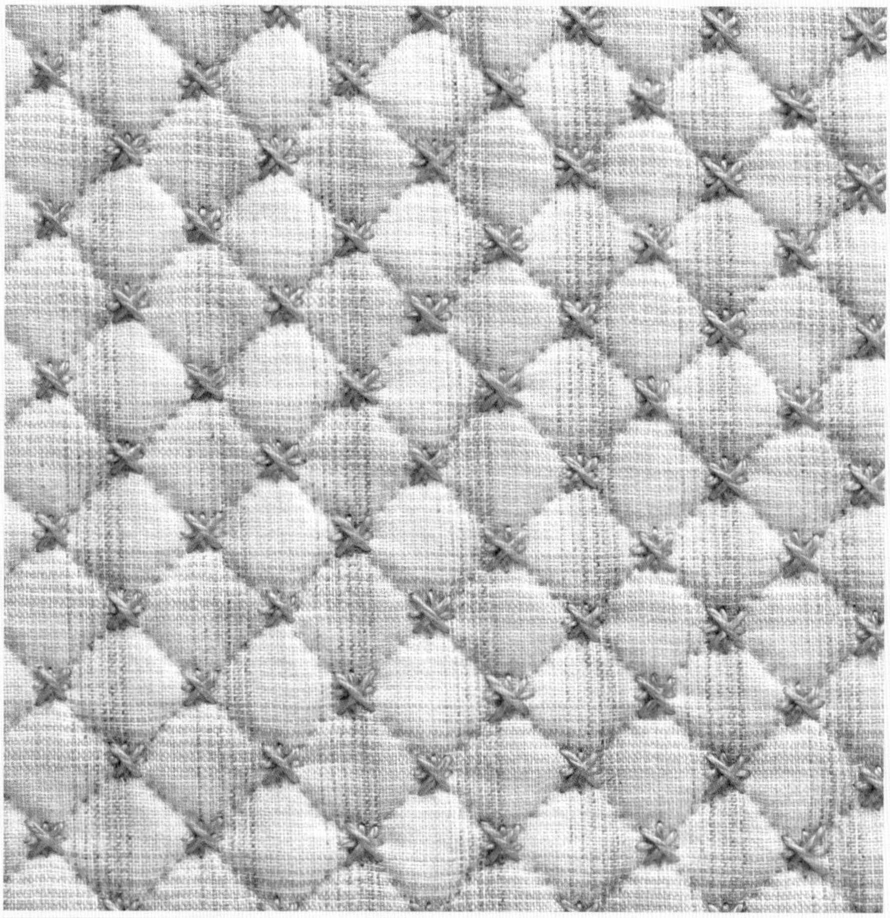

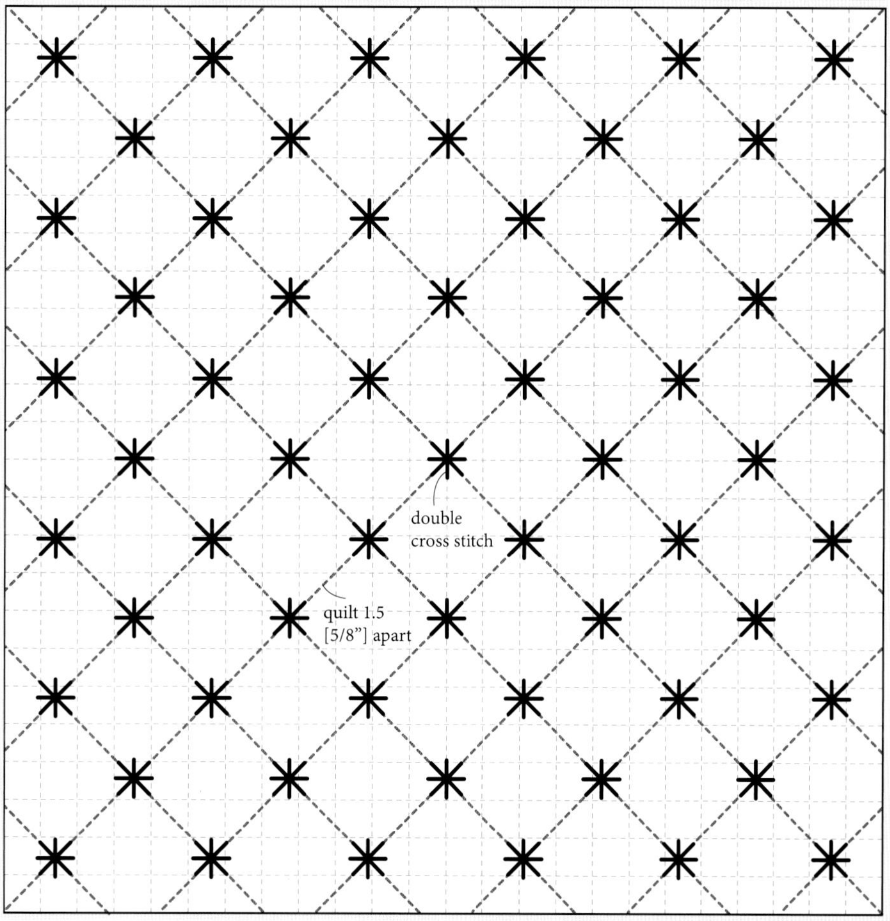
double
cross stitch
quilt 1.5
[5/8"] apart

◆ use 1 strand of perle cotton for the double cross stitches

k Handbag

I used a number of grey-tinged beige-toned fabrics to make this handbag. The main bag body fabric is created using pattern 62 (p. 89), while the embroidery design around the bag opening is pattern 102 (p. 134). Plan out the embroidery around the bag opening so that when you sew the sides together, the embroidery design lines up perfectly. I chose a metal handle to add sophistication and to keep the handbag from looking too sweet.

The designs are from patterns **62** and **102** (pp. 89 and 134). Instructions for the handbag are on p. 208.

63 *Zero*

"Zero" is of a mouth wide open. It might be fun to embroider in the date using these numbers when you are signing or labeling a quilt.

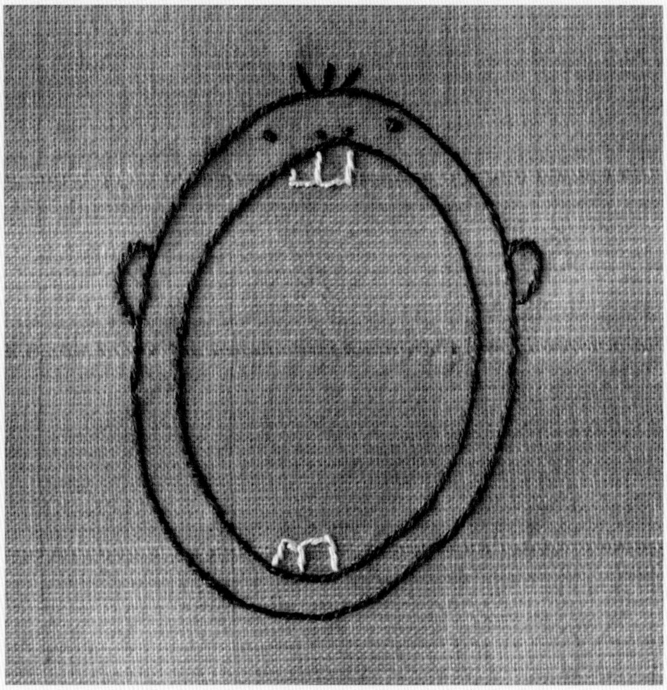

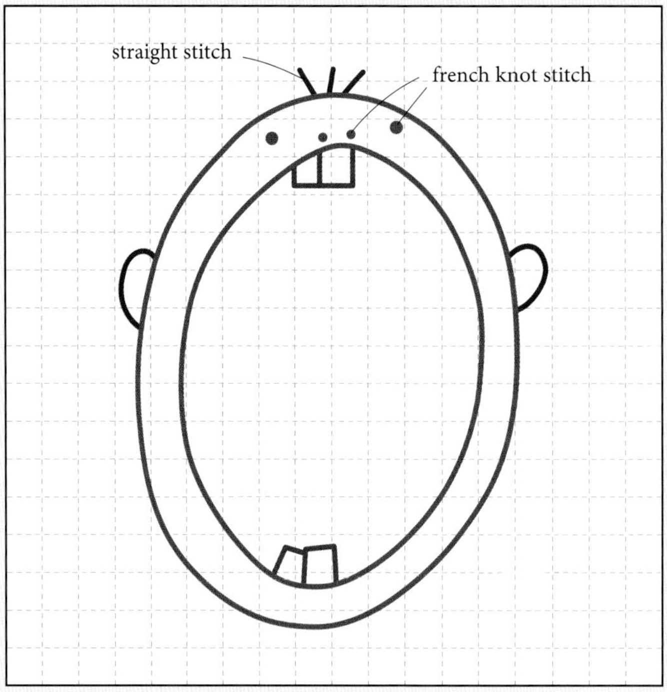

◆ use an outline stitch (2 strands) for any area not specified above

64 *One*

"One" is seen in the trunk of this tree. In order for the number to stand out, I drew a simple shape for the leaves. The background fabric was perfect for this design.

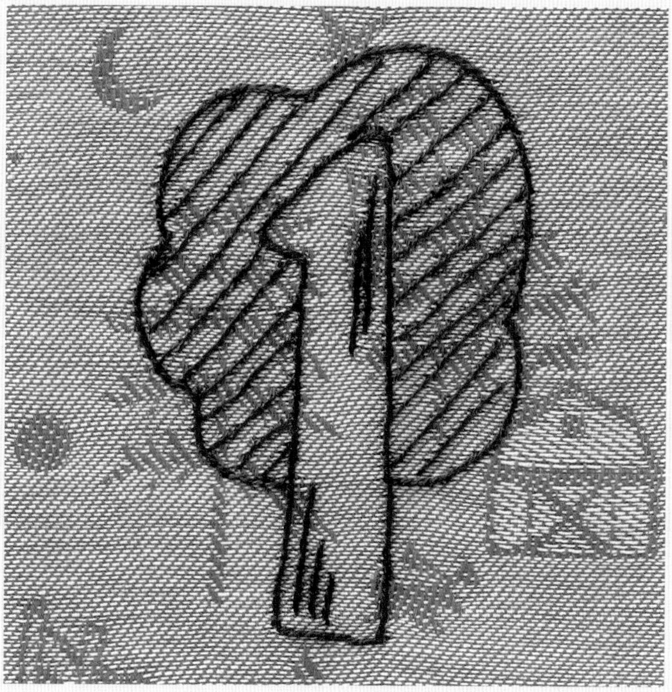

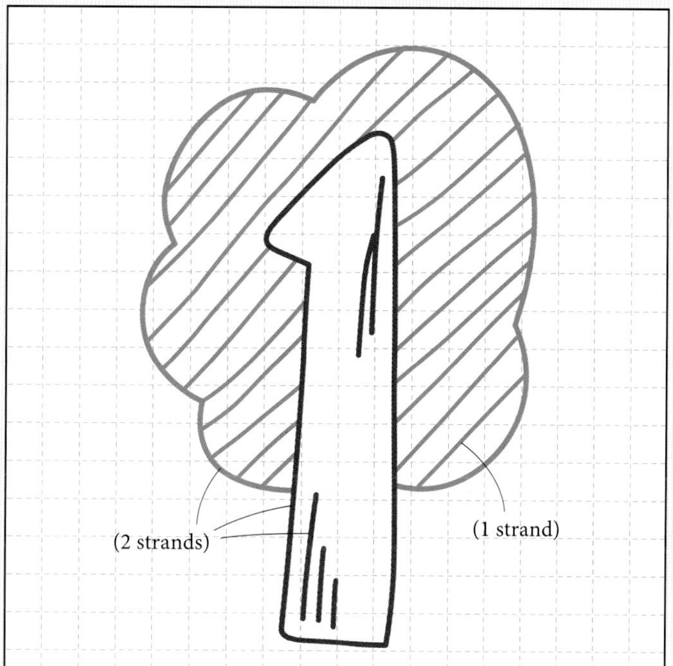

◆ use an outline stitch for the entire design

65 *Two*

"Two" is a swan floating on a pond. Use tiny little outline stitches to make a gently curved and graceful neck. I used a grey color, but white would work well against a darker fabric.

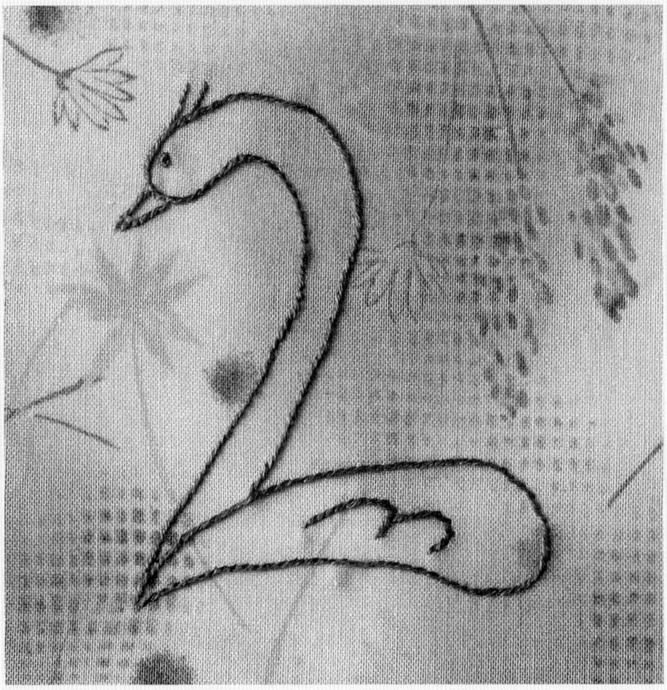

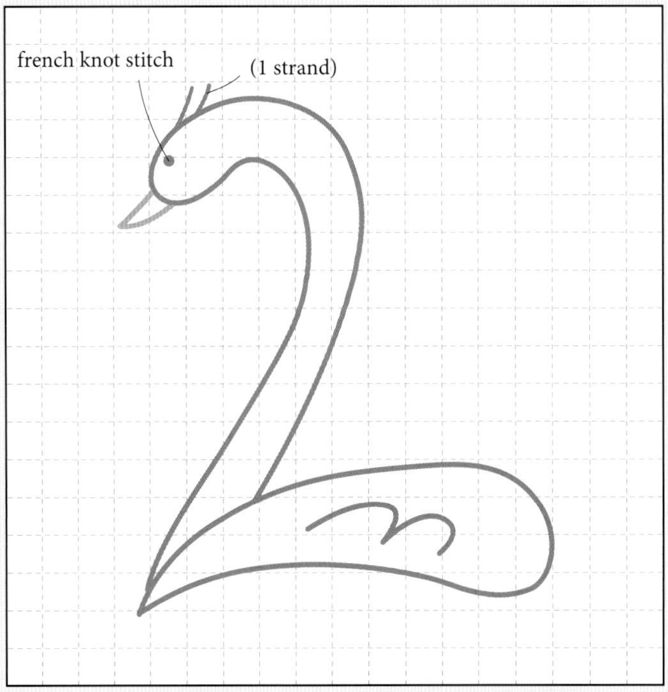

◆ use an outline stitch (2 strands) for any area not specified above

66 *Three*

"Three" is a combination appliqué and embroidery pattern. Appliqué the number three onto the background fabric, then embroider a blanket stitch around the edges. Finish by adding the other embroidery designs.

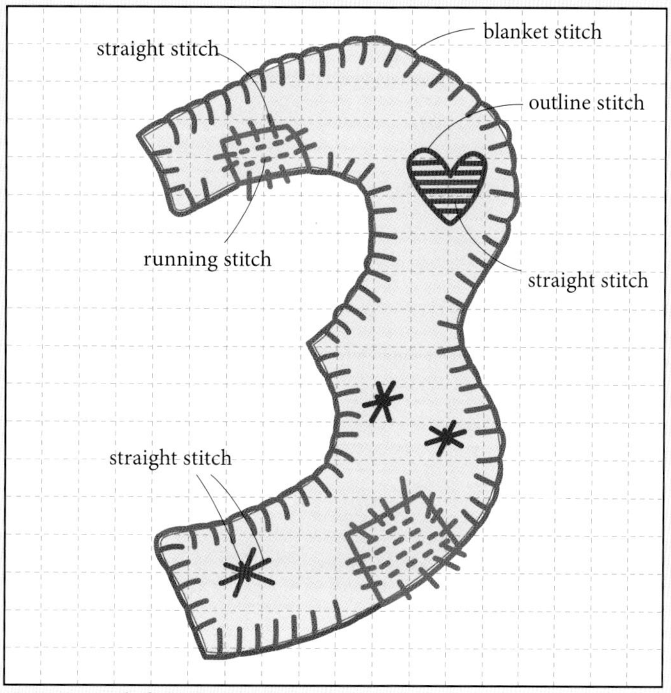
straight stitch
blanket stitch
outline stitch
running stitch
straight stitch
straight stitch

◆ use 2 strands for any area not specified above

67 *Four*

"Four" is a large building with lots of square windows. See the people walking by? It's fun to add little touches that make the designs unique.

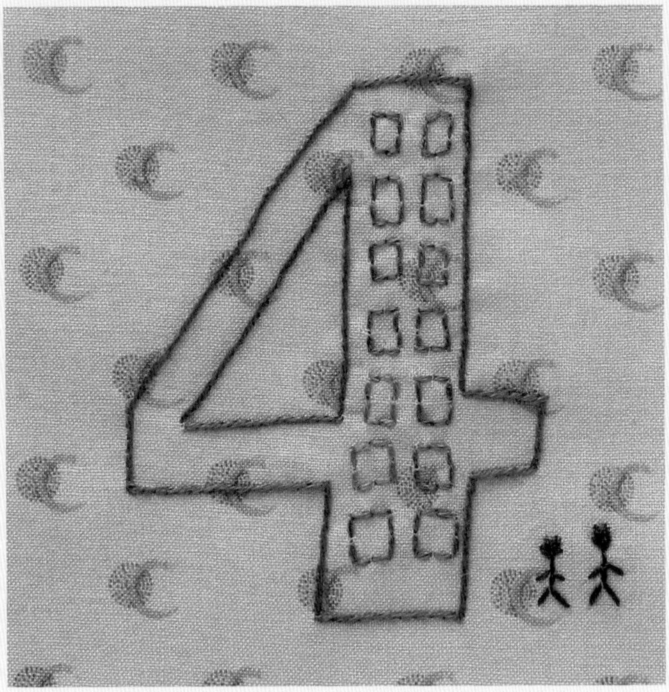

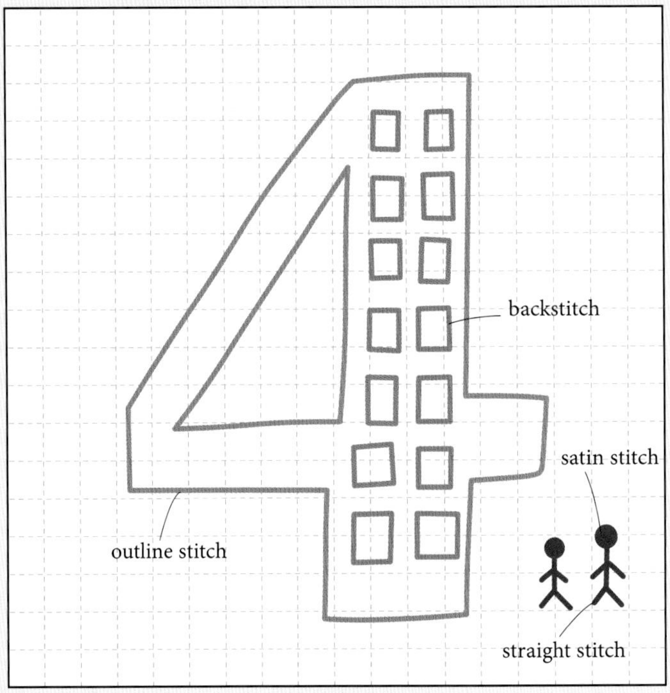
backstitch
satin stitch
outline stitch
straight stitch

◆ use 2 strands for any area not specified above

68 *Five*

"Five" is a hungry cat reaching for one fish after it already ate the other, leaving the bone. The cat's nose is done using a fly stitch.

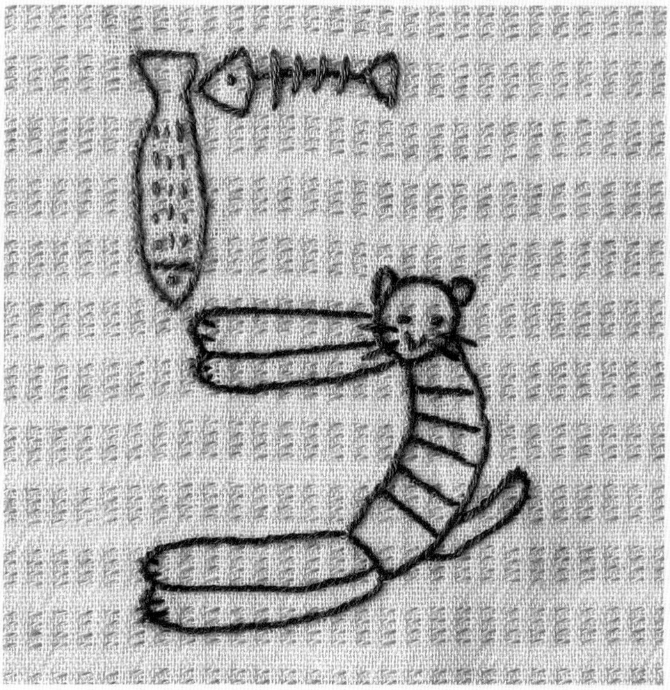

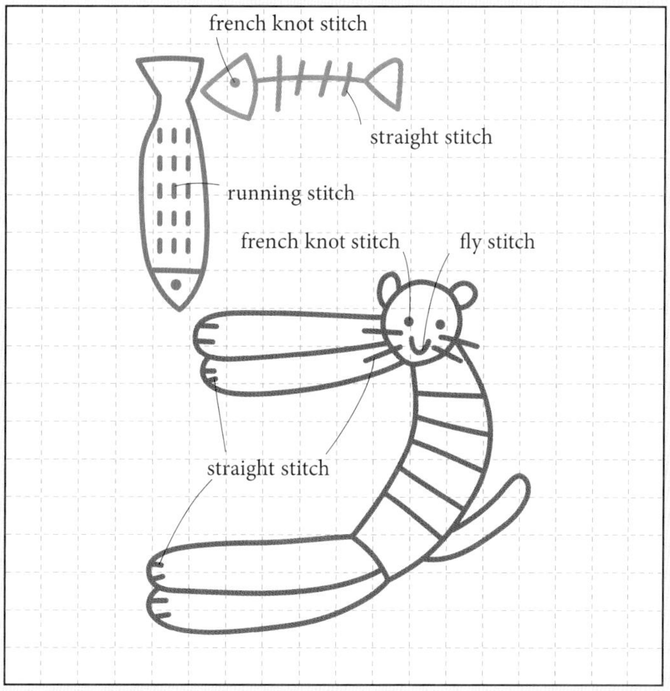
french knot stitch
straight stitch
running stitch
french knot stitch
fly stitch
straight stitch

◆ use an outline stitch (2 strands) for any area not specified above

69 *Six*

"Six" is done entirely in a running stitch. I first embroidered the circles to make the bottom portion of the number, then stitched the diagonal lines to finish. Use a floss color that contrasts with the background fabric for the best results.

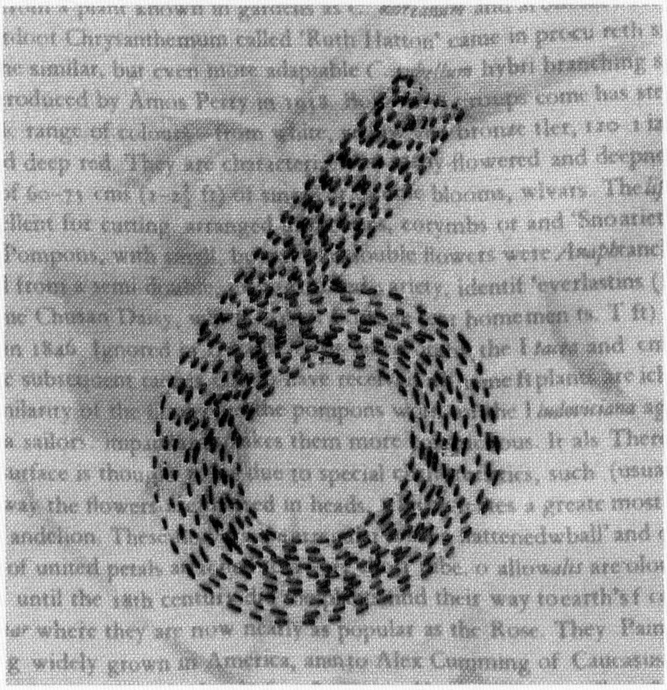

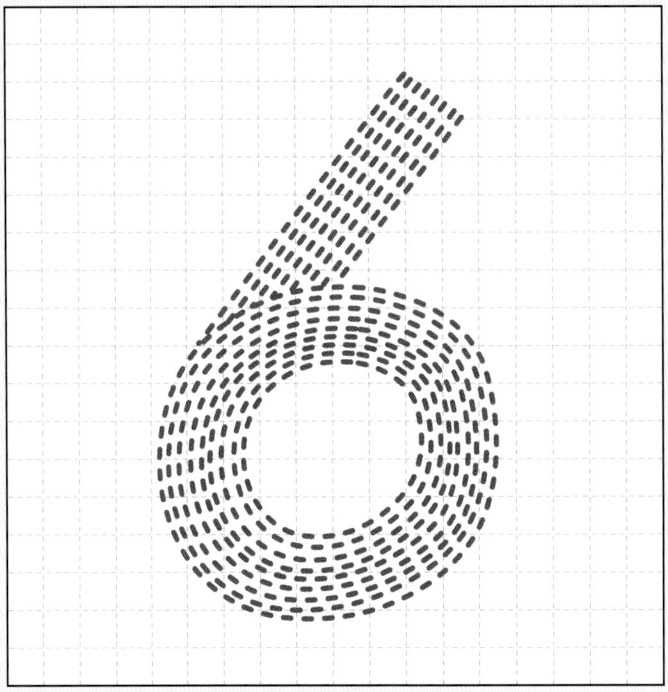

◆ use a running stitch (2 strands) for the entire design

70 *Seven*

"Seven" is all sharp angles and lines. Use one strand of perle cotton to make a strong statement. Take careful stitches as you work in order to make sure that the lines stay straight.

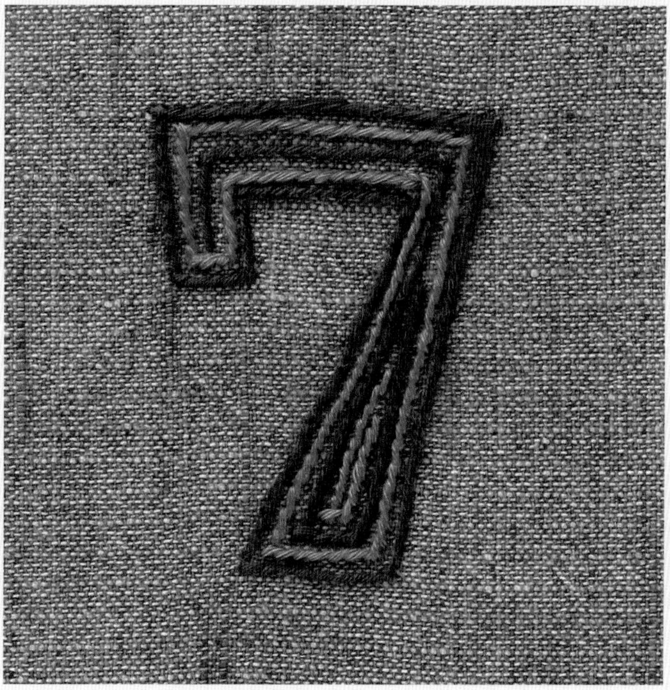

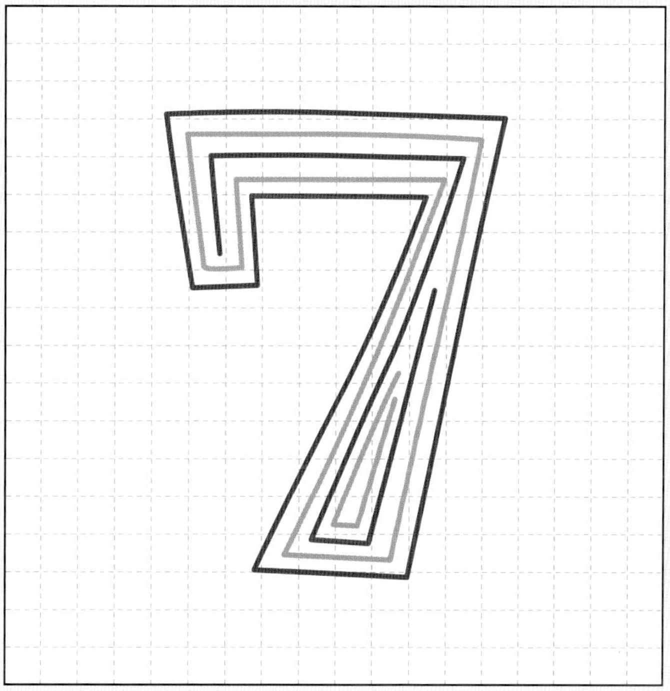

◆ use an outline stitch and perle cotton (1 strand) for the entire design

71 *Eight*

"Eight" is a uniquely combined set of two figure-eights that are done entirely in a threaded running stitch. The center row is done in grey, while the outer lines are threaded using two different colors. They are worked from both sides to achieve the look of a chain.

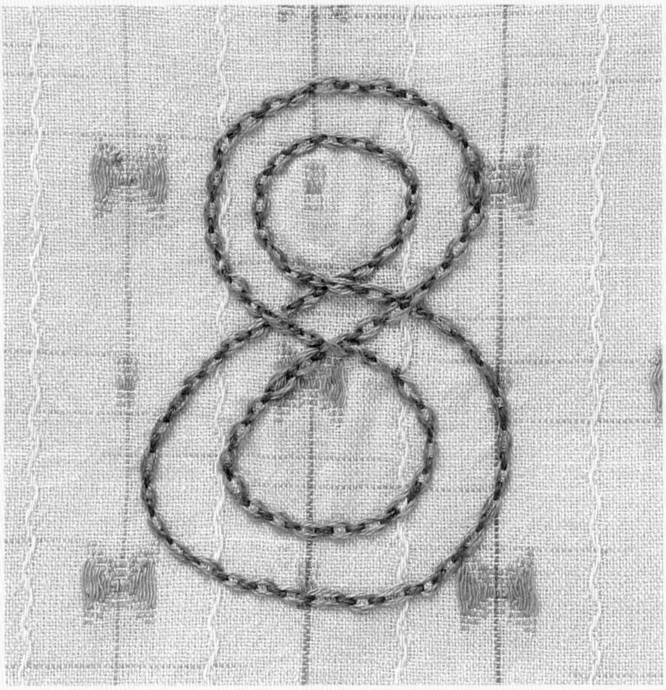

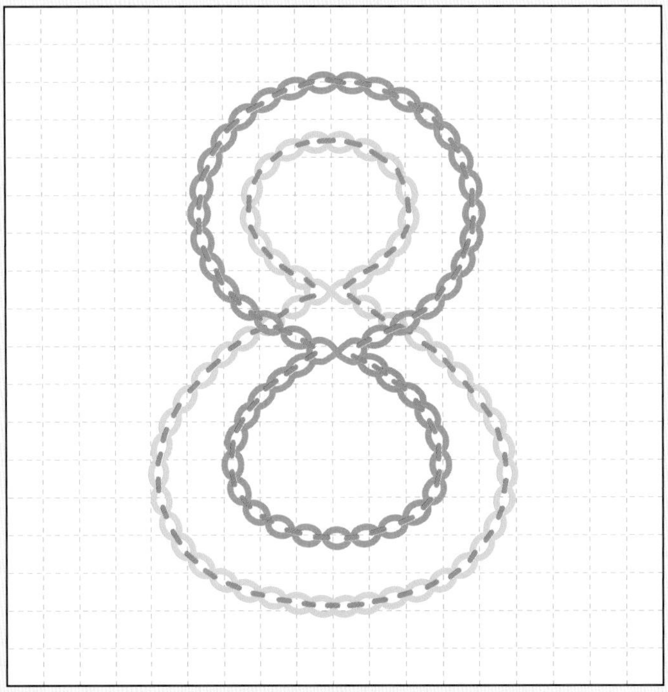

◆ use a threaded running stitch (3 strands) for the entire design

72 *Nine*

"Nine" is made of garlands of flowers, some of which are made into a wreath. Use a combination of lazy daisy and feather stitches for the wreath. I think an elliptical shape is more pleasing that a perfect circle.

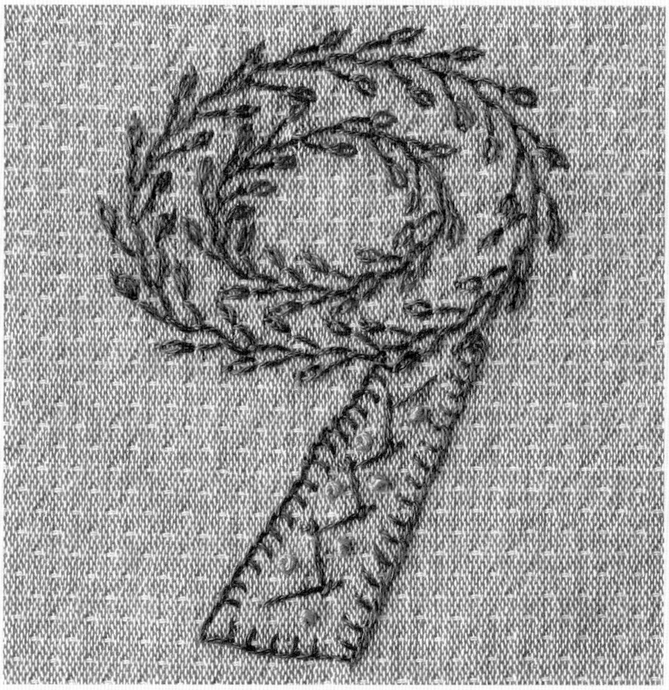

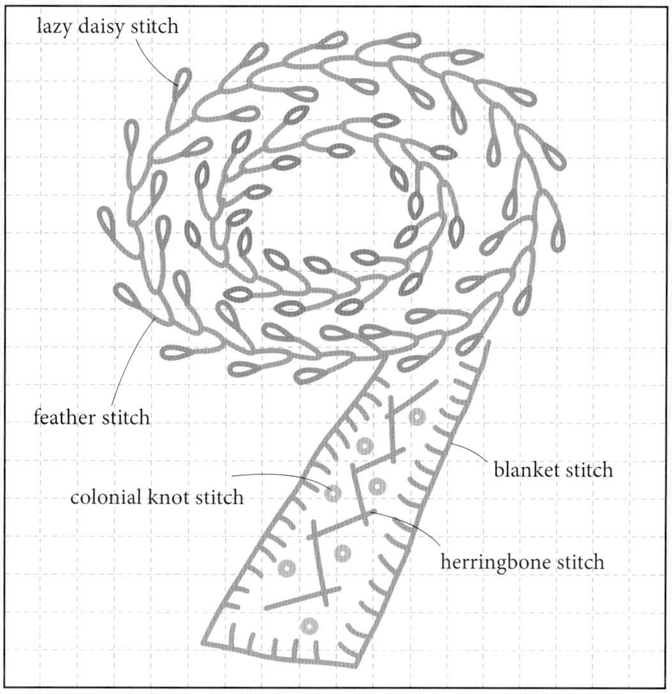
lazy daisy stitch
feather stitch
blanket stitch
colonial knot stitch
herringbone stitch

◆ use 2 strands for the entire design

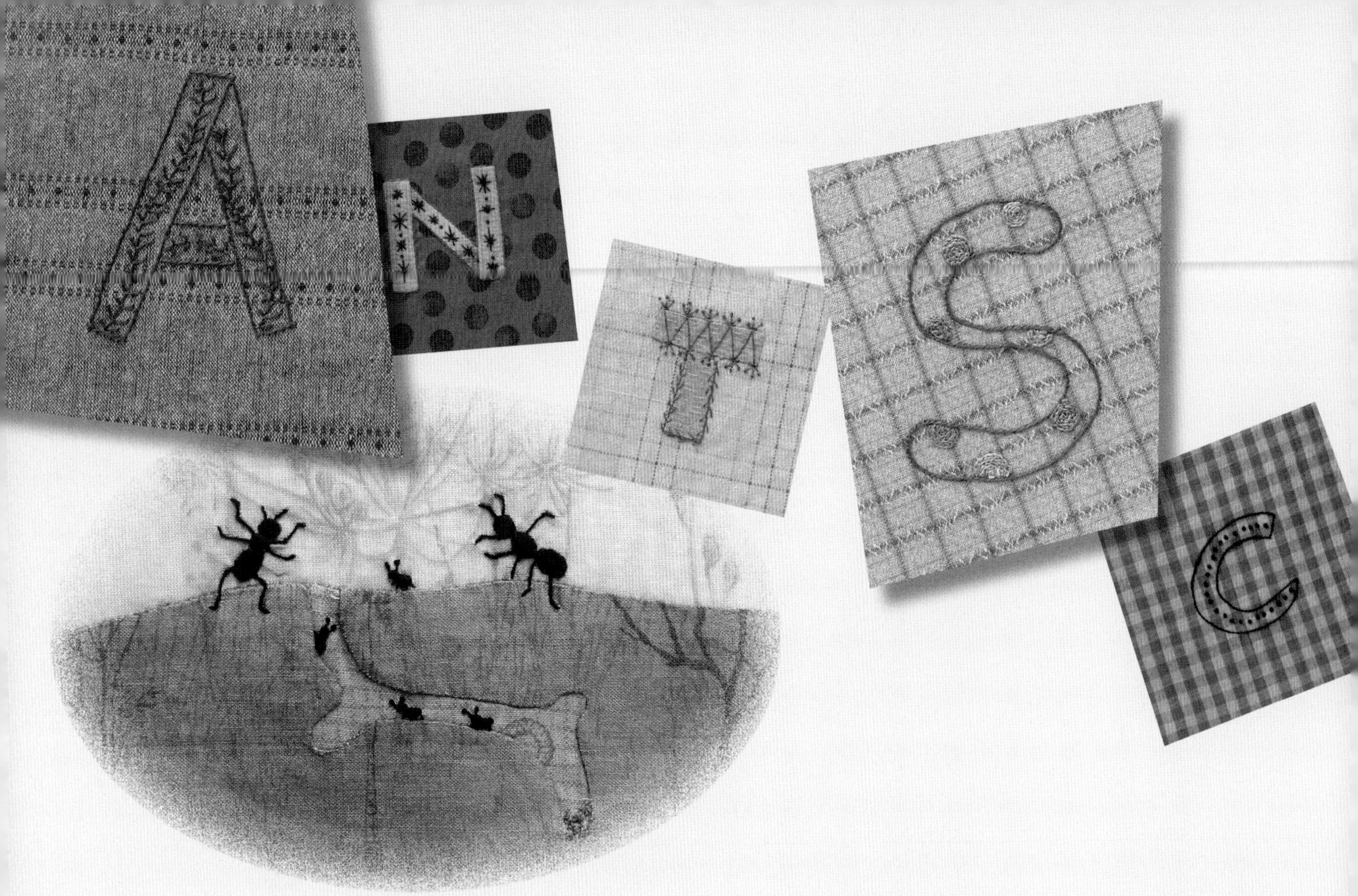
A
N
T
S
C

R
E
A
B

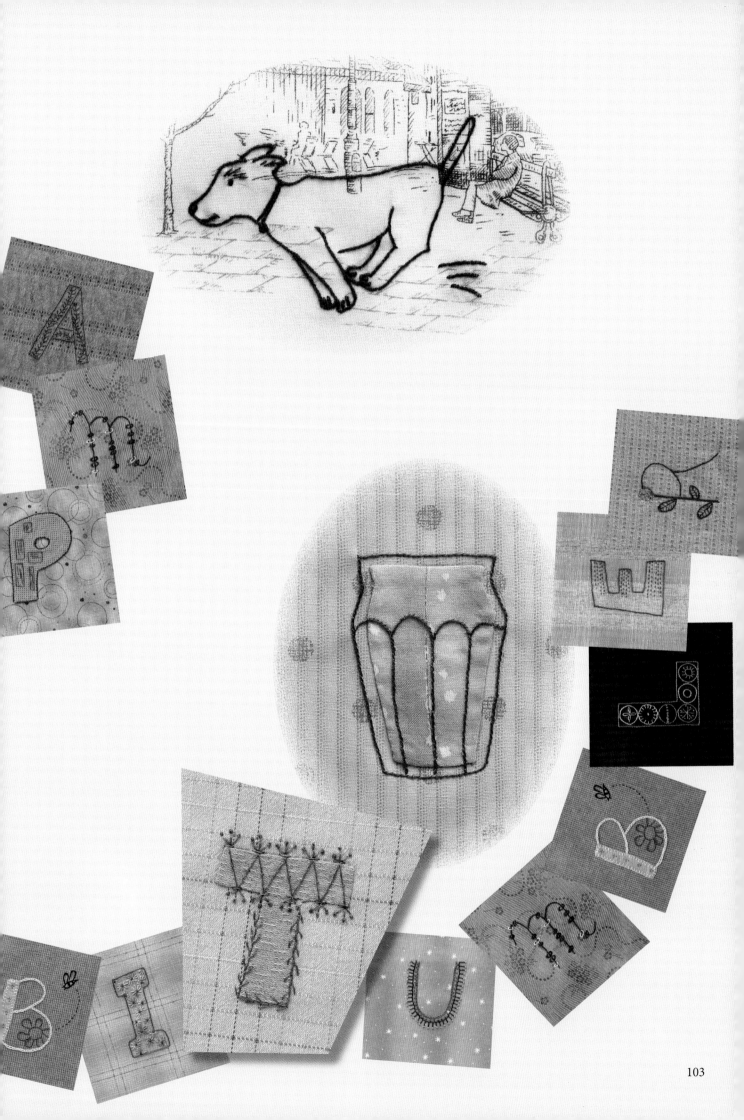

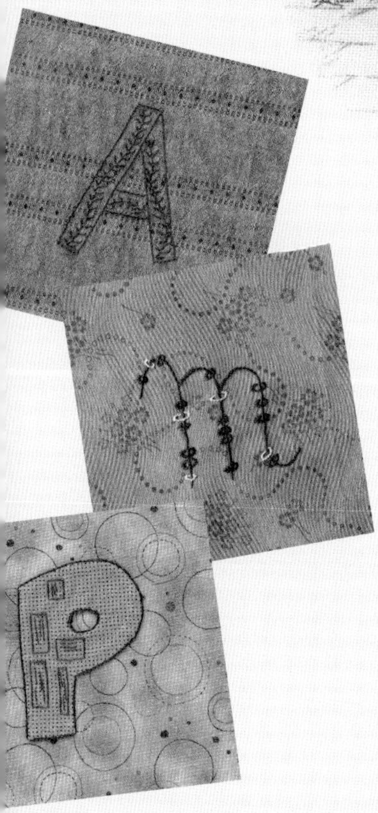

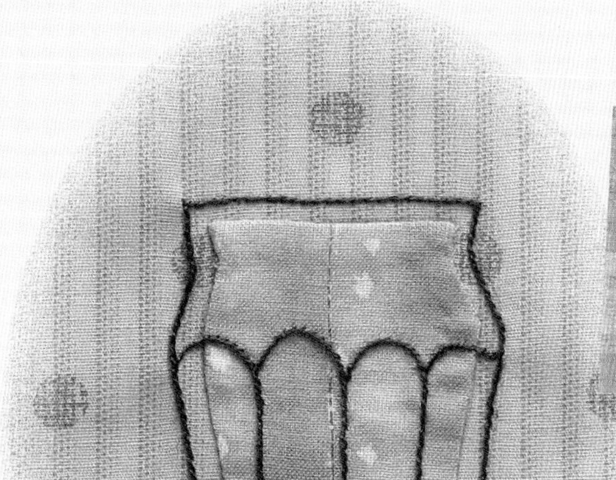

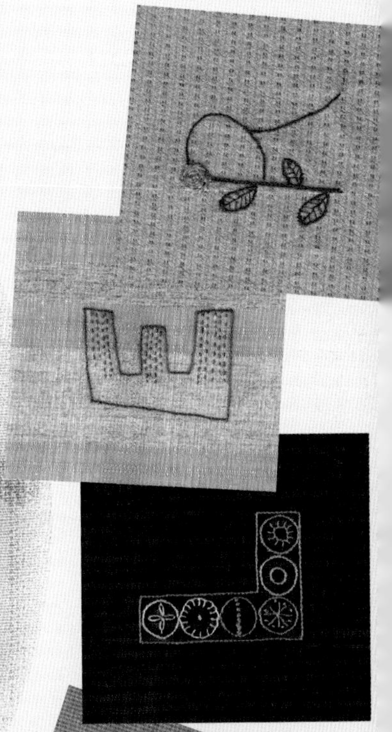

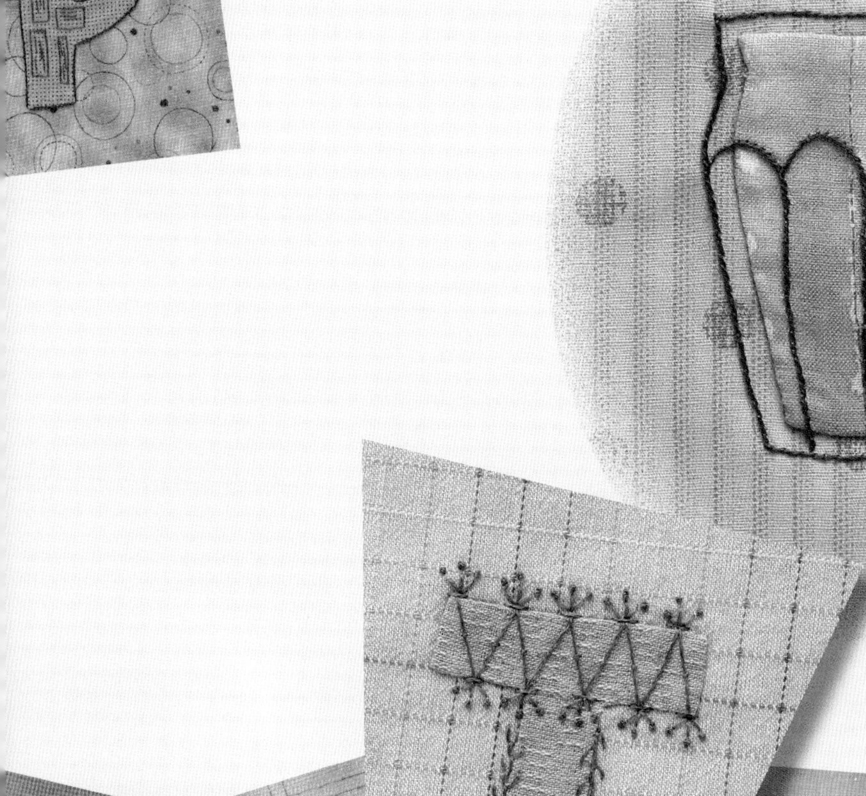

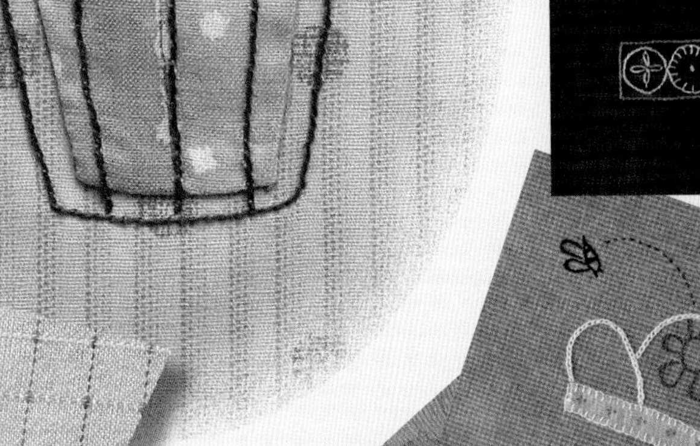

73 A of the Alphabet

I have chosen to use a variety of different embroidery stitches in the designs for the 26 letters of the alphabet. If you made all of them, as well as the numbers, you could have a very cute sampler. "A" is decorated with a continuous fern stitch.

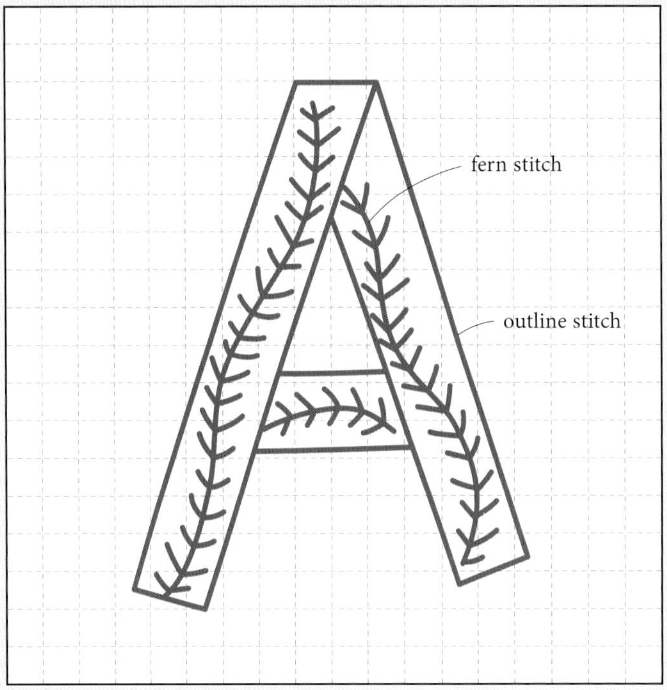

◆ use 2 strands for the entire design

74 *B of the Alphabet*

"B" shows a bee buzzing around a flower. Part of the letter is done using appliqué where I fussy cut the fabric so that the little flowers are lined up vertically. The background fabric has yellow in it to go with the concept of the bee.

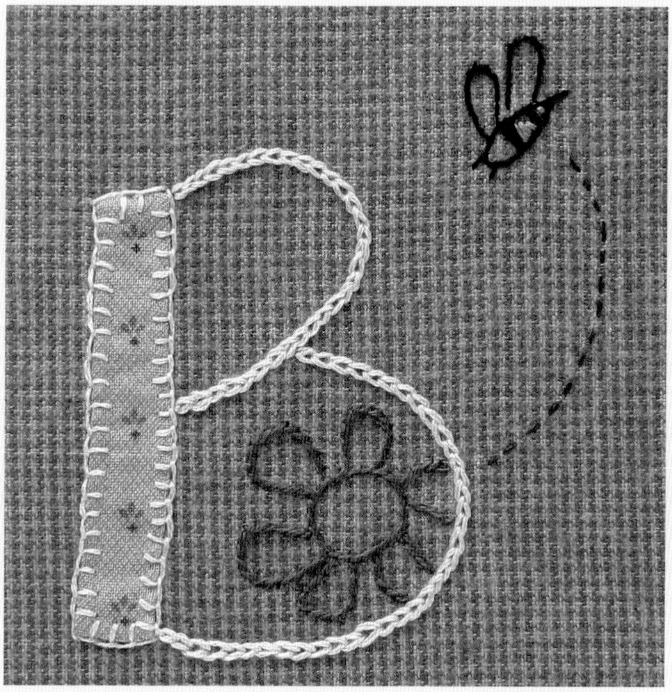

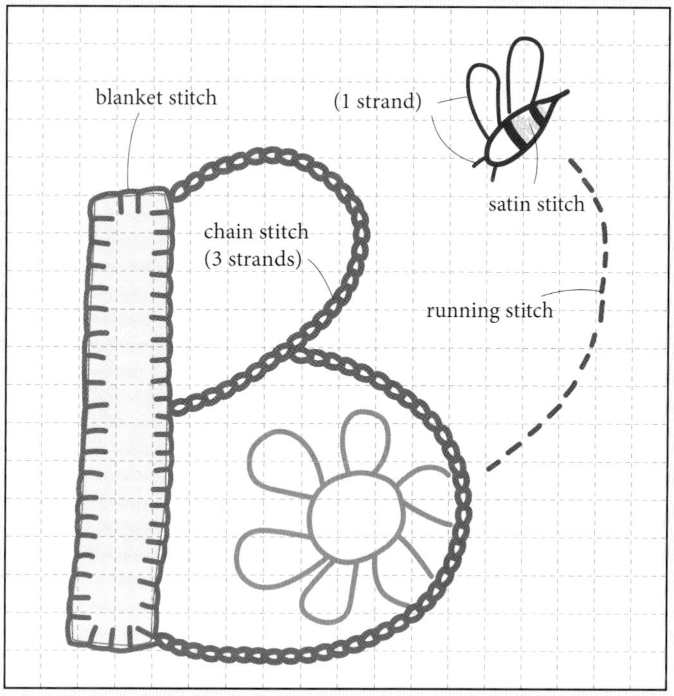
blanket stitch
(1 strand)
satin stitch
chain stitch
(3 strands)
running stitch

◆ use an outline stitch (2 strands) for any area not specified above

75 *C of the Alphabet*

"C" is simply made using an outline stitch and colonial knots to emphasize the curve. Stitch carefully to get a fluid line. The dark red floss stands out nicely against the blue gingham background fabric.

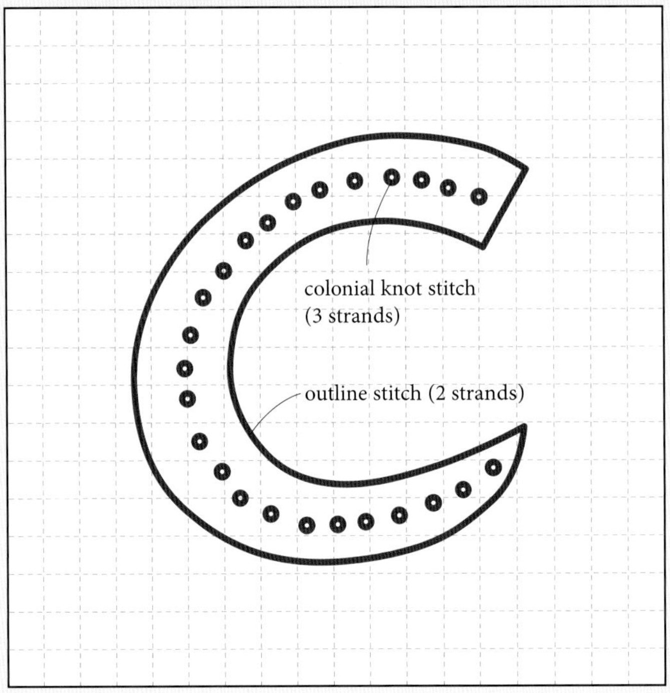

76 D of the Alphabet

I made the "D" as a three-dimensional letter. The depth comes from the embroidery on the backside of the appliqué.

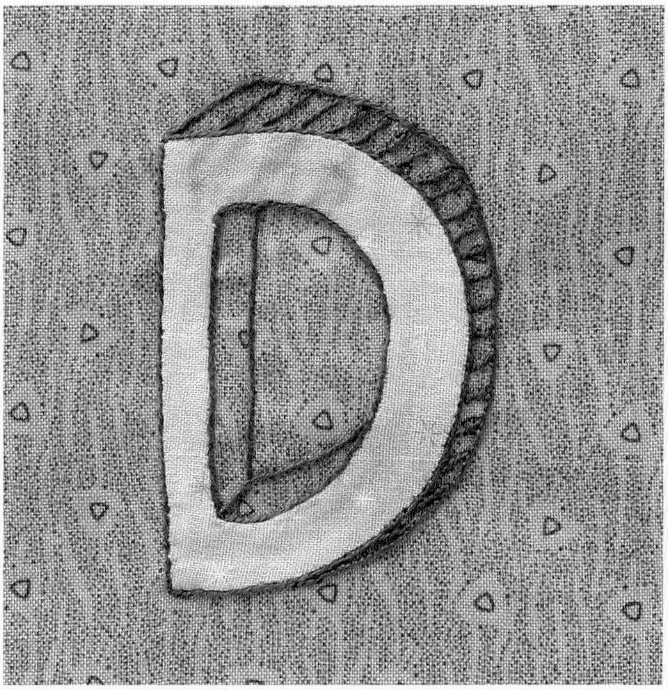

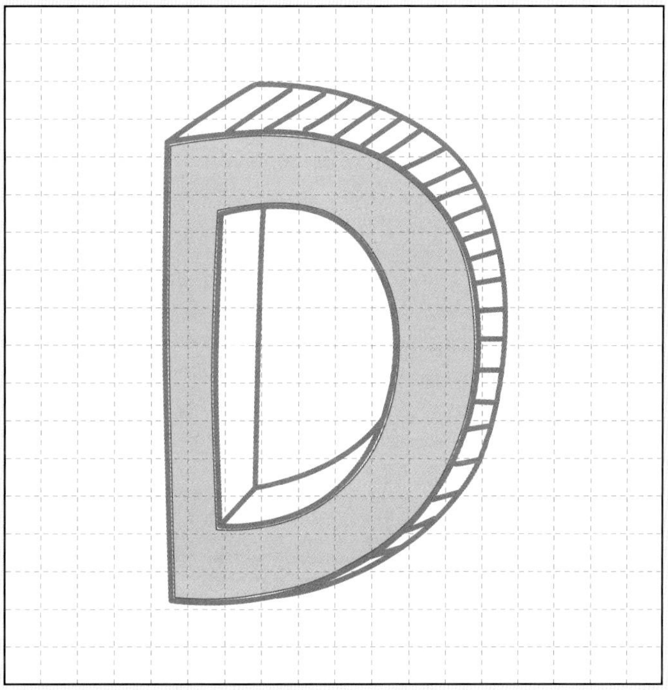

◆ use an outline stitch (2 strands) for the entire design

77 *E of the Alphabet*

Use random lengths of horizontal running stitches inside of the outlined "E" to create a sense of fading away when you make this letter of the alphabet.

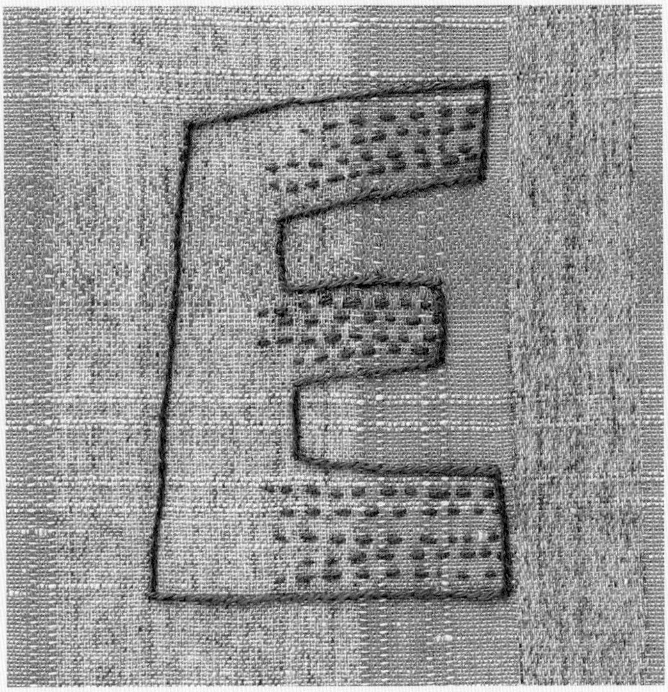

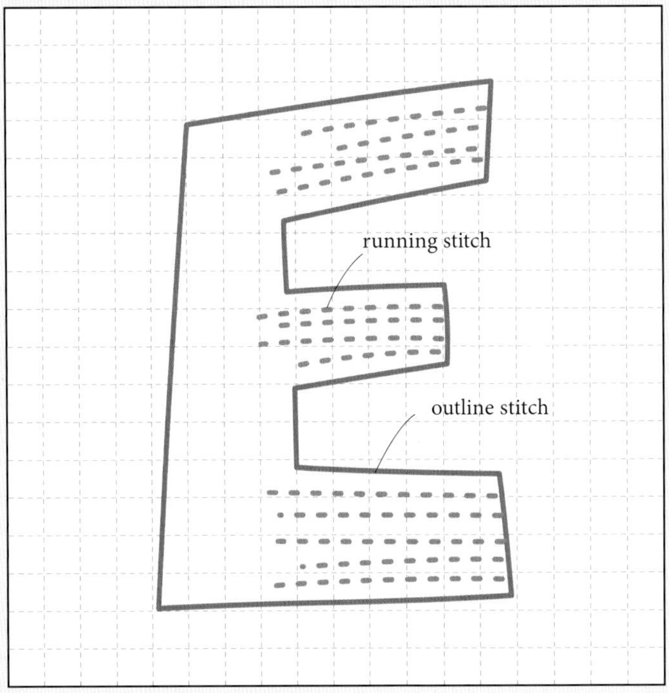

◆ use 2 strands for the entire design

78 *F of the Alphabet*

I thought of framboise when I chose to embroider the red strawberries in dark red floss against a woven plaid that had a fine red line running through. I deliberately placed the "F" at an angle to break up the balance point and add visual interest.

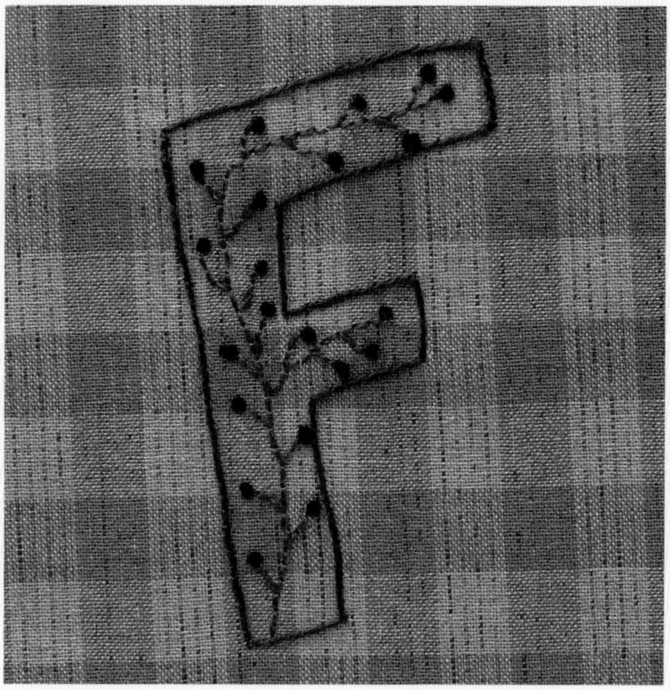

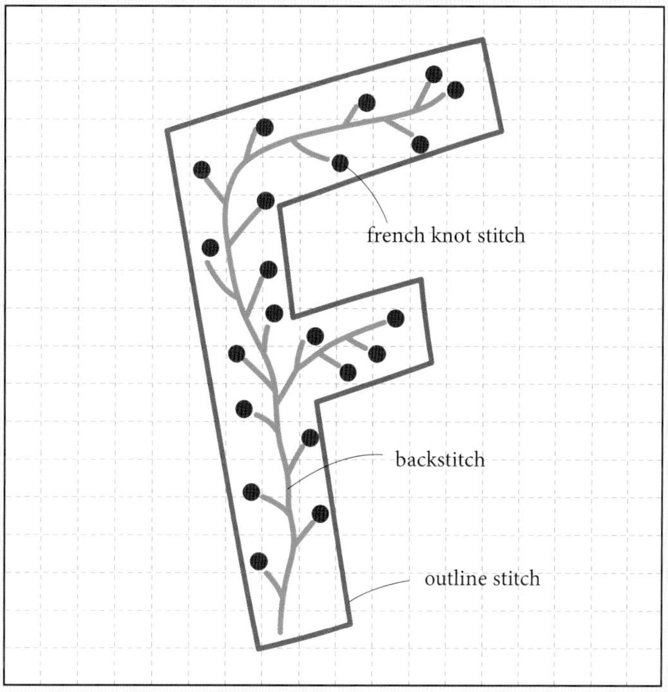
french knot stitch
backstitch
outline stitch

◆ use 2 strands for the entire design

79 *G of the Alphabet*

Begin to make the "G" by appliquéing the bottom "hook" section of the letter. Use an outline stitch to make the shape of the rest of the letter. Then add the herringbone stitch, in a different color, over the outline stitches. Embellish the center of the letter with double cross stitches in two different colors.

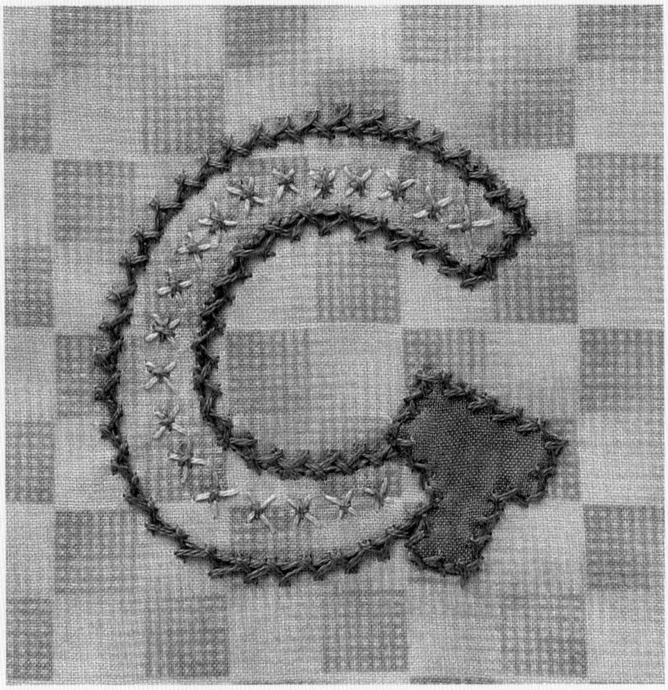

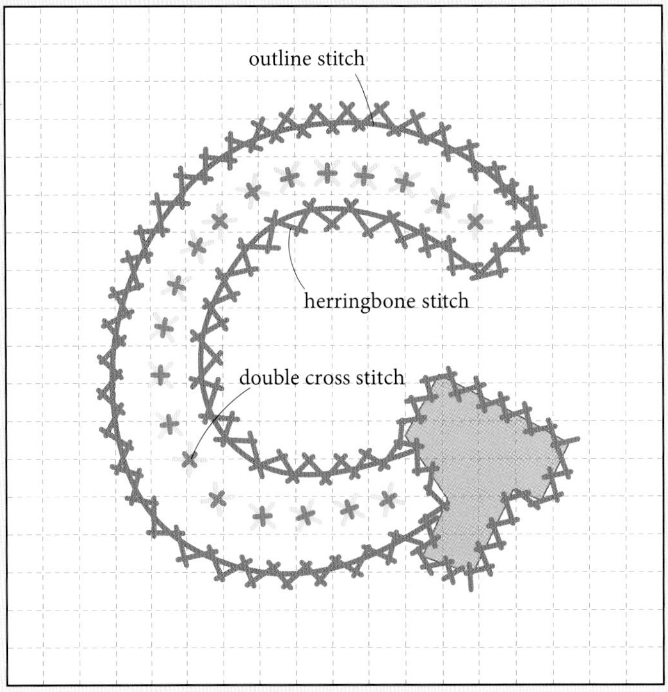

outline stitch
herringbone stitch
double cross stitch

◆ use 2 strands for the entire design

80 *H of the Alphabet*

I had to make a house for the letter "H." Appliqué the house with a chimney to the background fabric. Make the shape of the letter with an outline stitch and fill it in with the blanket stitch or the buttonhole filling stitch.

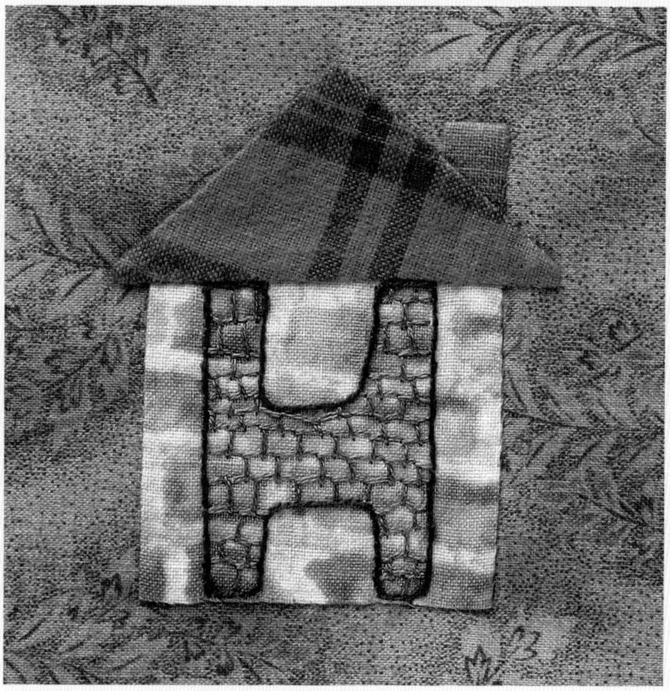

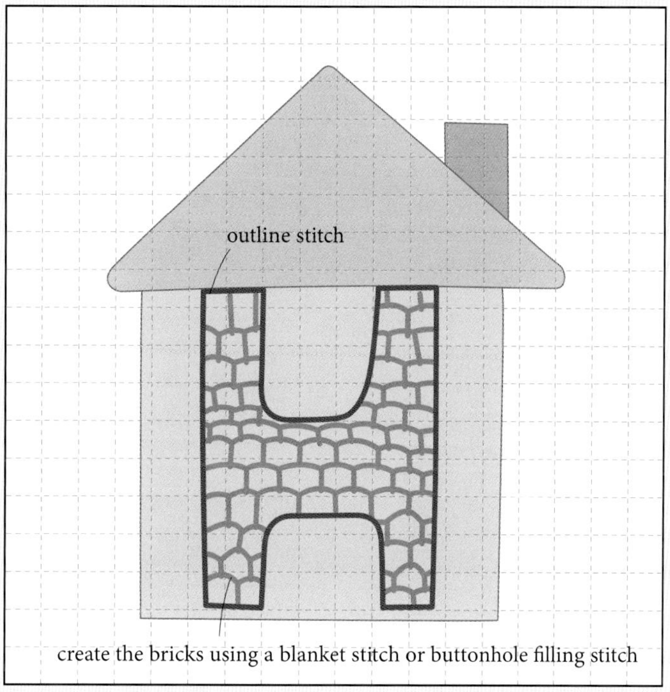

outline stitch
create the bricks using a blanket stitch or buttonhole filling stitch

◆ use 2 strands for the entire design

81 *I of the Alphabet*

I love how cute the "I" turned out with the letter filled with embroidered flowers. If you use a variegated floss, you will get interesting colored flowers without having to change out your floss as you stitch.

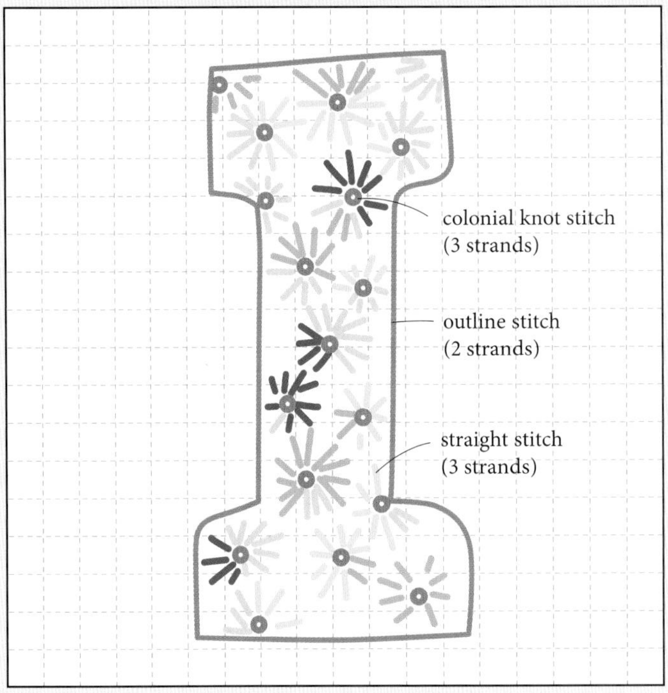
colonial knot stitch
(3 strands)
outline stitch
(2 strands)
straight stitch
(3 strands)

82 *J of the Alphabet*

For the letter "J" I first appliquéd fabric for the two sections to the background fabric. I cut out the "hook" part on the bias. I used several different stitches: the cross stitch, open cretan stitch, chevron stitch and colonial knots to embellish the letter.

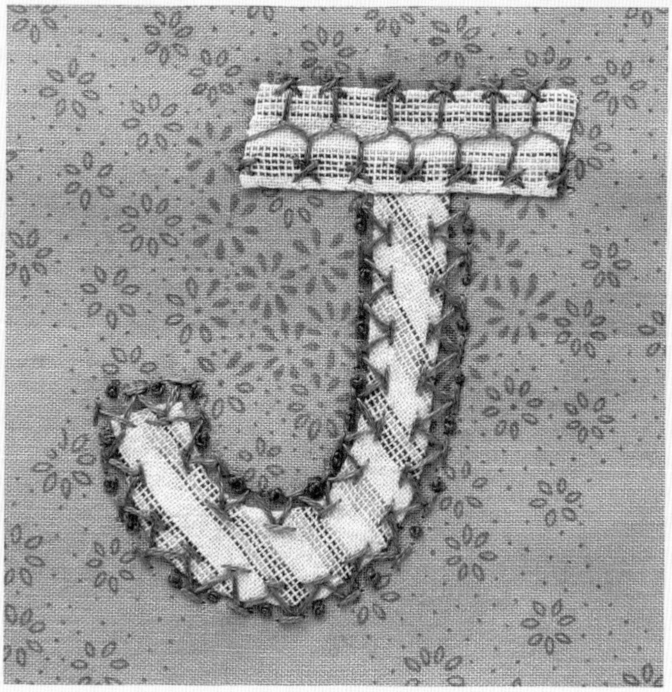

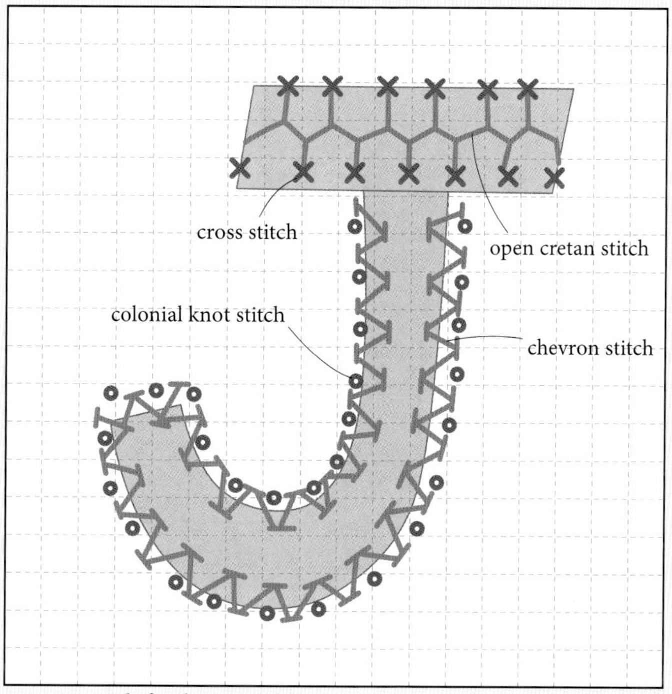

cross stitch
open cretan stitch
colonial knot stitch
chevron stitch

◆ use 2 strands for the entire design

83 *K of the Alphabet*

Although I only used the outline stitch for the entire pattern, I think it is interesting since the letter "K" is cleverly represented by a knife, fork and spoon.

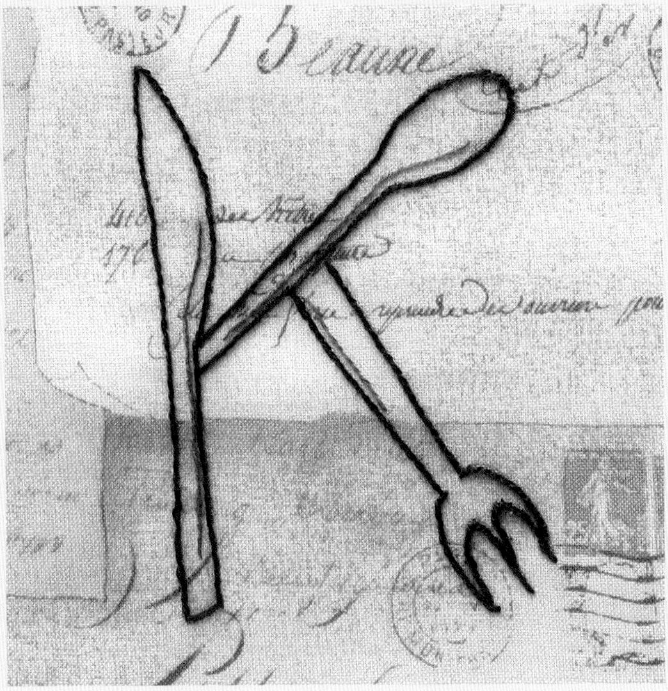

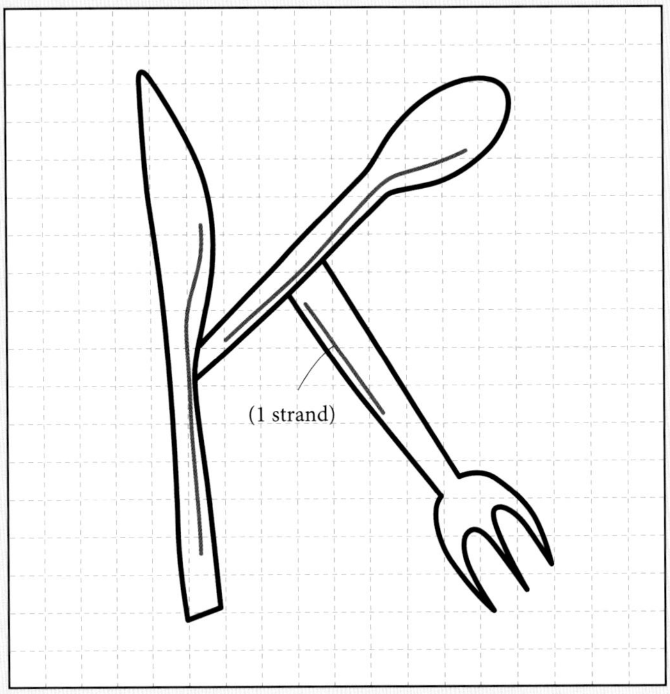

◆ use an outline stitch (2 strands) for any area not specified above

84 *L of the Alphabet*

I lined up six different circle designs inside the fat shape of the letter "L". I used many different stitches and colors, which plays nicely off the striped background fabric.

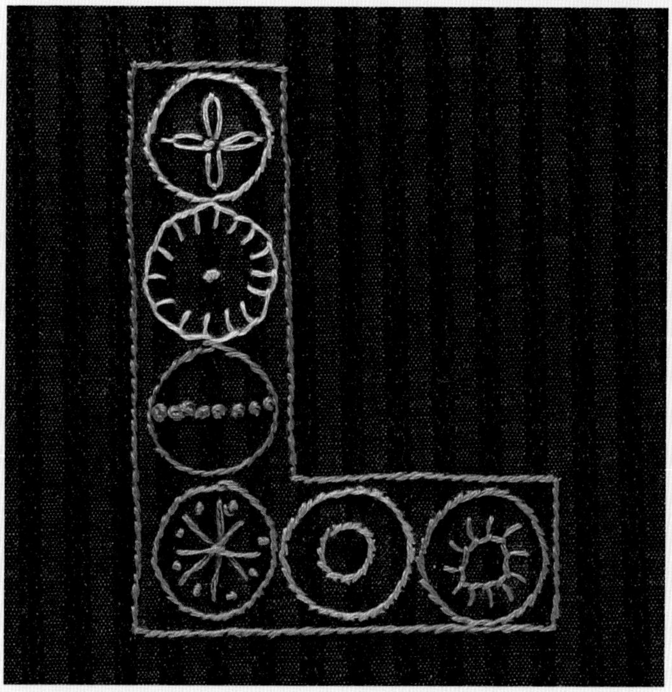

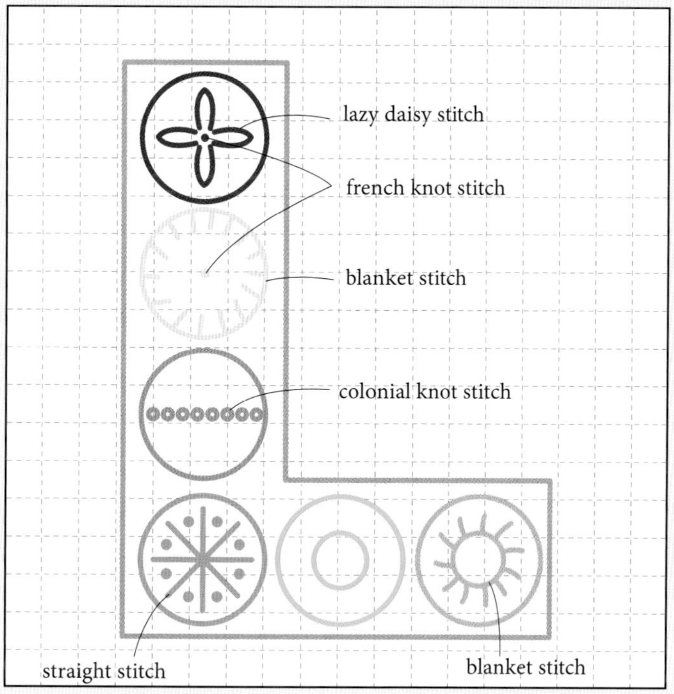
lazy daisy stitch
french knot stitch
blanket stitch
colonial knot stitch
straight stitch
blanket stitch

◆ use an outline stitch (2 strands) for any area not specified above

85 *M of the Alphabet*

I thought it would be fun to hook various sizes and colors of rings onto each of the strokes of the letter "M". Be careful to change the perspective of the rings that are on the curved sections so that they look realistic.

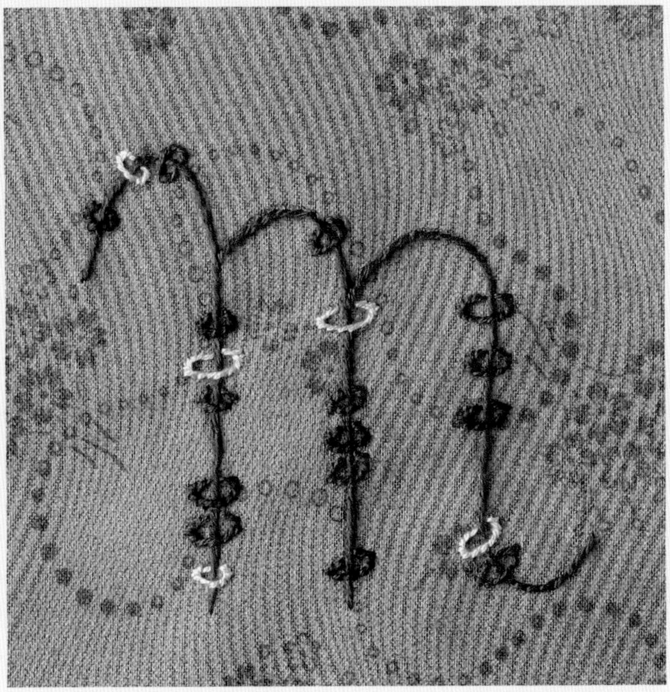

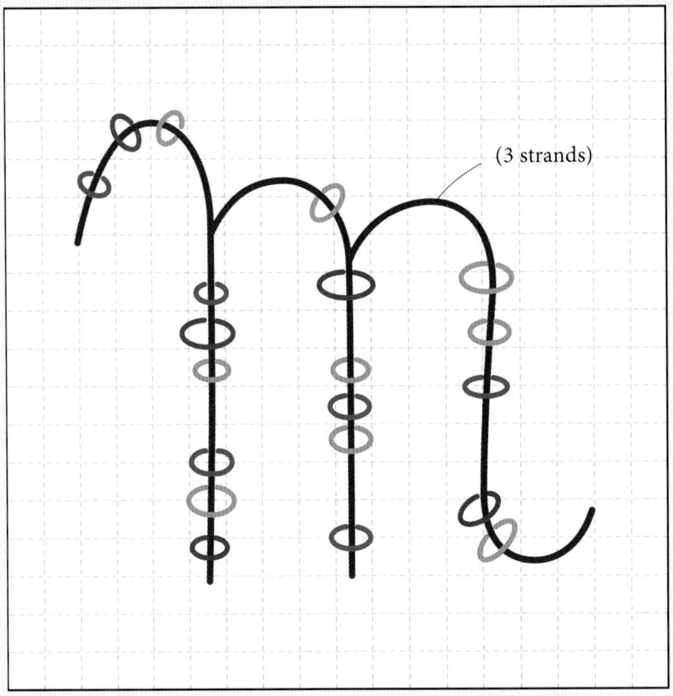

◆ use an outline stitch (2 strands) for any area not specified above

86 *N of the Alphabet*

Begin by appliquéing the diagonal line of the "N" with one kind of fabric. Follow this by the slightly fatter pieces from a different fabric for the two vertical ones, which ends up adding visual depth. Finish up by adding the embroidery.

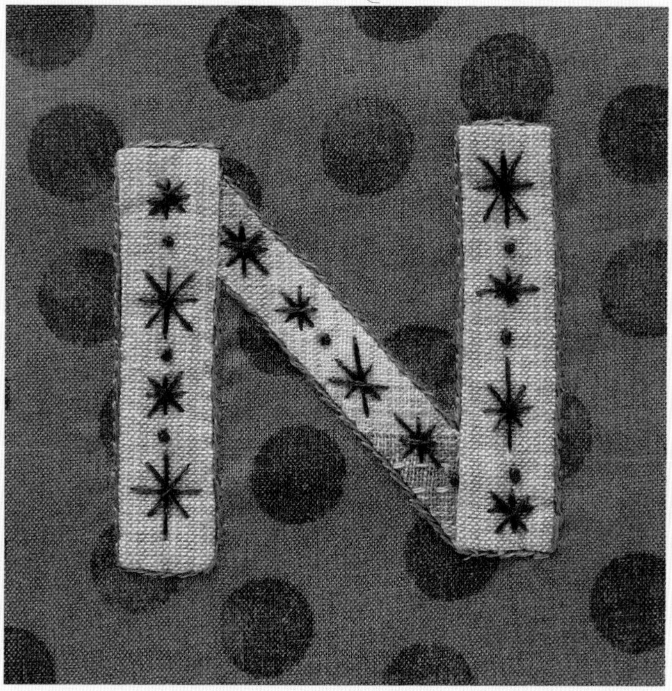

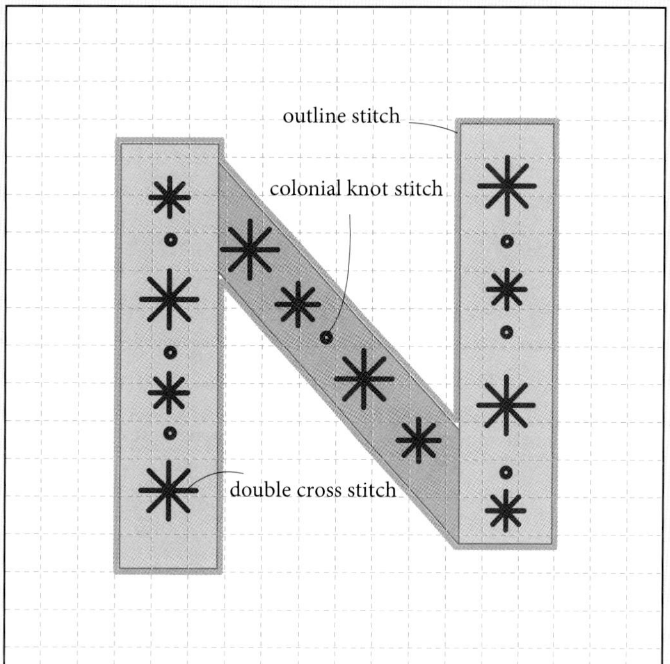
outline stitch
colonial knot stitch
double cross stitch

◆ use 2 strands for the entire design

87 *O of the Alphabet*

I made a sweet little wreath out of forget-me-nots for the letter "O" with their stems crossing at the bottom. First embroider the main stems to make the shape of the "O", then go back and add the leaves and flowers.

straight stitch
lazy daisy stitch
french knot stitch
outline stitch
(3 strands)

◆ use 2 strands for the entire design

88 *P of the Alphabet*

The "P" rather pops out in this pattern where the letter is first appliquéd to the background fabric. Outline the "P" with embroidery as well as add the little shapes after you appliqué the shape.

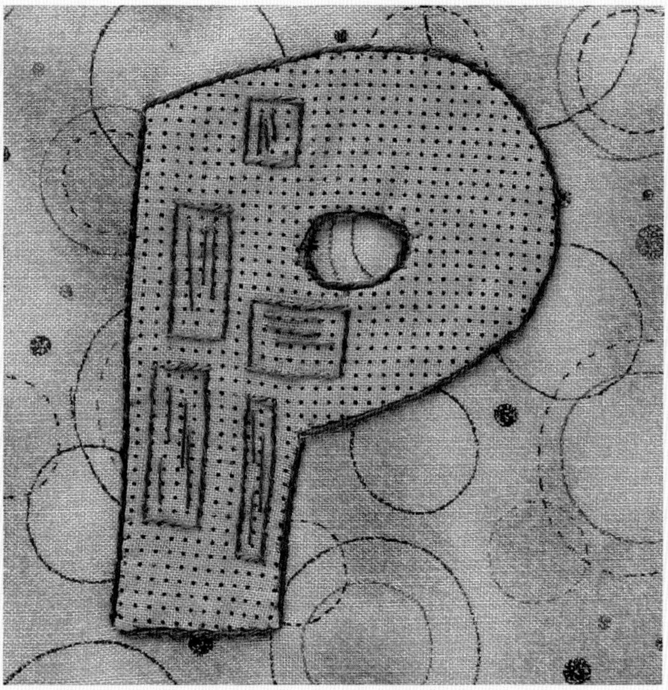

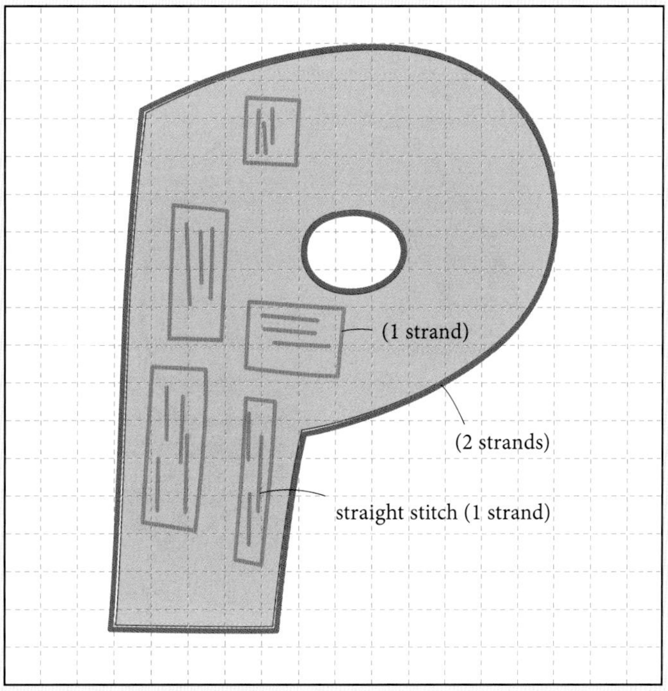

(1 strand)
(2 strands)
straight stitch (1 strand)

◆ use an outline stitch for the entire design

89 *Q of the Alphabet*

I chose to emphasize the weave of the background fabric by mimicking it in the letter "Q". Using a couched trellis stitch, the orange stitches hold the root of the "trellis" in shape inside the outline of the letter.

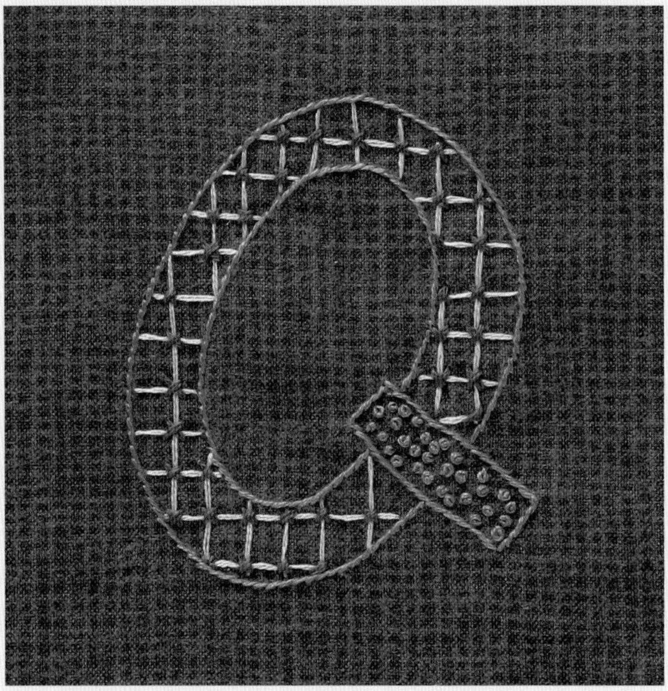

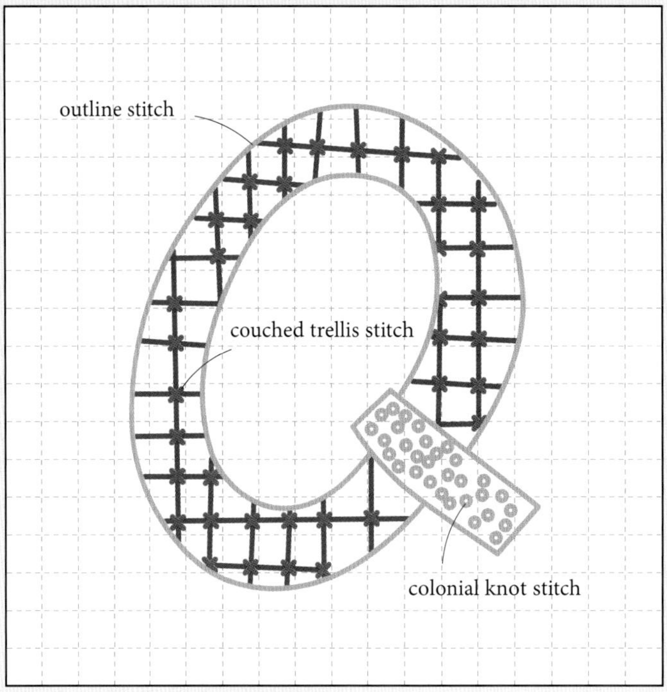

outline stitch
couched trellis stitch
colonial knot stitch

◆ use 2 strands for the entire design

90 *R of the Alphabet*

For the letter "R", I chose a background fabric with a lot of visual texture to set off the simple embroidery of a rose. After stitching the center of the flower, go back and weave over and under from the center out to create the rose petals. The large, dark and glossy leaves also reminded me of tea roses.

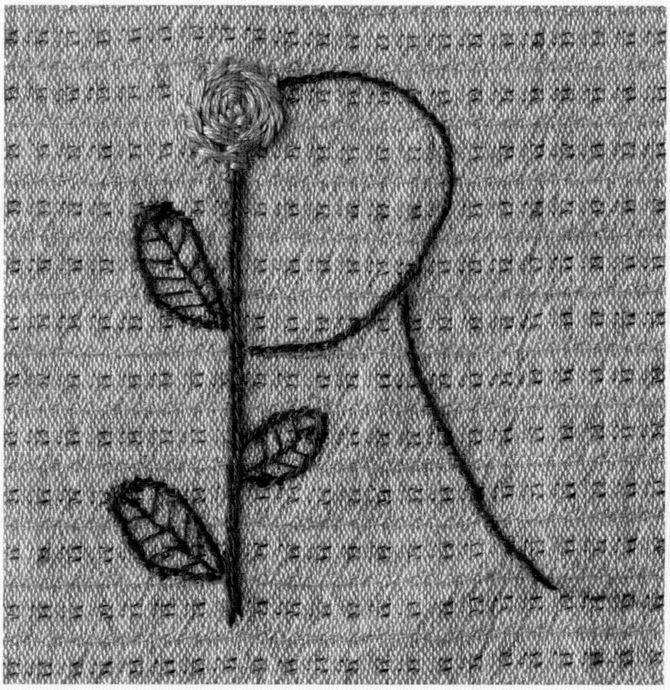

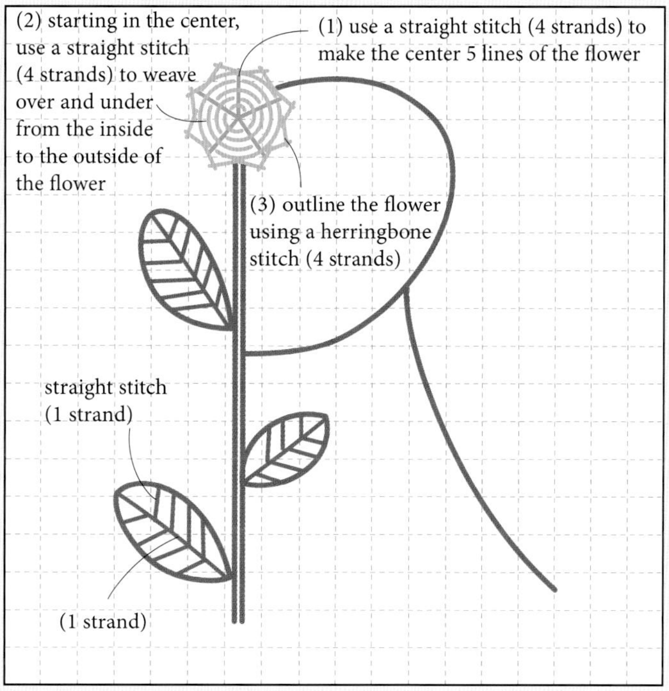

(2) starting in the center, use a straight stitch (4 strands) to weave over and under from the inside to the outside of the flower
(1) use a straight stitch (4 strands) to make the center 5 lines of the flower
(3) outline the flower using a herringbone stitch (4 strands)
straight stitch (1 strand)
(1 strand)

◆ use an outline stitch (2 strands) for any area not specified above

91 *S of the Alphabet*

I drew a simple curvy "S" and filled it in with bright and fun polka dots in yellow, green and pink. The dots are created by sewing a chain stitch around into circles. The design is visually interesting as I placed the background fabric at a slight angle.

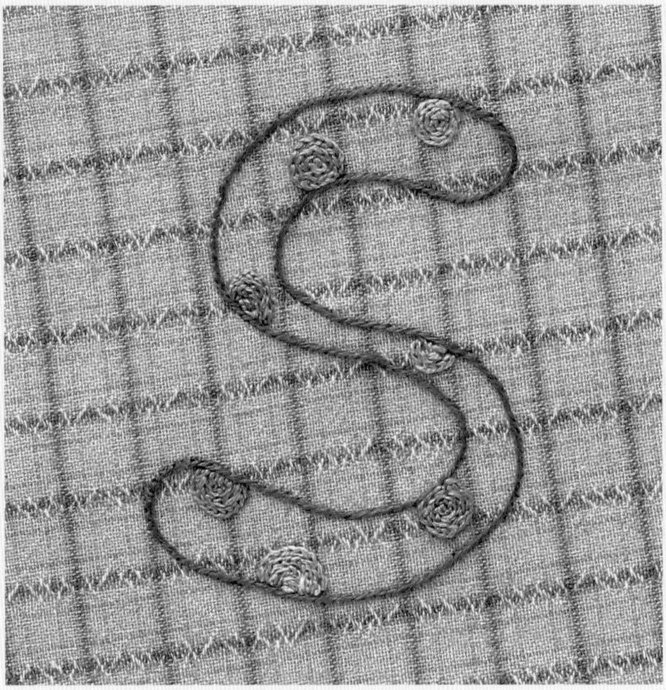

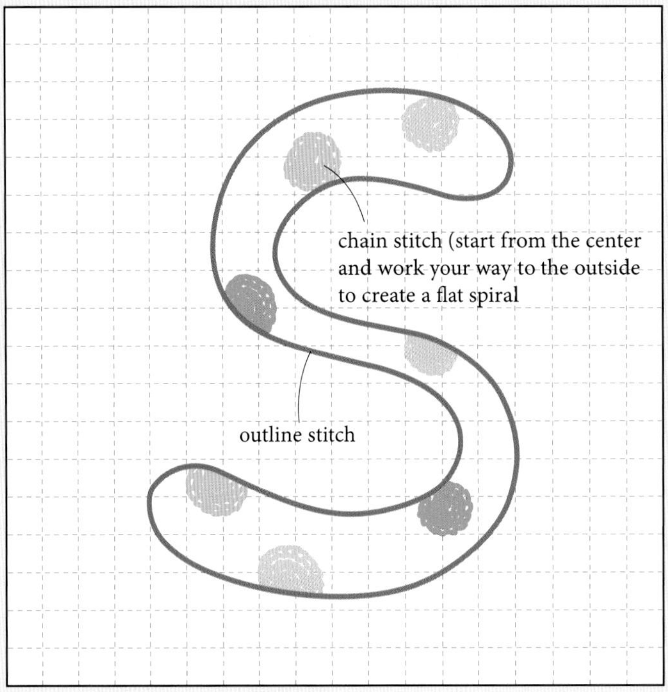

chain stitch (start from the center and work your way to the outside to create a flat spiral
outline stitch

◆ use 2 strands for the entire design

92 *T of the Alphabet*

I like the way the embroidery stitches are a primary focus for the letter "T". Use a chevron stitch for the upper portion of the "T", but since it is a long way for the floss to travel and it could easily get caught on something, I have taken a tiny securing stitch in the middle of each diagonal.

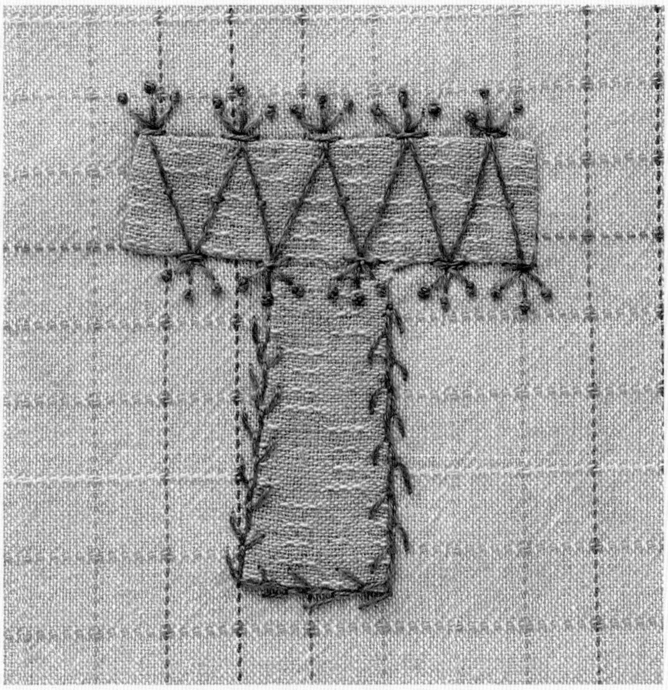

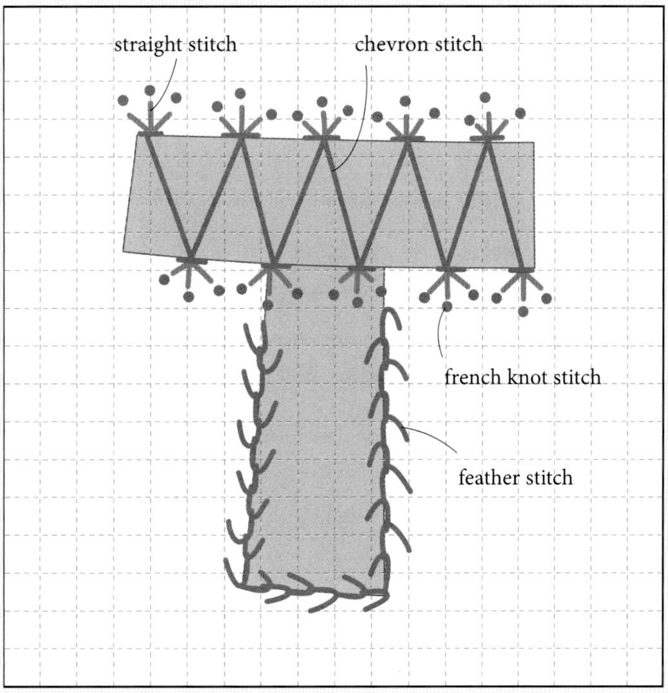
straight stitch
chevron stitch
french knot stitch
feather stitch

◆ use 2 strands for the entire design

93 *U of the Alphabet*

To make the letter "U", start with the chain stitch to create the shape. Then, right next to the line before, embroider french knots, blanket stitches, followed by french knots again to finish the design.

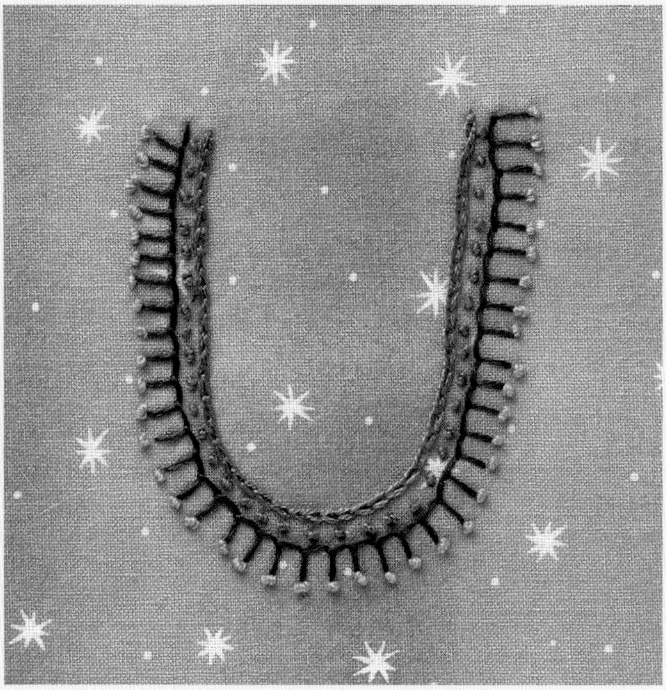

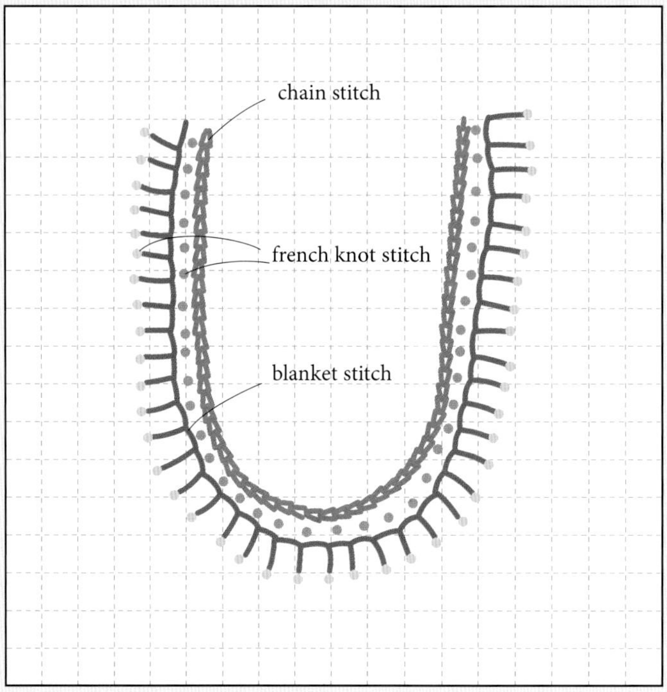

chain stitch
french knot stitch
blanket stitch

◆ use 2 strands for the entire design

94 *V of the Alphabet*

The letter "V" stands out beautifully when embroidered in the white against a darker background fabric. Start by stitching the outline of the "V" and fill it in with little flowers and colonial knots.

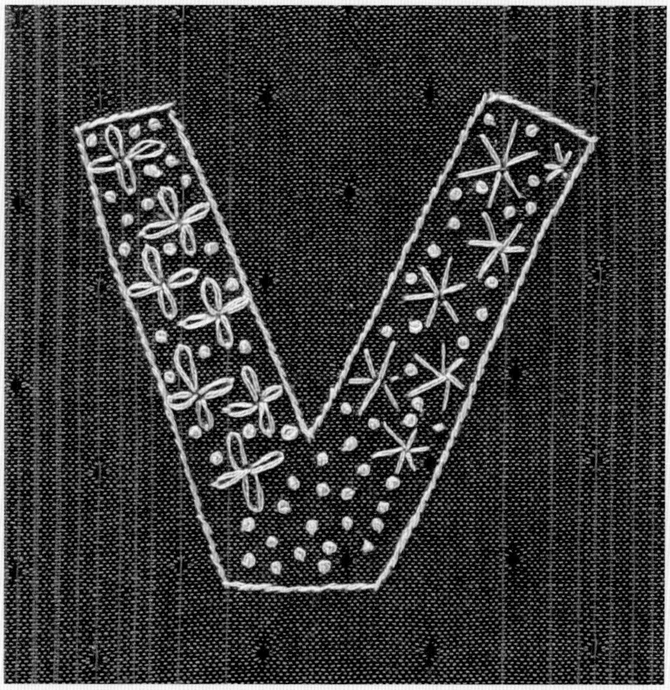

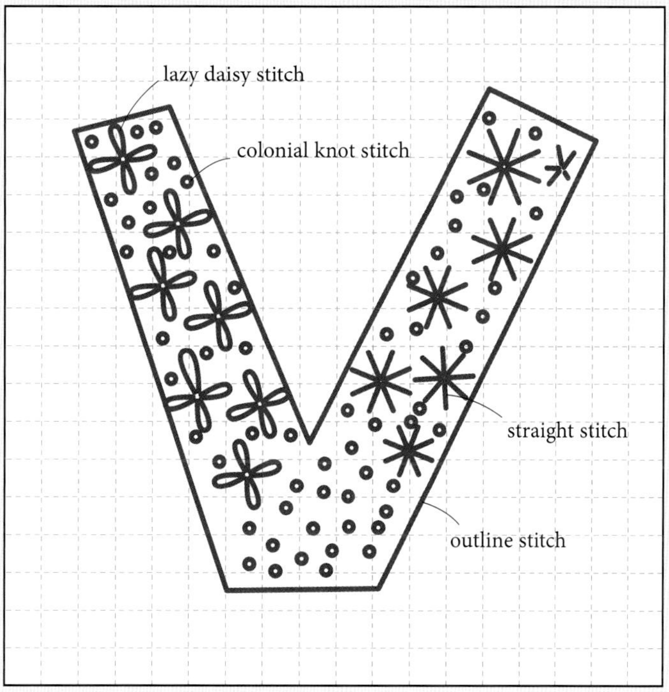

lazy daisy stitch
colonial knot stitch
straight stitch
outline stitch

◆ use 2 strands for the entire design

95 *W of the Alphabet*

The letter "W" turned out to be fun and casual. Using one strand of perle cotton for all of the stitches played well against the coarsely-woven background fabric.

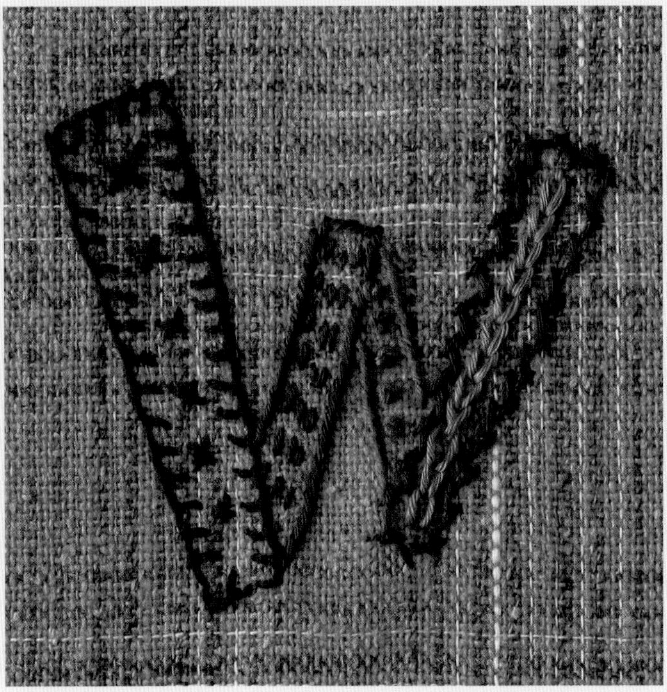

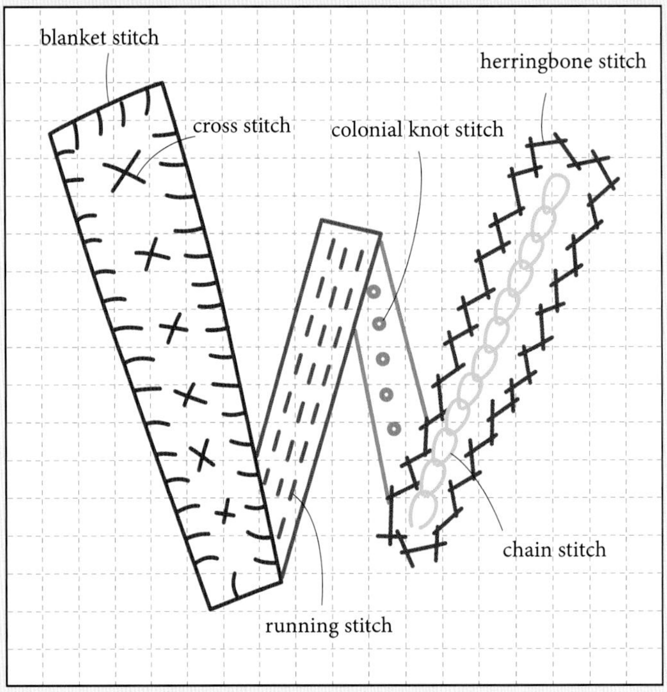

◆ use an outline stitch and perle cotton (1 strand) the entire design

96 *X of the Alphabet*

I incorporated both a pencil and ruler into the design for the letter "X". You can take the time to measure out the marks on the ruler, but I like to do them freehand.

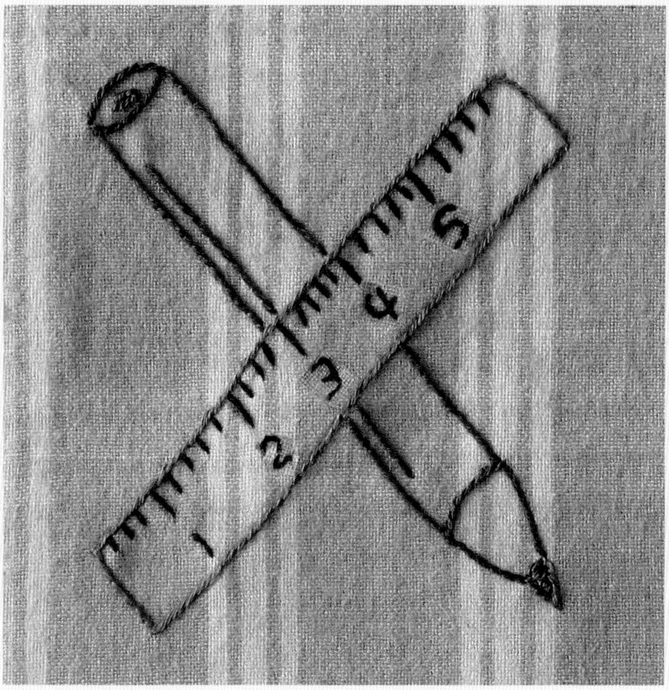

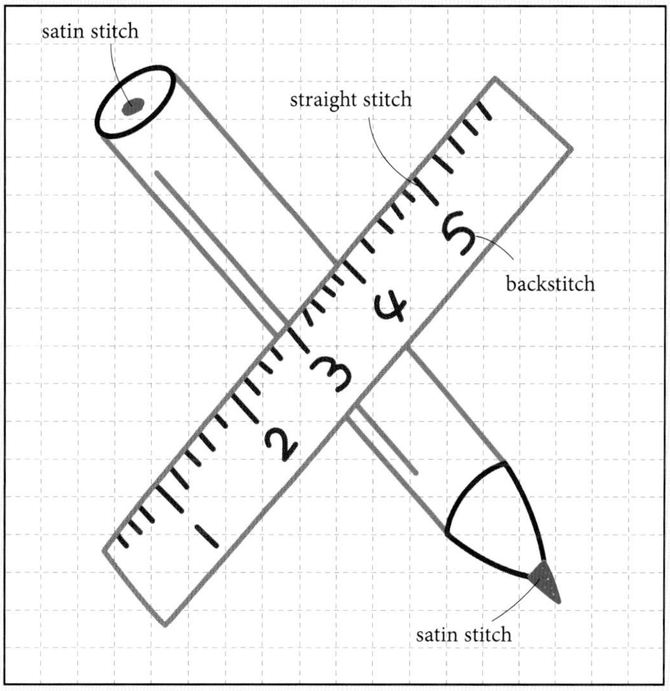

satin stitch
straight stitch
backstitch
satin stitch
1
2
3
4
5

◆ use an outline stitch (2 strands) for any area not specified above

97 *Y of the Alphabet*

A sheaf of wheat makes up the design for the letter "Y". I used an elongated lazy daisy stitch for each of the grains of wheat.

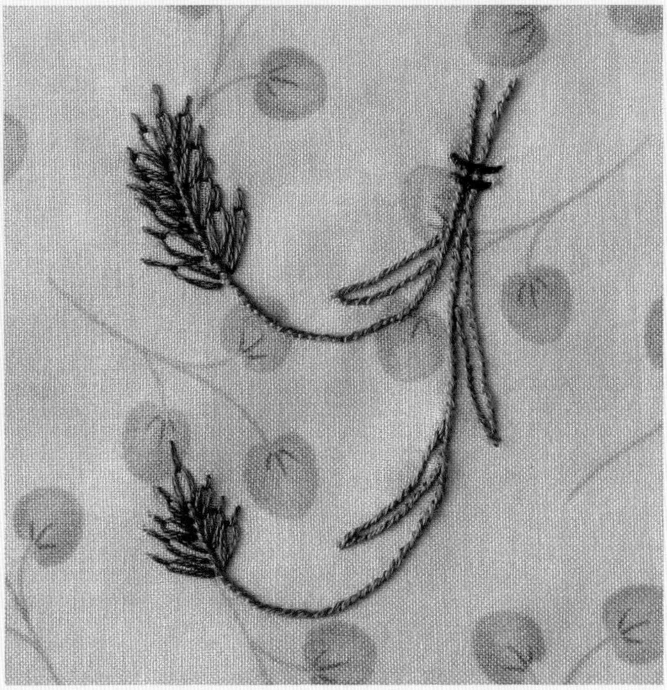

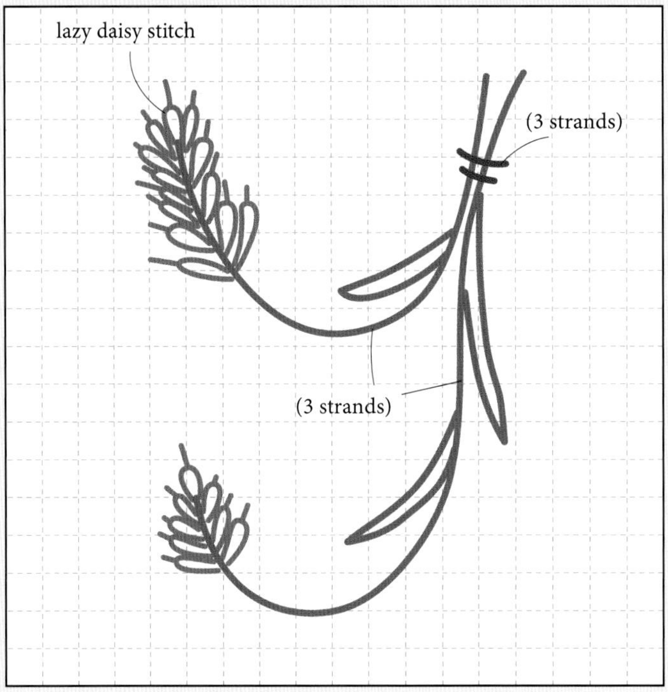
lazy daisy stitch
(3 strands)
(3 strands)

◆ use an outline stitch (2 strands) for any area not specified above

98 Z of the Alphabet

"Z" is uniquely made from a treble clef and bits of musical scores. I selected a background fabric that was calming in color and pattern, much like classical music often is.

french knot stitch
satin stitch
(3 strands)

◆ use an outline stitch (2 strands) for any area not specified above

99 *Radio Gymnastics*

In Japan, people often follow along on the radio and do gymnastics. Use all of the stick figures, like I did for the pencil case, or choose just a few. I used this design for the front of the pencil case on p. 131.

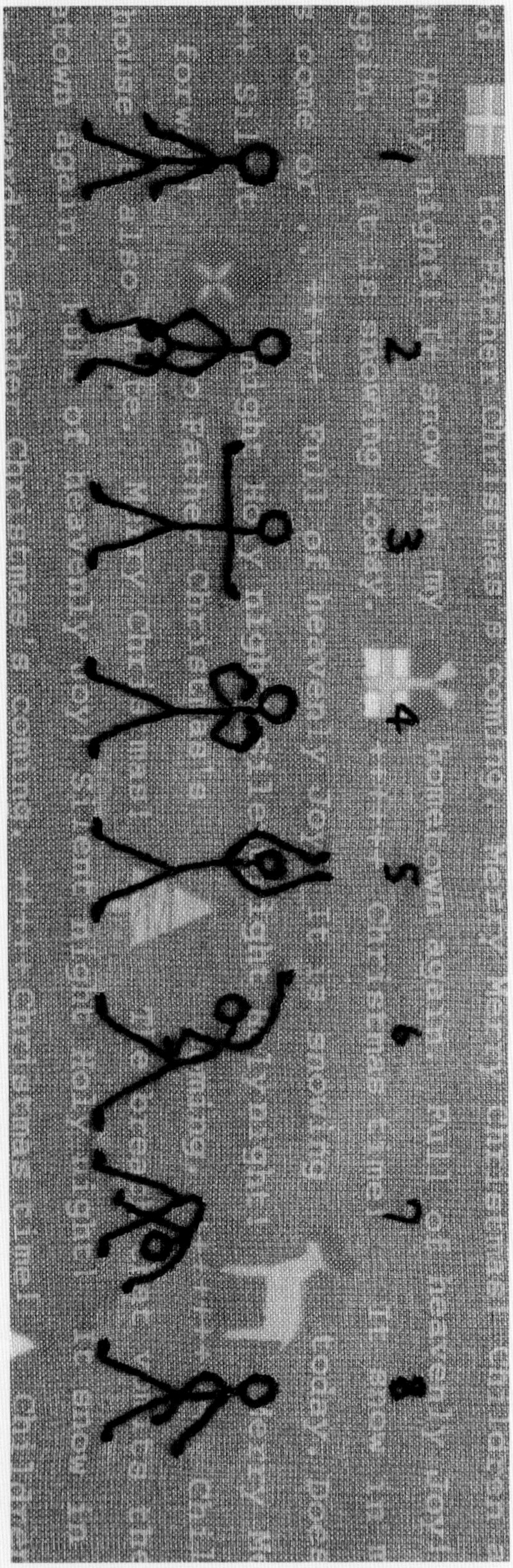

◆ use the outline stitch for the entire design

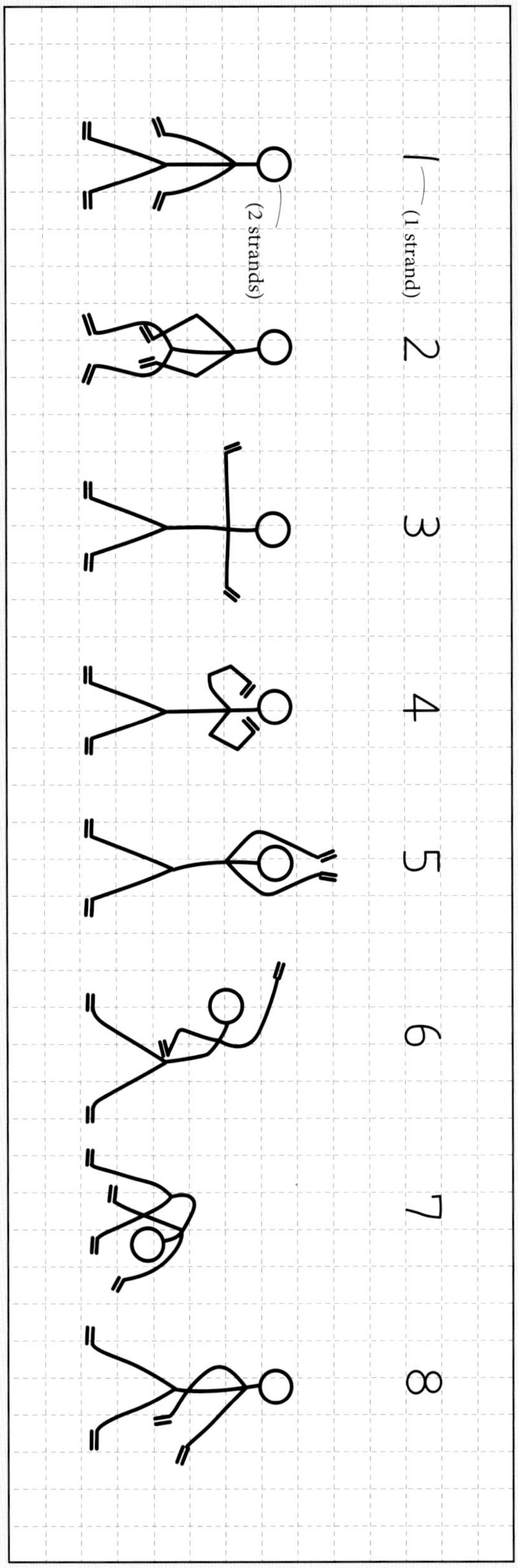

1 Pencil Case

I designed a pencil case that would accommodate the elongated design. I quilted the background fabric horizontally to go along with the text printed on it. I made a little zipper pull that looked like the stick figures.

The design is from pattern **99** (p. 130).
Instructions for the pencil case are on p. 210.

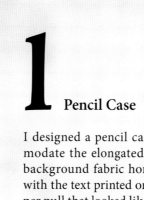

100 *Check on Cross*

I love the clean lines and uniformity of patterns done in cross stitch. It is easy to do this on a gingham check and use the pattern as a guide. If the gingham has tiny checks, use four of them for one cross stitch.

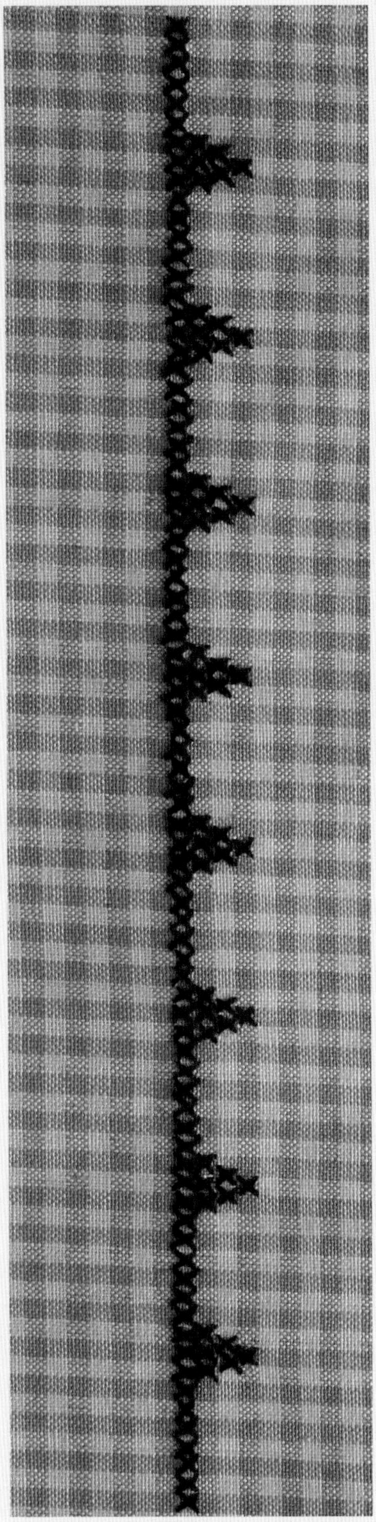

◆ use a cross stitch (2 strands) for the entire design

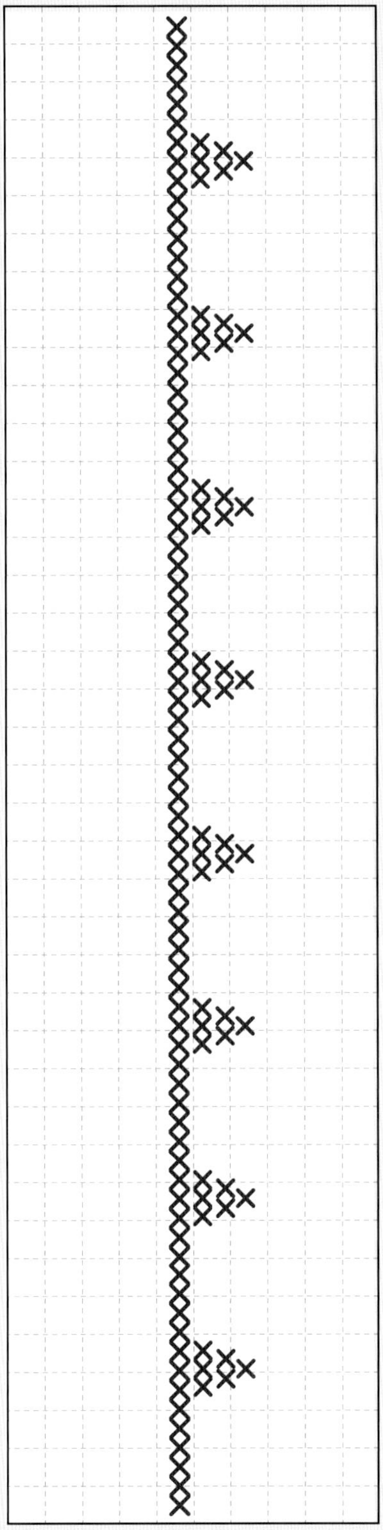

101 *Flower Chain*

This design is perfect for the borders or sashing of a quilt. Using a background fabric that has lines to use as guides (such as this one) makes it easy to keep repeatable patterns straight as you are working.

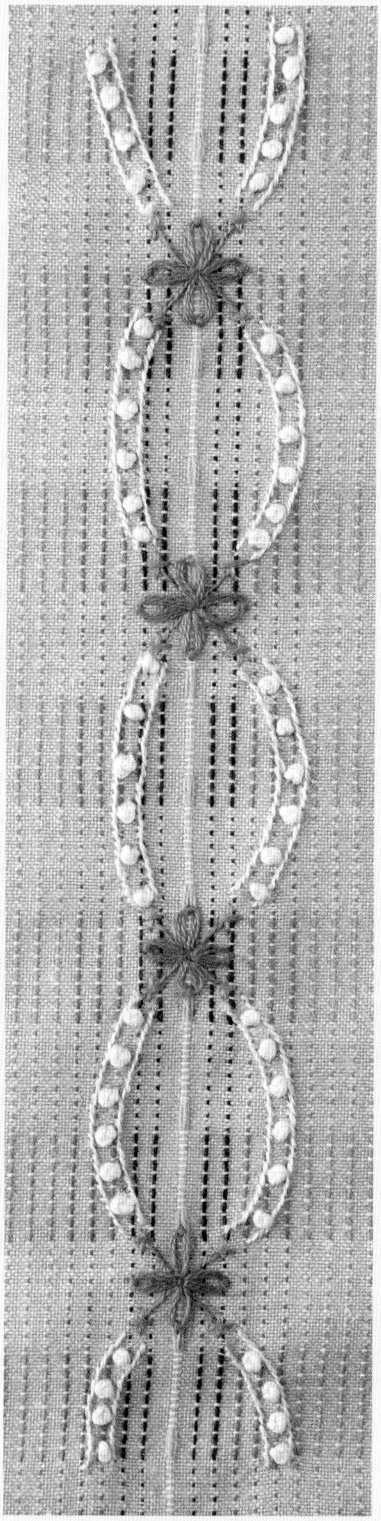

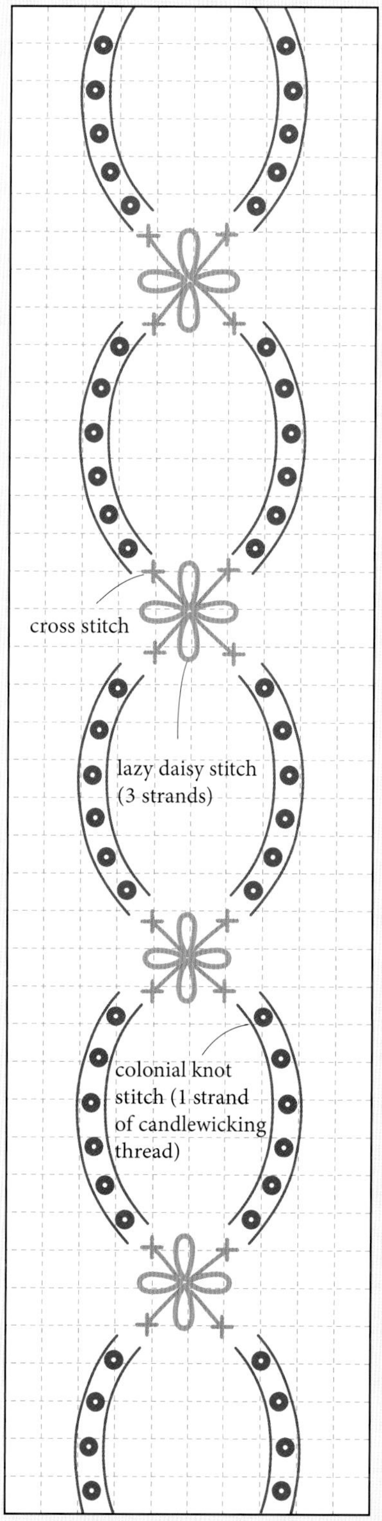
cross stitch
lazy daisy stitch (3 strands)
colonial knot stitch (1 strand of candlewicking thread)

◆ use an outline stitch (2 strands) for any area not specified above

102 *Tulips & Dandelions*

I often design quilts with a technique where I piece two similar fabrics together as a frame and hide the seam lines with appliqué or embroidery. I have done that with this tulip and dandelion design that sits on a gently curving feather stitch where the seam is. I used this design for the handbag on p. 90.

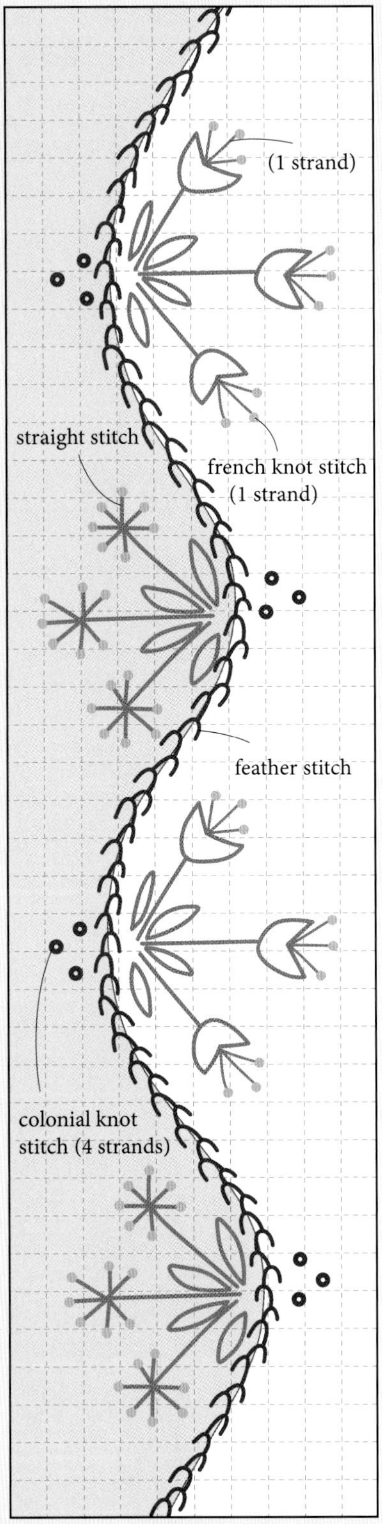
(1 strand)
straight stitch
french knot stitch (1 strand)
feather stitch
colonial knot stitch (4 strands)

◆ use an outline stitch (2 strands) for any area not specified above

103 *Green Bouquet*

The delicate print of the background fabric is a nice foil for the busy bouquet and ribbon design. I added a double cross stitch in white, secured by a tiny red stitch to add balance to the entire design. I used this design for the drawstring pouch on p. 147.

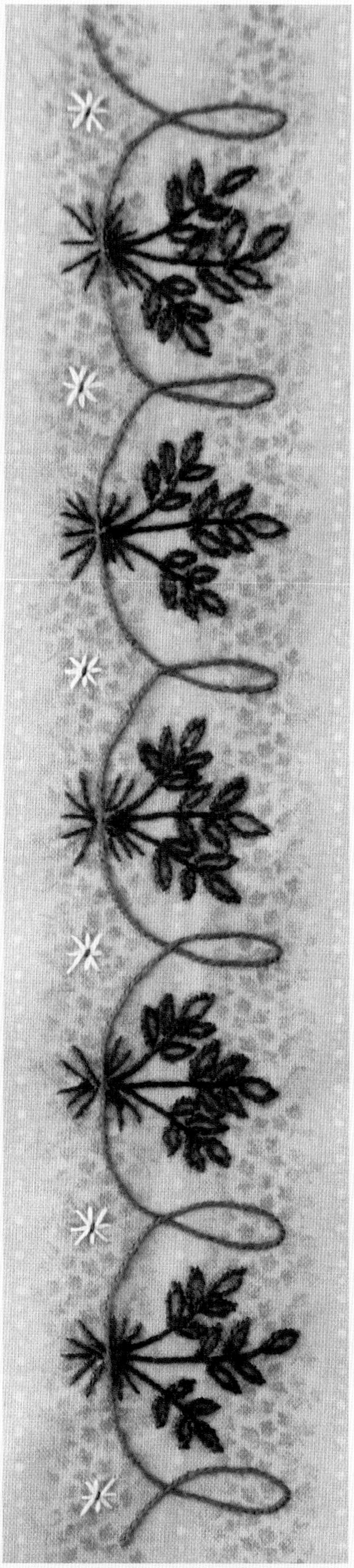

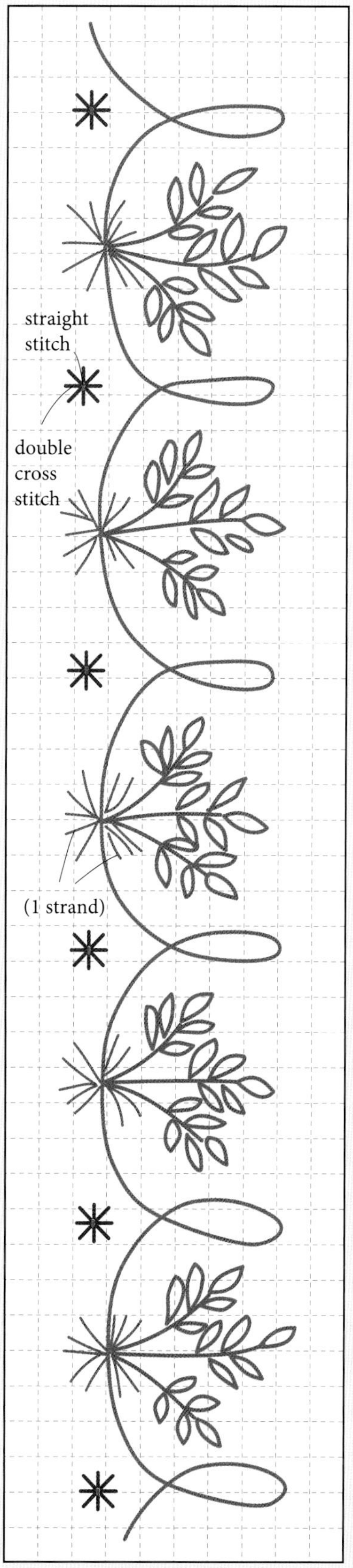

straight stitch
double cross stitch
(1 strand)

◆ use an outline stitch (2 strands) for any area not specified above

104

My Small House

◆ use an outline stitch (3 strands) for the entire design

I tried my hand at drawing a pattern using one continuous line. It turned out rather cute, even if the dog is as big as the house! The telephone pole is on the very right, however there is a sense of balance. I chose a busy print for the background to even out the simplicity of the pattern. I used this design for the notebook cover on p. 138.

m Notebook Cover

I made this simple little book cover and left it unquilted so that it is easy to use. When opened out, you can see the entire unbroken design. It would make a nice and easy handmade present for someone special.

The design is from pattern **104** (pp. 136-137).
Instructions for the notebook cover are on p. 211.

n Pouch

This little pouch is easy to use with the zipper that opens up wide in order to get things in and out. I freehand quilted the background fabric and appliquéd and embroidered the pinecones.

The design is from pattern **105** (pp. 140-141). Instructions for the pouch are on p. 212.

105

Pinecones

◆ use an outline stitch (2 strands) for any area not specified above

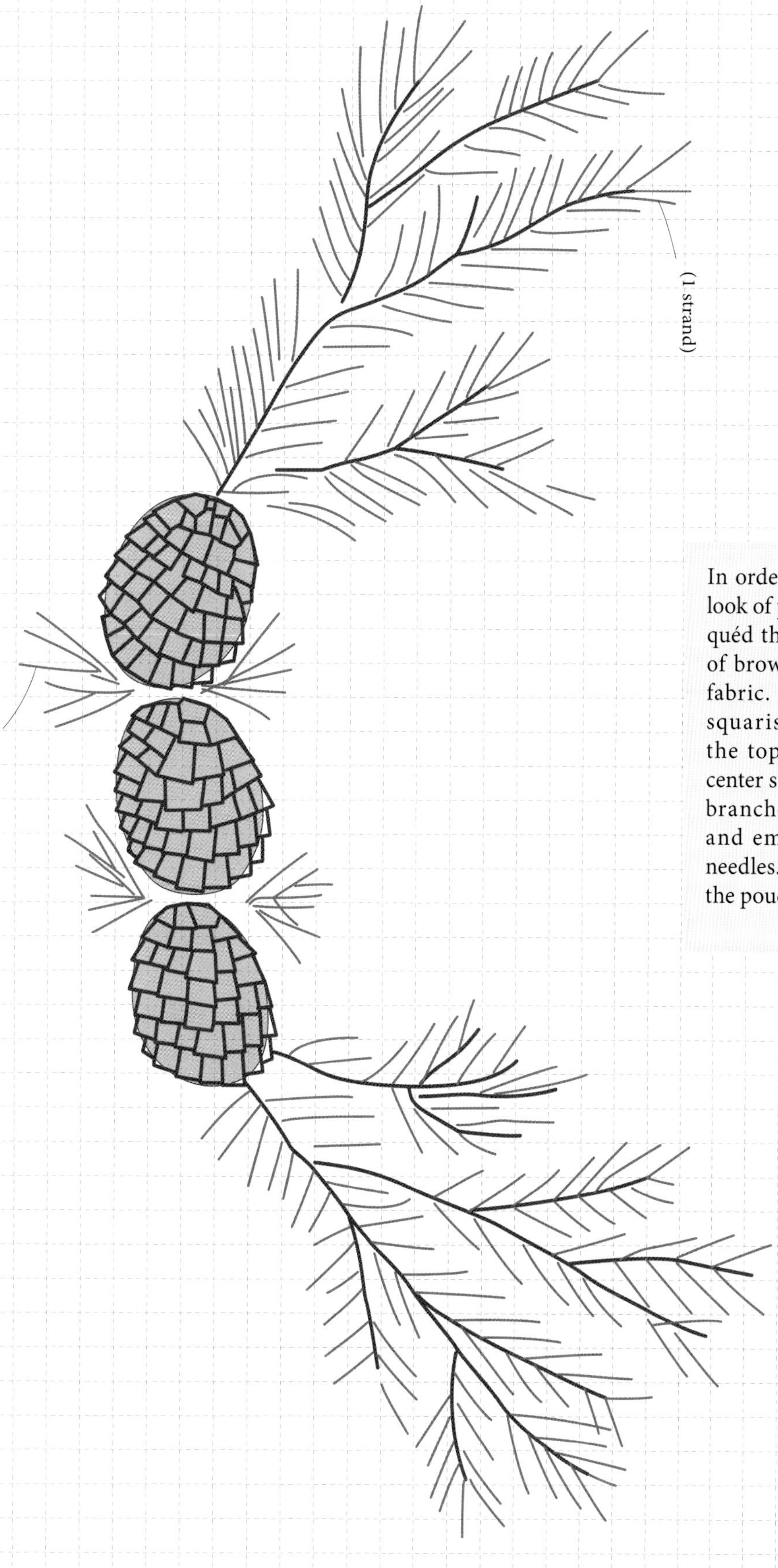

In order to achieve a realistic look of pinecones, I first appliquéd three egg-shaped pieces of brown to the background fabric. Then I embroidered squarish U-shapes all over the top of each. Stitch the center stem of each of the pine branches before going back and embroidering the pine needles. I used this design for the pouch on p. 139.

106

Poinsettia

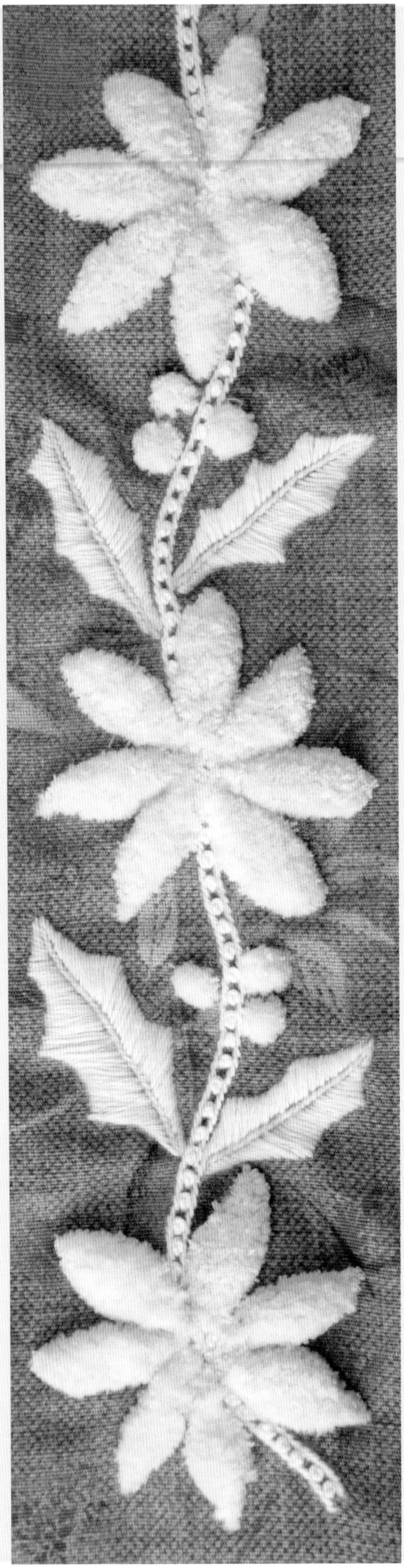

People are probably most familiar with red poinsettia plants, but the pink and white ones are beautiful as well. Combined in a repeatable pattern with holly leaves and berries in all white adds a level of sophistication. On p. 185 I have explained in detail how to do a velvet stitch to make the berries. It is a little challenging to use this weight of thread, but it adds a necessary dimension.

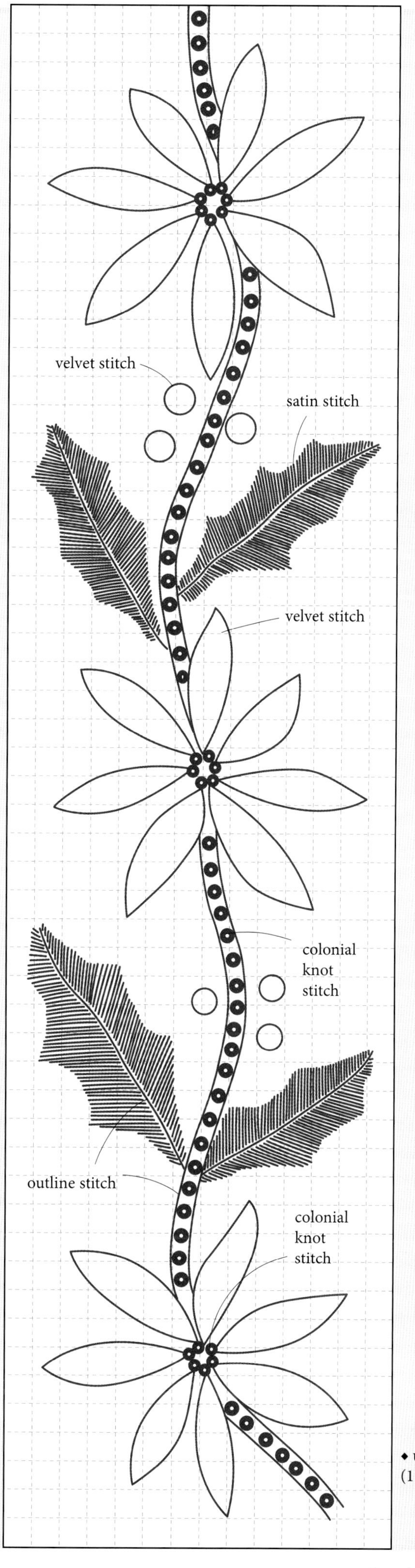
velvet stitch
satin stitch
velvet stitch
colonial knot stitch
outline stitch
colonial knot stitch

◆ use candlewicking thread (1 strand) for the entire design

107

Pagoda Tree

I have designed a number of patterns in this book that have trees, branches or leaves in them. This one will work for any kind of area in which you need a repeatable pattern. The soft "v" shape can be used in any number of combinations. I used this design for the mini bag on p. 146.

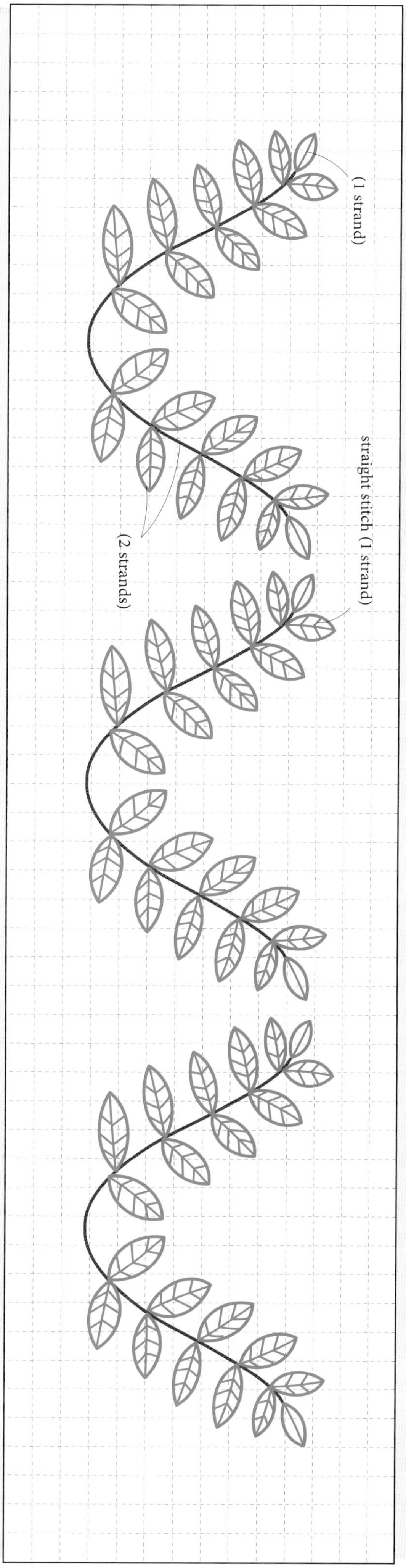
(1 strand)
straight stitch (1 strand)
(2 strands)

◆ use the outline stitch for the entire design

O Mini Bag

Sometimes I like to carry bags that are not quite as big or bulky. This mini bag is compact, but has a long strap so that it makes it easy to carry around. As I did not make it with a gusset, I sewed darts into the bottom corners to add a little fullness on the bag front. I used wooden beads for the zipper pulls.

The design is from pattern **107** (pp. 144-145). Instructions for the mini bag are on p. 214.

p Drawstring Bag

This drawstring bag is designed to be fairly simple. I sewed little rings through loops for the drawstring to go through, and made scalloped edges for the embroidery section and fabric that looks like a basket weave for the bag body. Finish the embroidery along the seams once the bag is sewn together.

The design is from pattern **103** (p. 135).
Instructions for the drawstring bag are on p. 216.

108

Thistle

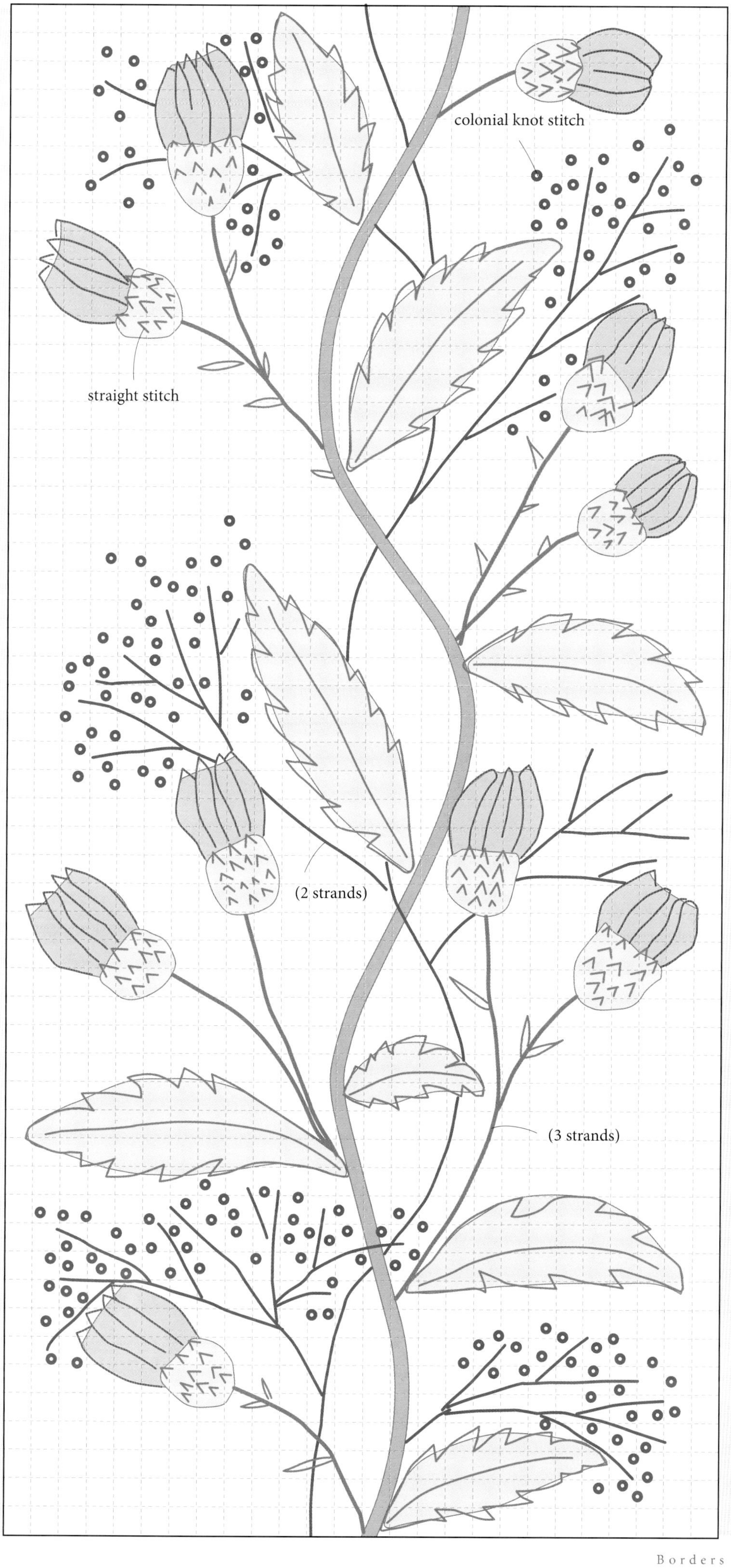
colonial knot stitch
straight stitch
(2 strands)
(3 strands)

The concept of "patchwork embroidery" is highlighted in this pattern. I chose a background fabric that complements the overall thistle flower design. The central stem, flowers and leaves are appliquéd down first. Along with the embroidery that enhances the appliqué, I added the white hazy grass intertwined throughout.

◆ use an outline stitch (1 strand) for any area not specified above

109

Small Rainbow

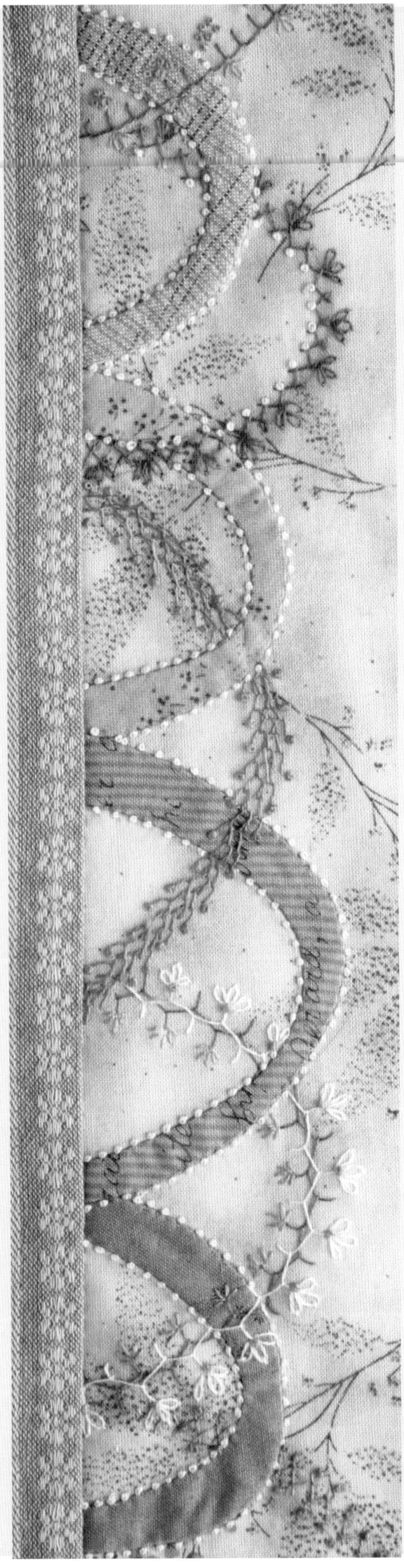

I appliquéd arches in various colored print fabrics onto the background. I then embroidered additional arches or outlined the appliqués to make it appear as though they are almost chasing each other in play. I used this design for the small basket on p. 152.

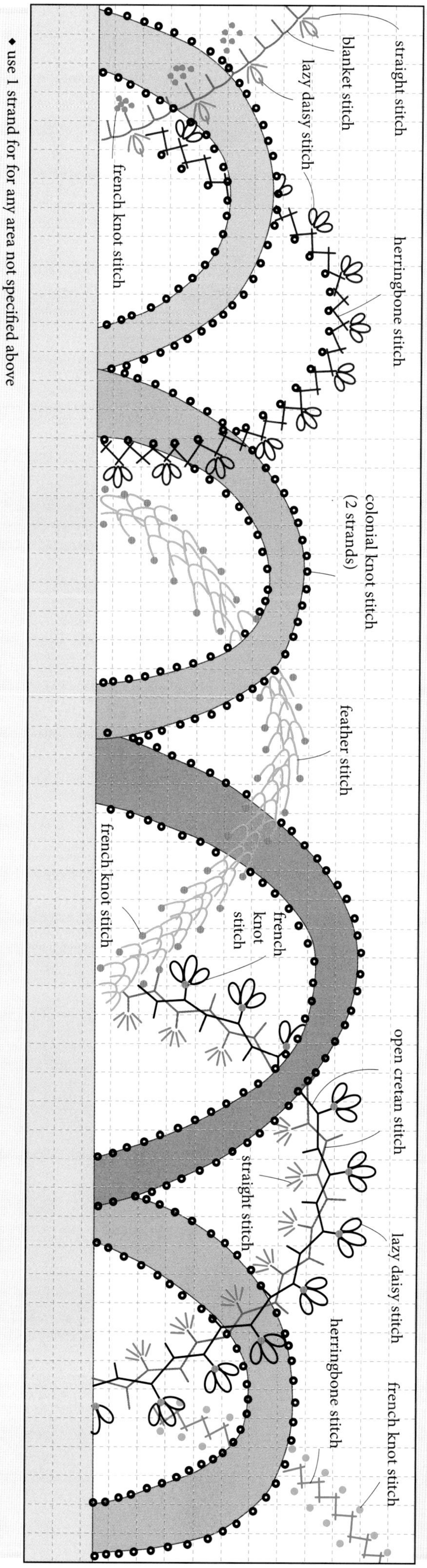
straight stitch
blanket stitch
lazy daisy stitch
french knot stitch
herringbone stitch
colonial knot stitch
(2 strands)
feather stitch
french knot stitch
french
knot
stitch
open cretan stitch
straight stitch
lazy daisy stitch
herringbone stitch
french knot stitch
◆ use 1 strand for for any area not specified above

q Small Basket

I used a combination of techniques and stitches that are commonly seen in crazy quilts to decorate this little basket. The background fabric has a delicate pattern that goes well with the colors of the arches of the rainbows. In order for the pattern to go around the entire basket, I added an extra appliquéd and embroidered arch on both sides.

The design is from pattern **109** (pp. 150-151).
Instructions for the small basket are on p. 218.

110

Maidenhair Fern

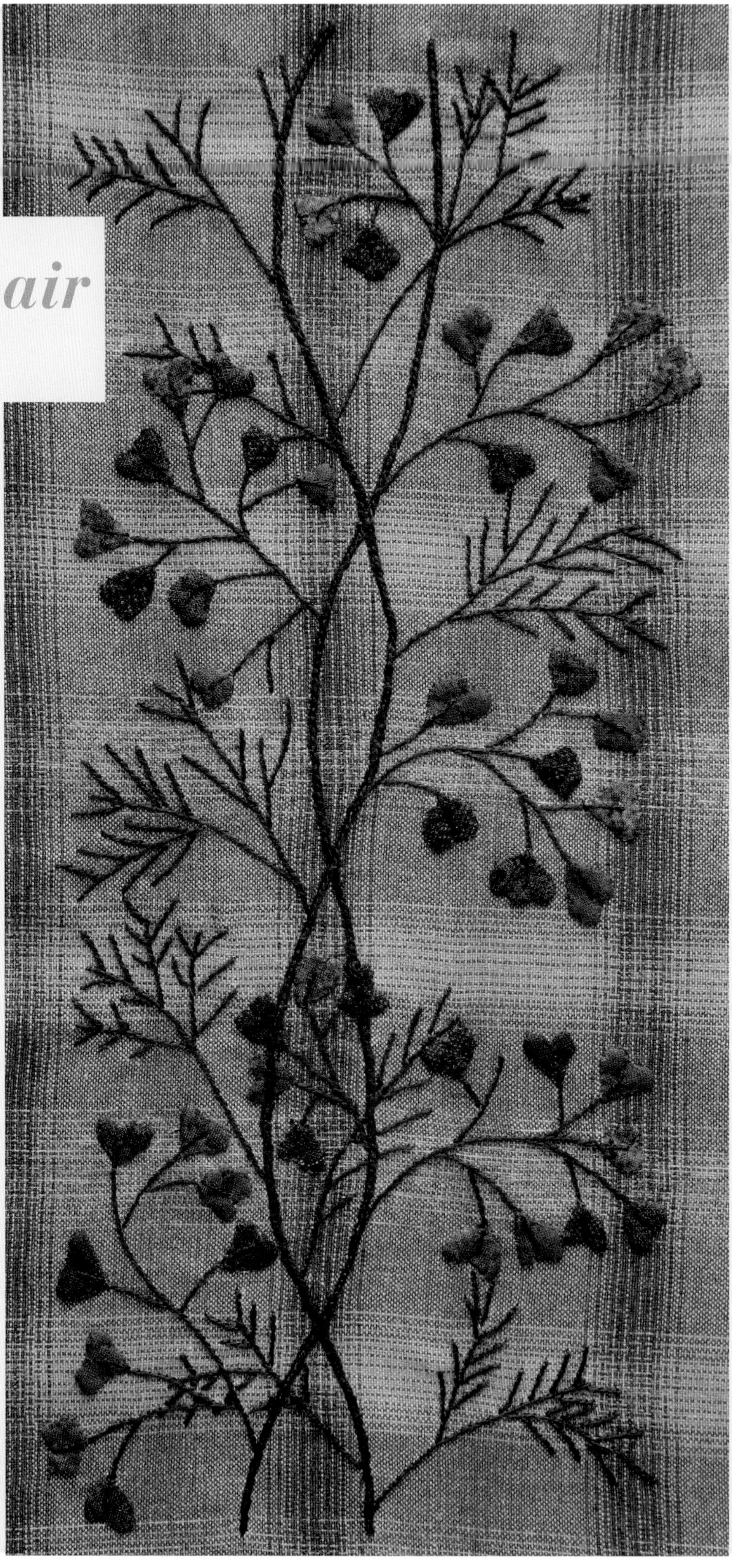

Tiny bright green leaves similar in shape to the ginko, maidenhair ferns make wonderful houseplants. Stitch two rows of the outline stitch in two different colors right next to each other to make the main stems. Appliqué the little leaves and fill in the areas with more embroidery. I used this design for the handbag on p. 158.

- use the outline stitch for the entire design

111 *Glass Vase*

Stitch a design with a glass vase and a beautiful bouquet of flowers by appliquéing the stems, flowers and leaves down first. For some of the leaves, outline them exactly, but for others, stitch the shape shifted to the sides. This technique, as well as choosing a background fabric that has a floral motif, makes the design appear to have more greenery than it does. I used this design for the handbag on p. 159.

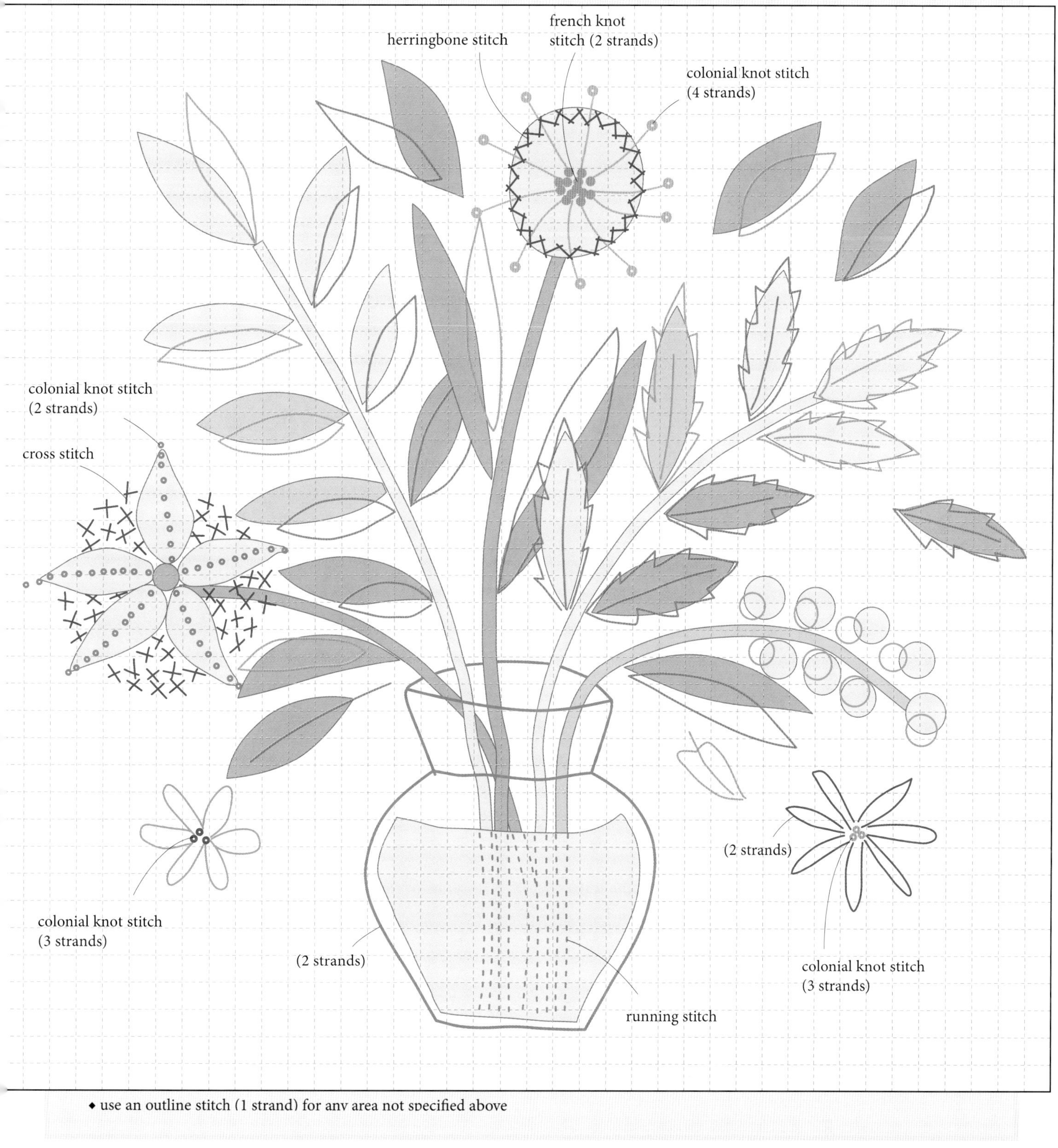
french knot
stitch (2 strands)
herringbone stitch
colonial knot stitch
(4 strands)
colonial knot stitch
(2 strands)
cross stitch
colonial knot stitch
(3 strands)
(2 strands)
(2 strands)
running stitch
colonial knot stitch
(3 strands)

◆ use an outline stitch (1 strand) for any area not specified above

r Handbag

This is a beautifully shaped unique handbag. The eye is drawn to the center panel. The maidenhair fern design is framed by tiny triangles. Use interfacing and machine quilt to achieve the firm sides and bottom.

The design is from pattern **110** (pp. 154-155). Instructions for the handbag are on p. 220.

S Handbag

The gently curved shape of the handbag is perfect for the soft water-color-like "patchwork embroidery" design. I added colonial knots to frame the embroidery and they look like the white dots in the bag body fabric.

The design is from pattern **111** (pp. 156-157).
Instructions for the handbag are on p. 222.

112

House-I

I love houses and buildings. I designed nine different patterns using the "patchwork embroidery" concept. The fabric with printed trees is the perfect background for these blocks that will become a wall hanging. This first of the nine buildings is of a log cabin with a steep roof. See the full set of houses and buildings in the wall hanging on pp. 168-169.

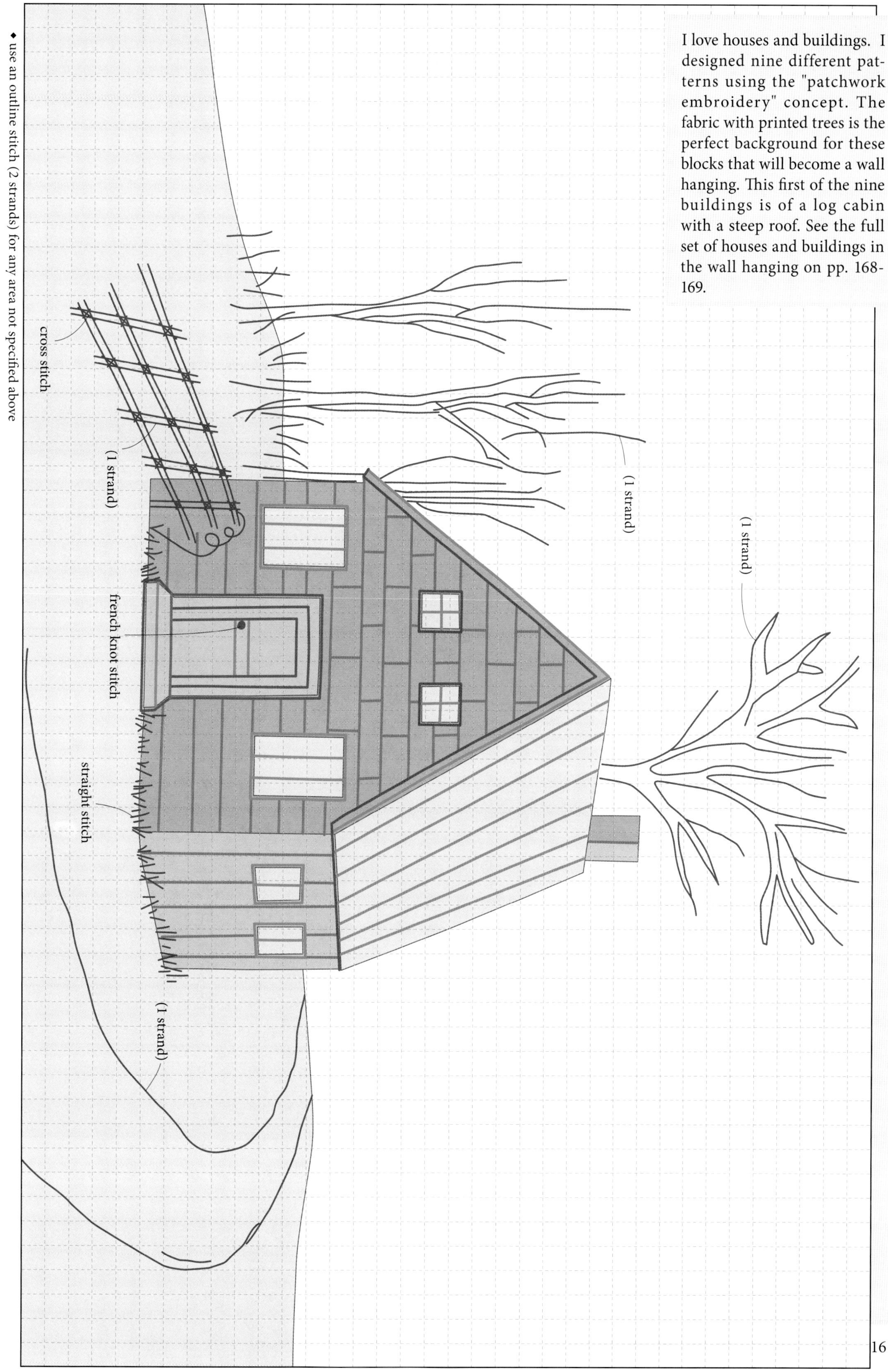

◆ use an outline stitch (2 strands) for any area not specified above
cross stitch
(1 strand)
french knot stitch
straight stitch
(1 strand)
(1 strand)
(1 strand)

113

House-II

This farm-style house has a gambrel roof. The two white trees are embroidered in front of the appliquéd buildings. They add perspective and depth of field with the tree fabric in the background. This is the second of the nine designs. See the full set of houses and buildings in the wall hanging on pp. 168-169.

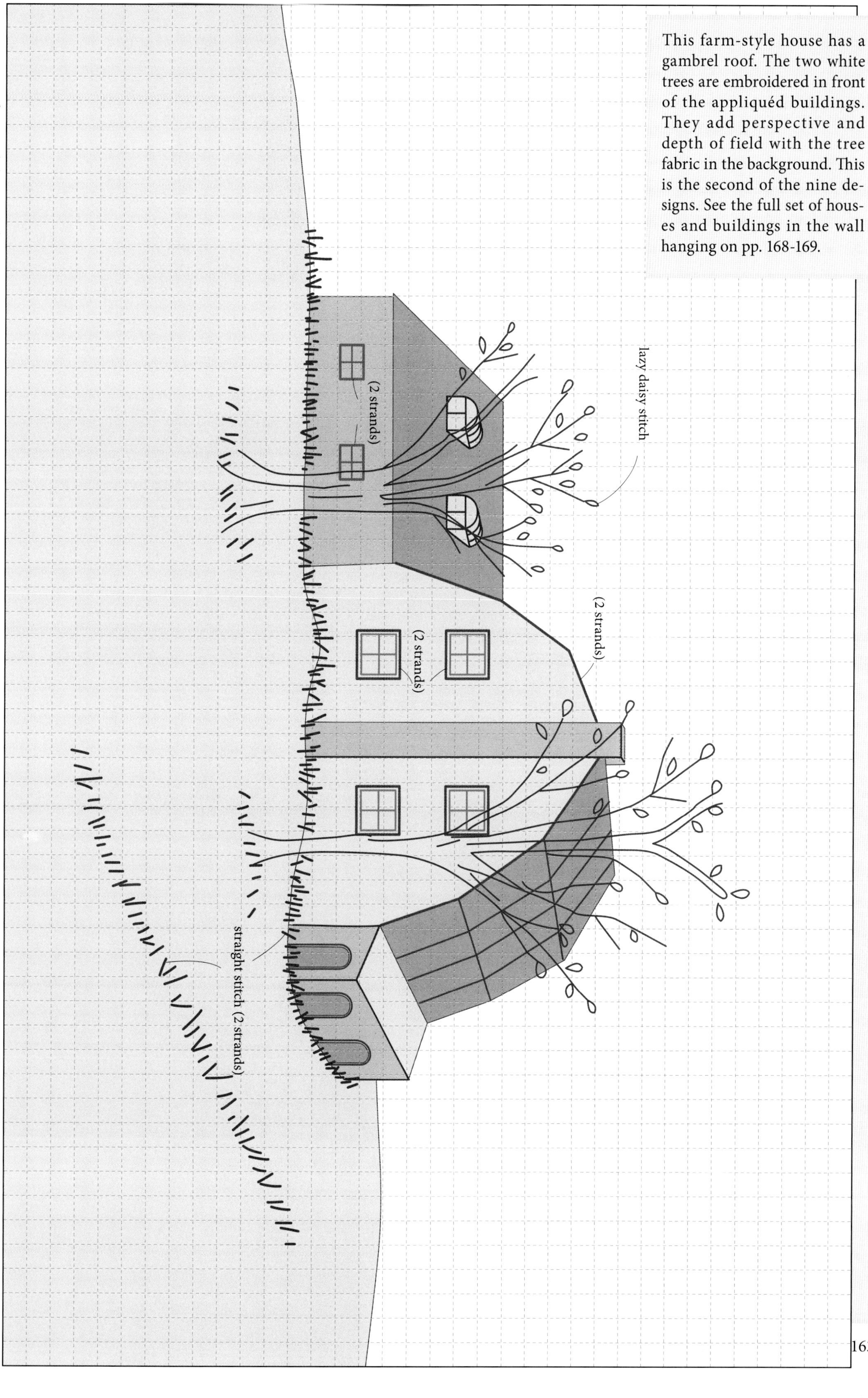

lazy daisy stitch
(2 strands)
(2 strands)
(2 strands)
(2 strands)
straight stitch (2 strands)

◆ use an outline stitch (1 strand) for any area not specified above

114

House-Ⅲ

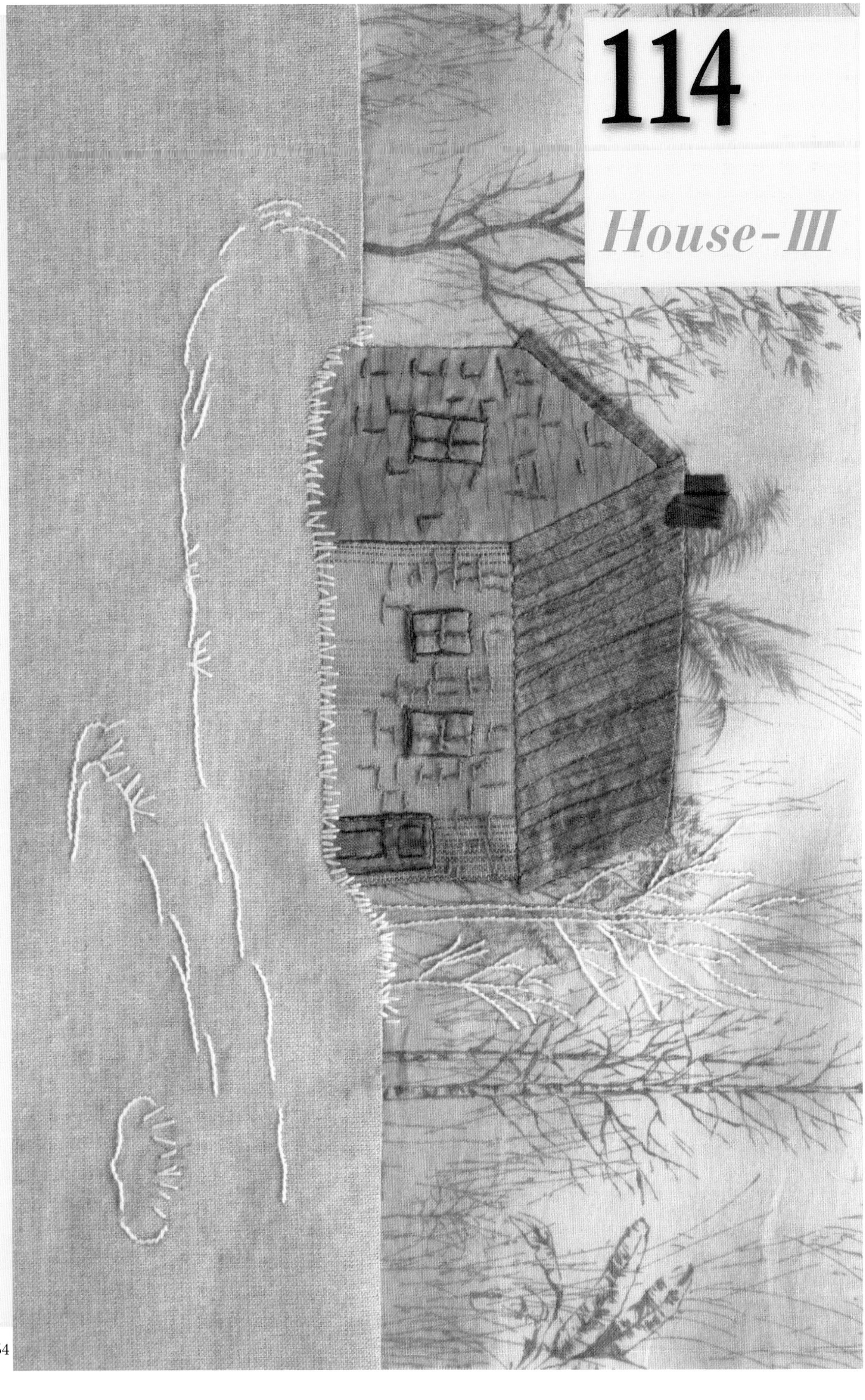

This is a house with a very basic shape that is made more interesting by the embroidery outlining the bricks in the walls. Appliqué all the various pieces of the house before starting to embroider. This is the third of the nine designs. See the full set of houses and buildings in the wall hanging on pp. 168-169.

(1 strand)
straight stitch
french knot stitch
(1 strand)
(1 strand)
(1 strand)

◆ use an outline stitch (2 strands) for any area not specified above

115

House-Ⅳ

I designed a grouping of buildings, large and small. I used different fabrics for the various pieces of the buildings. Tall trees, such as the fir tree, were embroidered behind the appliquéd houses. This is the fourth out of the nine buildings. See the full set of houses and buildings in the wall hanging on pp. 168-169.

◆ use an outline stitch (1 strand) for any area not specified above

t Wall Hanging

Sewing all of the nine house and building blocks together makes a perfect little sleepy town. Densely quilt the entire wall hanging. I change the direction of the quilting when doing the sky versus the ground. Embroider the remaining trees, grass and fencing to complete the wall hanging.

The designs are from the patterns 112-120 (pp. 160-167, 170-179). Instructions for the wall hanging are on p. 213.

116

House-V

The paddock sits in front of the house and is ready for horses or cows. All it needs is a rustic barn to complete the image. Use a straight stitch for the short grass around the house. This is the fifth of the nine buildings. See the full set of houses and buildings in the wall hanging on pp. 168-169.

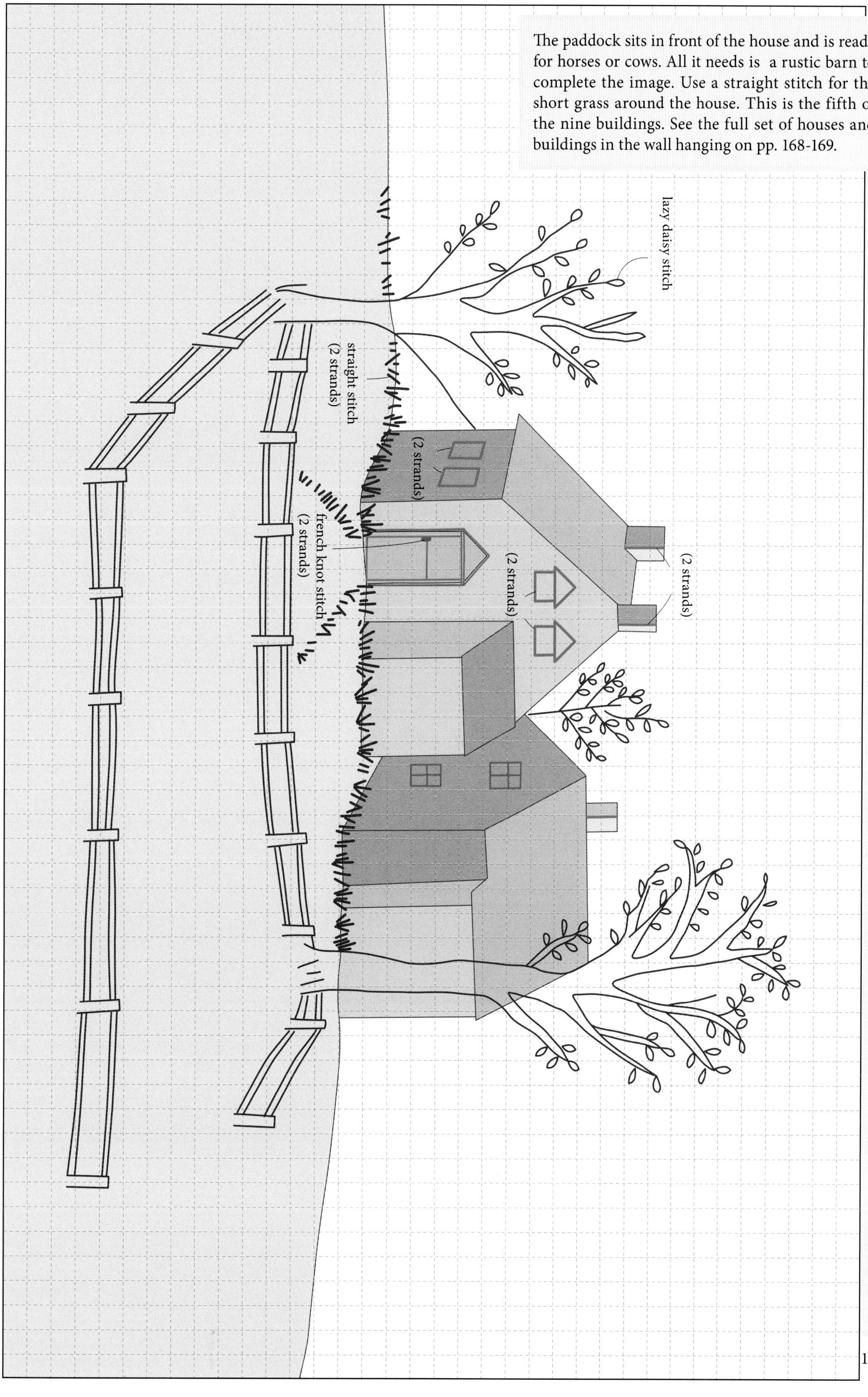

lazy daisy stitch
straight stitch (2 strands)
(2 strands)
french knot stitch (2 strands)
(2 strands)
(2 strands)

◆ use an outline stitch (1 strand) for any area not specified above

117

House -VI

The sixth of the nine designs, this large house is complete with a terrace and sunroom. There are trees planted all around the house. Use the shapes of the appliqué and the embroidery to show perspective from the front of the house to the back. See the full set of houses and buildings in the wall hanging on pp. 168-169.

(1 strand)
straight stitch
(1 strand)
(1 strand)
(1 strand)

◆ use an outline stitch (2 strands) for any area not specified above

118

House-VII

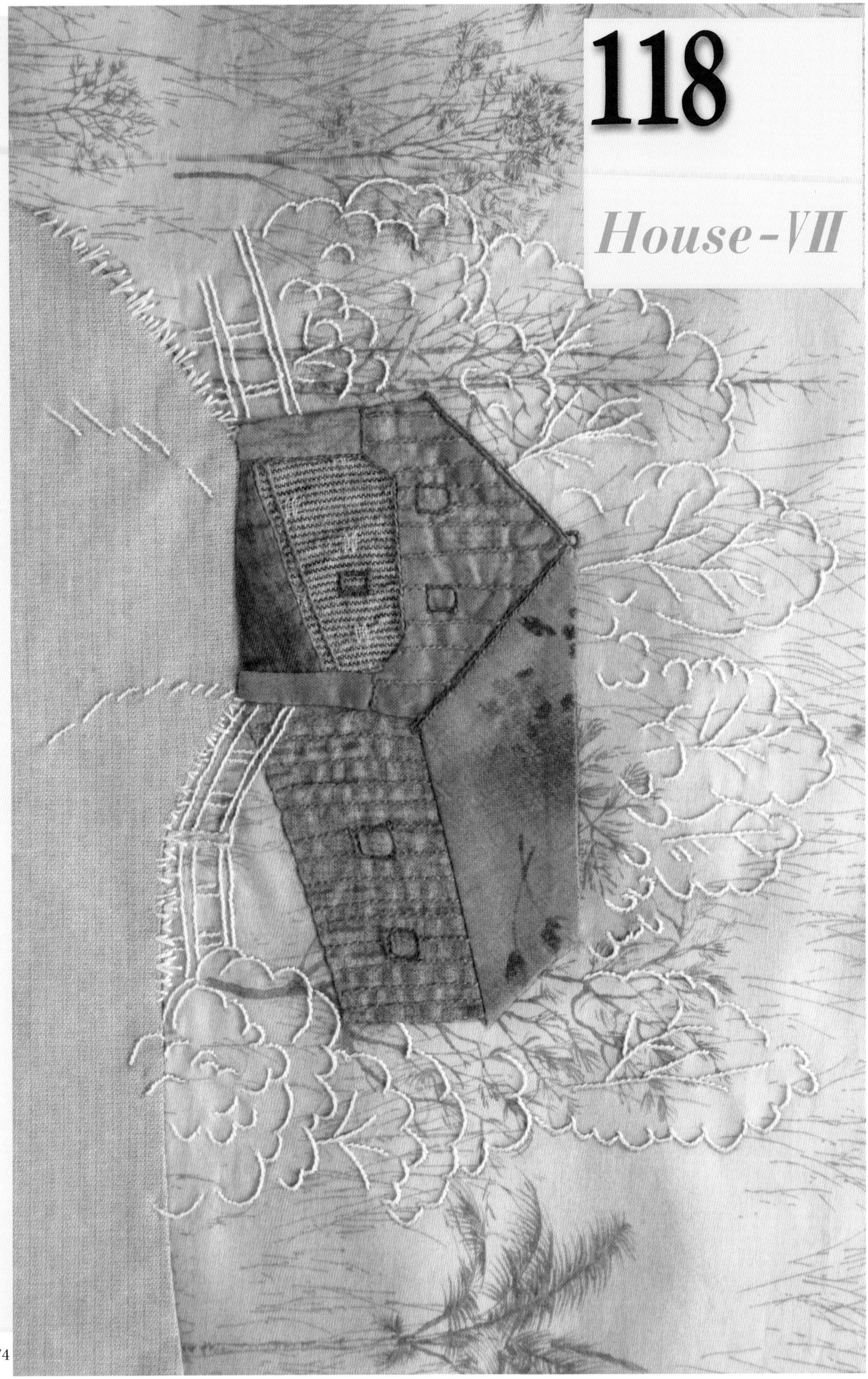

I love covered bridges and couldn't resist adding this to the wall hanging. Imagine driving through, protected from the wind and rain. I used embroidery to show the lines of the curving road. Stitch trees all around. This is the seventh of the nine designs. See the full set of houses and buildings in the wall hanging on pp. 168-169.

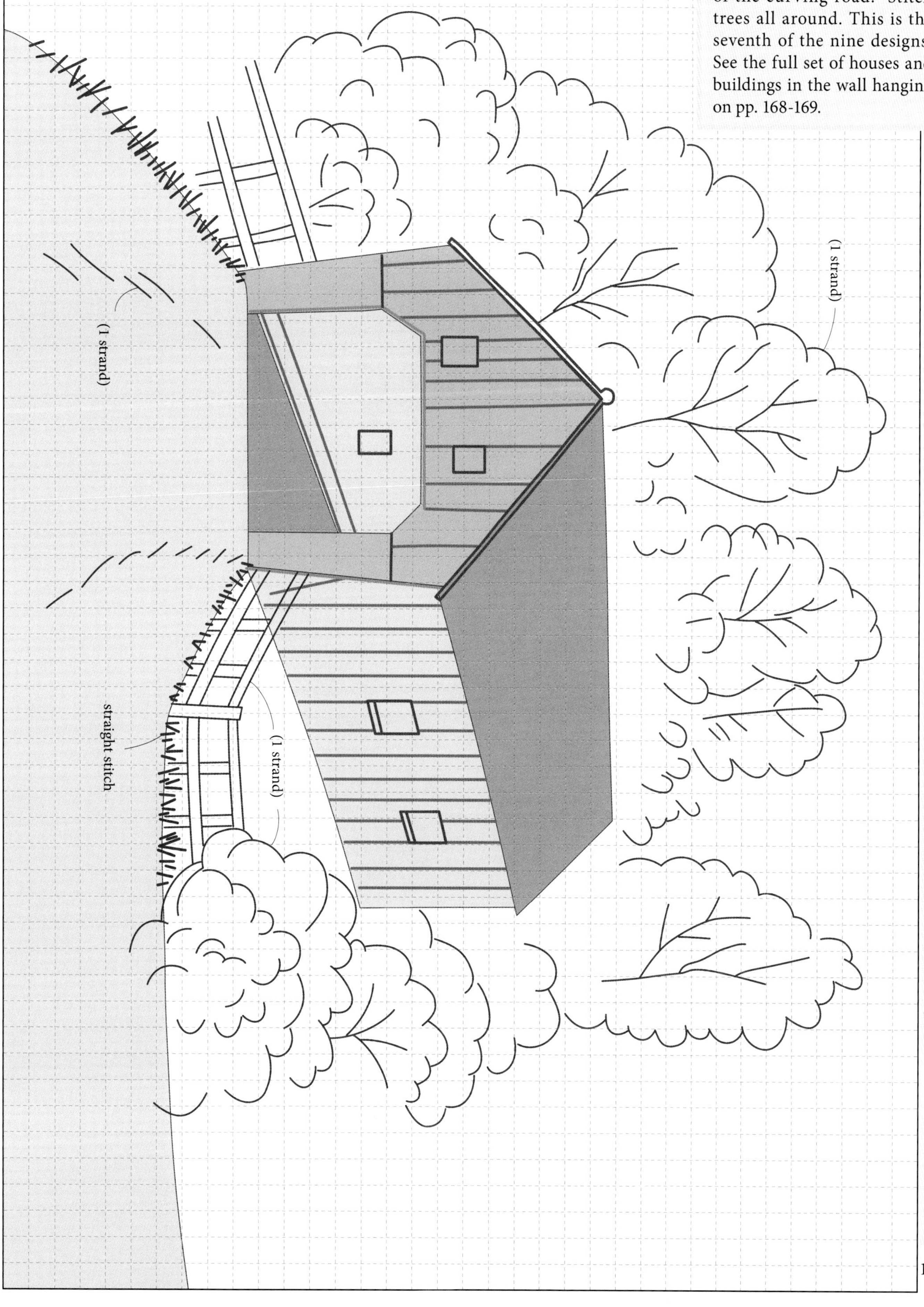

(1 strand)
(1 strand)
(1 strand)
straight stitch

◆ use an outline stitch (2 strands) for any area not specified above

119

House-Ⅷ

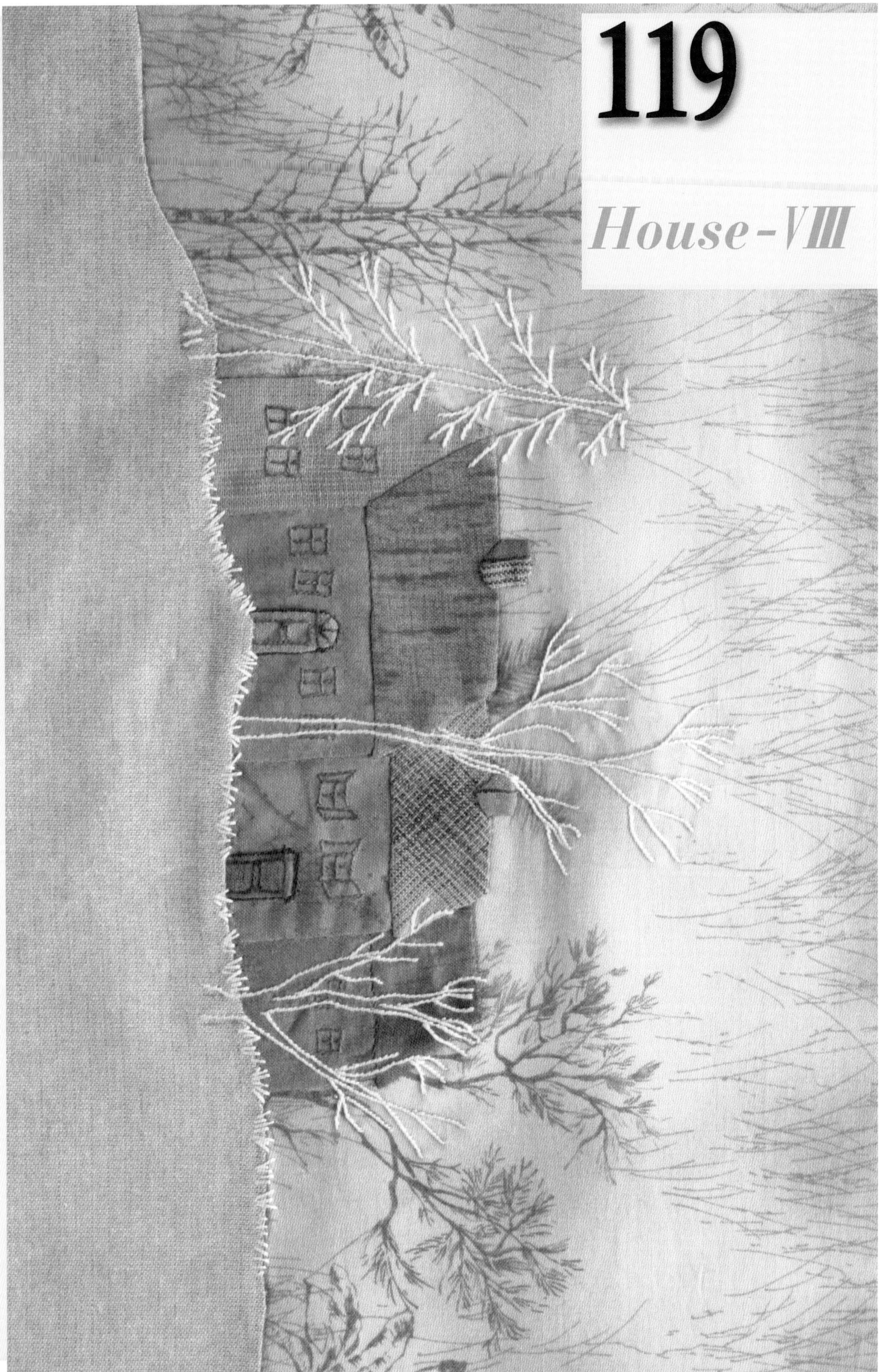

Guesthouses are charmingly lined up. The two different door designs stand out. Use your quilting designs to delineate paths and other areas in front of the guesthouses. This is the eighth of the nine designs. See the full set of houses and buildings in the wall hanging on pp. 168-169.

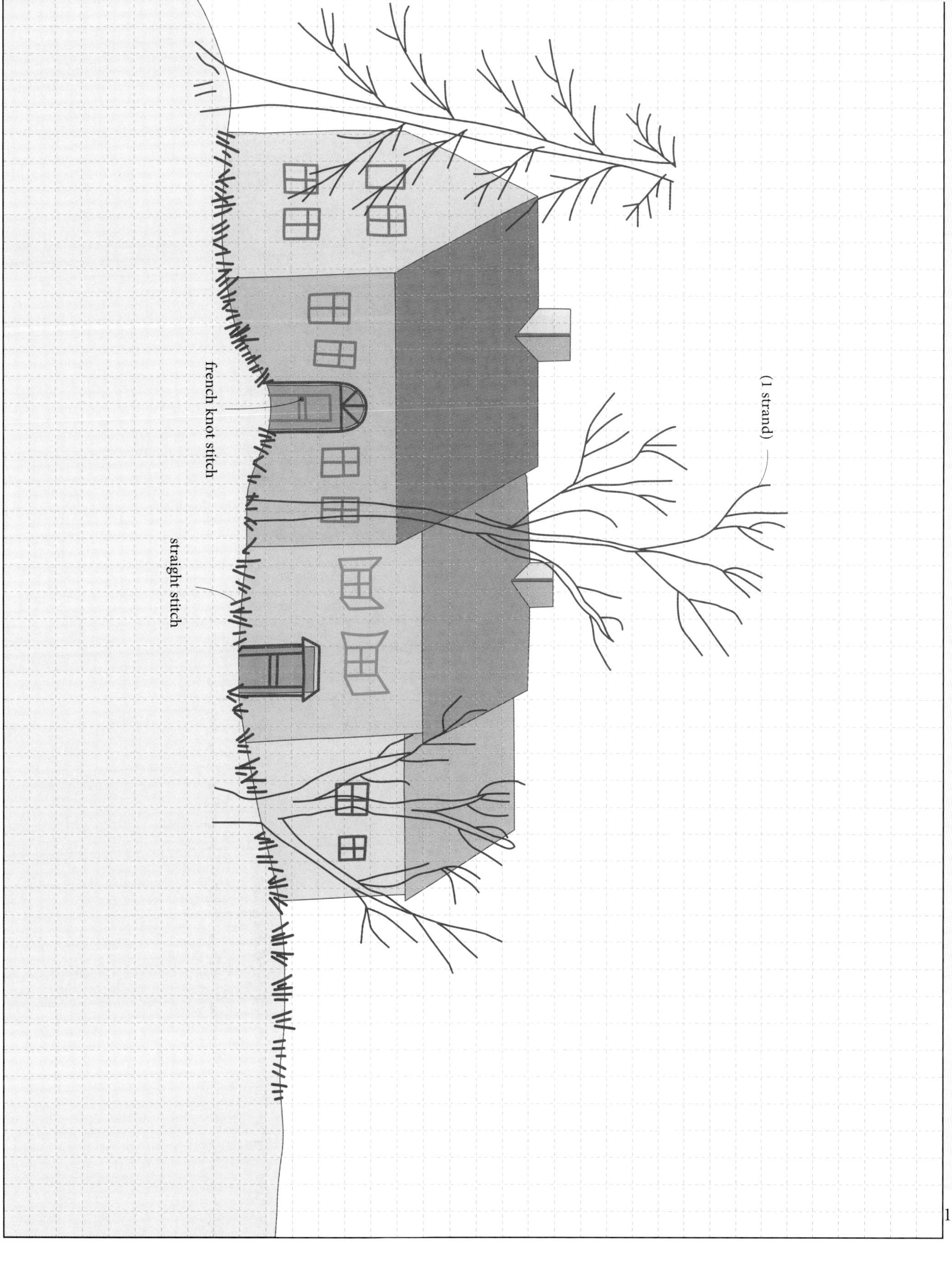
french knot stitch
straight stitch
(1 strand)

◆ use an outline stitch (2 strands) for any area not specified above

120

House-Ⅸ

This, the last of the nine designs, is a cute little country church with a bell tower and cross on top. Whenever I design many houses and buildings or towns, I try to make a number of the buildings ones that are easily recognizable and familiar, such as churches or barns. This church also has steps leading up to the doors. See the full set of houses and buildings in the wall hanging on pp. 168-169.

straight stitch (2 strands)
(2 strands)
(2 strands)
(3 strands)
(2 strands)

◆ use an outline stitch (1 strand) for any area not specified above

How to Use the Embroidery Patterns in this Book

- The photographs and patterns are shown full size. The photographs do not include a seam allowance.
- 0.5 cm [¼"] grid paper is used for all of the patterns. Enlarge or shrink the pattern before use if desired.
- Standard No. 25 embroidery floss is used unless otherwise specified. "x" strand(s) in the pattern indicates how many strands of embroidery floss are used for each embroidery stitch.
- Shaded areas in the patterns indicate the areas to be appliquéd and/or requiring piecing. Add seam allowances when cutting the fabric for both appliquéd and pieced work.

Understanding the Patterns

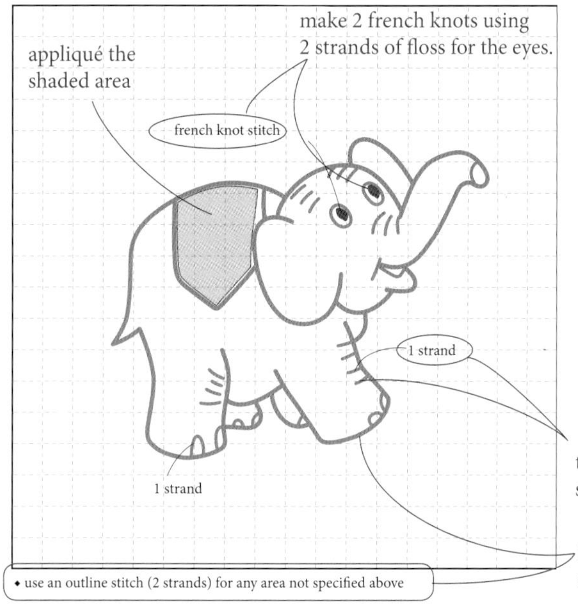

appliqué the shaded area
make 2 french knots using 2 strands of floss for the eyes.
french knot stitch
1 strand
1 strand
use an outline stitch (2 strands) for any area not specified above
the thin lines indicate using one strand of floss to do the outline stitch
for the lines that do not specify a specific strand count, use two strands of floss

Starting to Embroider

- Begin by embroidering the outlines and other main lines that are guidelines for detailed patterns, such as the outer lines of the design, grass stems, tree trunks and branches. (Apply appliqués and any piecing before starting to embroider.)
- Once the outlines are completed, embroider the detailed lines in the design, such as flower petals, small leaves and fine lines. With patterns that have animals or faces, embroider the eyes and mouth at the end so that you can check the balance. The key is to embroider them without worrying too much about design position; try to make them look bright and alive.

* See the pattern to the left (Pattern 11 on p. 18) as an example.

Walking through a Pattern Step-by-Step

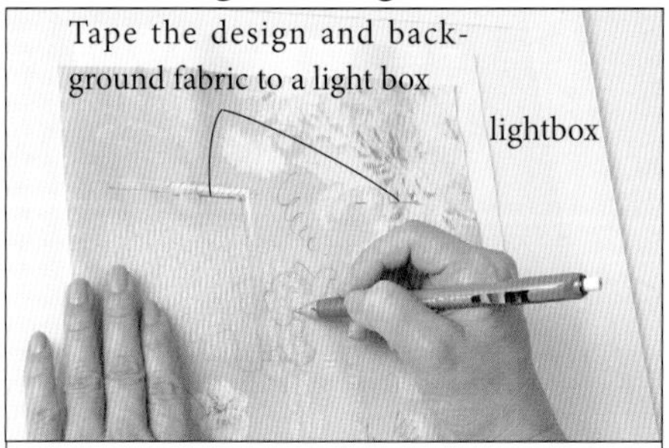

Tape the design and back-ground fabric to a light box
lightbox

1 Use a lightbox to trace the pattern design onto the background fabric. Use an erasable fabric pen or pencil for clean, neat lines.

2 Trace the detailed designs, including facial features. If you do not have a lightbox, use dressmaker's tracing paper or tape them up to a bright window.

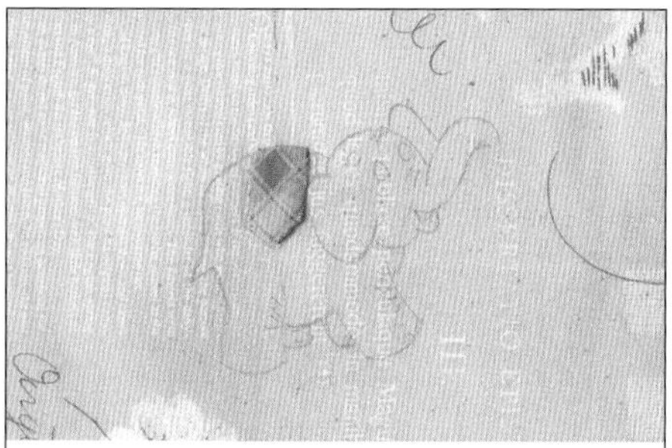

3 Do any appliqué or piecing first if required by the pattern (indicated by shaded areas on the pattern).

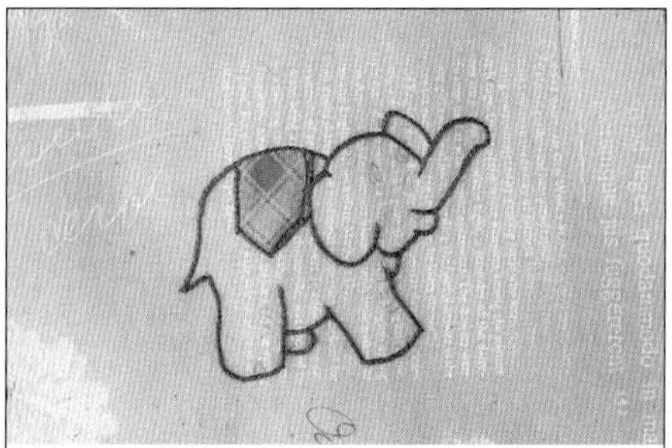

4 Embroider the entire outline of the design first, using an outline stitch with 2 strands of floss (as specified for this pattern).

5 Outline stitch the thin lines with 1 strand of floss. Embroider the eyes and mouth last, checking to see that they look balanced as you stitch.

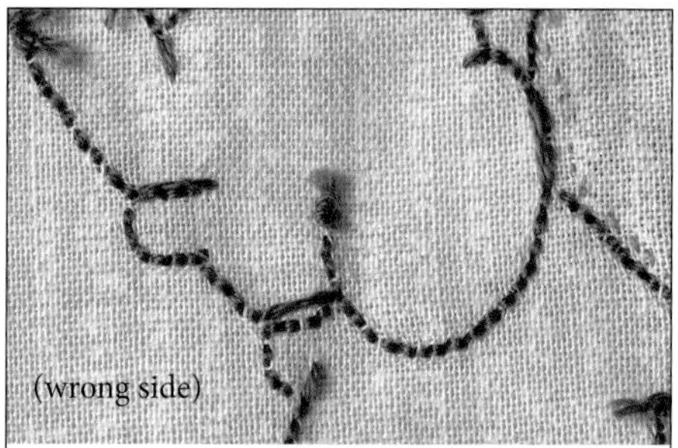

(wrong side)

6 Knot the floss on the back side before you begin and when you finish embroidering. Make sure they are small so that they don't show on the right side.

Embroidery Basics

Embroidery Basics when Incorporating Embroidery into Patchwork

Types of Embroidery Floss

1. No. 25 embroidery floss
This is the most popular type of embroidery floss. Six strands of fine floss are loosely twisted together; one skein is approximately eight meters [8¾ yards]. Use as many strands as needed.

2. Cosmo Multi Work (2 strands of No. 25 embroidery floss)
The floss comes on an easy-to-use bobbin and is recommended when using one or two strands of No.25 embroidery floss.

3. No. 5 embroidery floss (Cosmo Stitch Work)
This is a glossy thick embroidery floss. One strand is usually used. Also known as perle cotton.

4. Candlewicking thread
Thick loosely-twisted cotton thread that is perfect for the velvet stitch. One strand is usually used. White and light beige colors are most common, but colored threads can also be found.

Stretch the fabric in an embroidery hoop and adjust the screw to tighten.

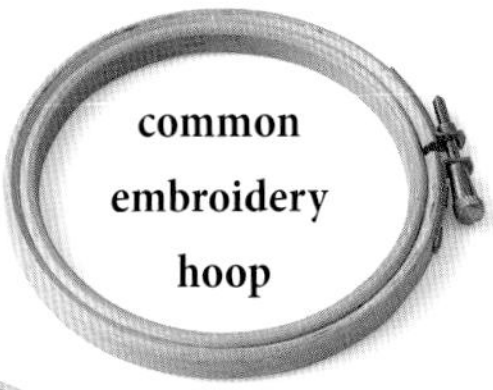
common
embroidery
hoop

One Touch
embroidery
hoop

One Touch hoops are easy to use without the screw.

Embroidery Needles

Embroidery needles have larger eyes for easy threading and are pointed for smooth piercing. The lower the number, the thicker and longer the needle. Use a thicker needle when using thicker floss (or more strands); use a thinner needle when using thinner floss (or less strands.) Try different types of needles to find which one is easiest for you to work with. A candlewicking needle is thick and has an even larger eye to accommodate the thick thread.

Embroidery Floss (full size)

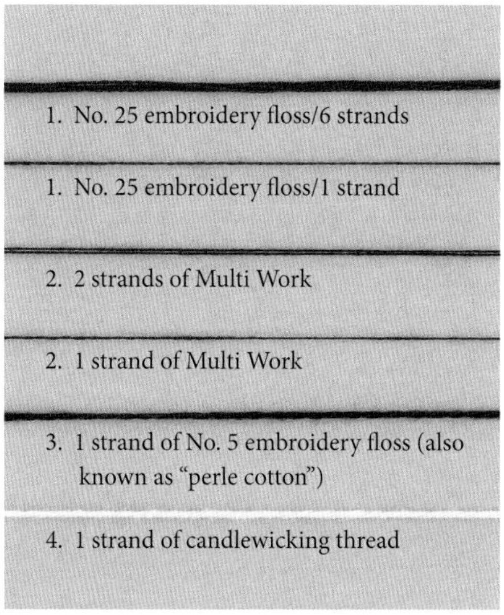
1. No. 25 embroidery floss/6 strands
1. No. 25 embroidery floss/1 strand
2. 2 strands of Multi Work
2. 1 strand of Multi Work
3. 1 strand of No. 5 embroidery floss (also known as "perle cotton")
4. 1 strand of candlewicking thread

Embroidery Needles (full size)

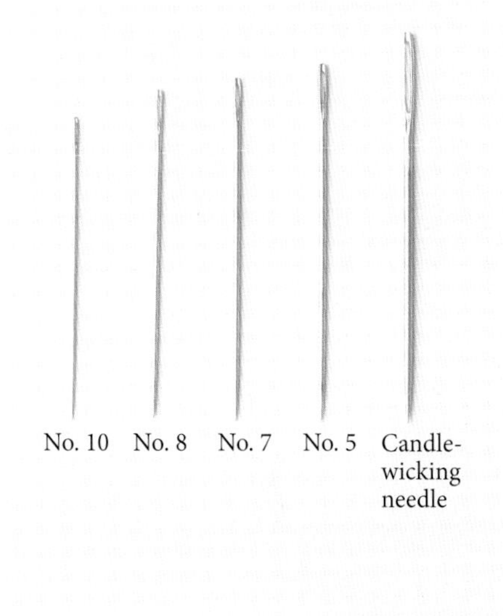
No. 10
No. 8
No. 7
No. 5
Candle-wicking needle

■ Using a One Touch embroidery hoop

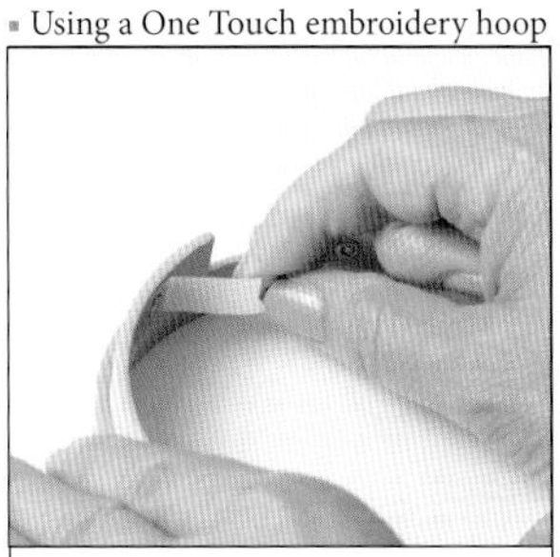

1 Remove the inner hoop by pulling the spring inward.

Embroidery Hoops

It is often easiest to use an embroidery hoop when embroidering. For many stitches, having the background fabric taut makes it easy to work as well as giving beautiful results. A small hoop with a 10 cm [4"] diameter is easy to hold and use. When working on a larger design, stop and move the hoop to work on various areas of the design so that you are always embroidering at the center of the hoop.

Embroidery Hoop Stand

(laptop double embroidery hoop)

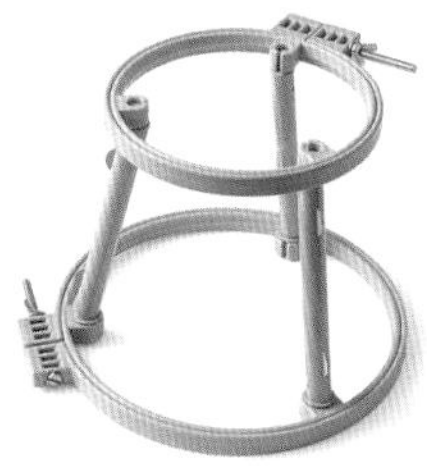

2 Center the design on the background fabric.

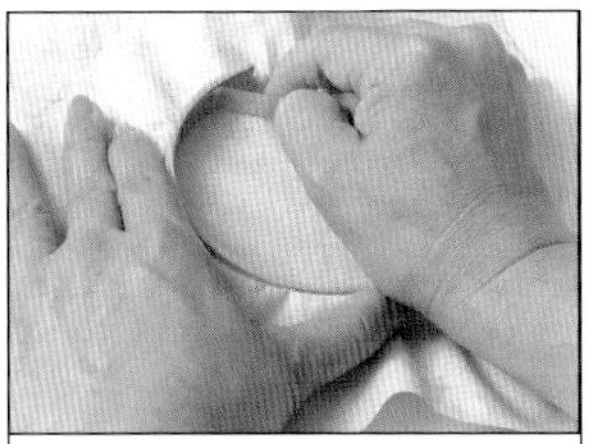

3 With the right side down, place it on the outer hoop, then snap the inner hoop into place by pulling the spring inward again.

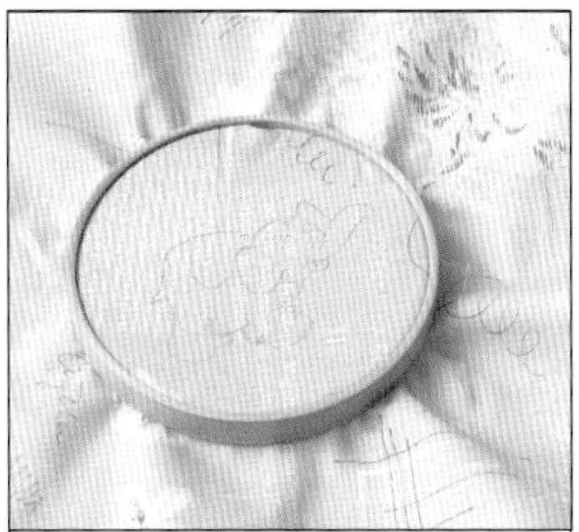

4 Many feel that these are easier to work with as there is no screw for the floss to catch on.

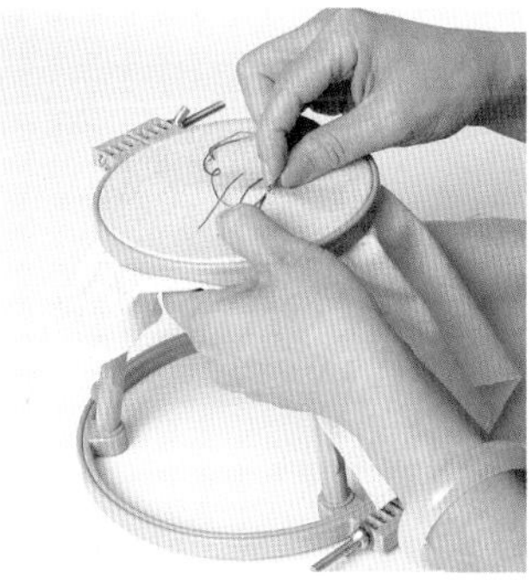

A stand type of hoop might make it easier to work as it leaves your hands free to embroider. It comes with different sizes of hoops on the top and bottom.

How to Use Embroidery Floss

■ No. 25 Embroidery Floss Before you start

No. 25 embroidery floss is used for most patterns in this book. This floss comes in varieties of colors and is easy to use because you can select the number of strands you need for any given pattern.

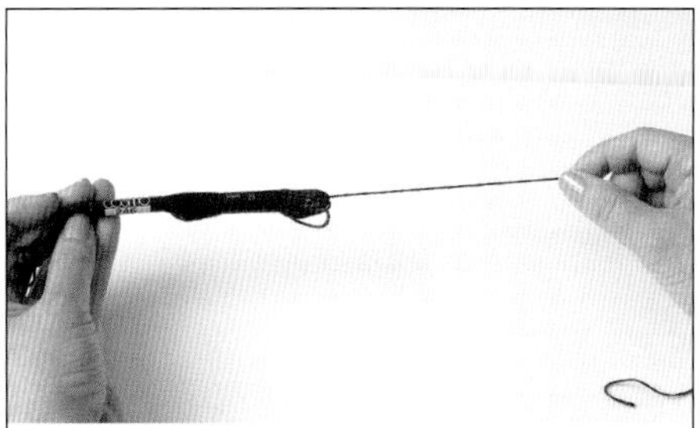

1 Holding the skein by the paper label, pull out the floss (note that all 6 strands are twisted into one) and cut the length you want to use.

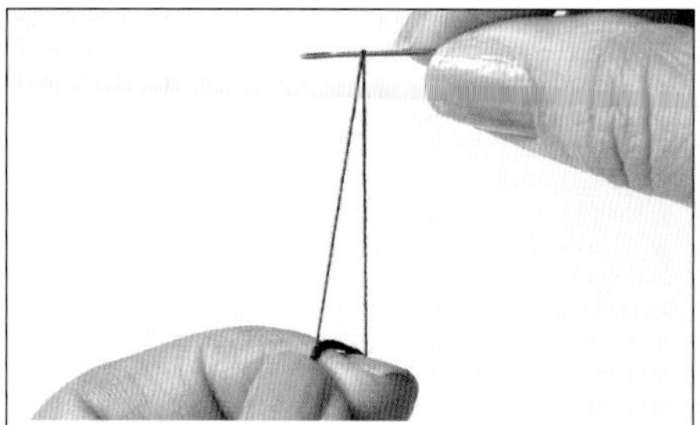

2 Wrap the floss from step 1 on your left index finger and pull out one strand at a time using the tip of the needle while holding the floss taut.

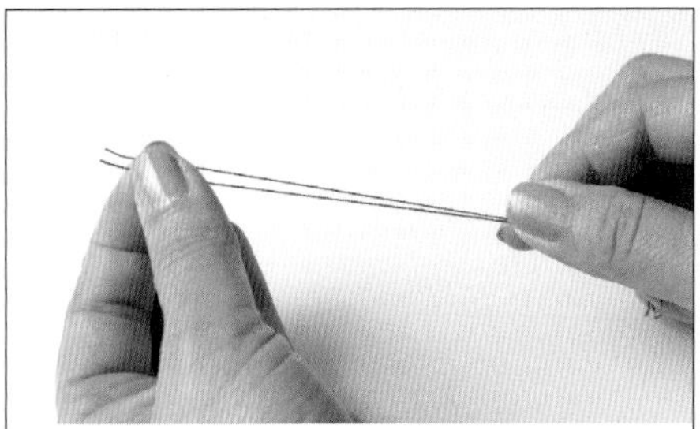

3 Once you have pulled out the number of strands you need, match the ends of the strands together. Smooth the strands together.

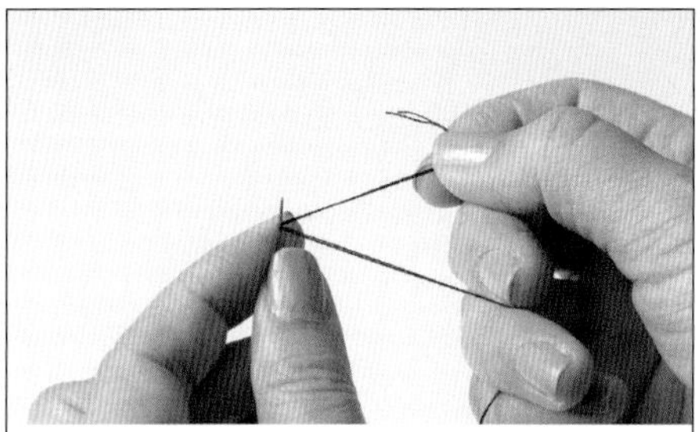

4 For easy threading, holding them taut, wrap the strands around the top of the needle and fold them in two.

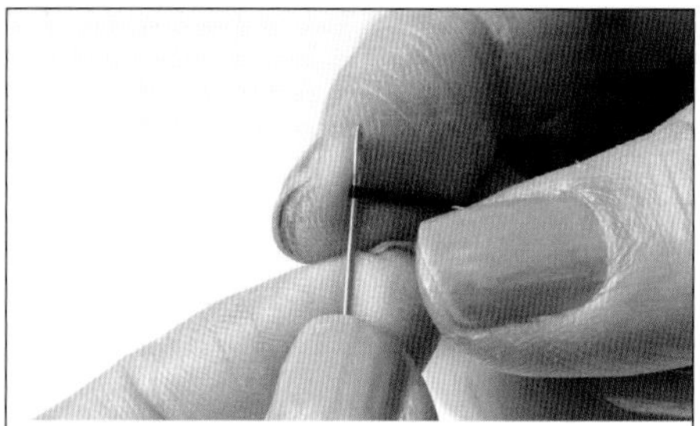

5 Pinch the strands of floss while keeping them taut at the top of the needle (the side of eye); pull the floss off the top while it is still pinched between your fingertips.

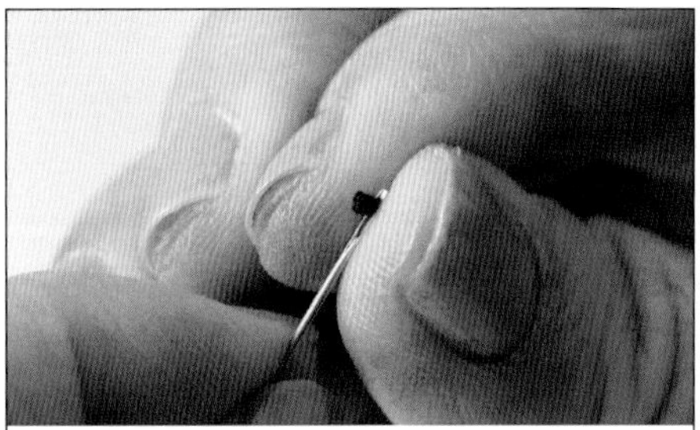

6 Thread the flattened floss through the eye of the needle.

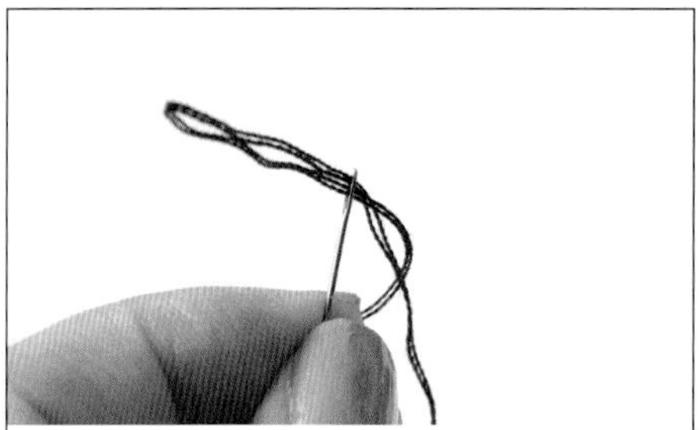

7 Pull the loop of floss through the eye until you have several centimeters (inches). Then pull one side of the floss all the way through so that the needle is threaded.

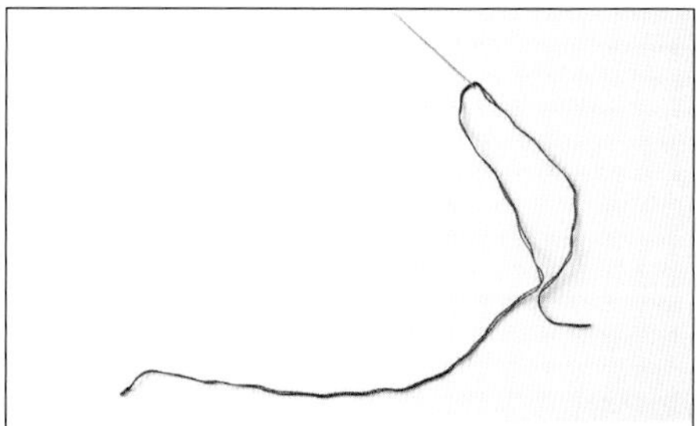

8 The optimum length is approximately 30-40 cm [11¾"-15¾"]. Use short lengths of floss as needed as they often begin to get fuzzy as you work if they are too long.

■ Knotting the Thread

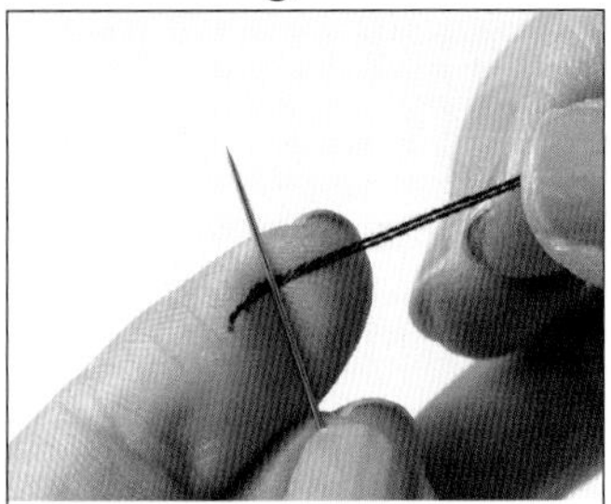

1 Lay the end of the floss on the left index finger and place the tip of the needle over it.

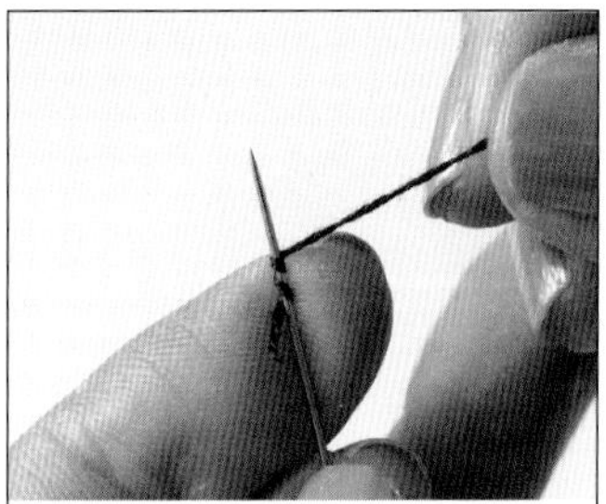

2 Support the needle with the left hand and wrap the floss twice while continuing to push the tip of the needle against the index finger.

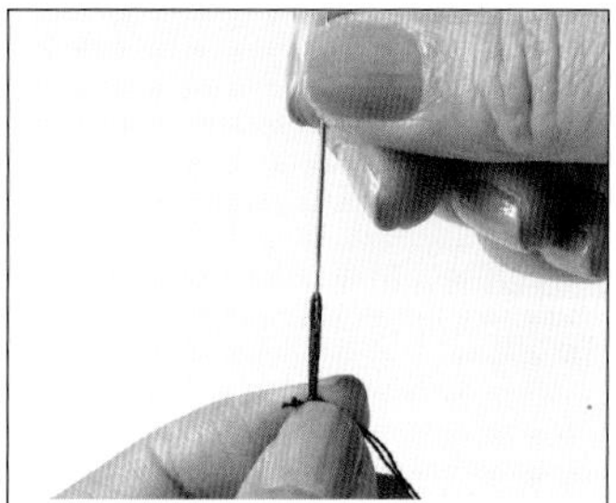

3 Firmly pinch the wrapped floss with your fingertips and pull the needle up and out while firmly holding on to the floss.

4 A small firm knot is made. Make knots at the beginning and end of embroidery except when using extremely thin or pure white fabrics on which the knot can be seen through.

The Outline Stitch and French Knot Stitch

Learn how to do two frequently used stitches including tips on how to do beautiful embroidery. Adjust the thickness (number) of the embroidery floss according to the thickness and size of the stitch you want to make. Practice embroidering on an extra piece of fabric before embroidering the actual pattern.

▪ Outline Stitch (full size)

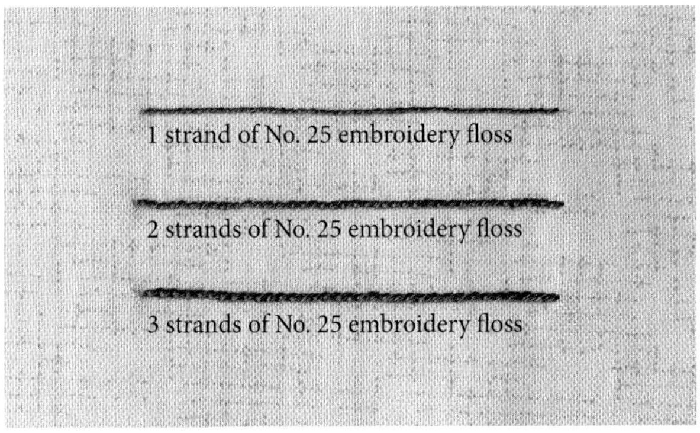

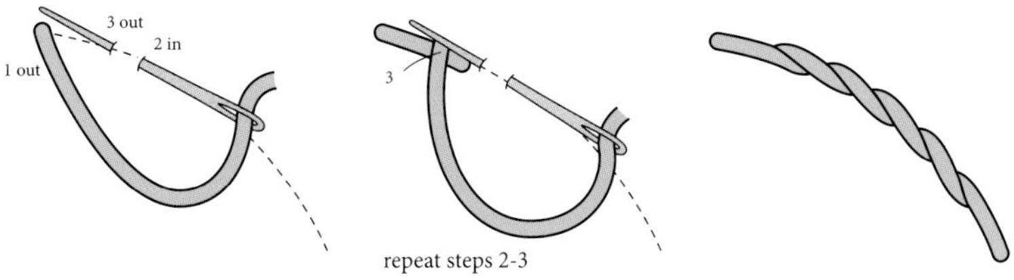

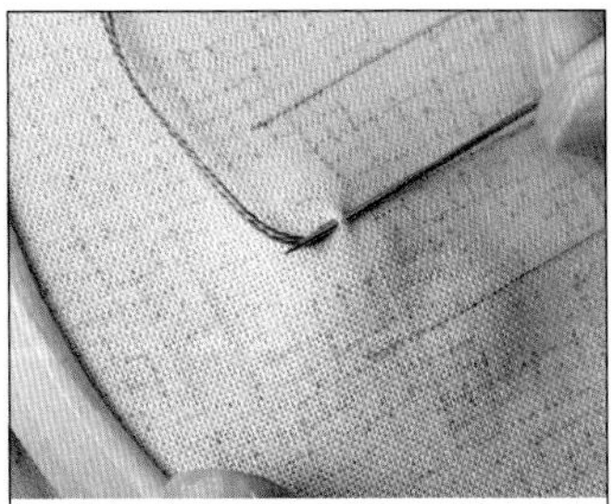

1 Following the directions above, make backstitches. Be careful not to split the stitch you have just created.

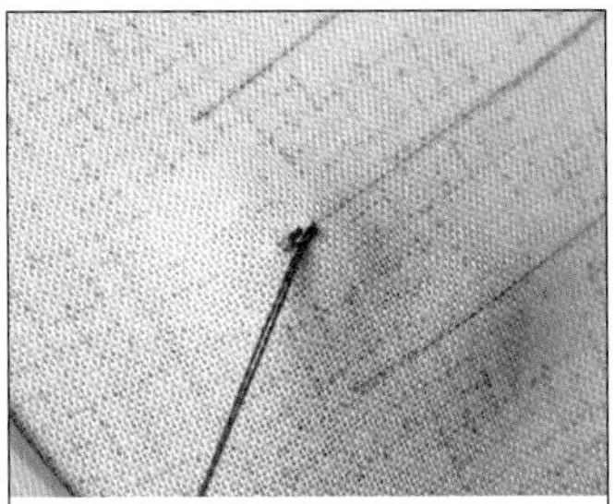

2 Do not pull the floss too tight. You don't want the stitches and fabric to become too taut.

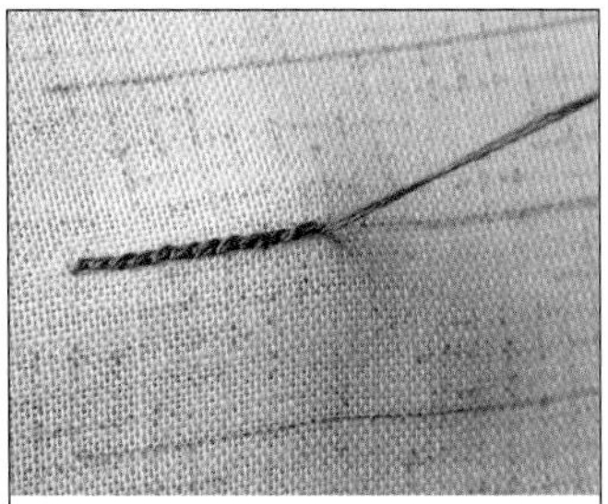

3 Embroider along the marked design line taking small stitches. It is easy to make beautiful curves and corners when you use small stitches.

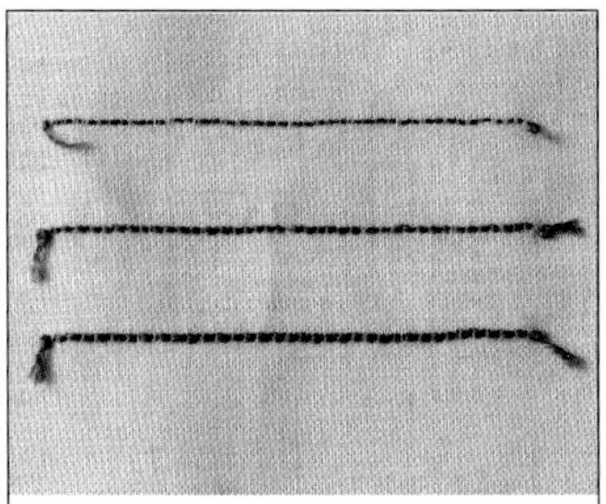

4 This is what the back side of outline stitches should look like.

▪ French Knot Stitch

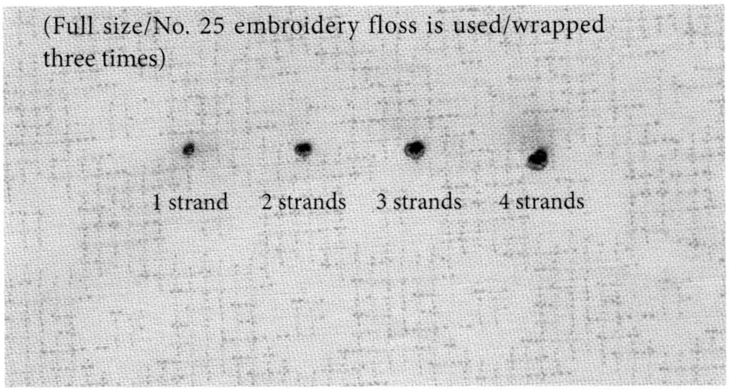
(Full size/No. 25 embroidery floss is used/wrapped three times)
1 strand
2 strands
3 strands
4 strands

With French knots, the size of the knots are adjusted by the thickness of the floss (or the number of strands) and the number of times you wrap the floss around the needle.

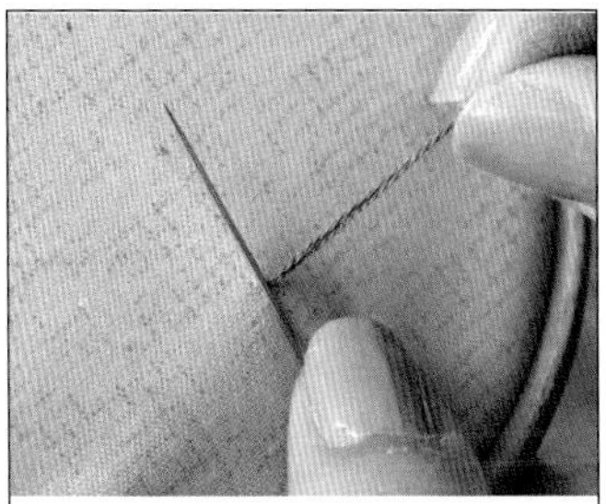

1 To begin, bring the needle up through the background fabric from underneath at the position marked on the design. Lay it next to the floss.

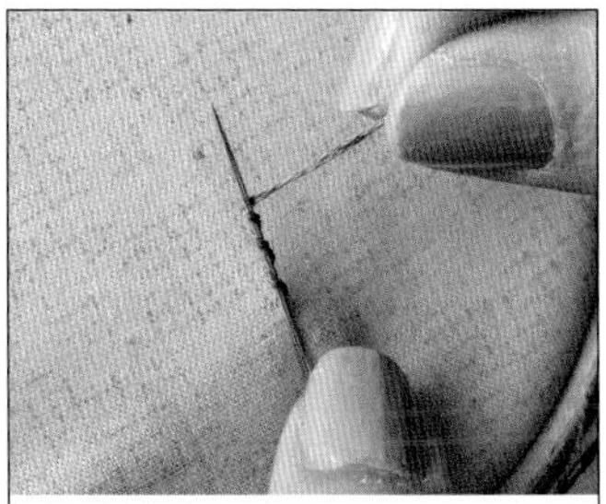

2 Press the needle down with the thumb and wrap the floss around the needle as many times as needed (three times is shown here.)

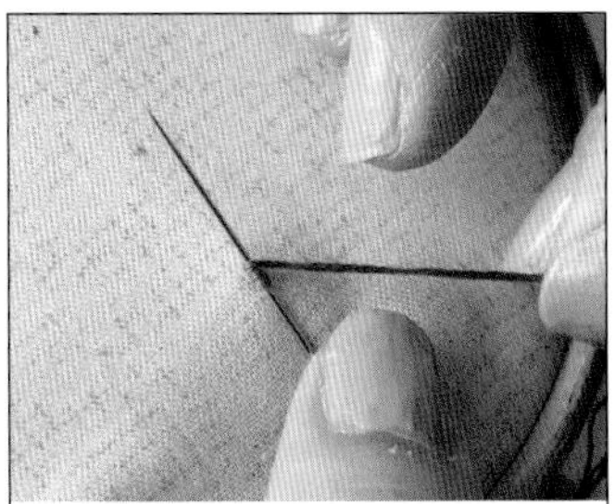

3 Tug the floss to gather the wrapped floss down toward the head of the needle. Use your thumb to press down on top of the wraps so they won't loosen.

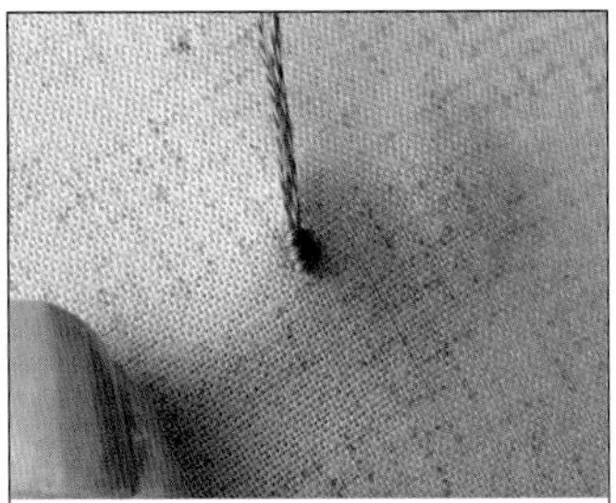

4 Pull the needle all the way through while continuing to press firmly down on the wrapped floss to tighten and create a knot.

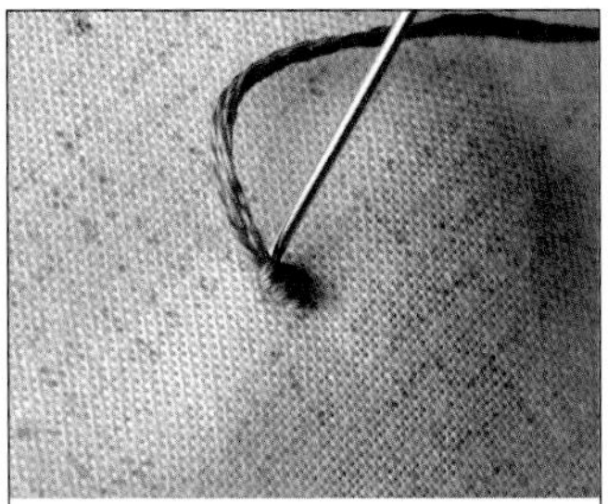

5 Push the tip of the needle down through the background fabric next to the knot. Tug on the floss to adjust the shape of the knot.

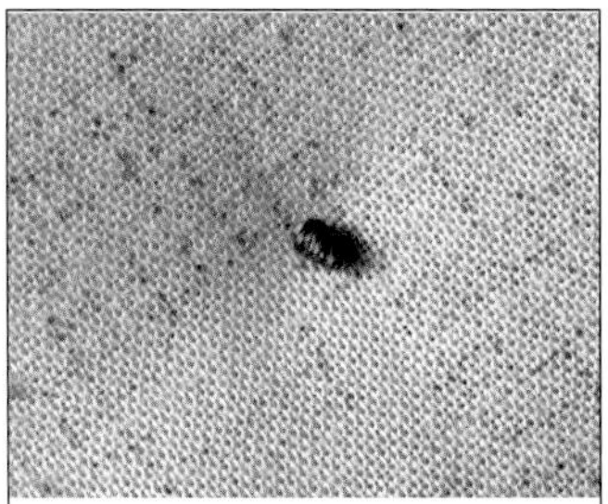

6 The stitch is completed. To create an oval shape, increase the number of times the floss is wrapped around the needle.

The Candlewick Stitch

Candlewick stitches were originally done all in white using wicking for candles. See the step-by-step pictures below on how to do a Colonial Knot Stitch and a Velvet Stitch, which are signature styles of candlewicking embroidery.

Colonial Knot Stitch

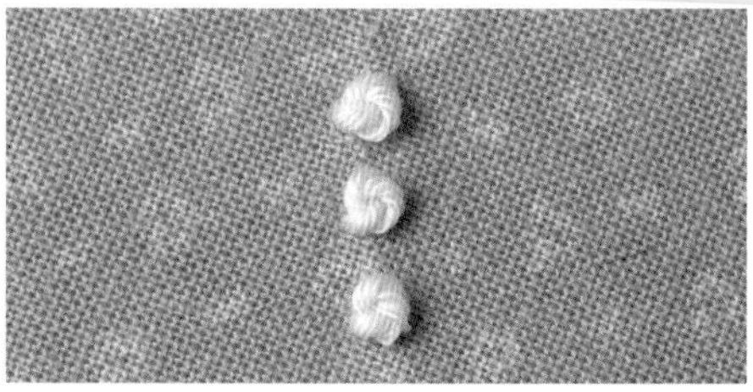

The colonial knot stitch is similar to a french knot, but it is easier to make flatter shapes and is often used when embroidering many of the same knot stitches. Any floss can be used, but for large knots, use candlewick thread.

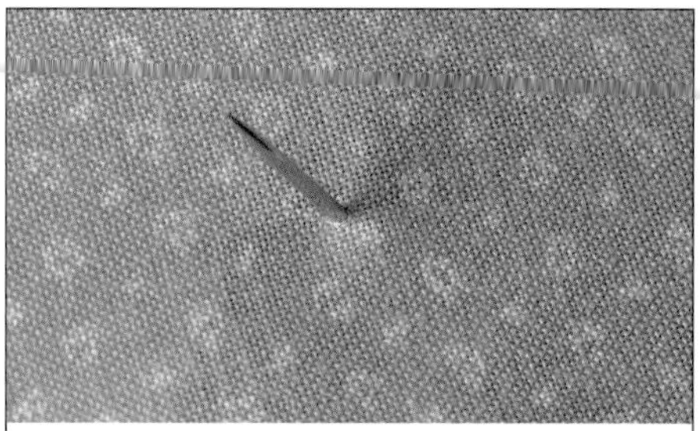

1 Bring the needle up through the background fabric from underneath at the marked position of the design.

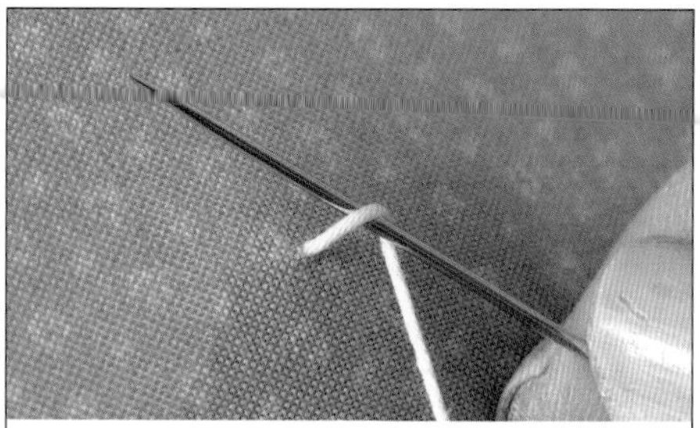

2 Bring the tip of the needle to the point where the thread is coming out and wrap the thread around the needle from left to right.

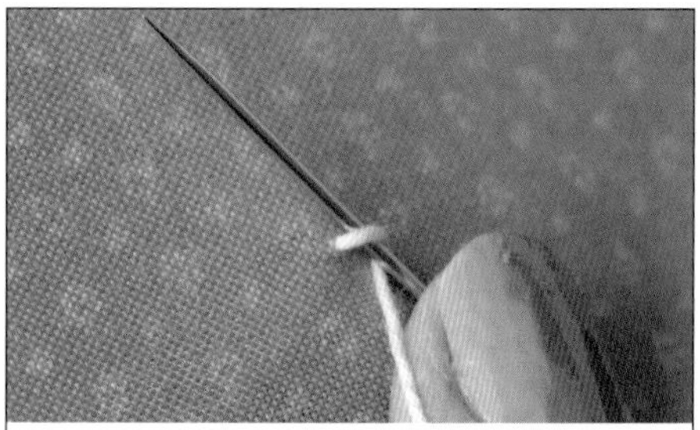

3 Wrap the thread around the needle once, then bring the thread down under and to the left of the needle.

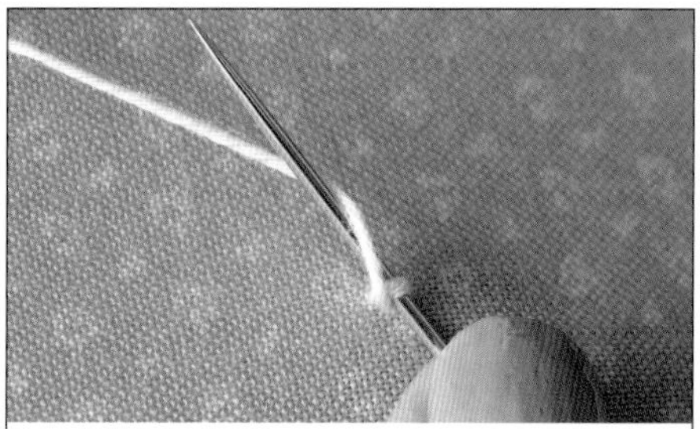

4 Bring the thread up and to the right over the needle so that the thread is wrapped on the needle.

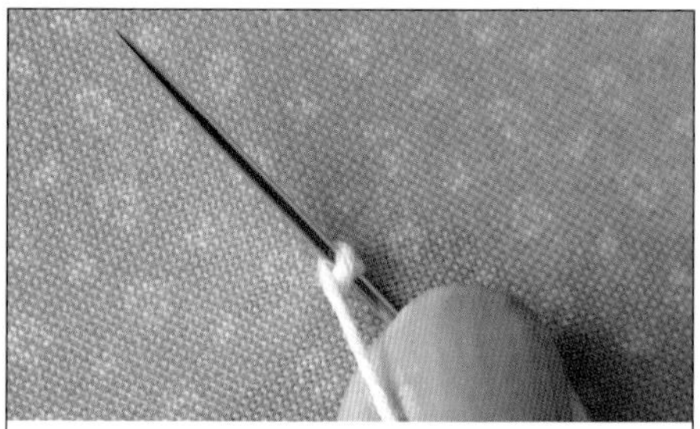

5 Pull the thread down and toward you to tighten the wrapped thread.

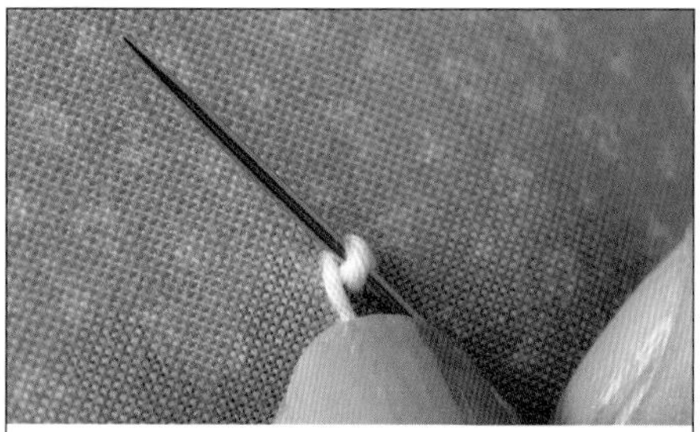

6 Press down on the wrapped thread with your left thumb to keep the thread from moving. Carefully pull the needle down and out a little bit at a time (toward the head of the needle) so that the wraps won't loosen.

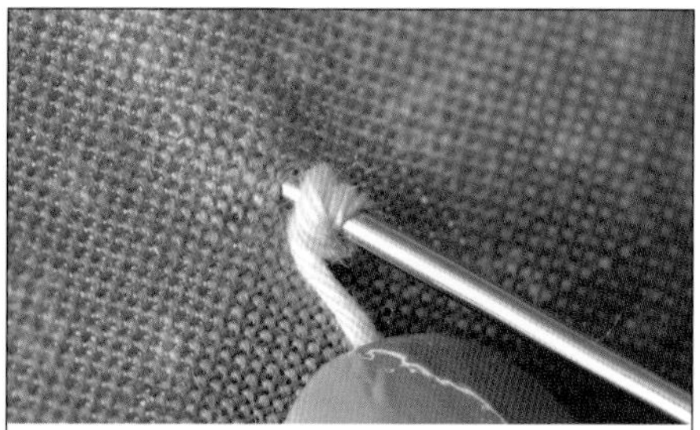

7 Don't let up on the thread while you push the tip of the needle back into the fabric next to the knot without pulling out the needle.

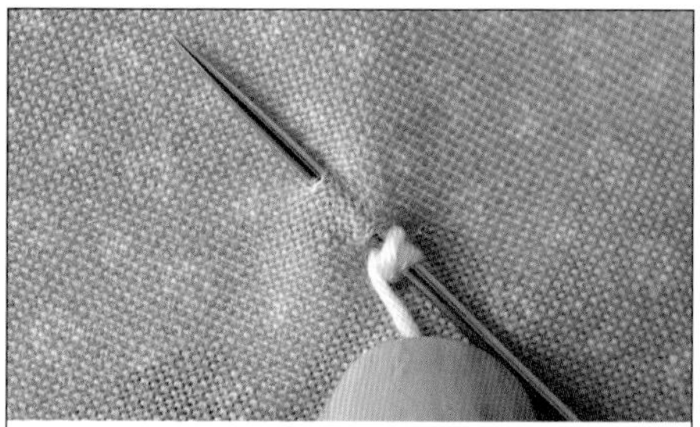

8 Continue to press down on the thread with left thumb to keep the knot and thread taut; bring the needle up at the next marked point.

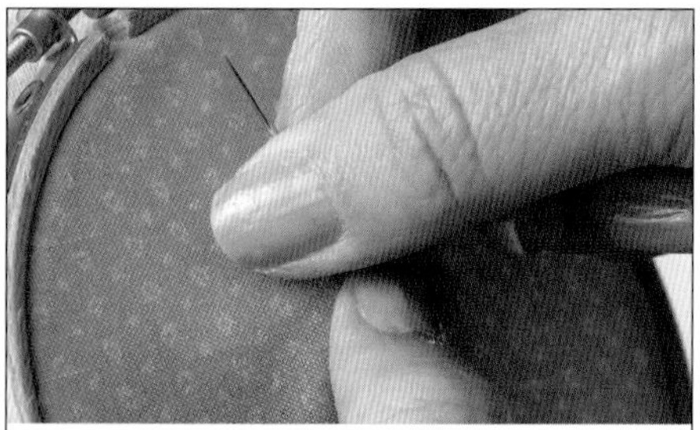

9 Pull the needle out while firmly pressing the knot with your left thumb. If it becomes hard to pull the needle eye through the knot, rotate it using the fingertips to pull it up slowly.

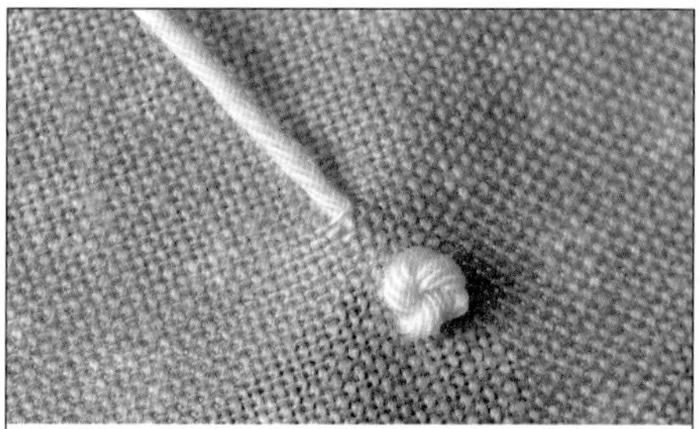

10 The colonial knot stitch is completed. If you are not making any more knots, rather than bringing the thread back out on the top, tie it off on the back side of the fabric.

Pattern 43 on p. 61 uses the colonial knot stitch using 4 strands of No. 25 embroidery thread.

A Velvet Stitch has a pom-pom-like, fluffy, three-dimensional finish. In order to get the pom-pom look, use loosely wrapped, easy-to-loosen candlewick thread when doing this stitch.

▪ Velvet Stitch

Make dense, evenly-sized loops to fill the designated area in the design. Adjust the loop's length according to the finished height you desire.

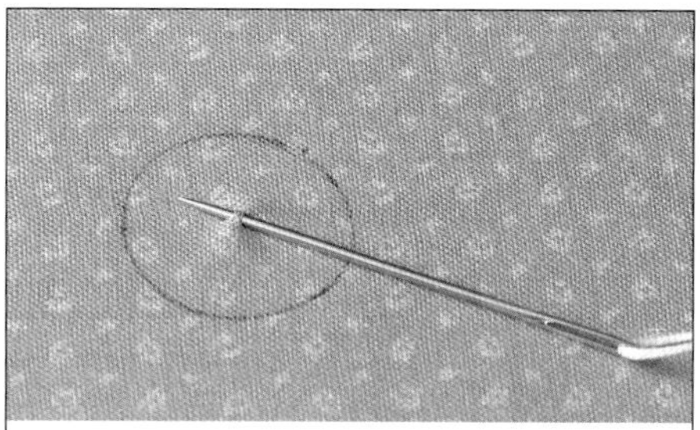

1 Start in the center of the design and take a stitch approximately 0.1 cm [$^{1}/_{16}$"] from where you pushed the needle in, leaving about 1 cm [⅜"] of thread sticking out.

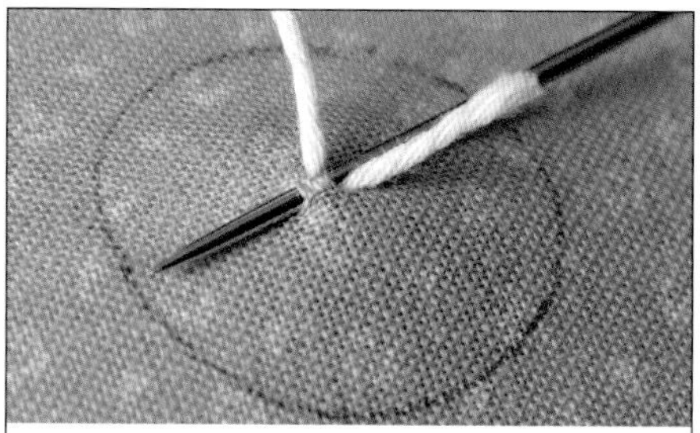

2 Take one half backstitch. Make sure the needle pierces the center of the thread that is underneath the fabric in step 1, which serves to secure the thread without knotting it.

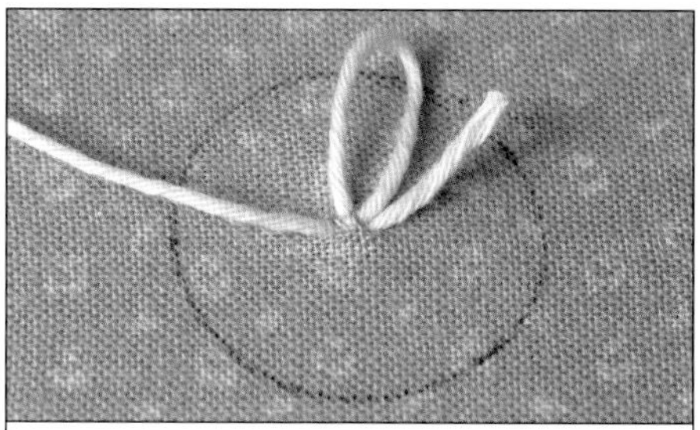

3 Pull the thread through until it makes a 1 cm [⅜"] loop on the surface. Continue to take small backstitches (as in step 2) to make many loops.

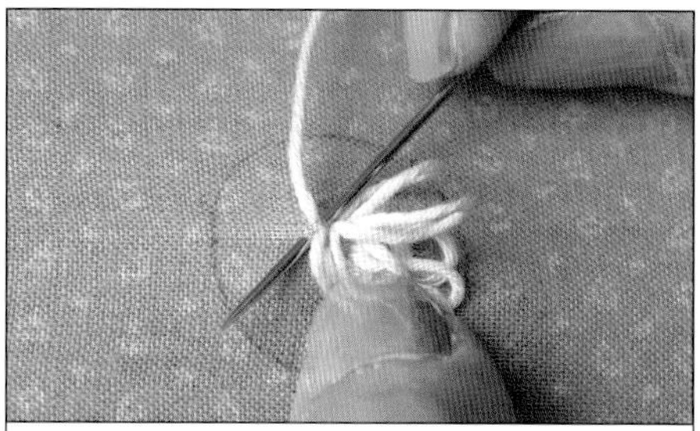

4 Take half backstitches as you work from the center outward, as if drawing a circle, to make dense loops. Press down on the loops with your finger to see where the center of the loops are as you work.

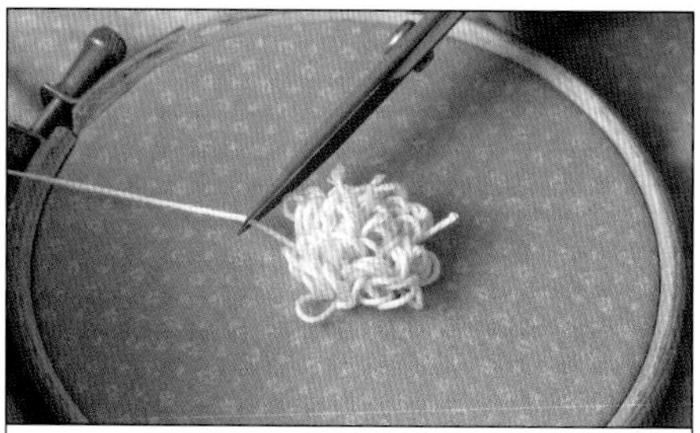

5 Fill in the entire design with loops, ending by stitching directly on the outer lines of the design. Cut the thread the same length as the loops without making a knot.

6 This is what the back side of the stitches should look like. The design is filled because the backstitches are sewn in a circular manner from the center.

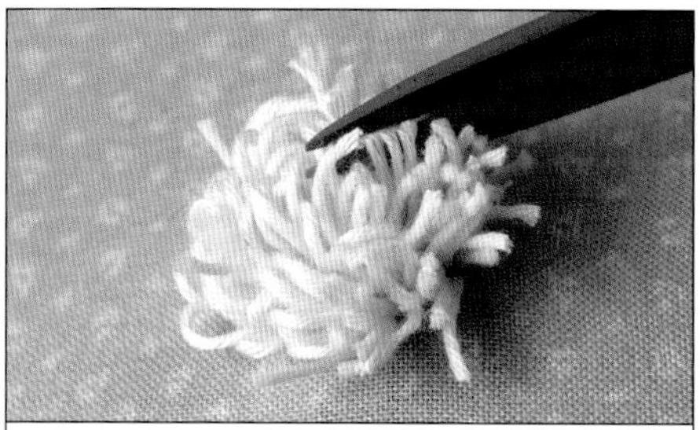

7 Cut all the loops using the tip of the scissors.

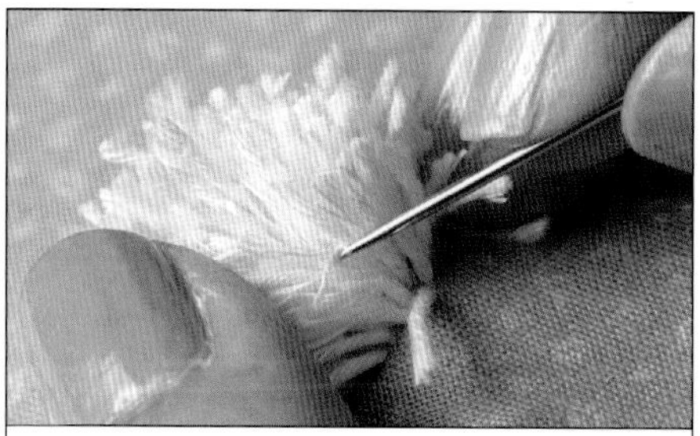

8 Using the tip of the needle, fray the threads one by one. Do not try to fray them from the roots. Split the tip of the thread and work your way down. Don't pull the thread too hard as you work.

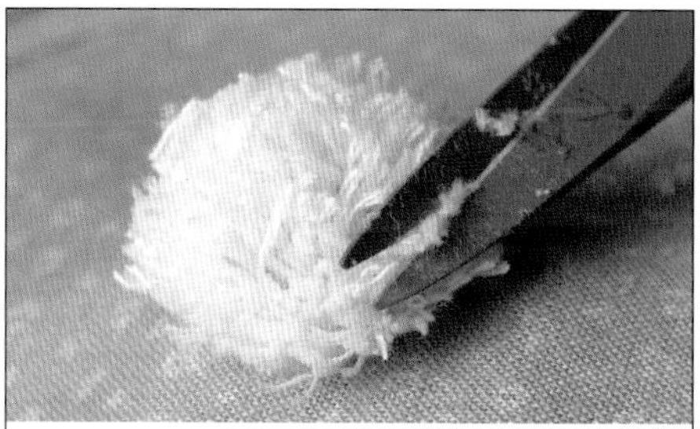

9 Once all threads are mostly frayed, shape the ball with scissors. Cut any uncut loops or any threads that are sticking out.

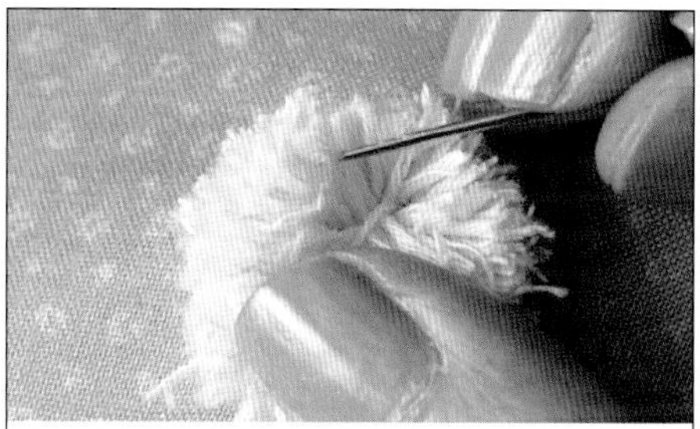

10 Fray the threads some more using the tip of the needle. Once the threads are frayed all the way from the roots and have become fluffy, trim and shape them using the scissors as desired.

11 This is the view of the velvet stitch from the side. Trim the perimeter threads shorter than the center for a three-dimensional look.

Basic Embroidery Stitches

▪ Backstitch

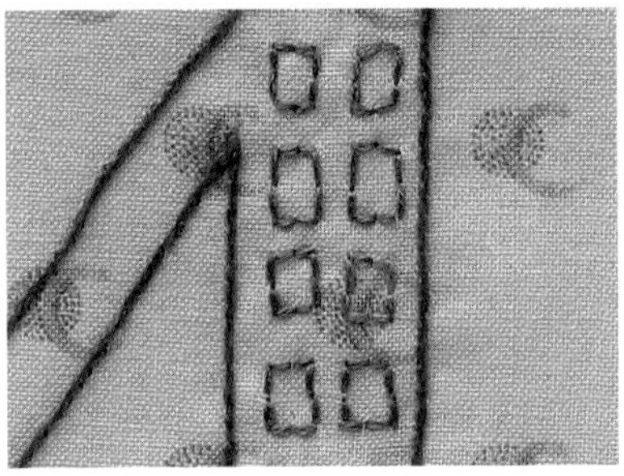

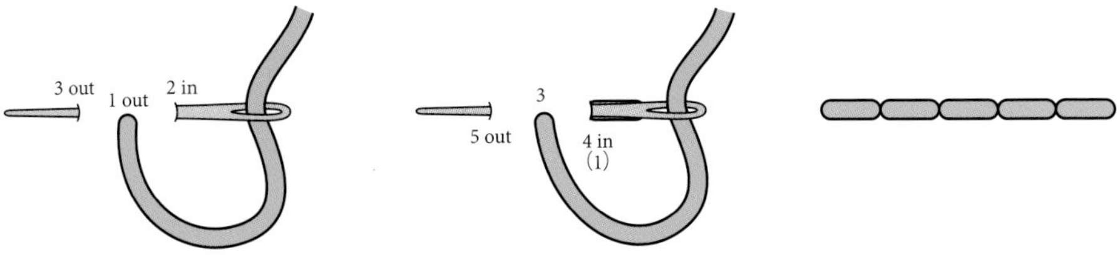

▪ Chain stitch

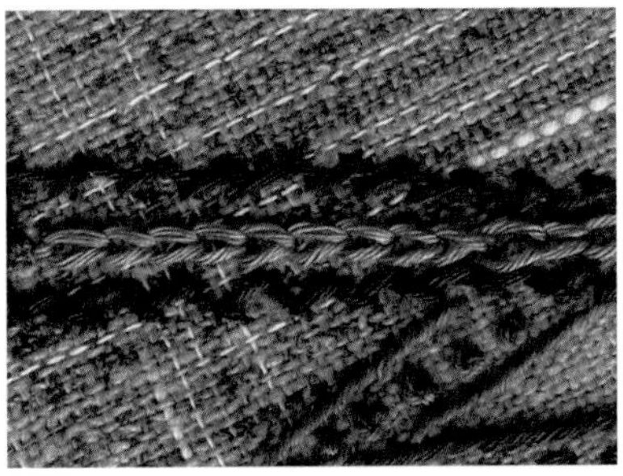

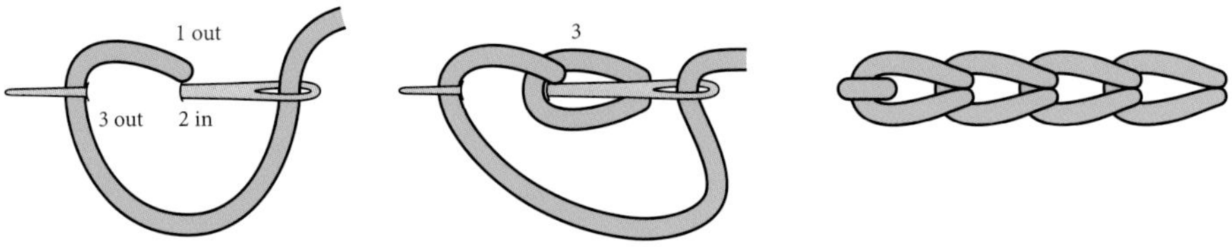

▪ Running Stitch

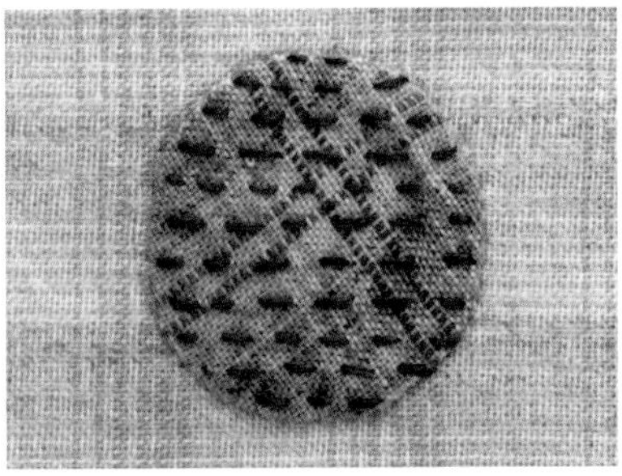

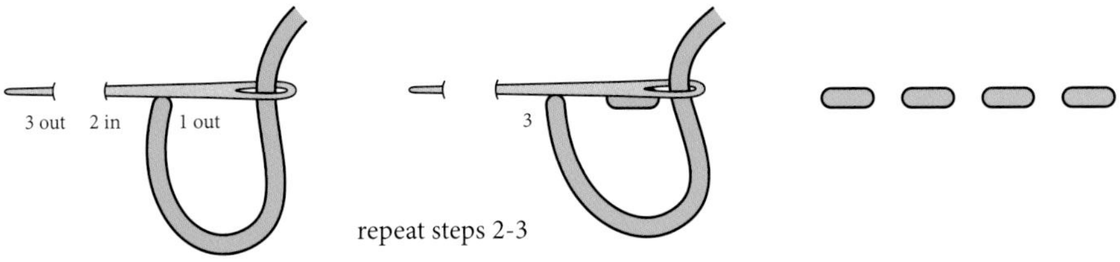

▪ Threaded Running Stitch

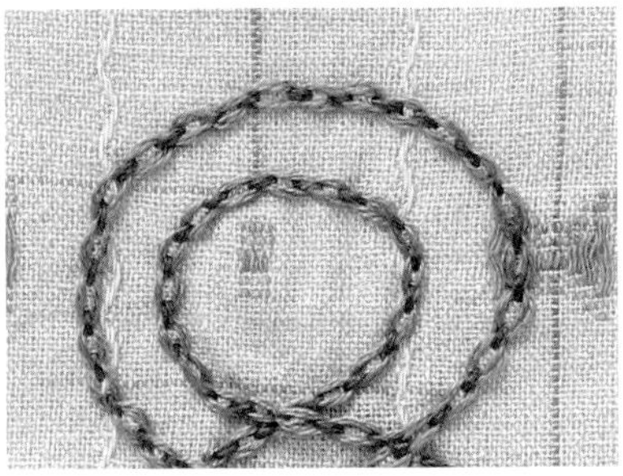

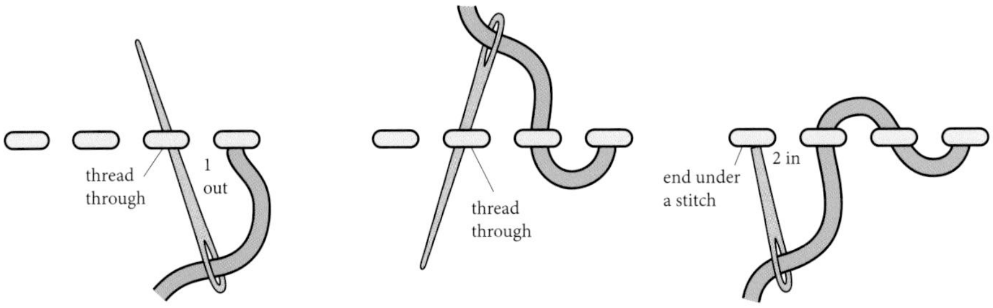

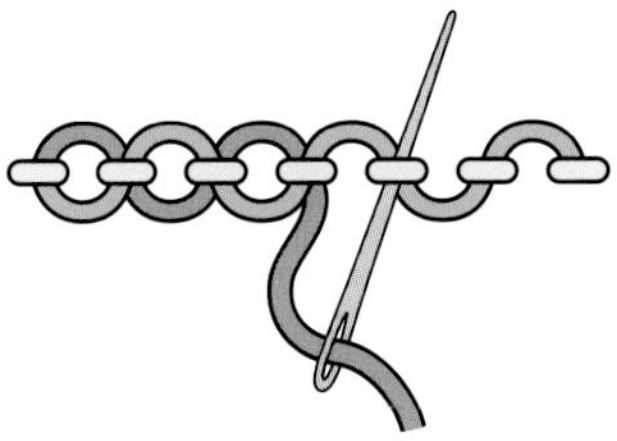

- Variation -

You can also thread the floss through from both sides.

■ Straight Stitch

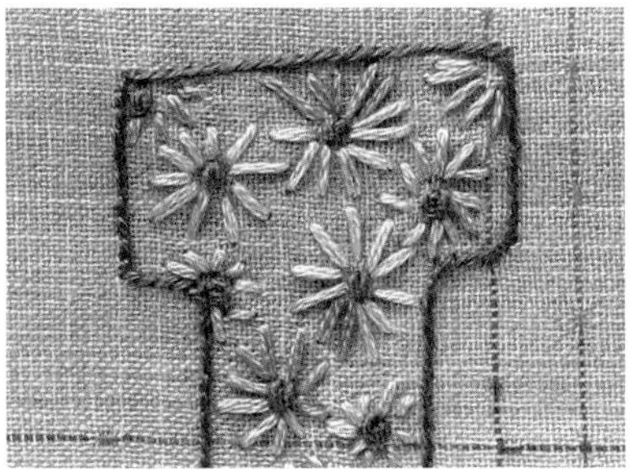

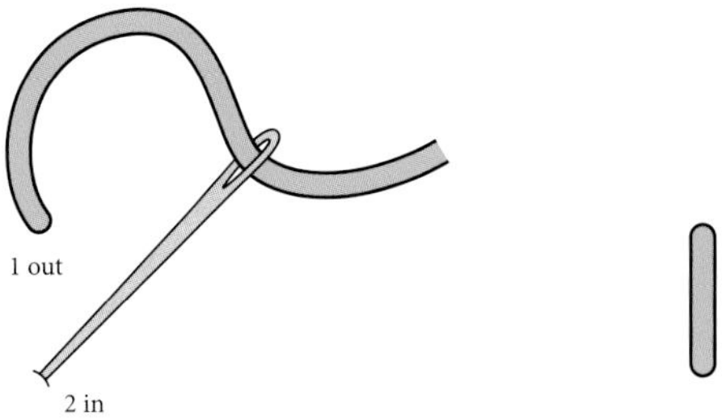

1 out
2 in

■ Cross Stitch

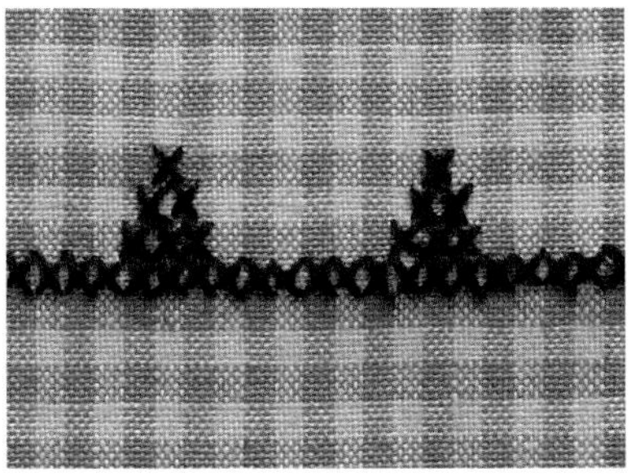

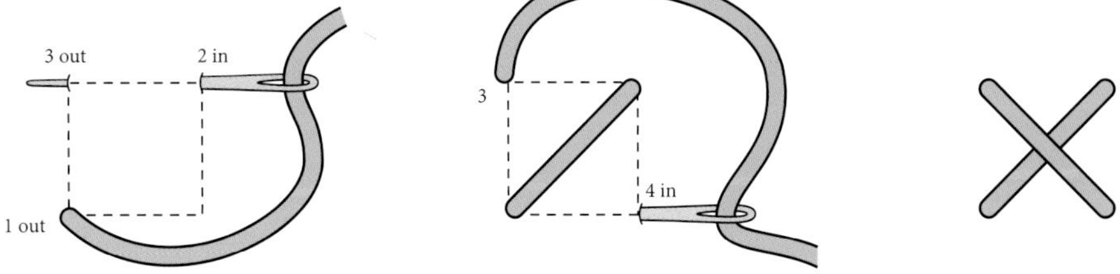

3 out
2 in
1 out
3
4 in

■ Double Cross Stitch

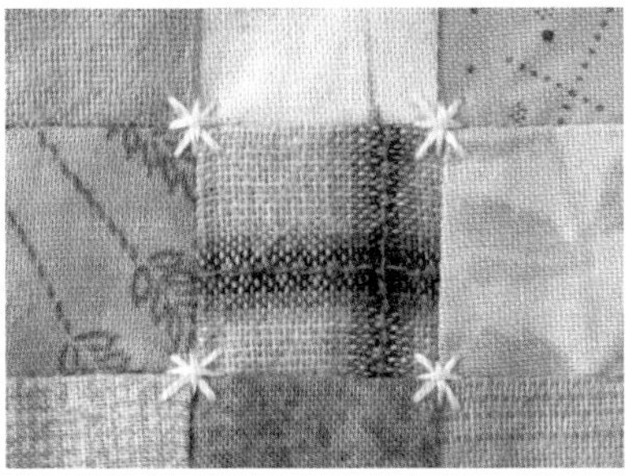

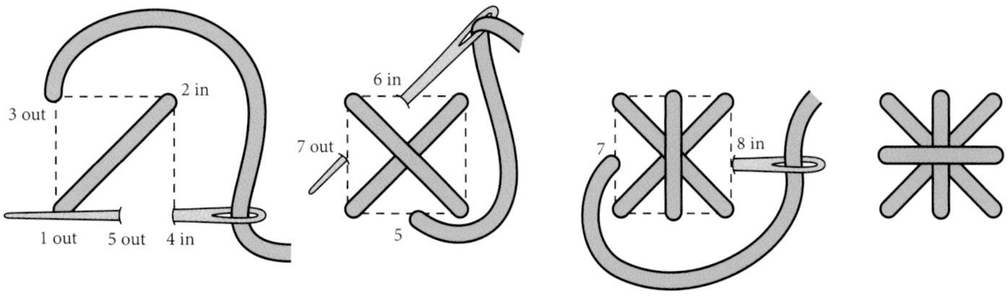

3 out
2 in
1 out
5 out
4 in
6 in
7 out
5
7
8 in

■ Lazy Daisy Stitch

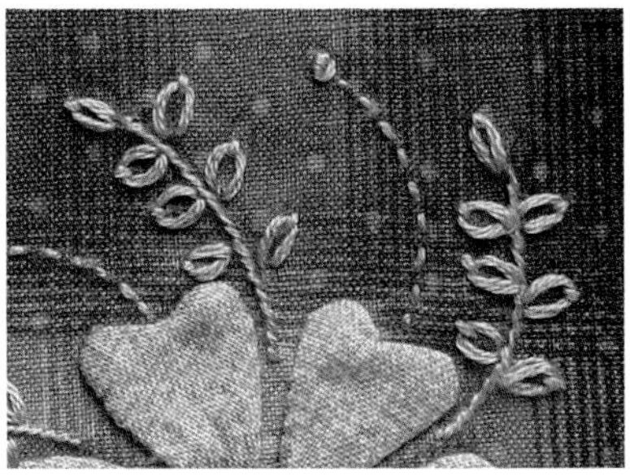

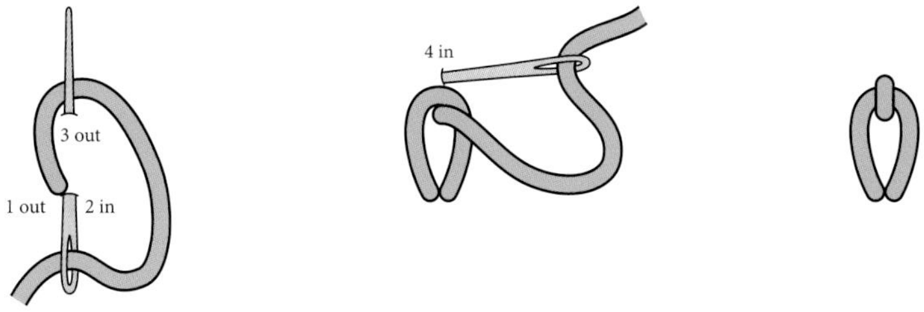

3 out
1 out
2 in
4 in

■ Fly Stitch

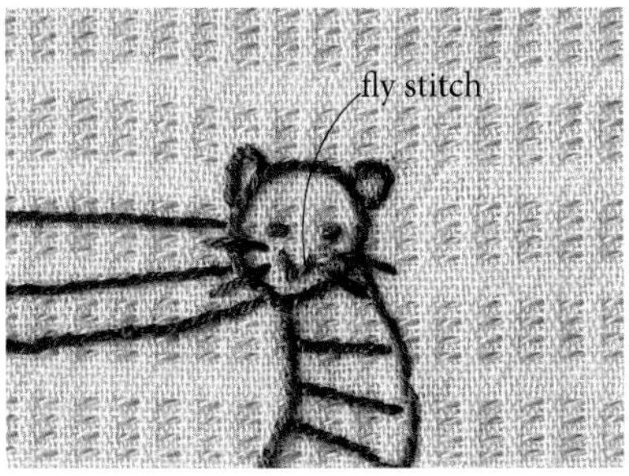

fly stitch

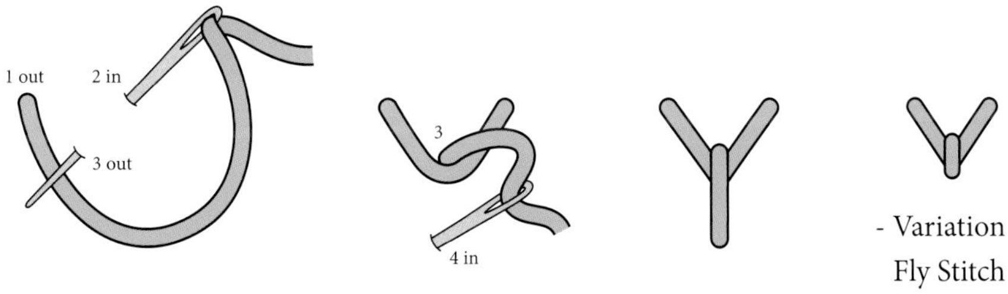

1 out
2 in
3 out
3
4 in

- Variation -
Fly Stitch

Blanket Stitch

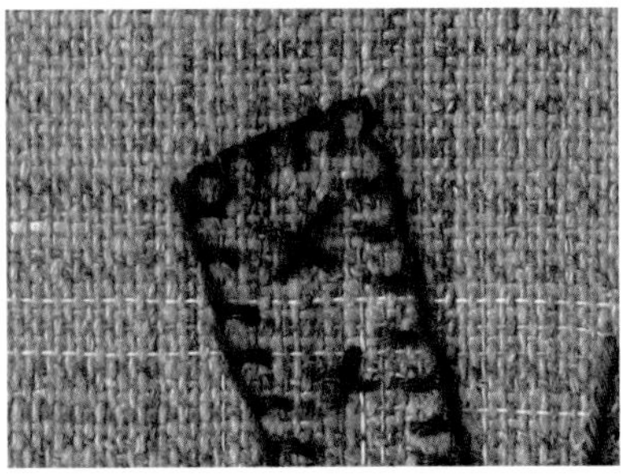

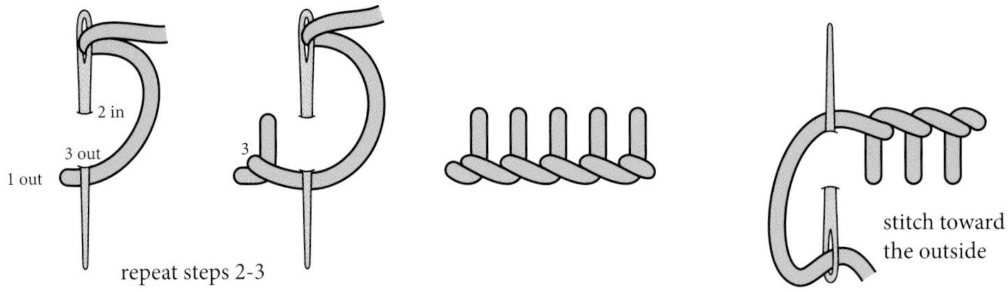

- Variation -

You can fill in any area with the blanket stitch (also called a buttonhole filling stitch.)

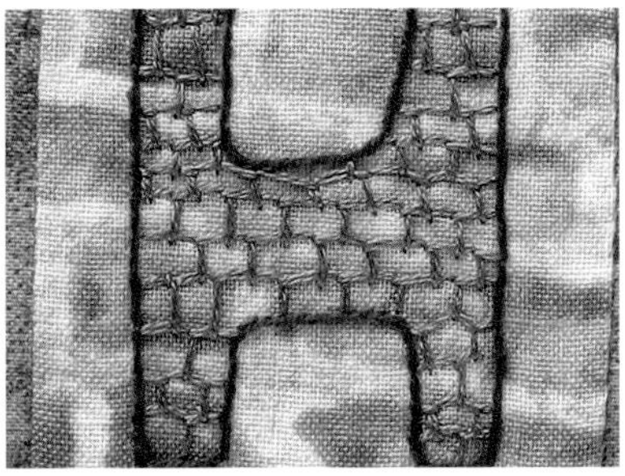

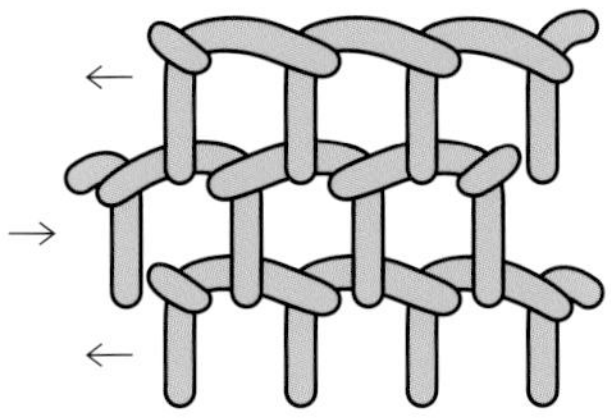

Herringbone Stitch

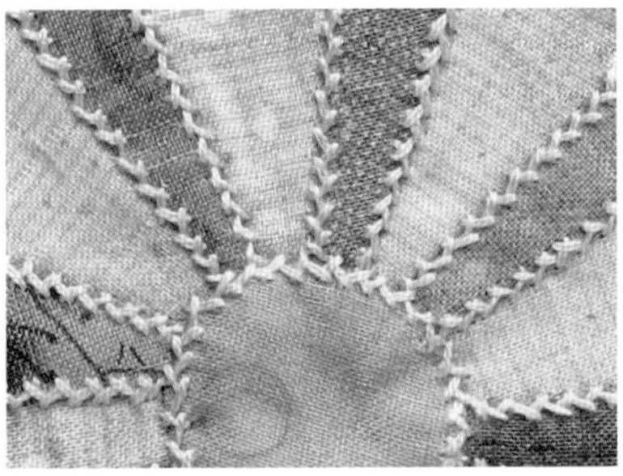

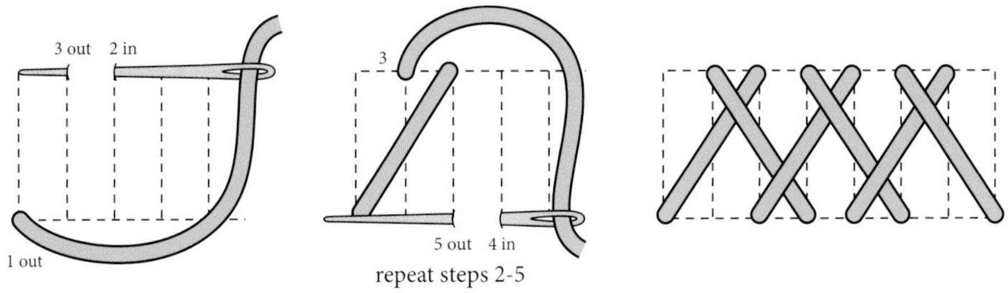

Double Herringbone Stitch

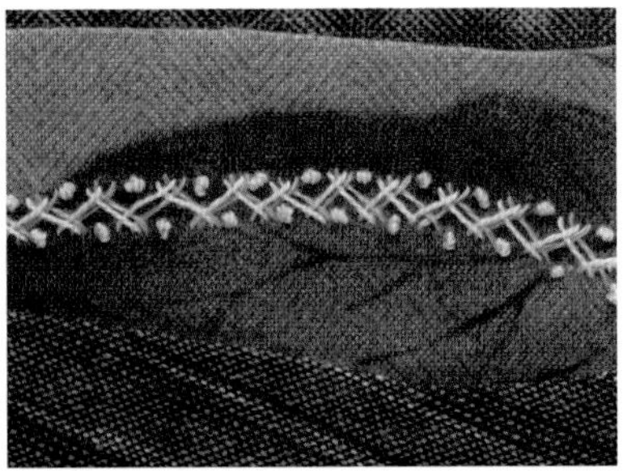

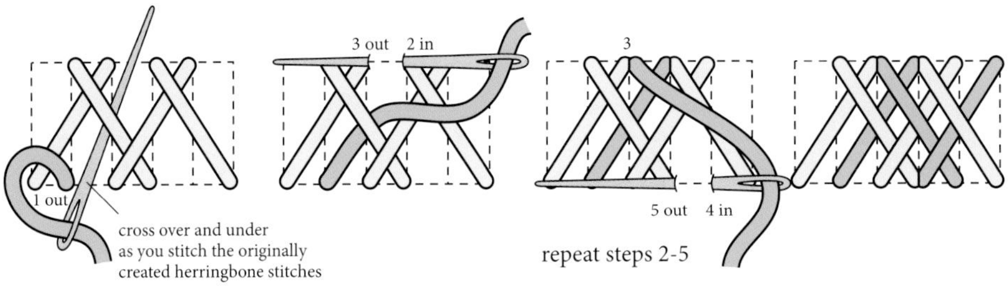

Feather Stitch

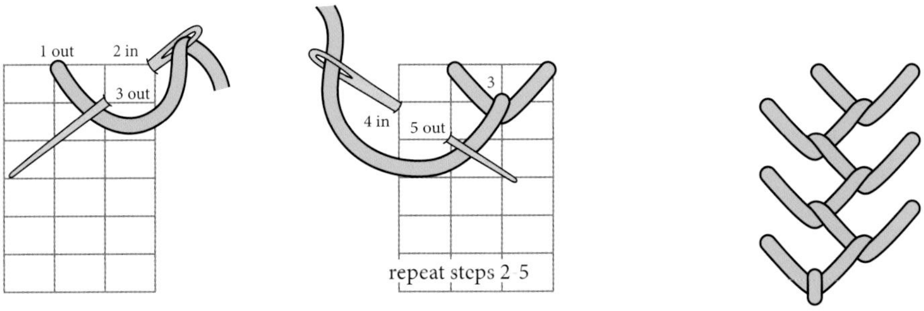

Fern Stitch

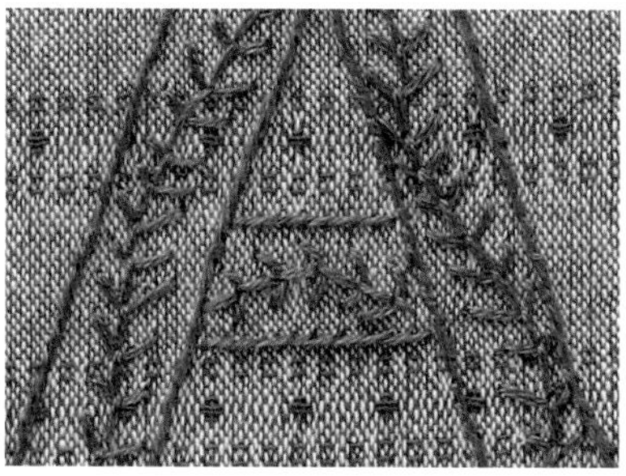

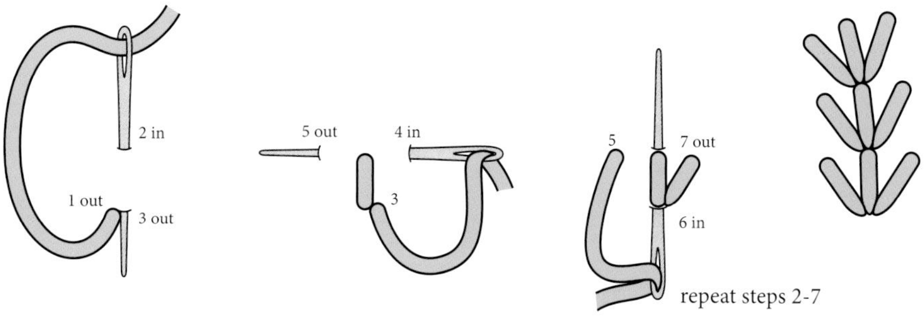

Open Cretan Stitch

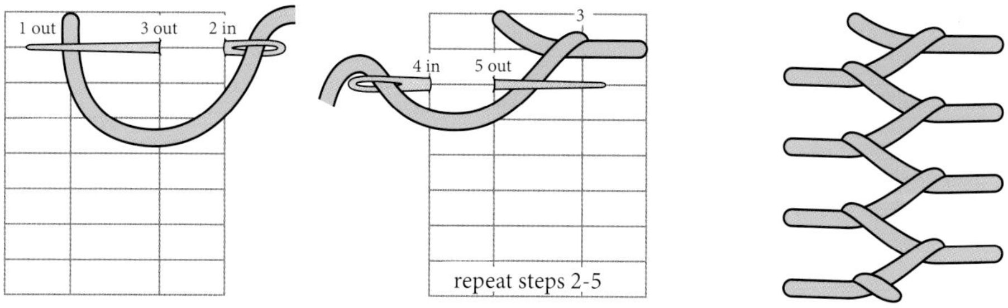

Chevron Stitch

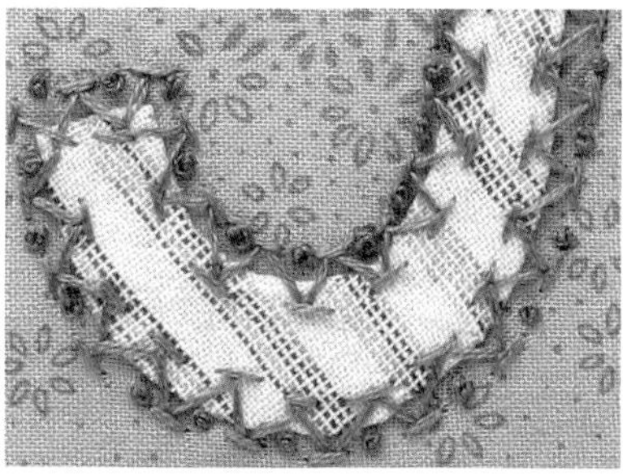

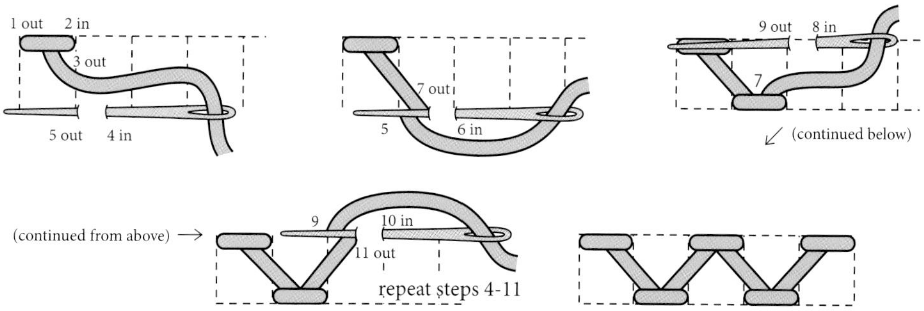

Couched Trellis Stitch

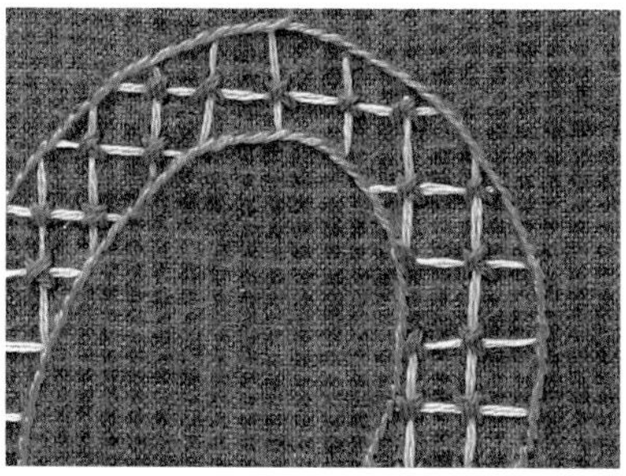

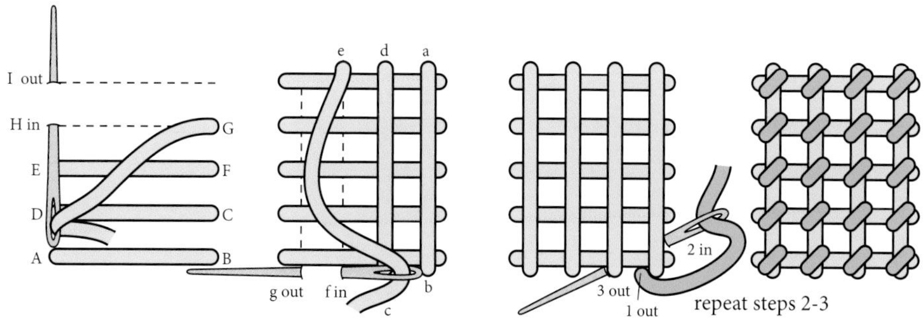

Satin Stitch

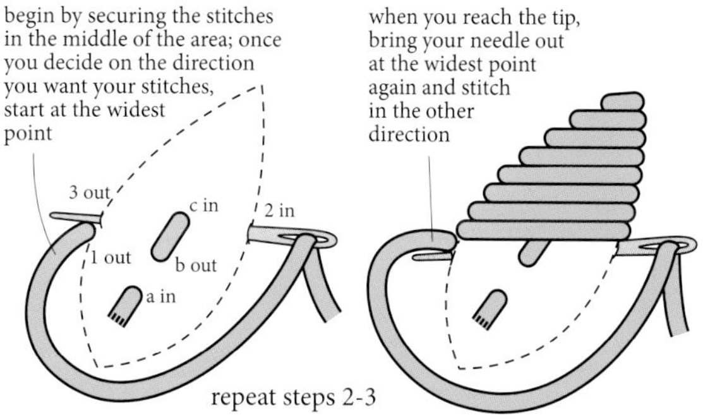
begin by securing the stitches in the middle of the area; once you decide on the direction you want your stitches, start at the widest point
when you reach the tip, bring your needle out at the widest point again and stitch in the other direction
3 out
c in
2 in
1 out
b out
a in
repeat steps 2-3

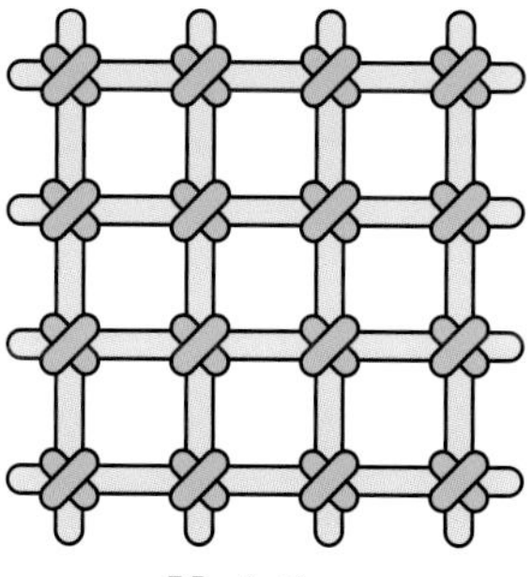

- Variation -

Couched Trellis Stitch

Before you begin...

► All measurements listed for the following projects are in centimeters (cm) and in inches [in brackets].
► The dimensions of the finished projects are listed for each, as well as shown in the drawings. Note that any pieced, appliquéd or quilted pieces tend to shrink somewhat during the sewing and quilting process. The final dimensions of the completed project will often be slightly smaller.
► Unless otherwise specified, seam allowances have not been added. Please add seam allowances for all pattern pieces. In general, add 0.3 - 0.5 cm [⅛"- ¼"] for appliqué pieces, 0.7 - 1 cm [¼" - ⅜"] for piecing or whatever amount you are most comfortable working with. If you are quilting the "patchwork embroidery" piece, cut the lining and batting several centimeters or inches larger than the top.
► If specific sizes of fabric are not given for the pattern, such as "assorted fat quarters or scraps," go through your stash to find appropriate pieces of fabric for the pattern pieces necessary for the given project.

a Wall Hanging

Shown on p. 12

Patterns used 1 ~ 9

The full-size embroidery patterns are on pp. 6-11 and pp. 14-16.

▸ Materials Needed

9 Beige and grey tone prints (background for the blocks)
- 15 × 15 cm each [5⅞" × 5⅞"]

Brown polka dots (borders)
- 60 × 60 cm [23⅝" × 23⅝"]

Backing - 60 × 60 cm [23⅝" × 23⅝"]

Batting - 60 × 60 cm [23⅝" × 23⅝"]

Grey print (bias binding)
- 3.5 × 200 cm [1⅜" × 78¾"]

Embroidery floss

▸ Finished measurements

48.4 × 48.4 cm [19⅛" × 19⅛"]

▸ Instructions

1 Embroider each of the nine designs onto the nine different background fabrics.

2 Piece them together to make the quilt center following the pattern below. Add the side borders, followed by the top and bottom borders.

3 Embroider the twig design along all the seams of the pieced blocks and border.

4 With wrong sides together and batting in between, baste. Quilt the entire quilt following the suggested quilting designs below in the dimensional diagram or as desired.

5 Bind the quilt with the bias binding. See p. 200 for instruction on binding a quilt.

▸ Tip

Be sure to quilt the backgrounds of each of the nine blocks as well as the borders.

Dimensional Diagram

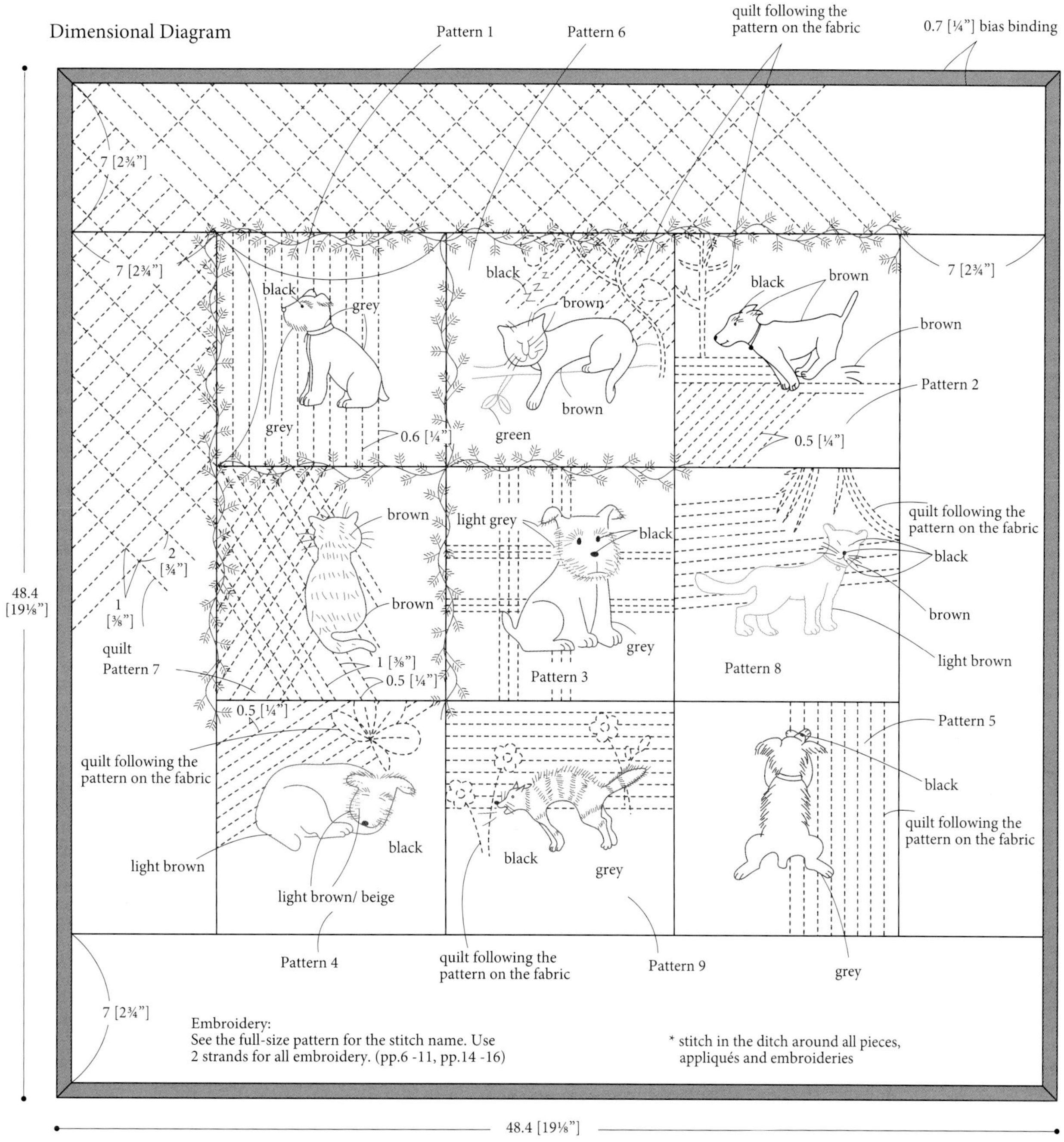

Twig Pattern (full-size pattern) - embroider along all the seams

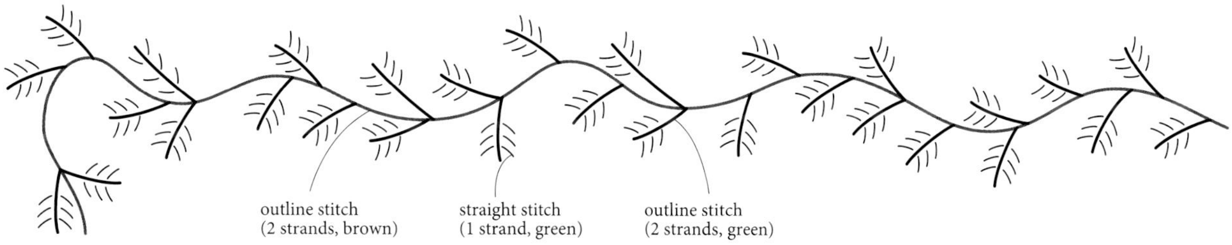

b Pouch

Shown on p. 24 and p. 25

Patterns used 15 ~ 16

The full-size embroidery patterns are on pp. 22-23.

► Materials Needed
Cream check (front background) - 15 × 15 cm [5⅞" × 5⅞"]
Grey print (back background) - 15 × 15 cm [5⅞" × 5⅞"]
Beige stripe (pouch body) - 30 × 30 cm [11¾" × 11¾"]
Brown print (pouch bottom) - 10 × 25 cm [4" × 9¾"]
Scraps - (tabs)
Lining - 35 × 35 cm [13¾" × 13¾"]
Batting - 35 × 35 cm [13¾" × 13¾"]
Brown homespun (bias binding) - 3.5 × 40 cm [1⅜" × 15¾"]
Bias strip (bottom gusset) - 2.5 × 15 cm [1" × 5⅞"]
Interfacing -10 × 10 cm [4" × 4"]
1 Zipper - 12.5 cm [5"] long
2 Beads - 1.2 cm [½"]
Cord - 0.1 × 10 cm [1/16" × 4"]
Embroidery floss

► Finished measurements
See the diagrams below.

► Instructions
1 Embroider the pouch front and back designs on the background fabric; piece together to create the pouch front top and back top.
2 With right sides together, piece the pouch front top and pouch back top with the pouch bottom.
3 With wrong sides together and batting in between, baste and quilt the pouch top and pouch lining.
4 Bind the zipper opening of the pouch body; sew in the zipper.
5 With right sides together, sew the side seams. Bind the raw edges (see p. 217).
6 Sew the bottom gusset. Bind the raw edges with the bias strips (see p. 212).
7 Make the zipper tabs.
8 Turn the pouch right side out and sew the gussets at the zipper opening of the pouch. Sandwich the seam allowances between the tabs; blindstitch; topstitch as shown.
9 Attach the beads for the zipper pull to the zipper clasp with the cord.

Pouch Body (Front, Back and Bottom)

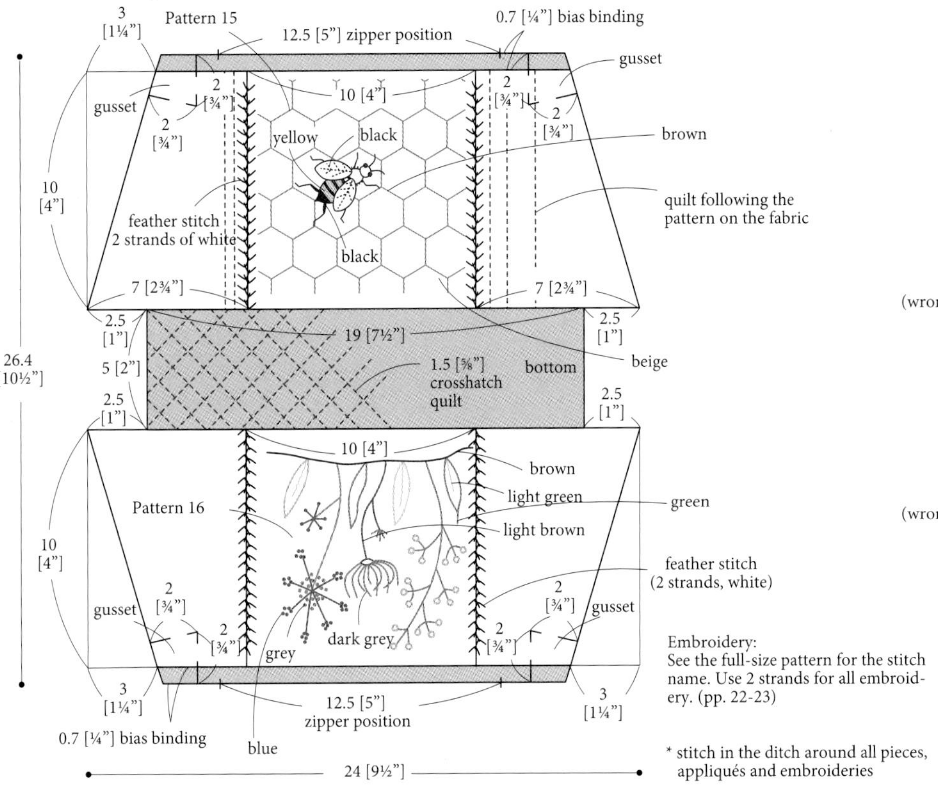

Embroidery:
See the full-size pattern for the stitch name. Use 2 strands for all embroidery. (pp. 22-23)

* stitch in the ditch around all pieces, appliqués and embroideries

Zipper Tabs - make 2

(top and lining - cut 2 each)

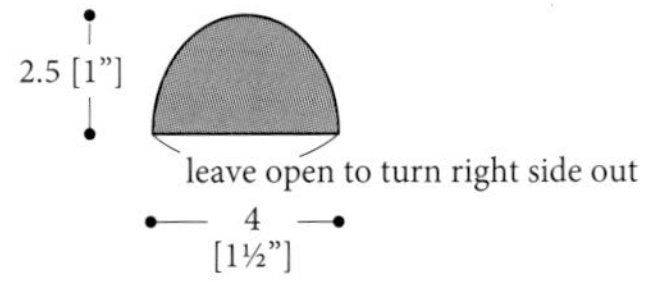

Making the Zipper Tabs

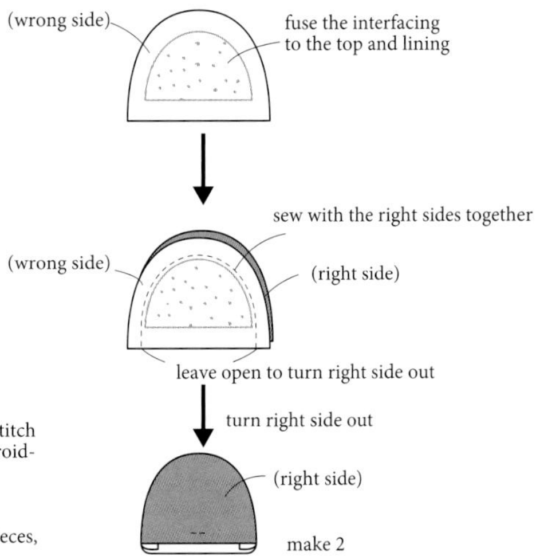

Making the Body

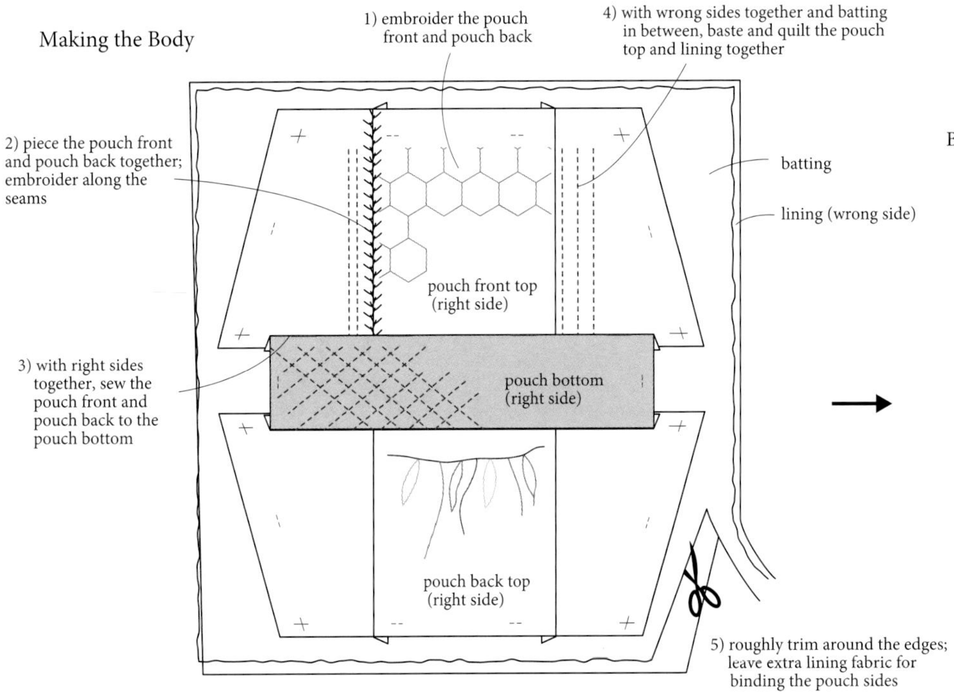

Binding the Zipper Opening

(see page. 201, Binding the Opening)

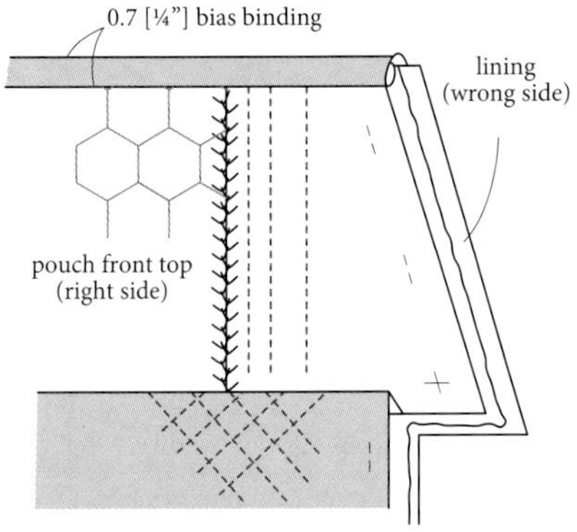

repeat for the other side

Sewing in the Zipper

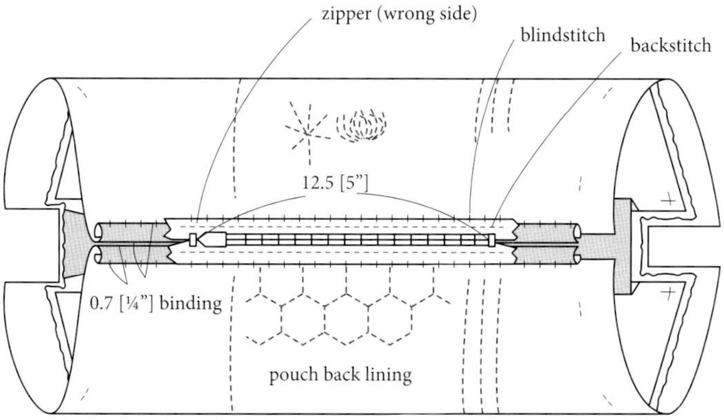
zipper (wrong side)
blindstitch
backstitch
12.5 [5"]
0.7 [¼"] binding
pouch back lining

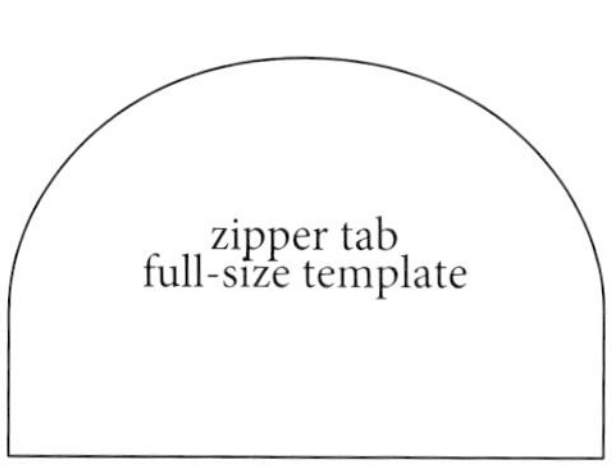
zipper tab
full-size template

with right sides together, form the pouch body into a cylinder shape; then with right sides together, center zipper on the bias binding and sew it in using a backstitch close to the zipper teeth; blindstitch the edges of the zipper tape down to the lining, being sure that the stitches are caught in the batting and cannot be seen on the right side

Sewing the Sides

sew the side seams; trim the top and the batting and pouch back lining down to 0.7 [¼"] (you will have the pouch front lining remaining); fold over the remaining lining twice to cover the raw edges and blindstitch down to the lining

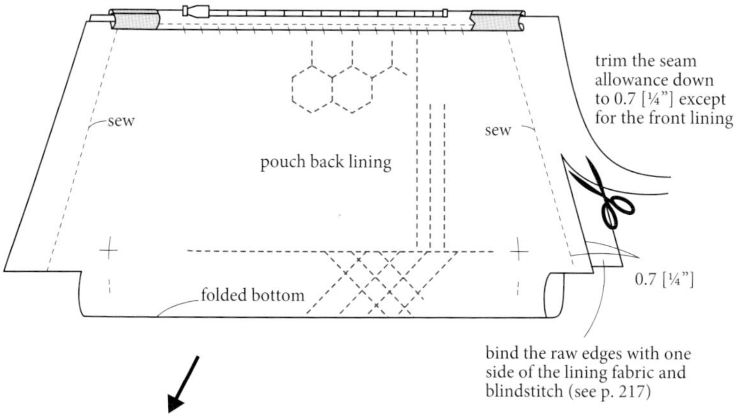
trim the seam allowance down to 0.7 [¼"] except for the front lining
sew
sew
pouch back lining
folded bottom
0.7 [¼"]
bind the raw edges with one side of the lining fabric and blindstitch (see p. 217)

Sewing the Gusset of the Bag/Zipper Opening

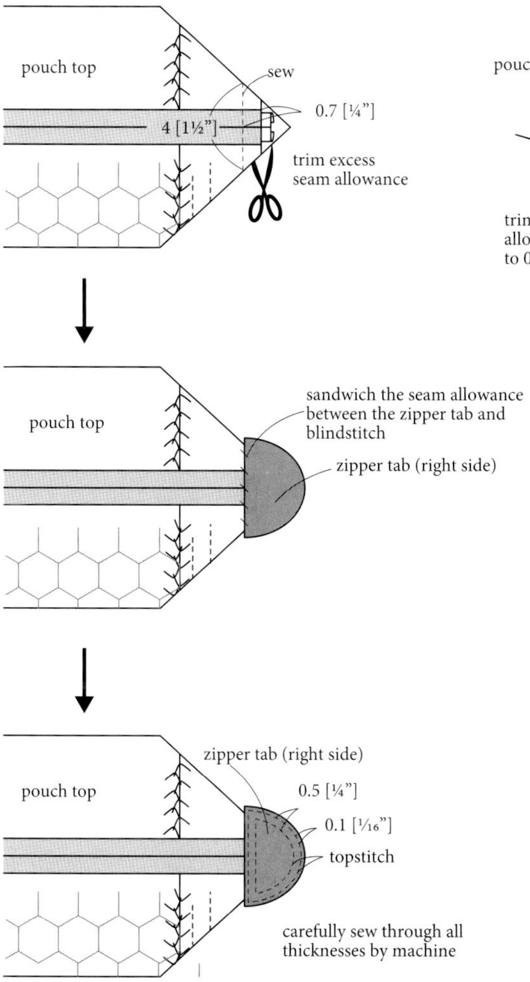
pouch top
sew
4 [1½"]
0.7 [¼"]
trim excess seam allowance
pouch top
sandwich the seam allowance between the zipper tab and blindstitch
zipper tab (right side)
pouch top
zipper tab (right side)
0.5 [¼"]
0.1 [1/16"]
topstitch
carefully sew through all thicknesses by machine

Sewing the Bottom Gusset

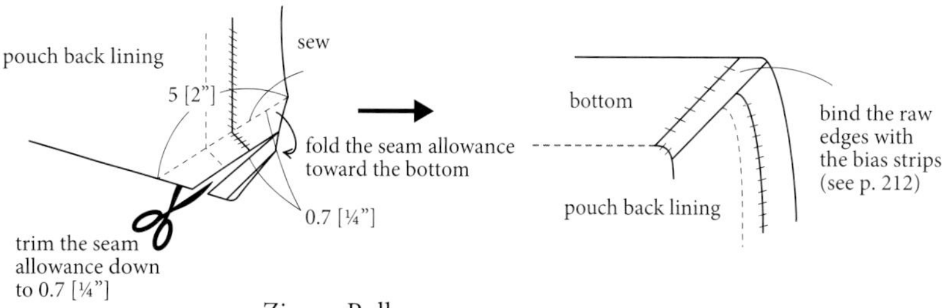
pouch back lining
sew
5 [2"]
fold the seam allowance toward the bottom
0.7 [¼"]
trim the seam allowance down to 0.7 [¼"]
bottom
pouch back lining
bind the raw edges with the bias strips (see p. 212)

Zipper Pull

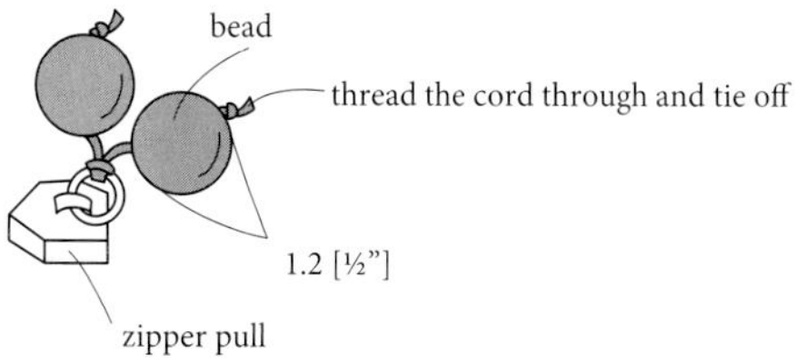
bead
thread the cord through and tie off
1.2 [½"]
zipper pull

Finished Pouch

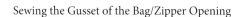

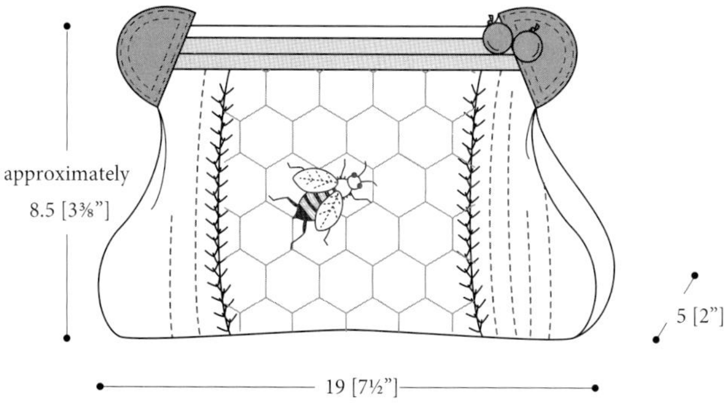
approximately 8.5 [3⅜"]
5 [2"]
19 [7½"]

C Coin Purse

Shown on p. 30

Patterns used 17-18

The full-size embroidery patterns are on pp. 26-27; the full-size templates for the purse body and bottom gusset can be found on Side A of the pattern sheet inserts.

► Materials Needed
Assorted fat quarters or scraps (piecing and appliqué)
Green plaid (bottom gusset)
- 10× 35 cm [4"× 13¾"] (on bias)
Lining - 30×50 cm [11¾" × 19¾"]
Batting - 30×50 cm[11¾" × 19¾"]
Lt beige lace
- 1× 50 cm [⅜" ×19¾"]
Sew-in purse frame
- 15×6 cm [5⅞" × 2⅜"] outside diameter
Embroidery floss

► Finished measurements
See the diagrams below.

► Instructions
1 Applique, embroider, piece the purse front A and back B.
2 With right sides together and batting against the back, sew the front A and lining together around the sides and bottom, leaving the top open.
3 Turn right side out, blindstitch the opening closed. Repeat for back B.
4 Make the bottom gusset following steps 2 and 3 above.
5 With right sides together, sew A and B to the gusset using a whipstitch.
6 Turn right side out. Insert the top edge of A and B into the channels of the purse frame; sew them on using a backstitch.
7 Glue the lace in place on the inside of the purse frame to cover the stitches.

► Tip
Mark the center of the purse frame and align it with the center of the purse body. When sewing the frame on the body, start sewing from the center outward to evenly divide the opening. When using your own purse frame, adjust the upper curve of the actual pattern to match to the size and length of your frame.

Purse Front A

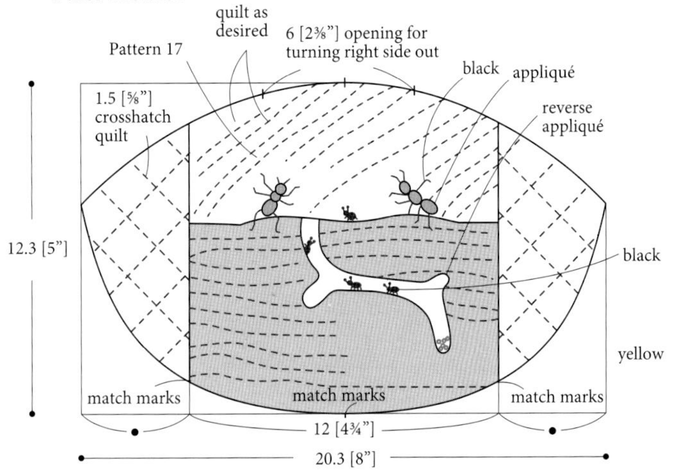

Purse Back B

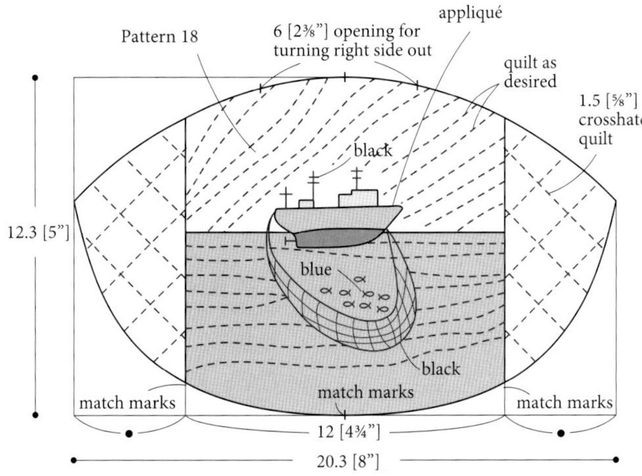

Bottom Gusset

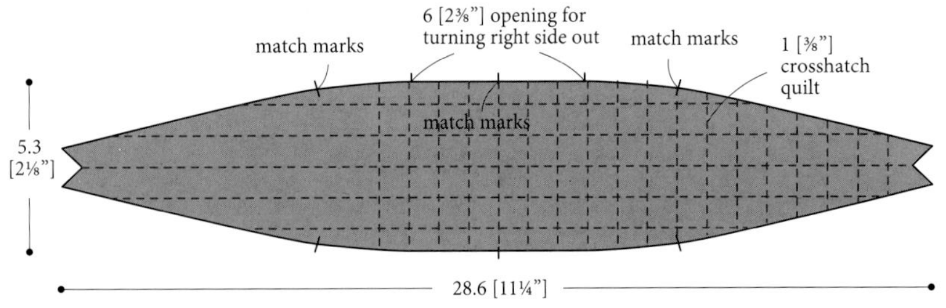

Embroidery:
See the full-size pattern for the stitch name and number of strands needed. (pp. 26-27)

* stitch in the ditch around all pieces, appliqués and embroideries

How to do Reverse Appliqué

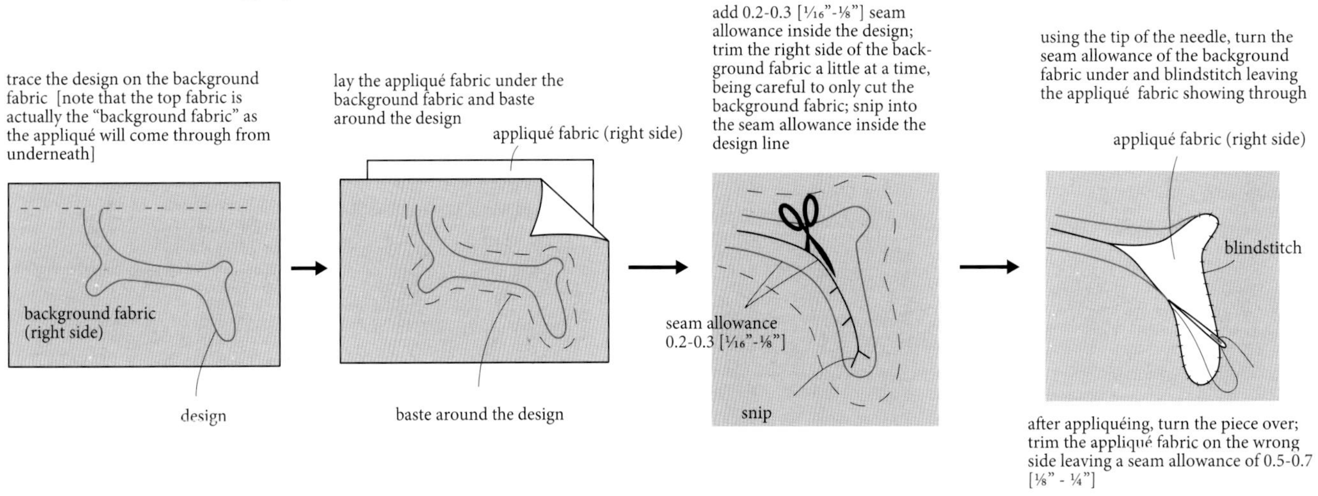
trace the design on the background fabric [note that the top fabric is actually the "background fabric" as the appliqué will come through from underneath]
background fabric (right side)
design
lay the appliqué fabric under the background fabric and baste around the design
appliqué fabric (right side)
baste around the design
add 0.2-0.3 [1/16"-⅛"] seam allowance inside the design; trim the right side of the background fabric a little at a time, being careful to only cut the background fabric; snip into the seam allowance inside the design line
seam allowance 0.2-0.3 [1/16"-⅛"]
snip
using the tip of the needle, turn the seam allowance of the background fabric under and blindstitch leaving the appliqué fabric showing through
appliqué fabric (right side)
blindstitch
after appliquéing, turn the piece over; trim the appliqué fabric on the wrong side leaving a seam allowance of 0.5-0.7 [⅛" - ¼"]

Making the Body

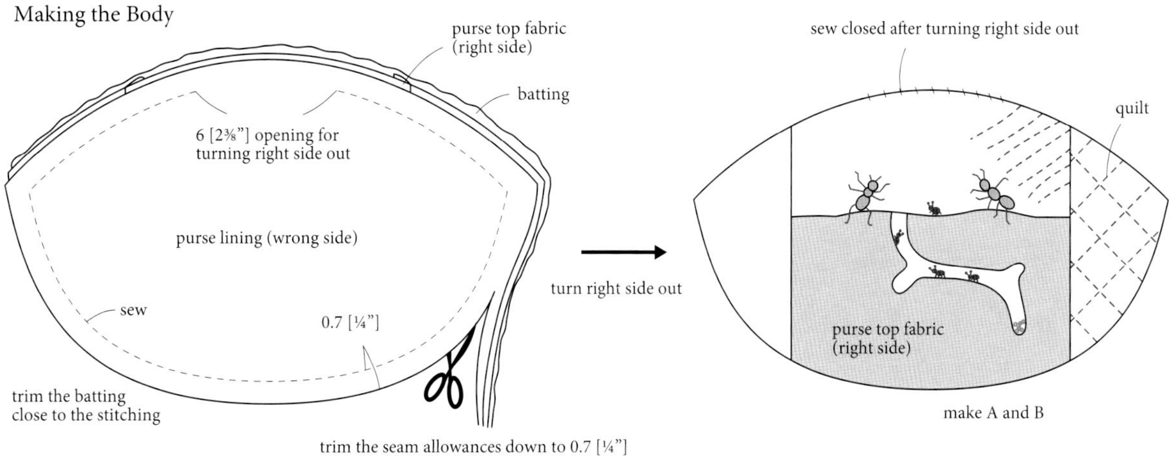
purse top fabric
(right side)
batting
6 [2⅜"] opening for
turning right side out
purse lining (wrong side)
sew
0.7 [¼"]
trim the batting
close to the stitching
trim the seam allowances down to 0.7 [¼"]
turn right side out
sew closed after turning right side out
quilt
purse top fabric
(right side)
make A and B

Making the Bottom Gusset

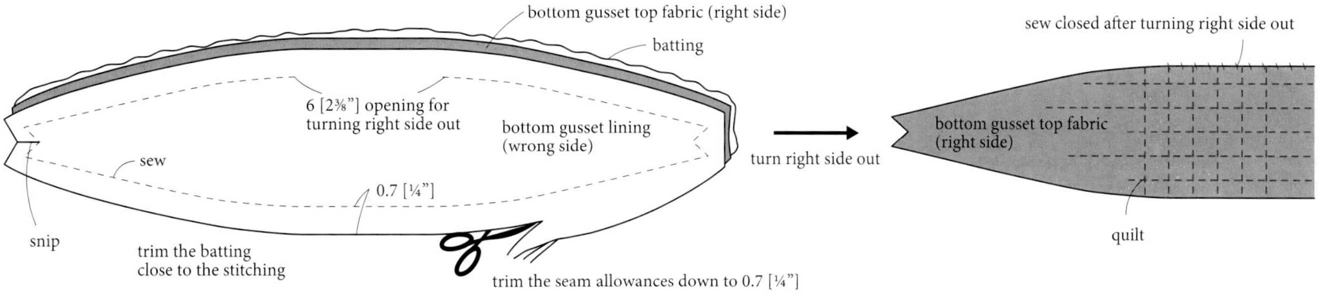
bottom gusset top fabric (right side)
batting
6 [2⅜"] opening for
turning right side out
bottom gusset lining
(wrong side)
sew
0.7 [¼"]
snip
trim the batting
close to the stitching
trim the seam allowances down to 0.7 [¼"]
turn right side out
sew closed after turning right side out
bottom gusset top fabric
(right side)
quilt

Sewing the Body and Bottom Gusset Together

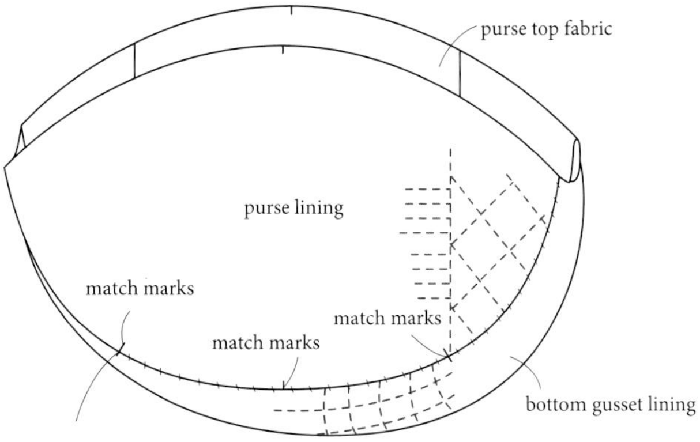
purse top fabric
purse lining
match marks
match marks
match marks
bottom gusset lining

with the right sides together, sew the purse body top (purse front A) to the gusset top with a whipstitch by passing the needle through the top fabric only; go back and use a mattress stitch to catch the lining fabrics together; repeat for the purse back B

Attaching the Purse Frame

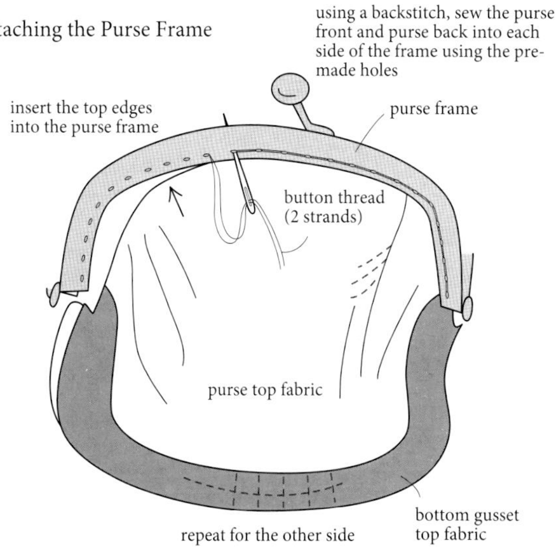
using a backstitch, sew the purse
front and purse back into each
side of the frame using the pre-
made holes
insert the top edges
into the purse frame
purse frame
button thread
(2 strands)
purse top fabric
repeat for the other side
bottom gusset
top fabric

Gluing the Lace to the Inside

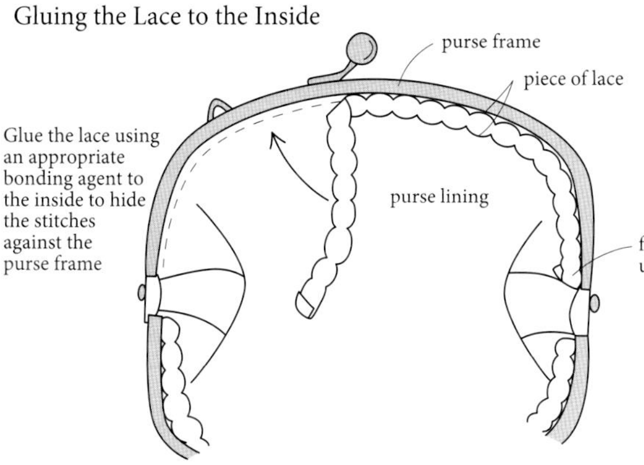
purse frame
piece of lace
Glue the lace using
an appropriate
bonding agent to
the inside to hide
the stitches
against the
purse frame
purse lining
fold the edge
under

Finished Pouch

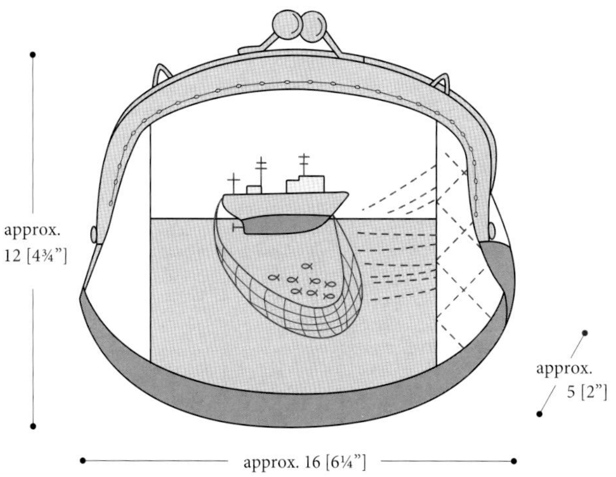
approx.
12 [4¾"]
approx.
5 [2"]
approx. 16 [6¼"]

d Mini Pouch

Shown on p. 31

Patterns used 19 ~ 20

The full-size embroidery patterns are on pp. 28-29; the full-size templates for the pouch body can be found on Side A of the pattern sheet inserts.

▸ Materials Needed
Beige prints (background fabrics) - 15 × 20 cm [5⅞" × 7⅞"] each
Brown print (gusset) - 10 × 50 cm [4" × 19¾"] (on bias)
Grey print (zipper tabs) - 5 × 15 cm [2" × 5⅞"]
Lining - 40 × 50 cm [15¾" × 19¾"]
Batting - 40 × 50 cm [15¾" × 19¾"]
Bias binding - 2.5 × 110 cm, [1" × 43¼"]
Interfacing - 10 × 25 cm [4" × 9¾"]
1 zipper - 17 cm [6"] long
Zipper pull (optional)
Embroidery floss - black, red

▸ Finished measurements
See the diagrams below.

▸ Instructions
1 Embroider the designs on the pouch front and back background fabrics.
2 With wrong sides together and batting in between, quilt the pouch front and lining together; repeat for the pouch back.
3 With wrong sides together and batting in between, quilt the zipper opening gussets (make 2).
4 Sew the zipper between the two zipper opening gusset pieces.
5 Make tabs and baste them in position on either end of the zipper.
6 With wrong sides together and batting in between, quilt the bottom gusset.
7 With right sides together, sew the zipper opening gusset to the bottom gusset to make a cylinder shape.
8 With right sides together, sew the pouch front and pouch back to the gusset, matching marks. Bind the raw edges with the bias binding.
9 Attach a fun zipper pull to the zipper clasp.

▸ Tip
When sewing the zipper to the zipper opening gusset, align the center of the zipper opening gusset (△) and the center of the zipper. Align the markings when sewing the body and the top and bottom gussets together.

Pouch Back A

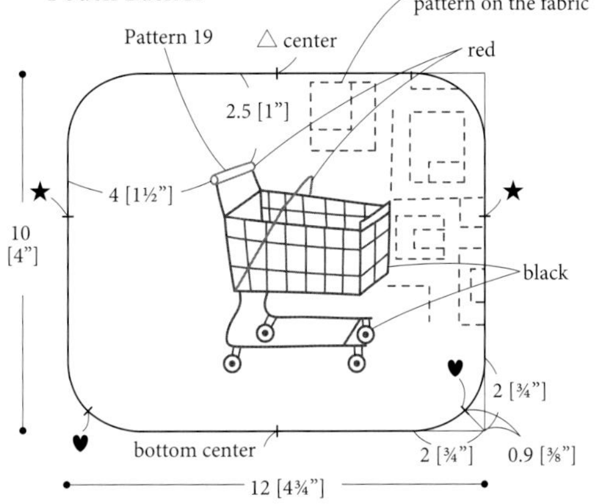

Embroidery:
See the full-size pattern for the stitch name and number of strands needed. (pp. 28-29)

* stitch in the ditch around all pieces, appliqués and embroideries

Pouch Front B

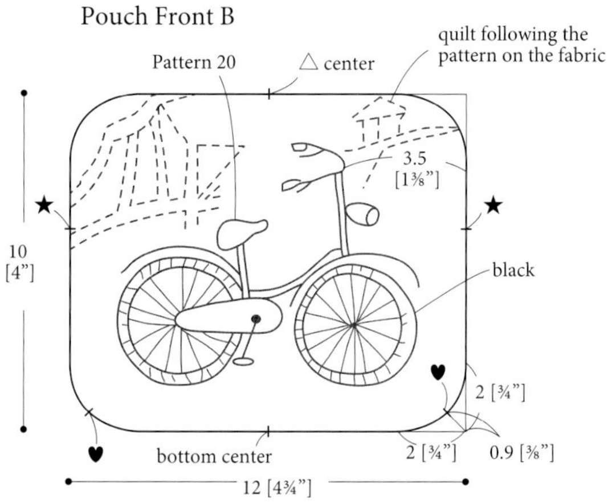

Bottom Gusset

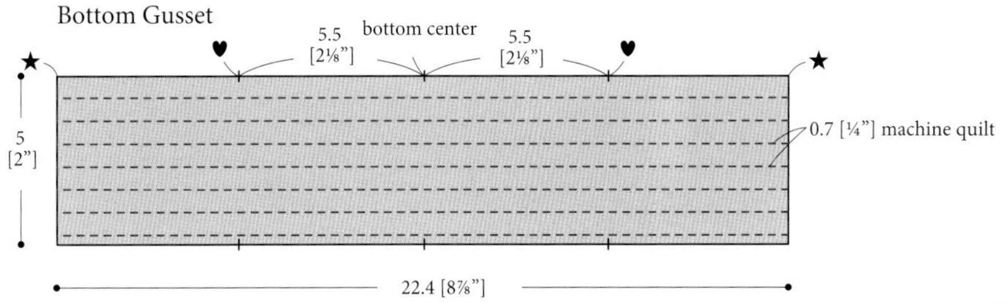

Zipper Tab (cut 2)

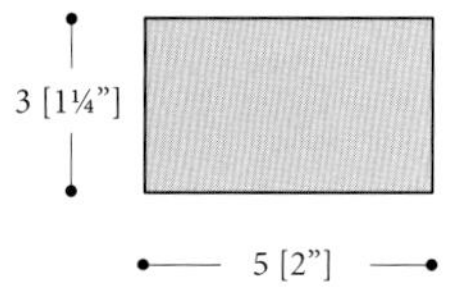

Zipper Opening Gusset - make 2

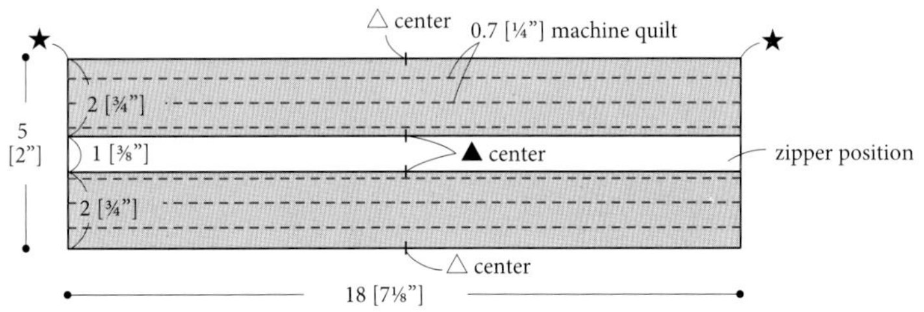

Making the Zipper Tabs

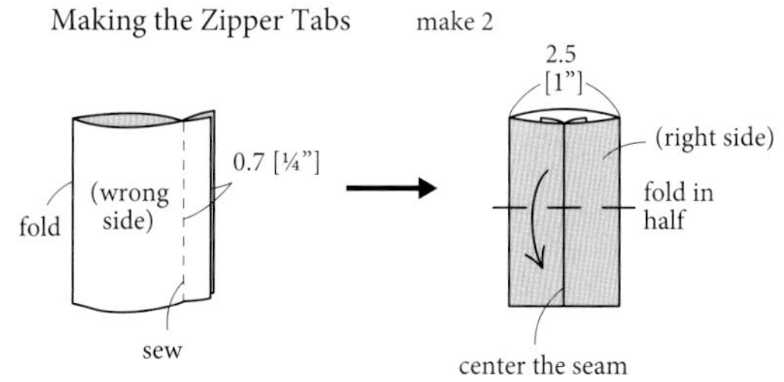

Making the Zipper Opening Gusset

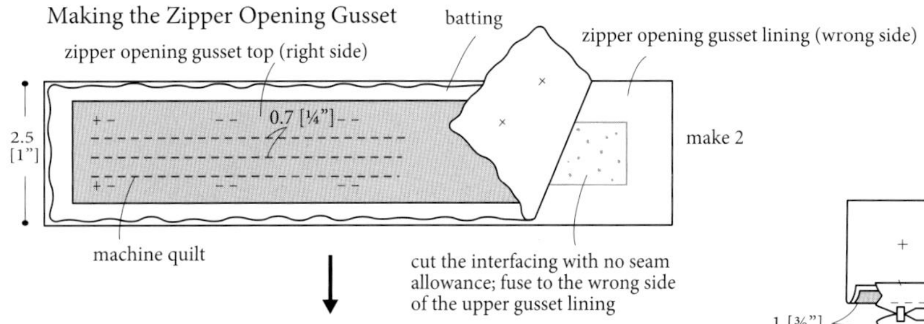

Sewing in the Zipper

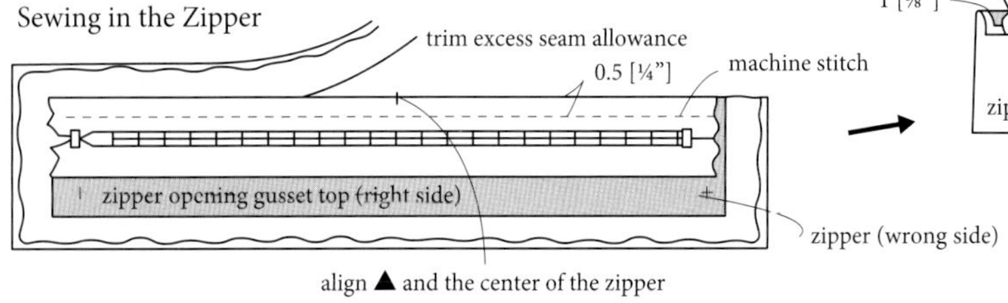

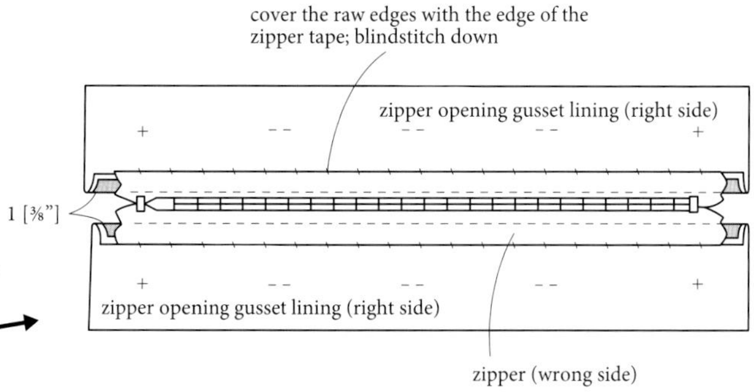

Basting the Tabs to the Zipper Opening Gusset

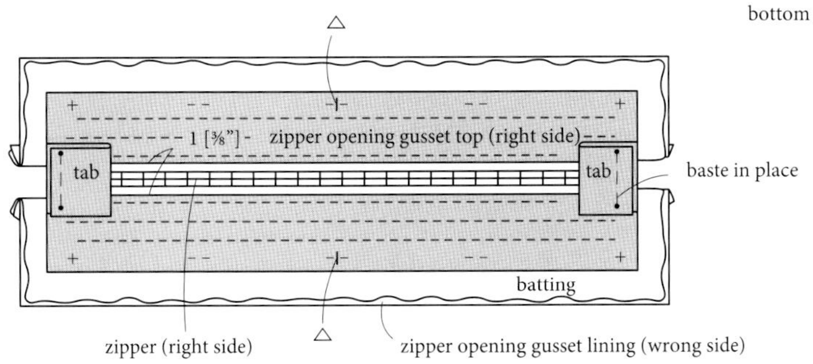

1 [⅜"]
zipper opening gusset top (right side)
tab
tab
baste in place
batting
zipper (right side)
zipper opening gusset lining (wrong side)

Making the Bottom Gusset

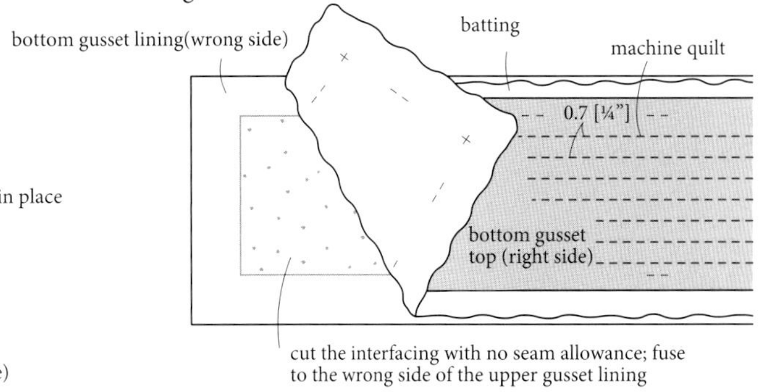

bottom gusset lining(wrong side)
batting
machine quilt
0.7 [¼"]
bottom gusset top (right side)
cut the interfacing with no seam allowance; fuse to the wrong side of the upper gusset lining

Sewing the Gussets Together

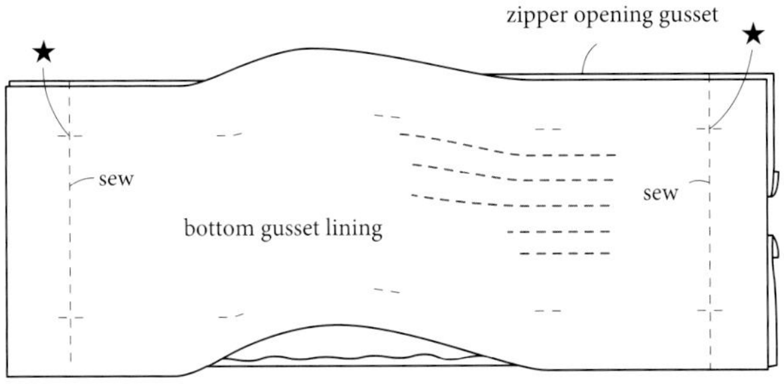

zipper opening gusset
sew
bottom gusset lining
sew

Binding the Raw Edges

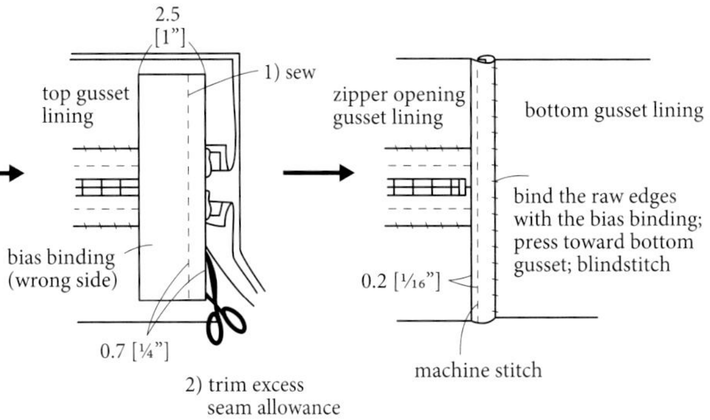

2.5 [1"]
1) sew
top gusset lining
bias binding (wrong side)
0.7 [¼"]
2) trim excess seam allowance
zipper opening gusset lining
bottom gusset lining
bind the raw edges with the bias binding; press toward bottom gusset; blindstitch
0.2 [1/16"]
machine stitch

Making the Pouch Body (Pouch Back A and Pouch Front B)

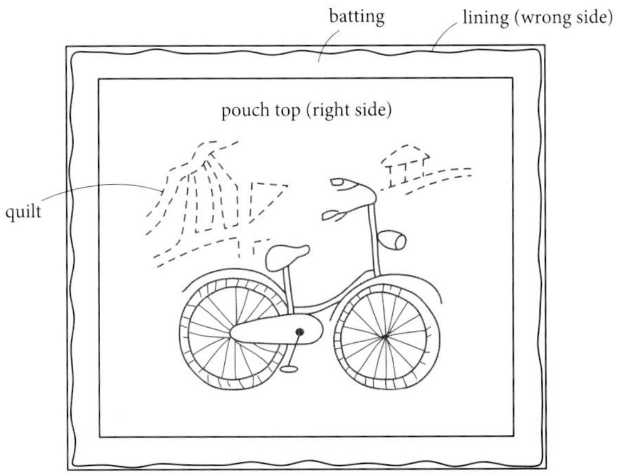

batting
lining (wrong side)
pouch top (right side)
quilt

Sewing the Pouch Together

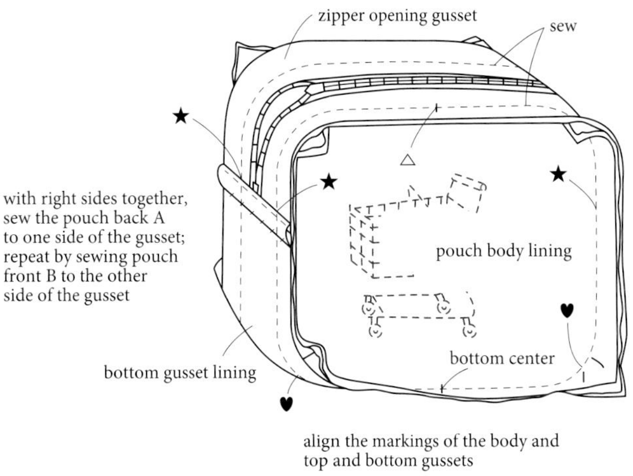

zipper opening gusset
sew
with right sides together, sew the pouch back A to one side of the gusset; repeat by sewing pouch front B to the other side of the gusset
pouch body lining
bottom center
bottom gusset lining
align the markings of the body and top and bottom gussets

Bind the Raw Edges

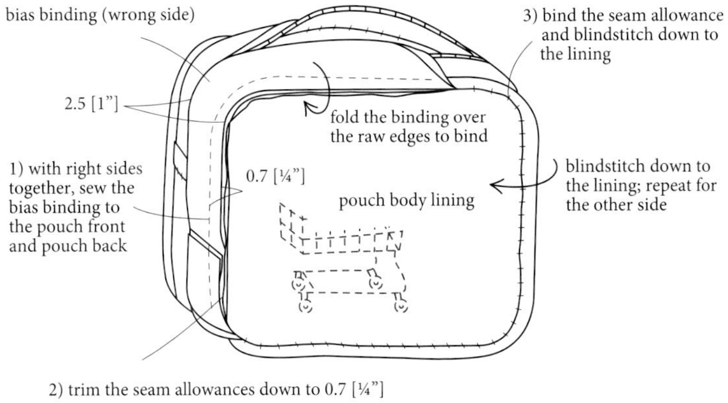

bias binding (wrong side)
3) bind the seam allowance and blindstitch down to the lining
2.5 [1"]
fold the binding over the raw edges to bind
1) with right sides together, sew the bias binding to the pouch front and pouch back
0.7 [¼"]
pouch body lining
blindstitch down to the lining; repeat for the other side
2) trim the seam allowances down to 0.7 [¼"]

Finished pouch

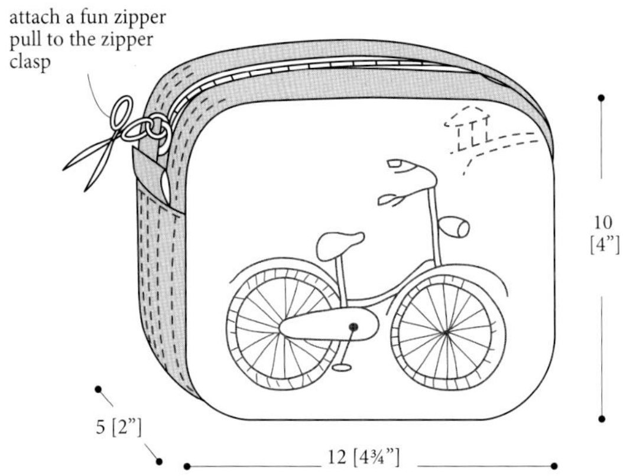

attach a fun zipper pull to the zipper clasp
10 [4"]
5 [2"]
12 [4¾"]

e Mini Pouch

Shown on p. 41

Pattern used 29

The full-size embroidery pattern is on p. 40; the full-size templates and dimensional diagrams can be found below.

► Materials Needed
Beige print (pouch front) - 15×15 cm [5⅞" × 5⅞"]
Brown print (pouch back) - 15×40 cm [5⅞" × 15¾"]
Brown plaid (bottom) - 10×15 cm [4" × 5⅞"]
Lining - 30×30 cm [11¾" × 11¾"]
Batting - 30×30 cm [11¾" × 11¾"]
Beige print (bias binding) - 3.5×40 cm [1⅜" × 15¾"]
Scraps - (zipper loop)
Interfacing - 5×12 cm [2" × 4¾"]
1 Zipper - 15 cm [5⅞"] long
2 Buttons (zipper pull)
- 2 cm [¾"] diameter
- 1.8 cm [⅝"] diameter
Embroidery floss - brown, white

► Finished measurements
See the diagrams below.

► Instructions
1 Embroider the designs on the pouch front and back background fabrics.
2 With right sides together and batting against the top, sew the front and lining together around the sides and bottom, leaving the top open.
3 Turn right side out; baste the opening edges; quilt.
4 Cut out the pouch back top and lining; with right sides together and lining against the top, sew around the sides and bottom; turn right side out; baste across the opening edges; quilt.
5 Make the bottom. Fuse the interfacing without seam allowance to the lining. With right sides together and batting against the top, sew all the way around; turn right side out; stitch opening closed; quilt
6 With right sides together, sew the pouch front and pouch back together along the sides.
7 With rights sides together, sew the pouch bottom to the pouch body.
8 Sew the zipper to the pouch and bind the opening.
9 Make the zipper pull loop and attach it together with buttons to make the zipper pull.

Pouch front

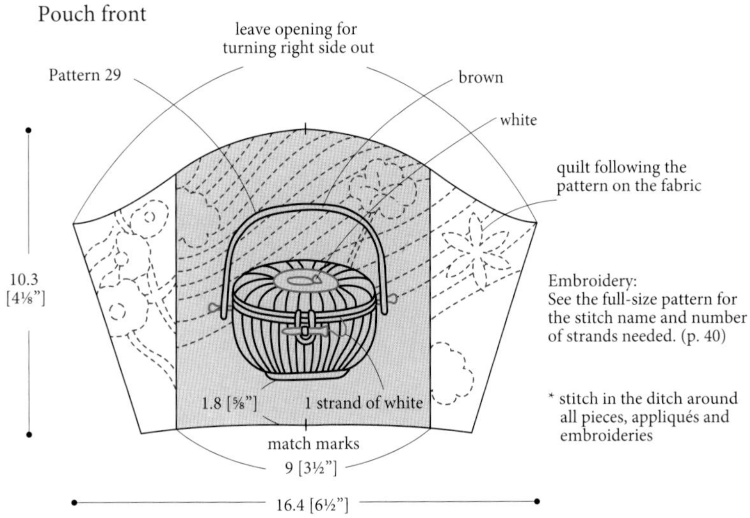

Pouch Back

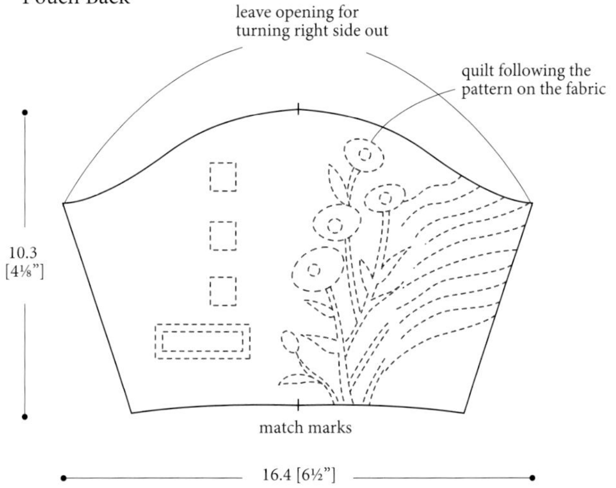

Pouch Bottom

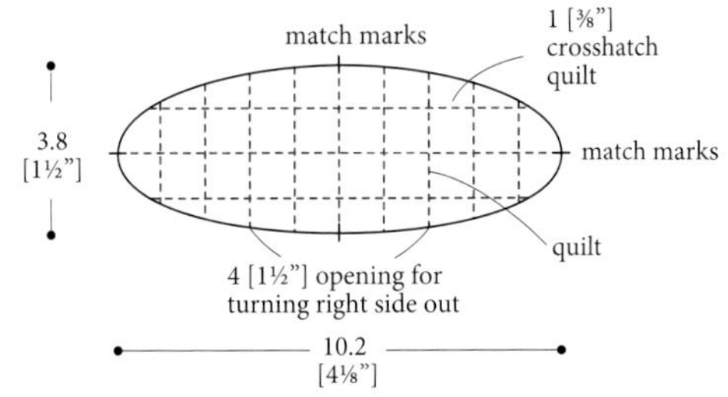

Zipper Pull Loop

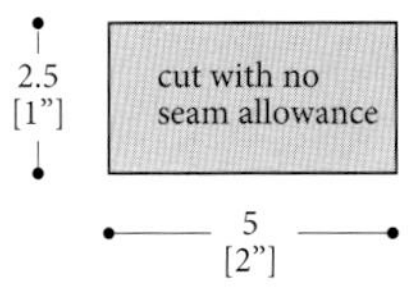

Make the Zipper Pull

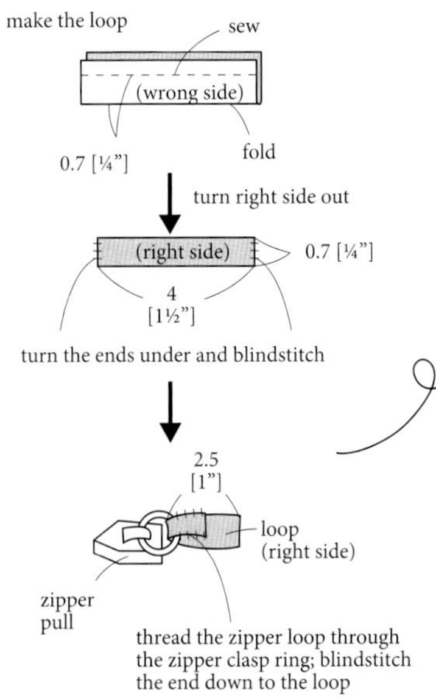

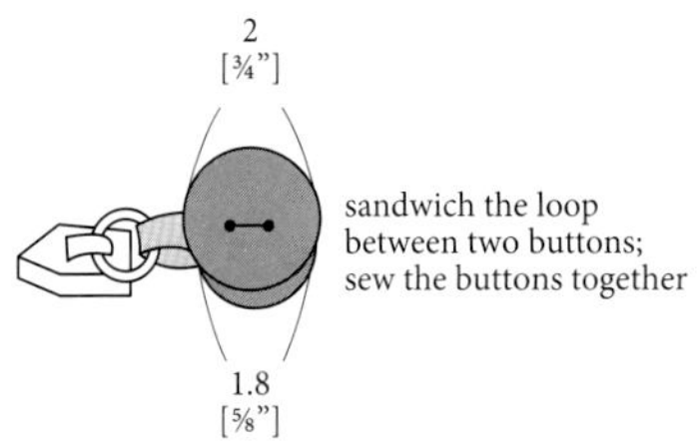

Full-Size Pattern

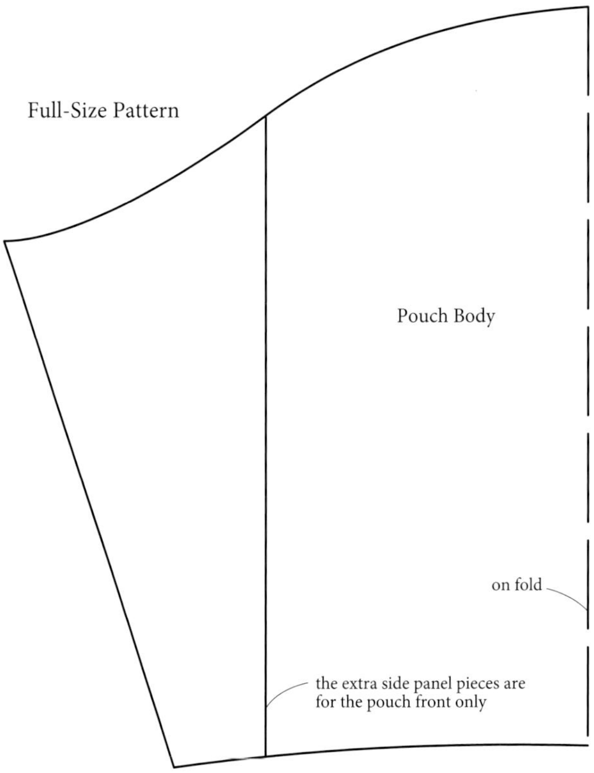

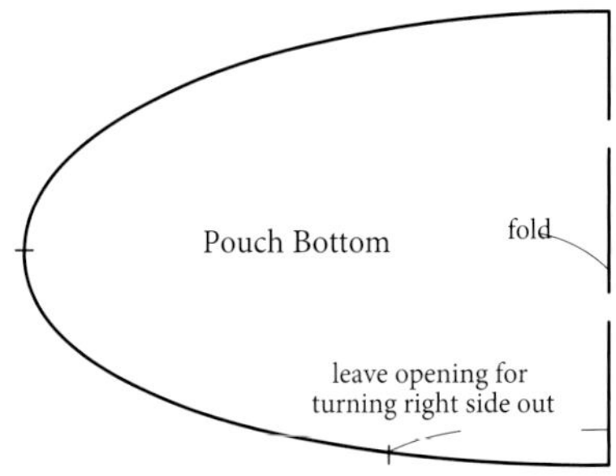

Making the Pouch Body

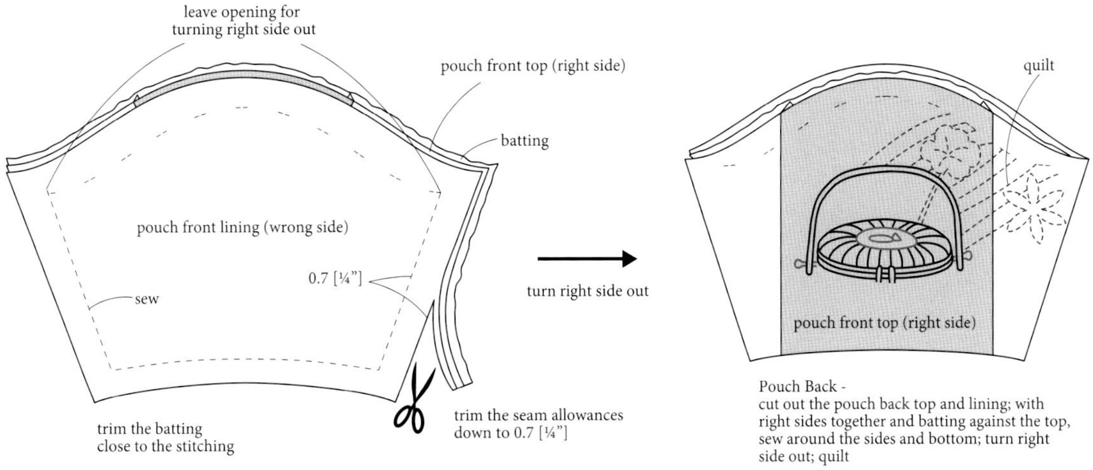

leave opening for turning right side out
pouch front top (right side)
batting
pouch front lining (wrong side)
0.7 [¼"]
sew
trim the batting close to the stitching
trim the seam allowances down to 0.7 [¼"]
turn right side out
quilt
pouch front top (right side)
Pouch Back - cut out the pouch back top and lining; with right sides together and batting against the top, sew around the sides and bottom; turn right side out; quilt

Making the Bottom

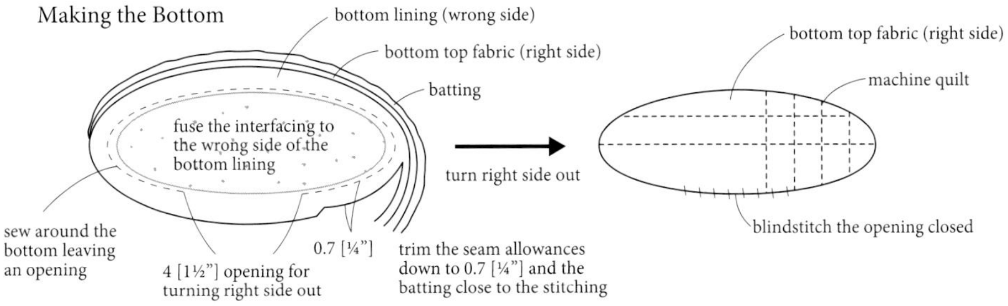

bottom lining (wrong side)
bottom top fabric (right side)
batting
fuse the interfacing to the wrong side of the bottom lining
sew around the bottom leaving an opening
4 [1½"] opening for turning right side out
0.7 [¼"]
trim the seam allowances down to 0.7 [¼"] and the batting close to the stitching
turn right side out
bottom top fabric (right side)
machine quilt
blindstitch the opening closed

Sewing the Pouch Together

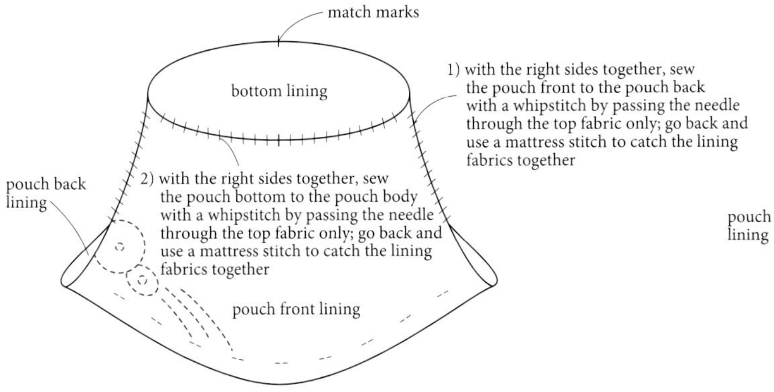

match marks
bottom lining
1) with the right sides together, sew the pouch front to the pouch back with a whipstitch by passing the needle through the top fabric only; go back and use a mattress stitch to catch the lining fabrics together
pouch back lining
2) with the right sides together, sew the pouch bottom to the pouch body with a whipstitch by passing the needle through the top fabric only; go back and use a mattress stitch to catch the lining fabrics together
pouch front lining

Sewing in the Zipper

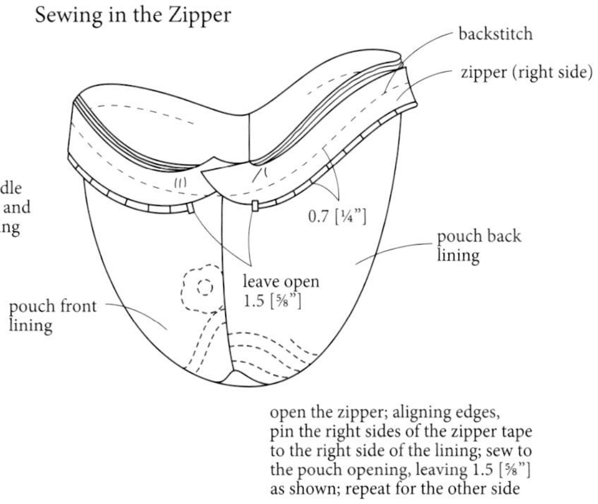

backstitch
zipper (right side)
0.7 [¼"]
pouch back lining
leave open 1.5 [⅝"]
pouch front lining
open the zipper; aligning edges, pin the right sides of the zipper tape to the right side of the lining; sew to the pouch opening, leaving 1.5 [⅝"] as shown; repeat for the other side

Binding the Pouch Opening

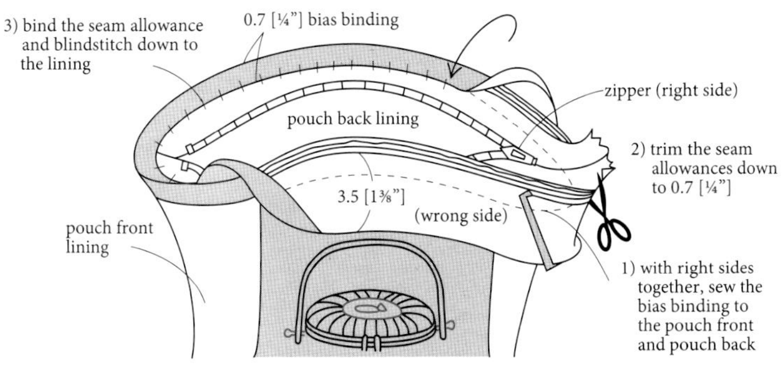

3) bind the seam allowance and blindstitch down to the lining
0.7 [¼"] bias binding
zipper (right side)
pouch back lining
2) trim the seam allowances down to 0.7 [¼"]
3.5 [1⅜"]
(wrong side)
pouch front lining
1) with right sides together, sew the bias binding to the pouch front and pouch back

Finished Pouch

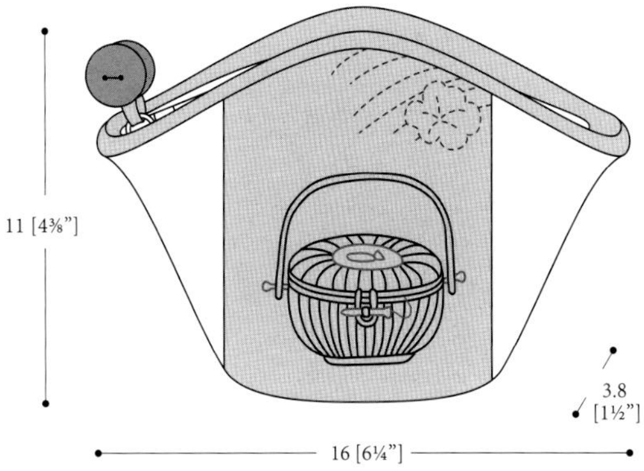

11 [4⅜"]
3.8 [1½"]
16 [6¼"]

f Wall Hanging

Shown on p. 58

Patterns used **38 ~ 41**

The full-size embroidery patterns are on pp. 51- 57; the dimensional diagrams can be found below.

► Materials Needed

Beige plaid (background)
- 110 × 30 cm [43¼" × 11¾"]

Brown plaid (border and sashing)
110 × 80 cm [43¼" × 31½"]

Backing
- 85 × 80 cm [33½" × 31½"]

Batting
- 85 × 80 cm [33½" × 31½"]

Dk brown plaid (bias binding)
- 3.5 × 300 cm [1⅜" × 118"]

Embroidery floss - dk brown

► Finished measurements

73.4 × 69.4 cm [28⅞" × 27⅜"]

► Instructions

1 Embroider the designs for each tree on the background fabrics.
2 Sew the two vertical pieces of sashing between each of the two blocks; sew the horizontal piece of sashing between the two sections to create the center square; Cut and sew on the borders to create the quilt top.
3 With wrong sides together and batting in between, baste the quilt; quilt each of the areas of the quilt as shown or as desired.
4 Bind the quilt with bias binding to finish.

► Tips

Stitch-in-the-ditch around all the embroideries and freehand quilt the background fabric in each block to give the appearance of wind currents.

Make sure that the amount of quilting is even across the entire quilt.

Cut the brown plaid on the bias for the sashing and on the straight of grain for the borders.

Dimensional Diagram

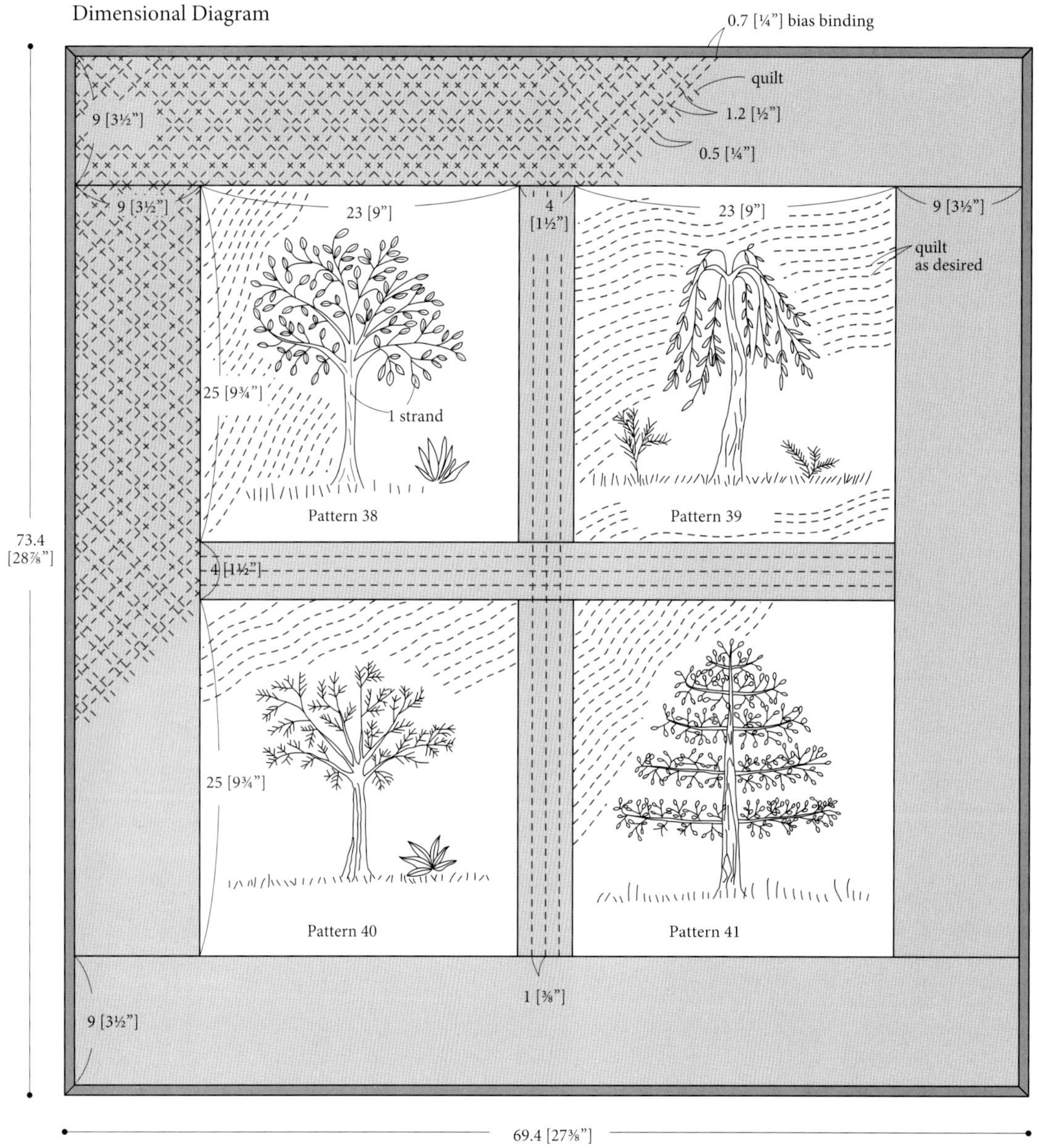

Embroidery:
See the full-size pattern for the stitch name. Use dk brown and 2 strands of floss unless otherwise specified. (pp. 51-57)

* stitch in the ditch around all pieces, appliqués and embroideries

Binding the Edges of the Wall Hanging

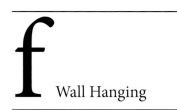

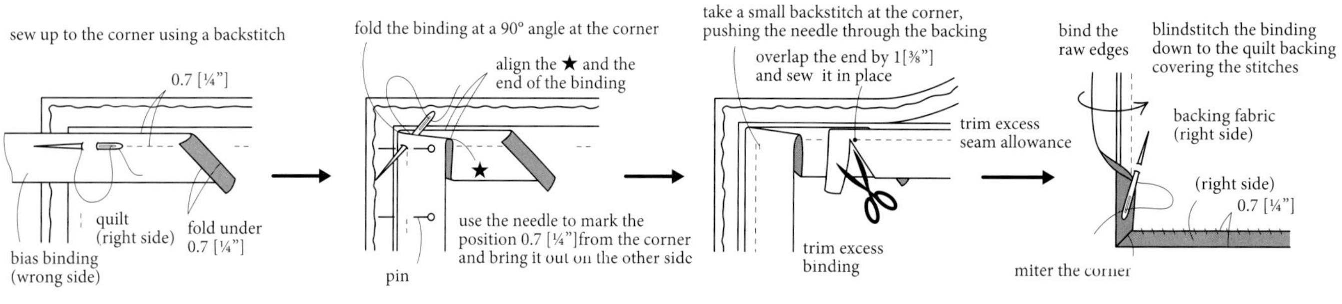

i Coin Purse

Shown on p. 79

Pattern used 54

The full-size embroidery pattern is on p. 78; the full-size templates for the purse body can be found on pattern sheet insert A.

► Materials Needed
5 Brown prints (piecing)
- 20 × 10 cm each [7⅞" × 4"]
Brown homespun (purse back)
- 20 × 20 cm [7⅞" × 7⅞"]
Lining - 40 × 25 cm [15¾" × 9¾"]
Batting - 40 × 25 cm [15¾" × 9¾"]
Dk brown plaid (bias binding)
- 3.5 × 40 cm [1⅜" × 15¾"]
Bias binding (for the zipper edges)
- 2.5 × 10 cm [1" × 4"]
1 zipper -13.5 cm [5¼"] long,
Red and green fringe
- 1.4 × 45 cm [⅝" × 17¾"]
Waxed cord (zipper pull)
- 0.1 × 10 cm [1/16" × 4"]
1 Bead - 1.2 [½"]
1 Oval bead - 2.2 [⅞"] long
Embroidery floss

► Finished measurements
See the diagrams below.

► Instructions
1 Appliqué, embroider, and piece the purse front and back.
2 With wrong sides of front and lining together and batting in between, baste and quilt the purse front.
3 Bind the top edge of the purse front.
4 With wrong sides of front and lining together and batting in between, baste and quilt the purse back. Bind the top edge of the purse back.
5 Sew the zipper to the the lining side of the purse front and purse back.
6 With right sides together and with the fringe sandwiched in between with edges aligned, sew around the edges. Trim the seam allowances down to 0.7 [¼"] except for the front lining. Bind the edges.
7 Attach the zipper decoration.

► Tip
Piece and embroider only the purse front piece. See full-size templates of the pattern sheet inserts for the embroidery on the left.

Purse Front

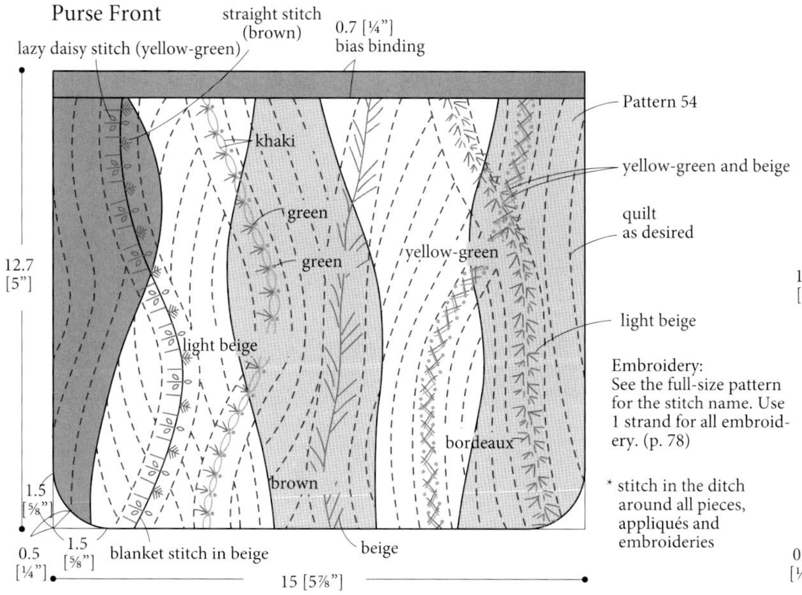

Purse Back

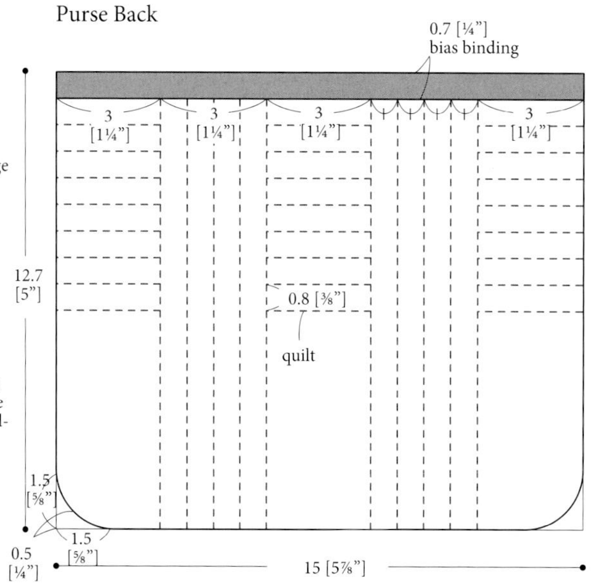

Binding the Opening

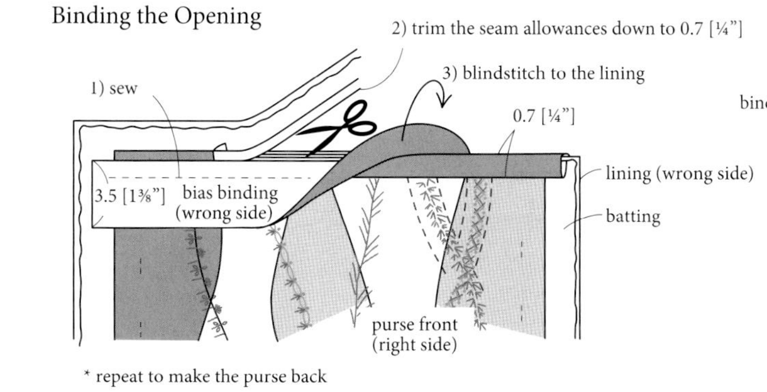

Sewing in the Zipper

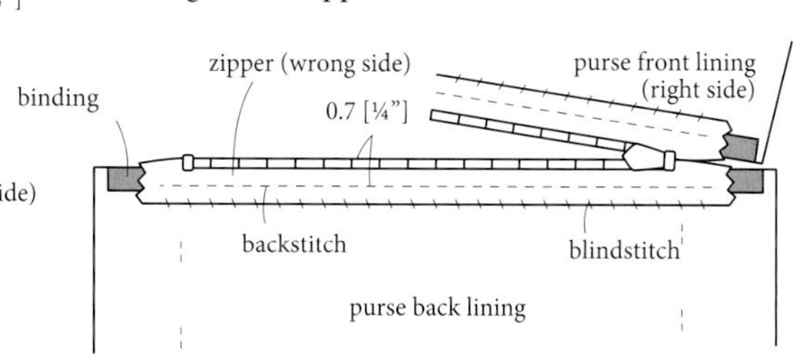

Zipper pull decoration

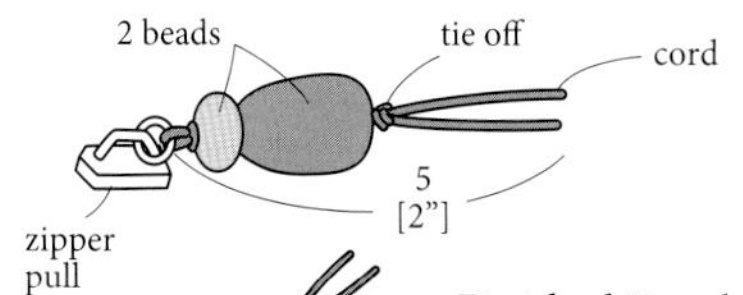

Sewing the Purse Together

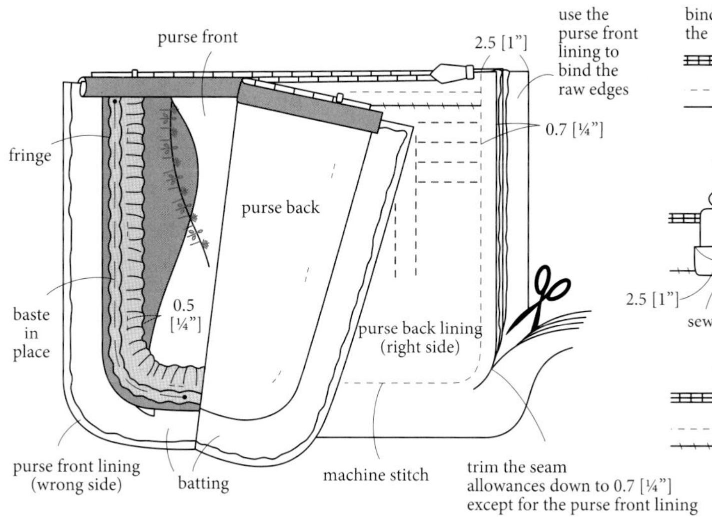

Binding the Raw Edges

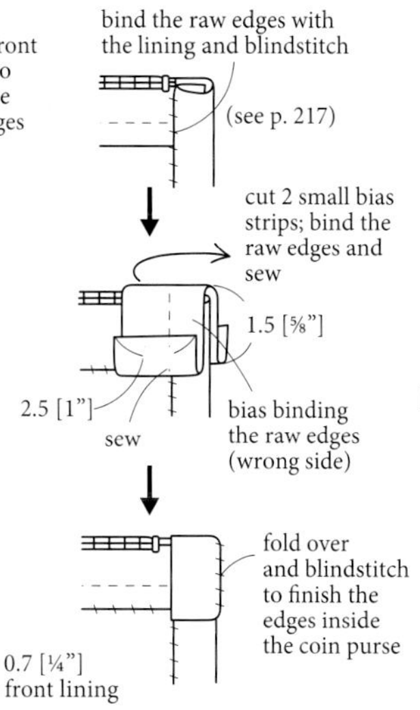

Finished Pouch

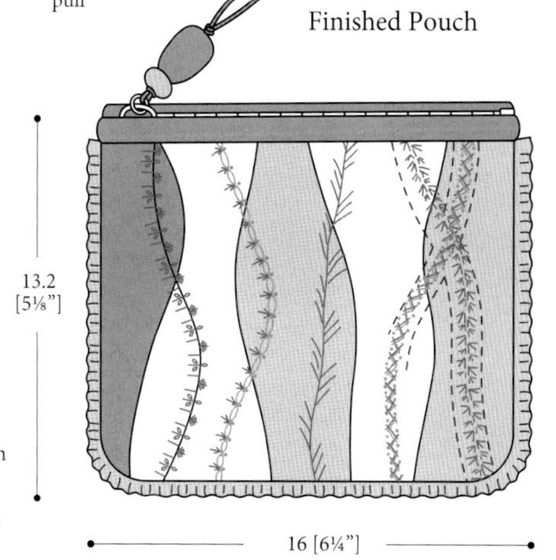

g Keepsake Box

Shown on p. 66

Pattern used 47

The full-size embroidery pattern is on p. 65; the full-size templates for the lid can be found on pattern sheet insert A.

▶ Materials Needed
Grey homespun and beige prints (frame and background)
- 20 × 20 cm [7⅞" × 7⅞"] each
Assorted fat quarters or scraps (piecing and appliqué)
Grey homespun (sides of lid)
- 35 × 25 cm [13¾" × 9¾"]
Brown homespun (box body top)
- 40 × 40 cm [15¾" × 15¾"]
Lining
- 40 × 80 cm [15¾" × 31½"]
Muslin (facing)
- 40 × 80 cm [15¾" × 31½"]
Batting
- 40 × 80 cm [15¾" × 31½"]
Linen trim
-1.5 × 80 cm [⅝" × 31½"]
Clear template plastic
Embroidery floss

▶ Finished measurements
See the diagrams below.

▶ Instructions
1 Piece, appliqué and embroider the design for the top of the lid. With right sides together, sew the sides of the lid to the center piece.
2 With wrong sides together, layer the lid top and facing with batting in between; baste; quilt.
3 Sew the trim around the side of the lid as shown. With right sides together, sew the quilted top and lining together at the "v's" of each corner of the sides referring to the diagram.
4 Turn right side out and machine stitch on the three sides where they meet the center of the lid.
5 Insert the template plastic pieces in the center of the lid; sew the remaining side to secure the piece.
6 Insert the template plastic pieces in each of the four sides; turn the seam allowances of the openings under and blindstitch closed.
7 Fold each of the four sides up to form a box; blindstitch at each corner side seam to secure.
8 Make the box body in the same way as the lid.

▶ Tip
Use a curved needle when sewing the sides of the box and lid together.

Embroidery:
See the full-size pattern for the stitch name and number of strands needed. (p. 65)

* Stitch in the ditch around all pieces, appliqués and embroideries

Box Lid

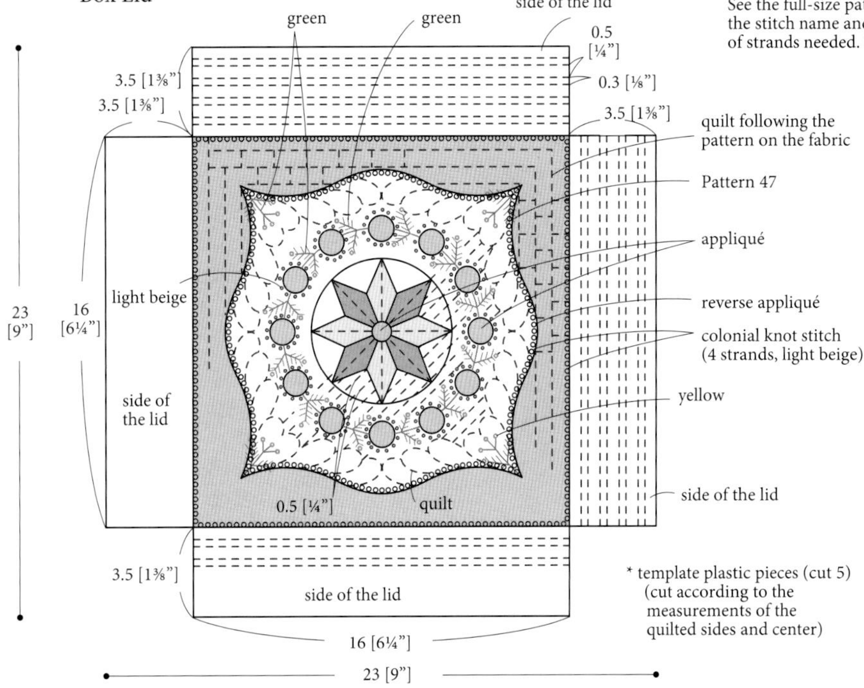

green
green
side of the lid
0.5 [¼"]
0.3 [⅛"]
3.5 [1⅜"]
3.5 [1⅜"]
3.5 [1⅜"]
quilt following the pattern on the fabric
Pattern 47
appliqué
reverse appliqué
colonial knot stitch (4 strands, light beige)
yellow
light beige
23 [9"]
16 [6¼"]
side of the lid
0.5 [¼"]
quilt
side of the lid
3.5 [1⅜"]
side of the lid
16 [6¼"]
23 [9"]
* template plastic pieces (cut 5) (cut according to the measurements of the quilted sides and center)

Making the Lid

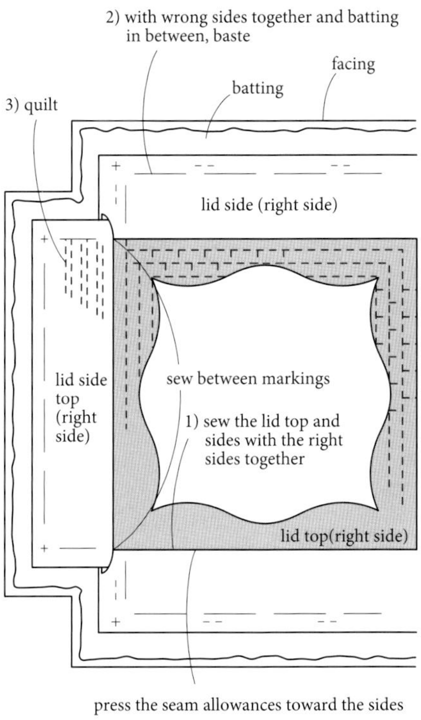

2) with wrong sides together and batting in between, baste
facing
batting
3) quilt
lid side (right side)
lid side top (right side)
sew between markings
1) sew the lid top and sides with the right sides together
lid top(right side)
press the seam allowances toward the sides

Box Body

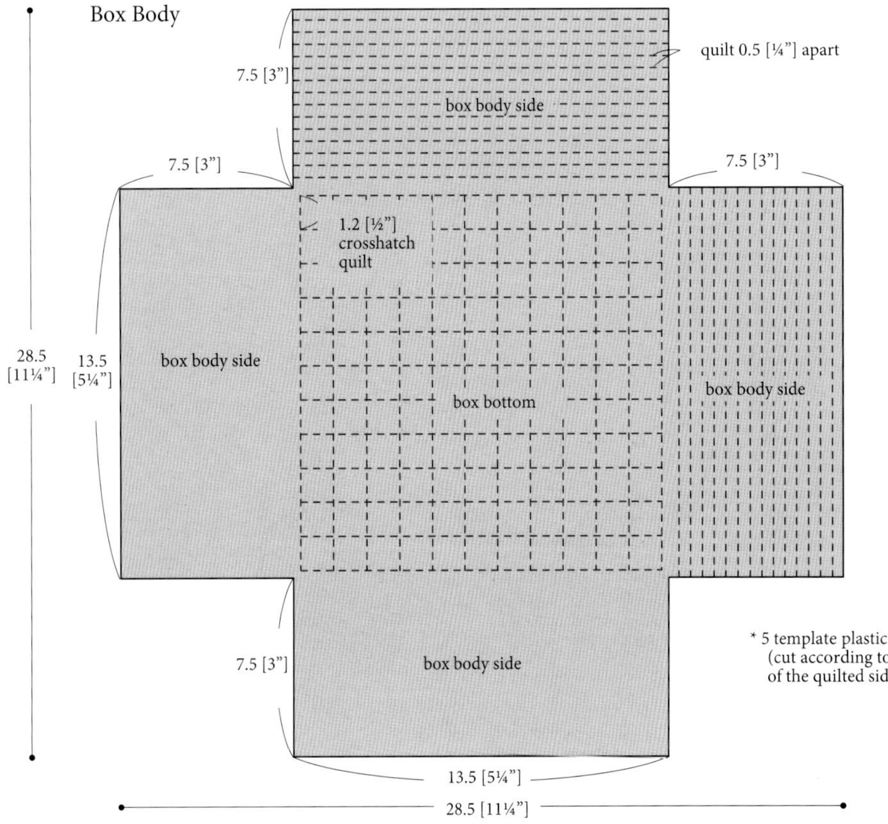

quilt 0.5 [¼"] apart
7.5 [3"]
box body side
7.5 [3"]
7.5 [3"]
1.2 [½"] crosshatch quilt
28.5 [11¼"]
13.5 [5¼"]
box body side
box bottom
box body side
7.5 [3"]
box body side
13.5 [5¼"]
28.5 [11¼"]

* 5 template plastic pieces (cut according to the measurements of the quilted sides and center box bottom)

Sewing the Trim to the Sides of the Lid

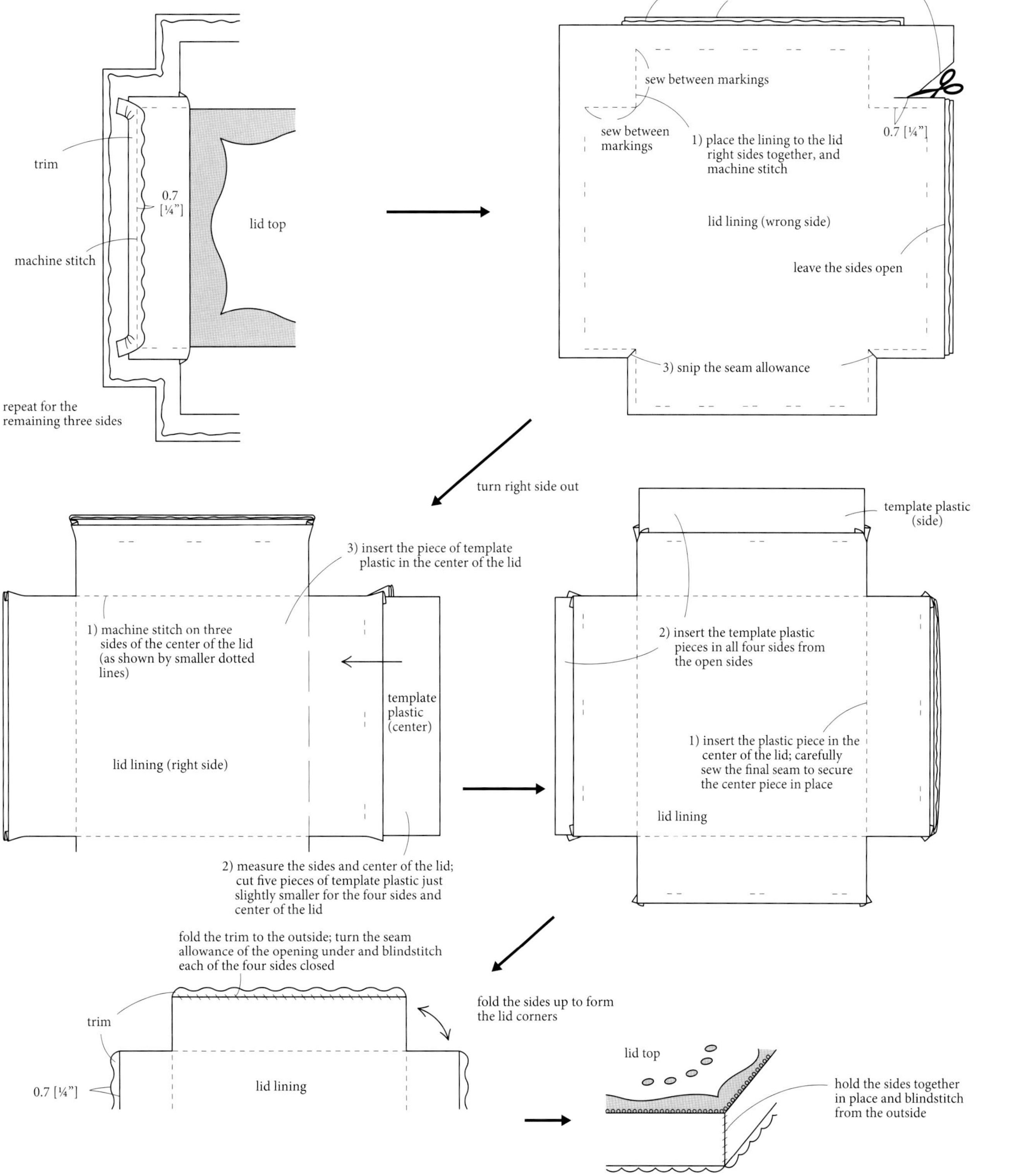

batting
facing
2) trim the seam allowances down to 0.7 [¼"]
trim
0.7 [¼"]
lid top
machine stitch
repeat for the remaining three sides
sew between markings
sew between markings
1) place the lining to the lid right sides together, and machine stitch
0.7 [¼"]
lid lining (wrong side)
leave the sides open
3) snip the seam allowance
turn right side out
3) insert the piece of template plastic in the center of the lid
1) machine stitch on three sides of the center of the lid (as shown by smaller dotted lines)
template plastic (center)
lid lining (right side)
2) measure the sides and center of the lid; cut five pieces of template plastic just slightly smaller for the four sides and center of the lid
template plastic (side)
2) insert the template plastic pieces in all four sides from the open sides
1) insert the plastic piece in the center of the lid; carefully sew the final seam to secure the center piece in place
lid lining
fold the trim to the outside; turn the seam allowance of the opening under and blindstitch each of the four sides closed
trim
0.7 [¼"]
lid lining
fold the sides up to form the lid corners
lid top
hold the sides together in place and blindstitch from the outside

Putting the Box Together

make the box body in the same way as the lid (without the facing as you will not have the extra appliqué/embroidery for the box body)

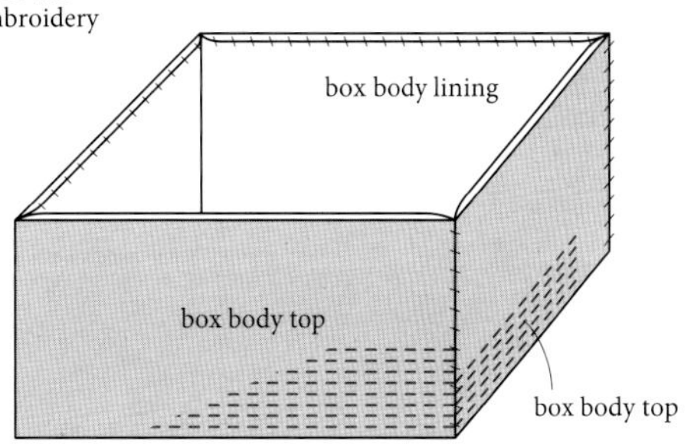

box body lining
box body top
box body top

Finished Box

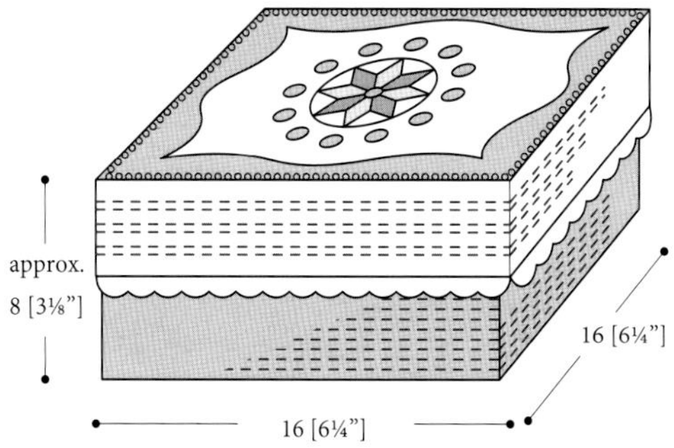

approx. 8 [3⅛"]
16 [6¼"]
16 [6¼"]

h Round Keepsake Box

Shown on p. 71

Pattern used 51

The full-size embroidery pattern is on p. 73.

▶ Materials Needed
Lt brown print (lid)
- 25×25 cm [9¾" ×9¾"]
Green print scraps (appliqué)
Lt brown homespun (lid side)
- 7×60 cm [2¾" ×23⅝"]
Brown faux wood print (box side, side lining, inside bottom)
- 40×90 cm [15¾" ×35⅜"]
Brown homespun (outer bottom)
- 20×20 cm [7⅞" ×7⅞"]
Dk brown faux wood print (opening bias binding)
- 7×55 cm [2¾" ×21⅝"]
Lining (lid and band)
- 30 × 60 cm [11¾" ×23⅝"]
Muslin (facing)
- 110 × 30 cm [43¼" ×11¾"]
Batting - 110×50 cm [43¼" ×19¾"]
Lt brown homespun (binding)
- 3.8×60 cm [1½" ×23⅝"]
Brown homespun (bias for piping)
- 2.5×60 cm [1" ×23⅝"]
Cord (for piping)
- 0.3 ×60 cm [⅛" ×23⅝"] long
Fusible interfacing
- 30×60 cm [11¾" ×23⅝"]
Clear template plastic
1 bead - 0.7 cm [¼"] diameter
1 bead - 2.5 cm [1"] diameter
1 button - 2 cm [¾"] diameter
Embroidery floss

▶ Finished measurements
See the diagrams below.

▶ Instructions
1 Piece, appliqué and embroider the top of the lid. With wrong sides together and batting in between, baste; quilt.
2 Sew the quilted band (or side) of the lid and the lining fused with interfacing into two cylinder shapes; with wrong sides together, adhere them to each other with spray adhesive.
3 With right sides together, sew the lid and lid band together with the piping cord sandwiched in between. Insert the template plastic; blindstitch and bind the edges. Attach the lid pull using the beads and a button.
4 Following the directions on the facing page, make the box bottom sides (16 pieces) and bottom. Secure the 16 pieces with the bias binding for the inside opening.
5 Finish the box bottom as shown on the following page.

Box Lid (cut lining to the same dimensions)

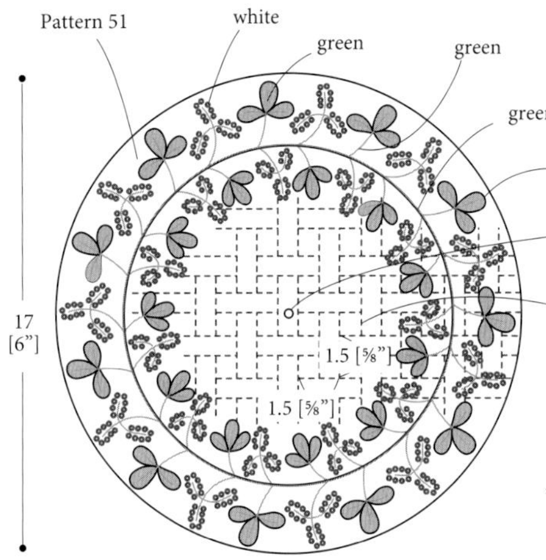

* 1 piece of template plastic - 16.5 cm [6½"] diameter

Side Pieces for the Box
(top and lining fabric - 16 pieces each)

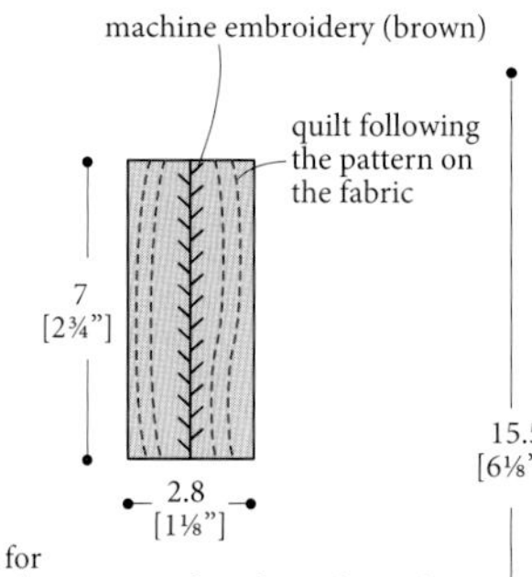

* template plastic (cut 16)
7.5 × 2.6 [3" × 1"]

Box Bottom (outer and inside lining)

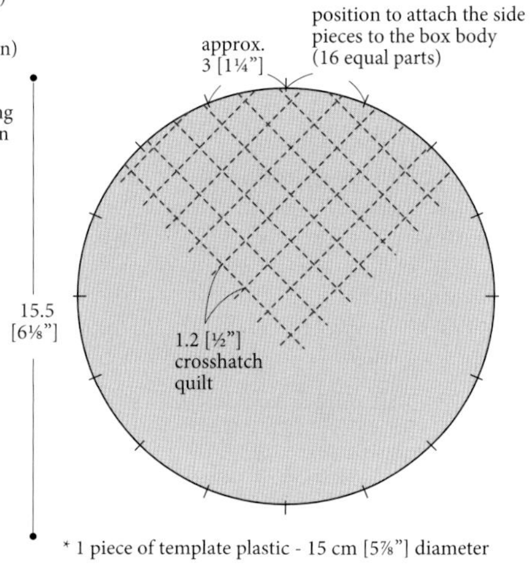

* 1 piece of template plastic - 15 cm [5⅞"] diameter

Lid Band (cut lining to the same dimensions)

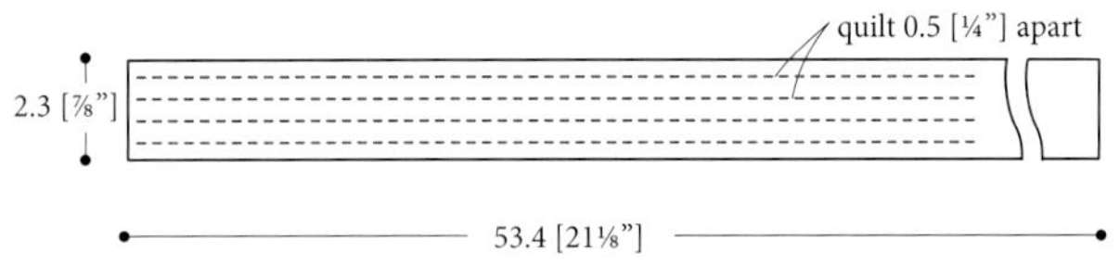

Bias Binding for the Inside of the Opening (for top of box sides)

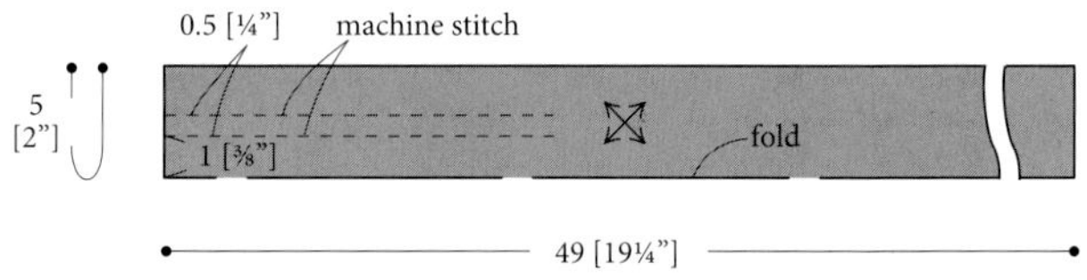

Making the Piping Cord

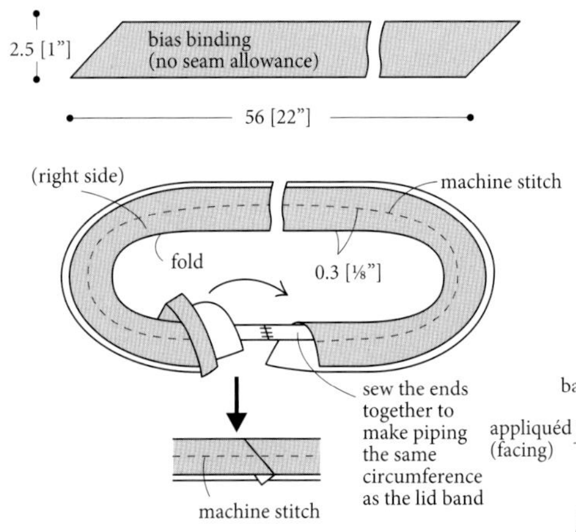

Making the Lid Band (side)

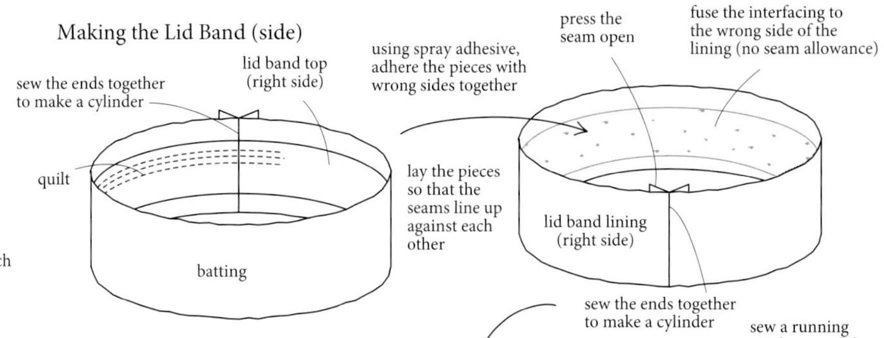

Sewing the Lid Together

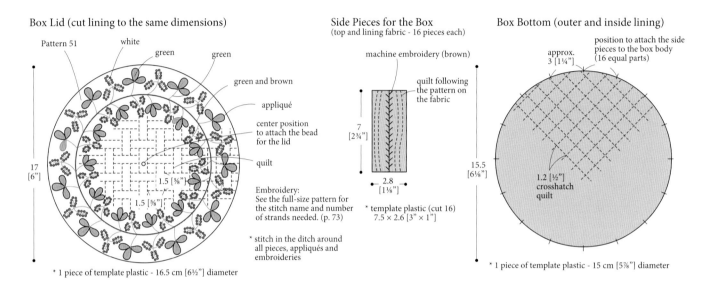

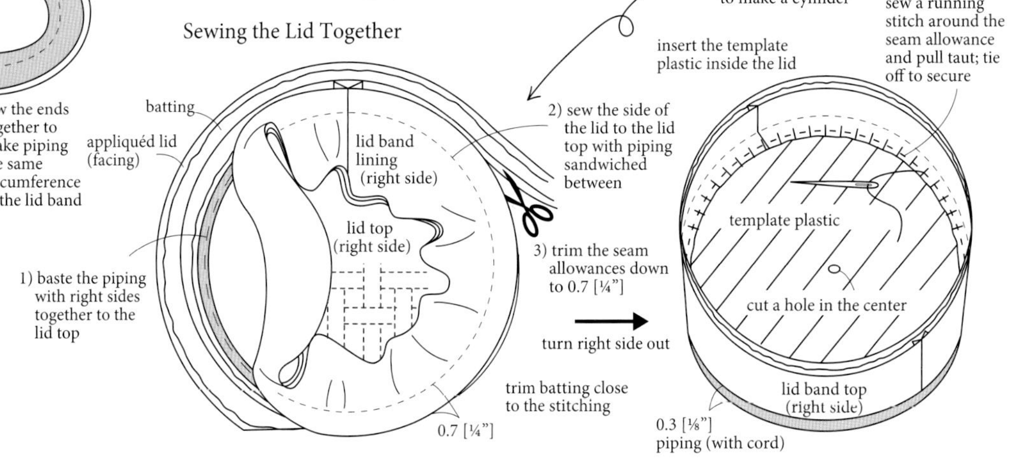

Making the Lining for the Lid

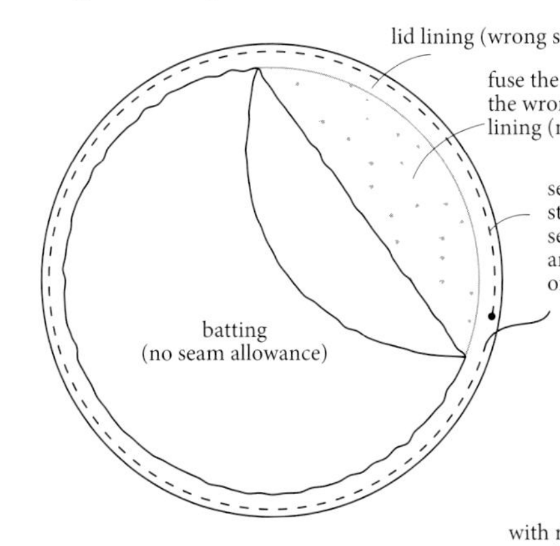
lid lining (wrong side)
fuse the interfacing to the wrong side of the lining (no seam allowance)
sew a running stitch around the seam allowance and pull taut; tie off to secure
batting (no seam allowance)

Finishing the Lid

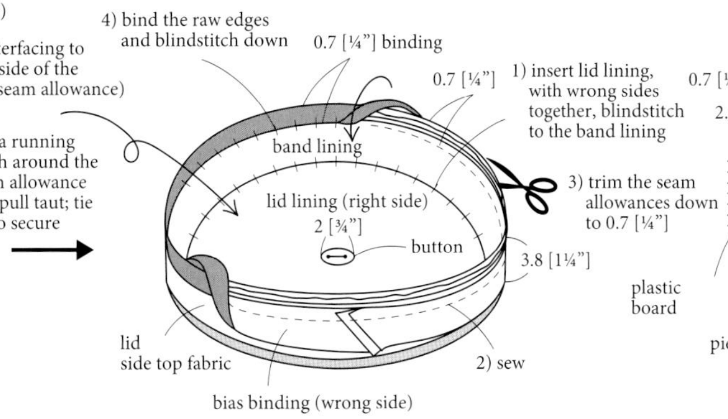
4) bind the raw edges and blindstitch down
0.7 [¼"] binding
0.7 [¼"]
1) insert lid lining, with wrong sides together, blindstitch to the band lining
band lining
lid lining (right side)
3) trim the seam allowances down to 0.7 [¼"]
2 [¾"]
button
3.8 [1¼"]
lid side top fabric
2) sew
bias binding (wrong side)

Attaching the Lid Pull

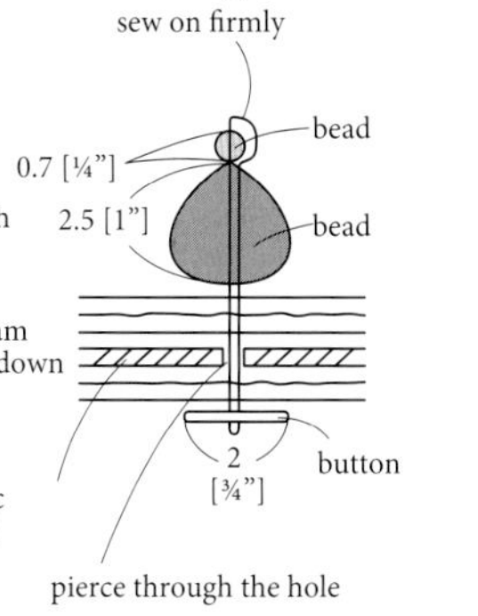
sew on firmly
bead
0.7 [¼"]
2.5 [1"]
bead
plastic board
2 [¾"]
button
pierce through the hole

Making the Sides of the Box

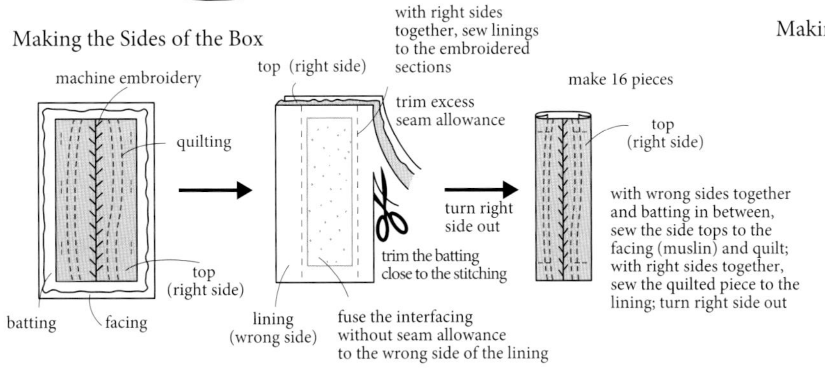
machine embroidery
quilting
top (right side)
batting
facing
top (right side)
with right sides together, sew linings to the embroidered sections
trim excess seam allowance
trim the batting close to the stitching
turn right side out
lining (wrong side)
fuse the interfacing without seam allowance to the wrong side of the lining
make 16 pieces
top (right side)
with wrong sides together and batting in between, sew the side tops to the facing (muslin) and quilt; with right sides together, sew the quilted piece to the lining; turn right side out

Making the Outer Box Bottom

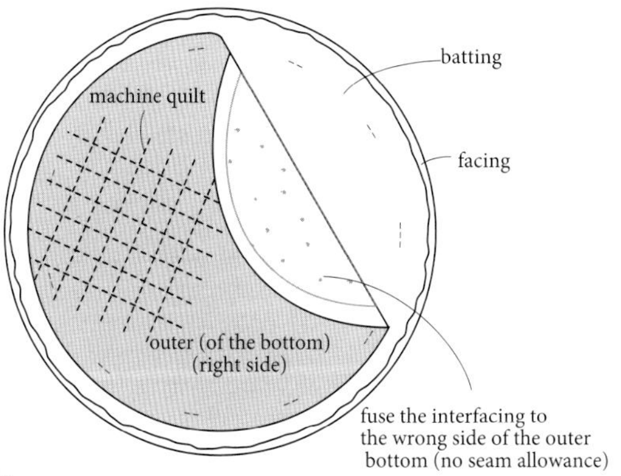
batting
machine quilt
facing
outer (of the bottom) (right side)
fuse the interfacing to the wrong side of the outer bottom (no seam allowance)

Sewing the Box Bottom Together

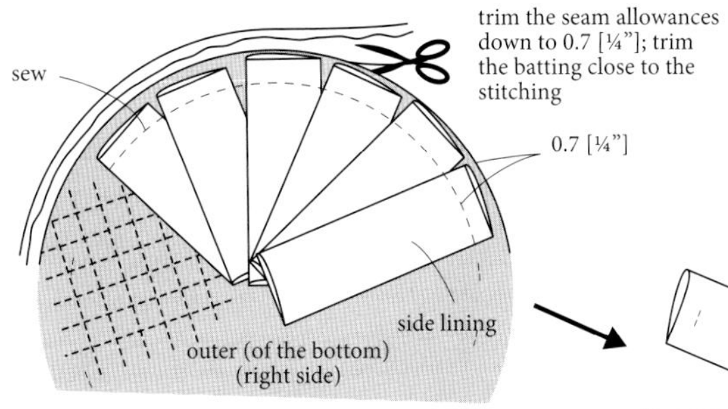
sew
trim the seam allowances down to 0.7 [¼"]; trim the batting close to the stitching
0.7 [¼"]
side lining
outer (of the bottom) (right side)

Inserting the Template Plastic

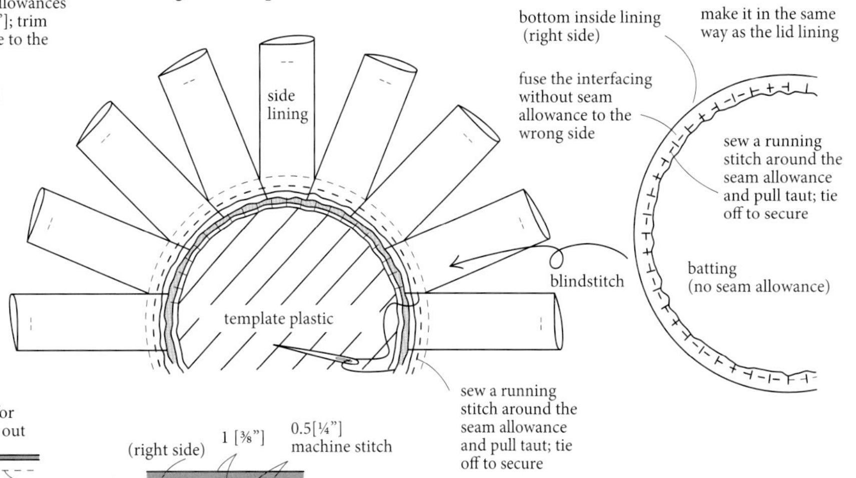
side lining
template plastic
blindstitch
sew a running stitch around the seam allowance and pull taut; tie off to secure
bottom inside lining (right side)
make it in the same way as the lid lining
fuse the interfacing without seam allowance to the wrong side
sew a running stitch around the seam allowance and pull taut; tie off to secure
batting (no seam allowance)

Making the Bias Binding for the Lid Opening

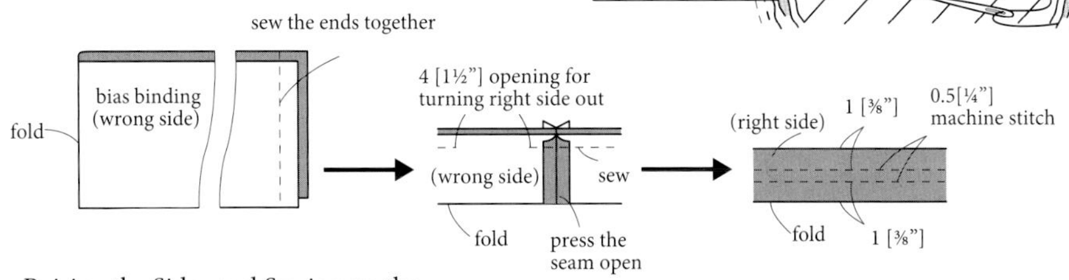
sew the ends together
bias binding (wrong side)
fold
4 [1½"] opening for turning right side out
(wrong side)
sew
fold
press the seam open
(right side)
1 [⅜"]
0.5[¼"] machine stitch
fold
1 [⅜"]

Raising the Sides and Sewing on the Bias Binding for the Inside Opening

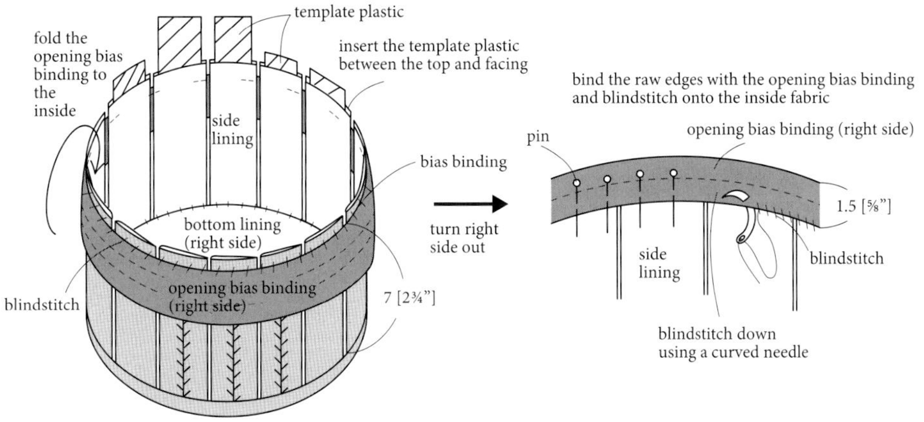
template plastic
fold the opening bias binding to the inside
insert the template plastic between the top and facing
side lining
bias binding
bottom lining (right side)
opening bias binding (right side)
blindstitch
7 [2¾"]
turn right side out
bind the raw edges with the opening bias binding and blindstitch onto the inside fabric
pin
opening bias binding (right side)
1.5 [⅝"]
side lining
blindstitch
blindstitch down using a curved needle

Finished Box

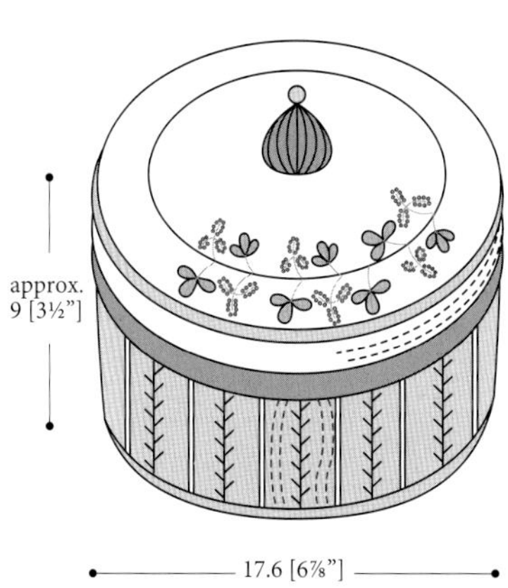
approx. 9 [3½"]
17.6 [6⅞"]

j Shoulder Bag

Shown on p. 82

Pattern used 56

The full-size embroidery pattern is on p. 81.

► Materials Needed
Grey homespun (squares for piecing, appliqué)
-30 × 45 cm [11¾" × 17¾"]
Beige stripes (squares for piecing)
- 30 × 30 cm[11¾" × 11¾"]
Assorted scraps (circle appliqué)
Beige stripes (bag body, gusset)
- 70 × 40 cm [27½" × 15¾"]
Grey homespun (facing, tabs)
- 30 × 10 cm [11¾" × 4"]
Lining- 90 × 50 cm [35⅜" × 19¾"]
Batting - 90 × 50 cm [35⅜" × 19¾"]
Grey homespun (bias binding)
- 3.5 × 120 cm [1⅜" × 47¼"]
Interfacing - 65 × 10 cm [25⅝" × 4"]
Magnetic closure - 1.6 cm [⅝"]
2 D-rings - 2.3 cm [1"] inside diameter
1 Shoulder strap - 1.5 cm [⅝"]wide
Embroidery floss

► Finished measurements
See the diagrams below.

► Instructions
1 Piece, appliqué and embroider the flap top.
2 With wrong sides together and batting in between, baste; quilt the bag flap top and lining; bind three sides (measure the sides after quilting and finish them at the dimensions in parenthesis).
3 With wrong sides together and batting in between, baste and quilt the bag body front and lining; repeat for the bag body back.
4 With right sides together, pin the flap to the bag body back in position, sew; cover with the facing fabric and topstitch as shown.
5 With wrong sides together and batting in between, baste and machine quilt the gusset.
6 Make the tabs and sew them to the gusset in position shown.
7 Sew the body and gusset with the right sides together and bind the raw edges. Turn right side out.
8 Bind the bag opening.
9 Cover the magnetic closure with fabric and sew it to the lining of the flap and the front of the bag body.
10 Attach the store-bought shoulder strap to the D-rings to finish.

Shoulder Bag Flap

* ( ) are the dimensions after quilting. Remeasure the piece after quilting and redraw the finished line using the measurements in ( ).

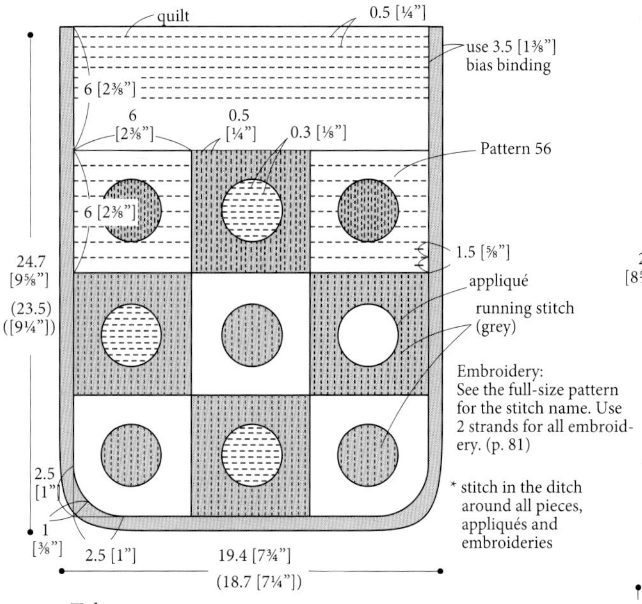

Bag Body (2 pieces)

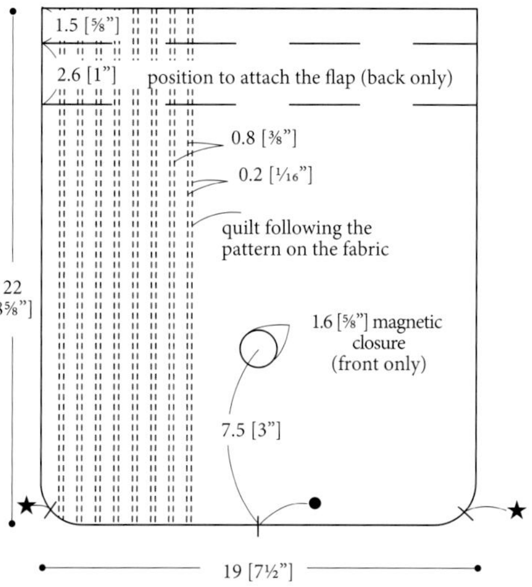

Gusset

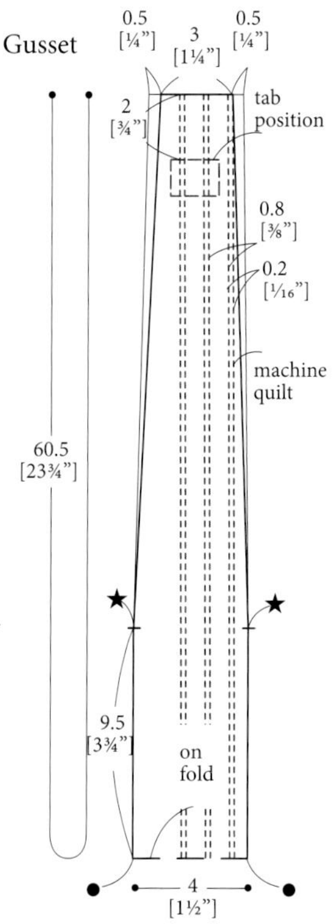

Facing for Sewing the Flap to the Bag Body

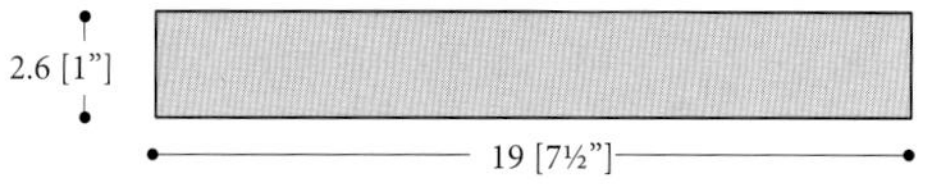

Tabs
(top and lining - 2 each)

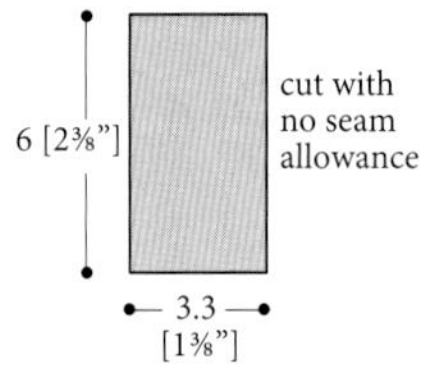

Making the Tabs

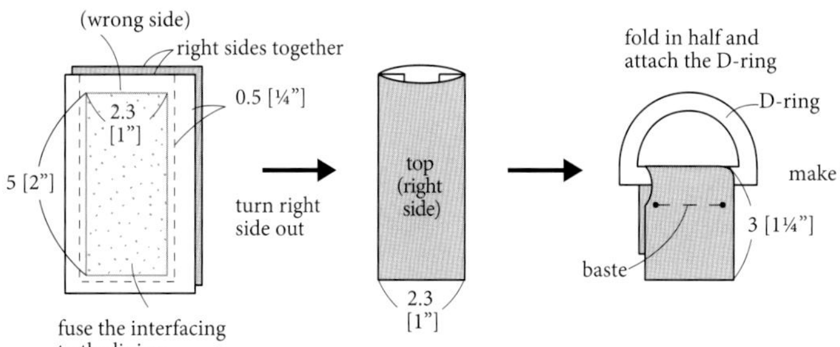

Making the Flap

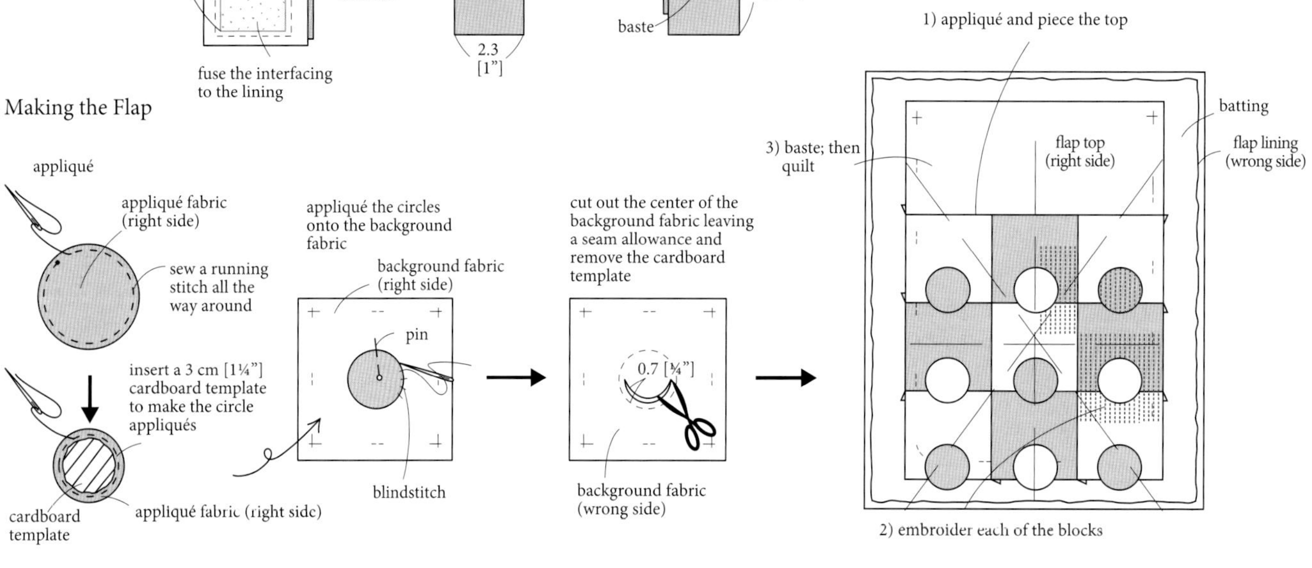

Binding the Flap

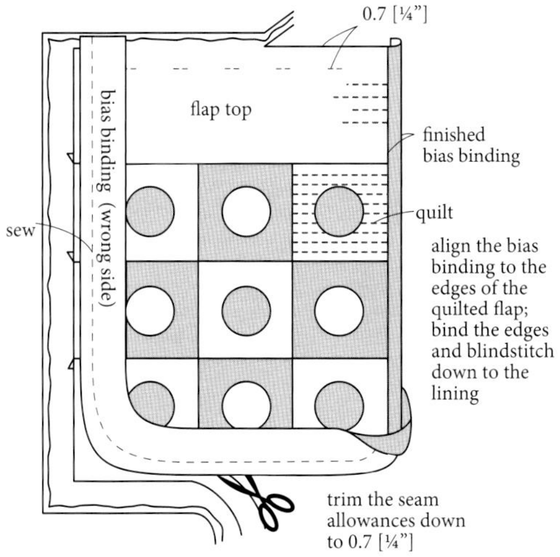
0.7 [¼”]
flap top
bias binding (wrong side)
finished bias binding
quilt
sew
align the bias binding to the edges of the quilted flap; bind the edges and blindstitch down to the lining
trim the seam allowances down to 0.7 [¼”]

Making the Bag Body

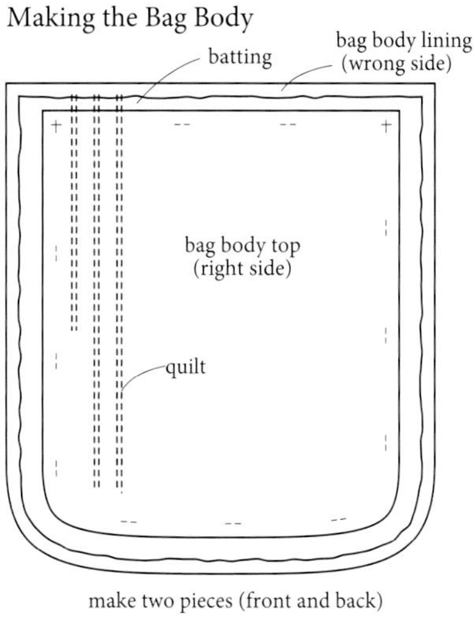
batting
bag body lining (wrong side)
bag body top (right side)
quilt
make two pieces (front and back)

Sewing the Bag Back Body and Flap Together

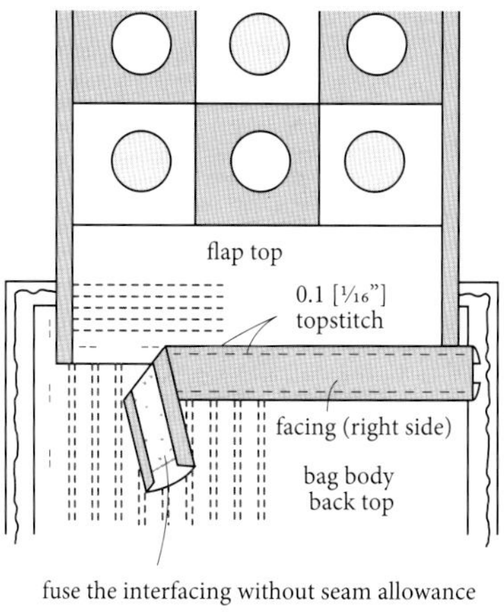
flap top
0.1 [1⁄16”] topstitch
facing (right side)
bag body back top
fuse the interfacing without seam allowance

Making the Gusset

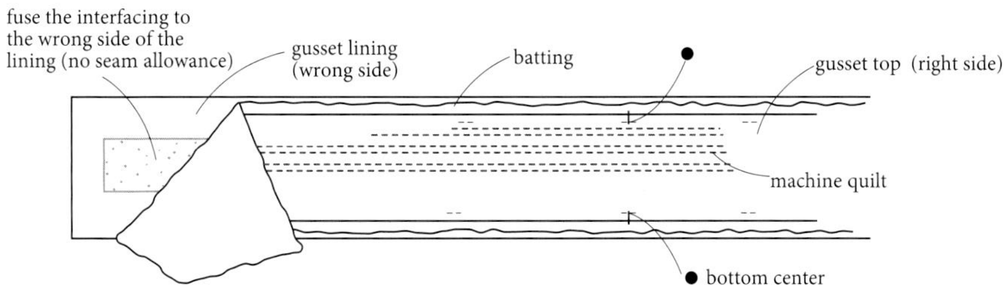
fuse the interfacing to the wrong side of the lining (no seam allowance)
gusset lining (wrong side)
batting
gusset top (right side)
machine quilt
bottom center

Attaching the Tab to the Gusset

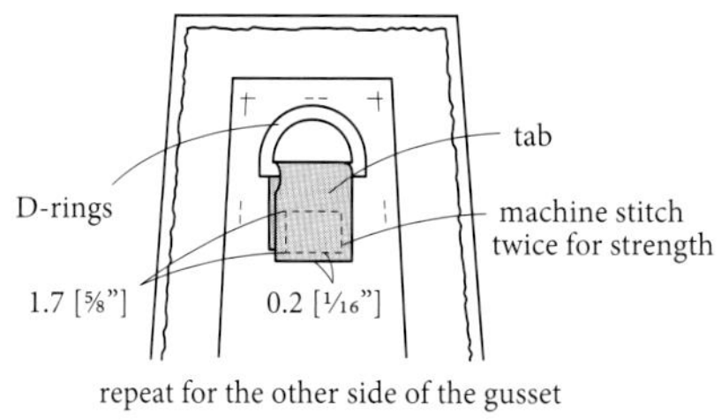
D-rings
tab
machine stitch twice for strength
1.7 [⅝”]
0.2 [1⁄16”]
repeat for the other side of the gusset

Sewing the Bag Body and Gusset Together

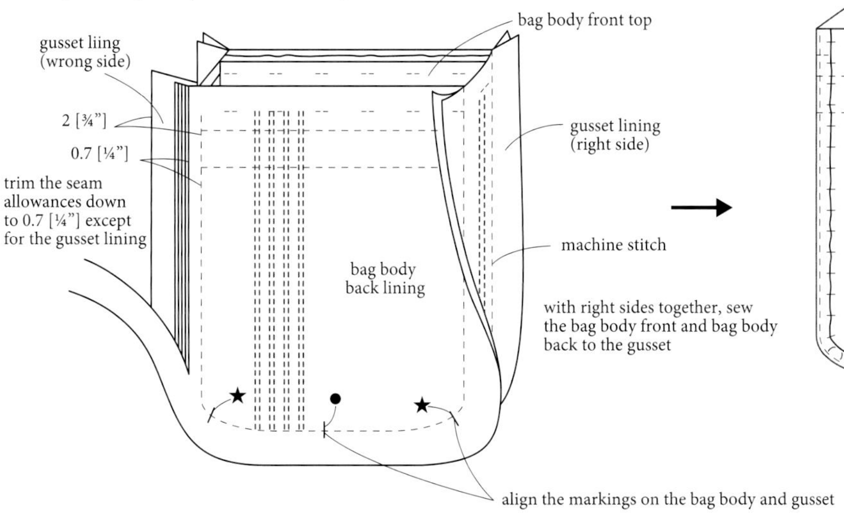
gusset liing (wrong side)
bag body front top
2 [¾”]
0.7 [¼”]
trim the seam allowances down to 0.7 [¼”] except for the gusset lining
gusset lining (right side)
machine stitch
bag body back lining
with right sides together, sew the bag body front and bag body back to the gusset
align the markings on the bag body and gusset

Binding the Raw Edges

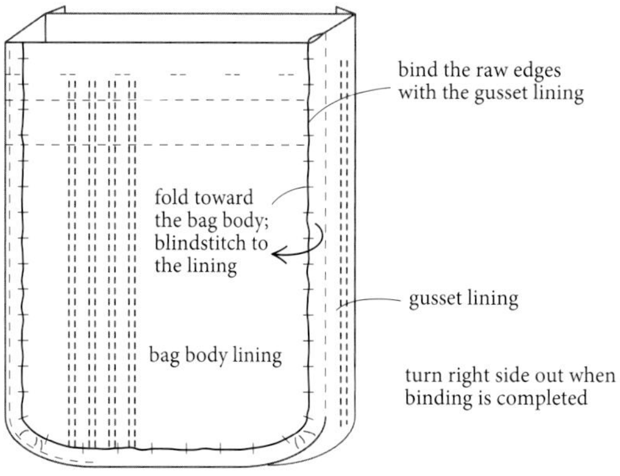
bind the raw edges with the gusset lining
fold toward the bag body; blindstitch to the lining
gusset lining
bag body lining
turn right side out when binding is completed

Finished Bag

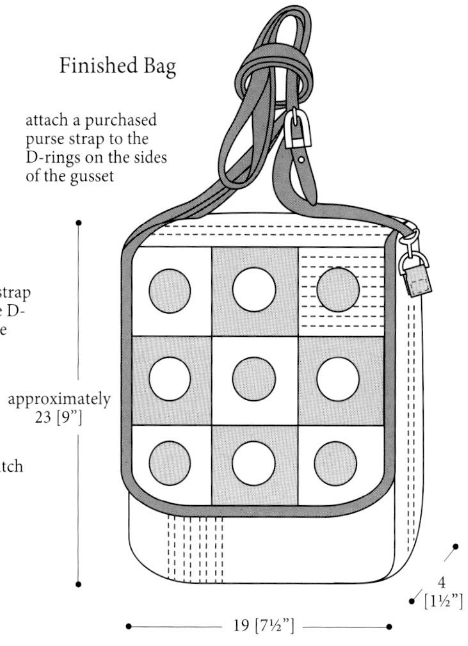
attach a purchased purse strap to the D-rings on the sides of the gusset
approximately 23 [9”]
4 [1½”]
19 [7½”]

Binding the Bag Opening

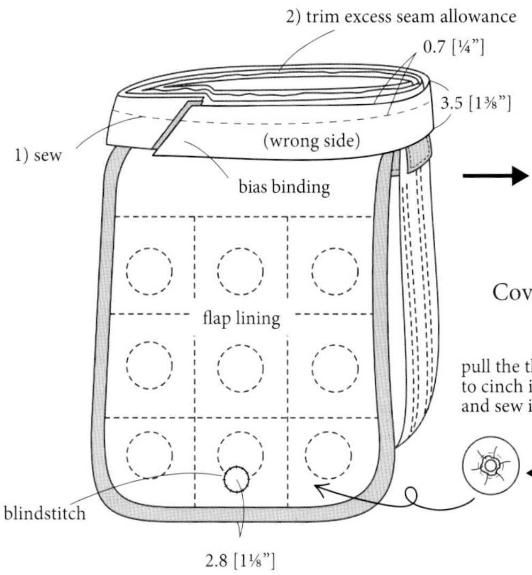
2) trim excess seam allowance
0.7 [¼”]
3.5 [1⅜”]
1) sew
(wrong side)
bias binding
flap lining
blindstitch
2.8 [1⅛”]

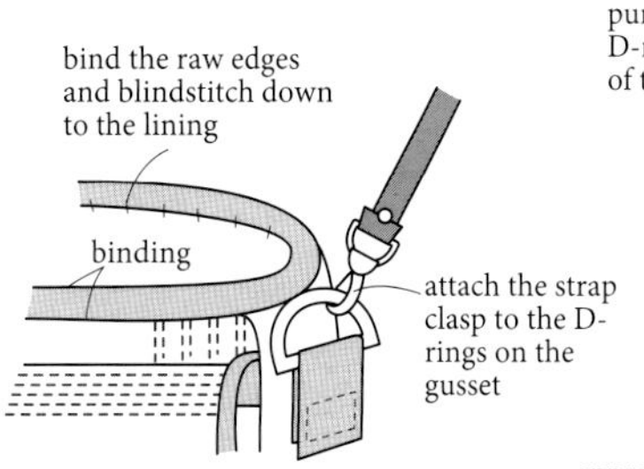
bind the raw edges and blindstitch down to the lining
binding
attach the strap clasp to the D-rings on the gusset

Covering the Magnetic Closure

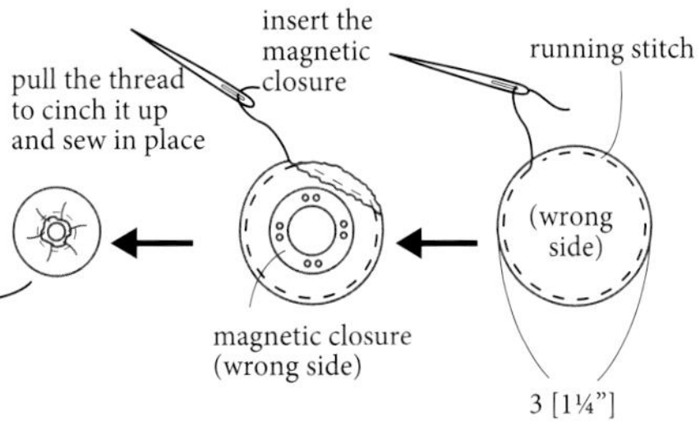
pull the thread to cinch it up and sew in place
insert the magnetic closure
running stitch
(wrong side)
magnetic closure (wrong side)
3 [1¼”]

k Handbag

Shown on p. 90

Patterns used **62 + 102**

The full-size embroidery pattern is on p. 89 and p. 134.

▸ Materials Needed
Lt brown homespun (bag body)
- 30 × 80 cm [11¾" × 31½"]
Grey homespun (bag opening, facing, handle strips)
- 30 × 50 cm [11¾" × 19¾"]
Grey print (bag opening)
- 10 × 50 cm [4" × 19¾"]
Bag lining
- 25 × 70 cm [9¾" × 27½"]
Batting
- 50 × 80 cm [19¾" × 31½"]
Bias binding
- 2.5 × 50 cm [1" × 19¾"]
Interfacing
- 10 × 45 cm [4" × 17¾"]
1 Metal purse handle
- 12 cm [4¾"] inside diameter
Perle cotton (grey)
Embroidery floss

▸ Finished measurements
See the diagrams below.

▸ Instructions
1 With wrong sides together and batting in between, quilt and embroider the bag body front, leaving the embroideries on the side seam area unstitched. Repeat for the bag body back.
2 With right sides together, sew the side seams. Finish the embroidery at the seams. Sew bottom gussets.
3 Make the bag lining and insert it inside the bag body with wrong sides together. Take tucks along the bag opening and baste to temporarily keep them in place.
4 Appliqué and embroider the top fabric for bag opening. Layer against the batting; quilt. With right sides together, fold in half and sew the ends to make a cylinder.
5 Fuse the interfacing to the facing; with right sides together, fold in half and sew the ends to make a cylinder.
6 With right sides together and bag body opening sandwiched in between, align the bag opening and facing; sew.
7 Make the handle strips and baste them in place. Bind the raw edges of the bag opening with the bias binding.
8 Sew in the handles

▸ Tips
Make sure that the seams at the center of the wave pattern appliqué meet when sewing together at the sides.

Bag Opening (cut the facing to the same dimensions - cut on the bias)

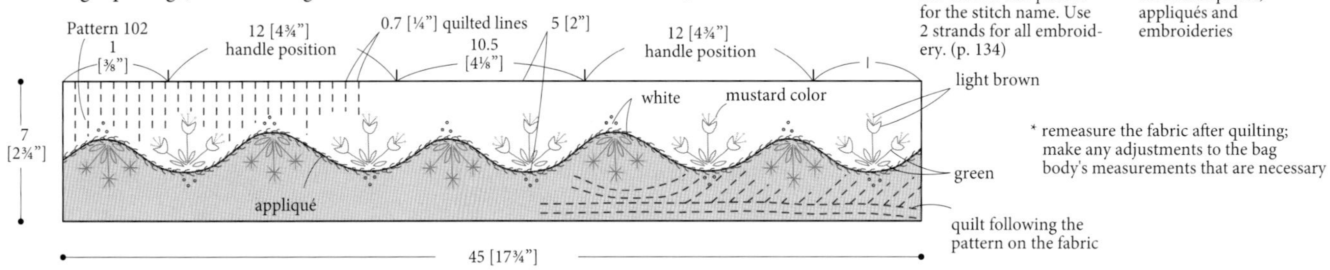
Embroidery:
See the full-size pattern for the stitch name. Use 2 strands for all embroidery. (p. 134)
* stitch in the ditch around all pieces, appliqués and embroideries
Pattern 102
1 [⅜"]
12 [4¾"] handle position
0.7 [¼"] quilted lines
10.5 [4⅛"]
5 [2"]
12 [4¾"] handle position
white
mustard color
light brown
7 [2¾"]
* remeasure the fabric after quilting; make any adjustments to the bag body's measurements that are necessary
green
appliqué
quilt following the pattern on the fabric
45 [17¾"]

Bag Body (bag lining is the same dimension - 2 pieces each)

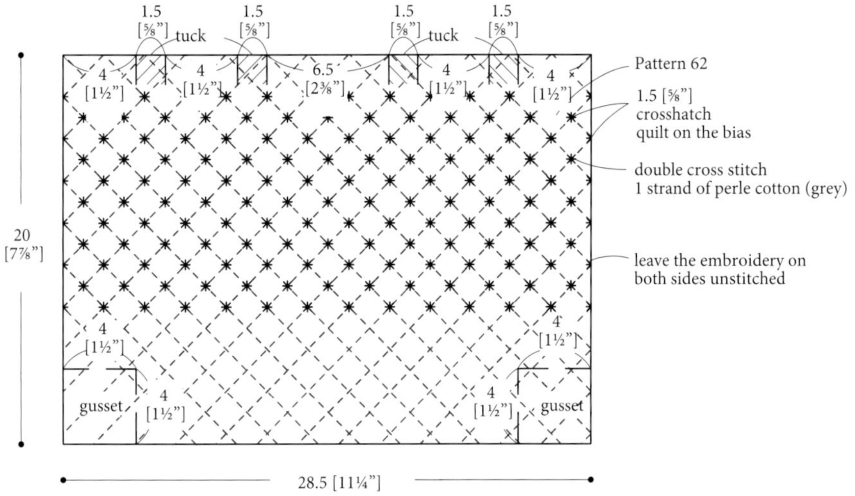
1.5 [⅝"]
tuck
1.5 [⅝"]
1.5 [⅝"]
tuck
1.5 [⅝"]
4 [1½"]
4 [1½"]
6.5 [2⅝"]
4 [1½"]
4 [1½"]
Pattern 62
1.5 [⅝"] crosshatch quilt on the bias
double cross stitch
1 strand of perle cotton (grey)
20 [7⅞"]
leave the embroidery on both sides unstitched
4 [1½"]
4 [1½"]
gusset
4 [1½"]
4 [1½"]
gusset
28.5 [11¼"]

Fabric Strips for Attaching the Handles (2 pieces)

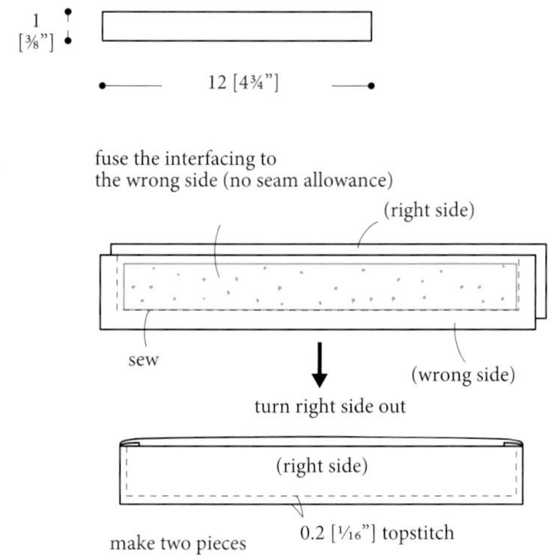
1 [⅜"]
12 [4¾"]
fuse the interfacing to the wrong side (no seam allowance)
(right side)
sew
(wrong side)
turn right side out
(right side)
make two pieces
0.2 [1⁄16"] topstitch

Making the Bag Body

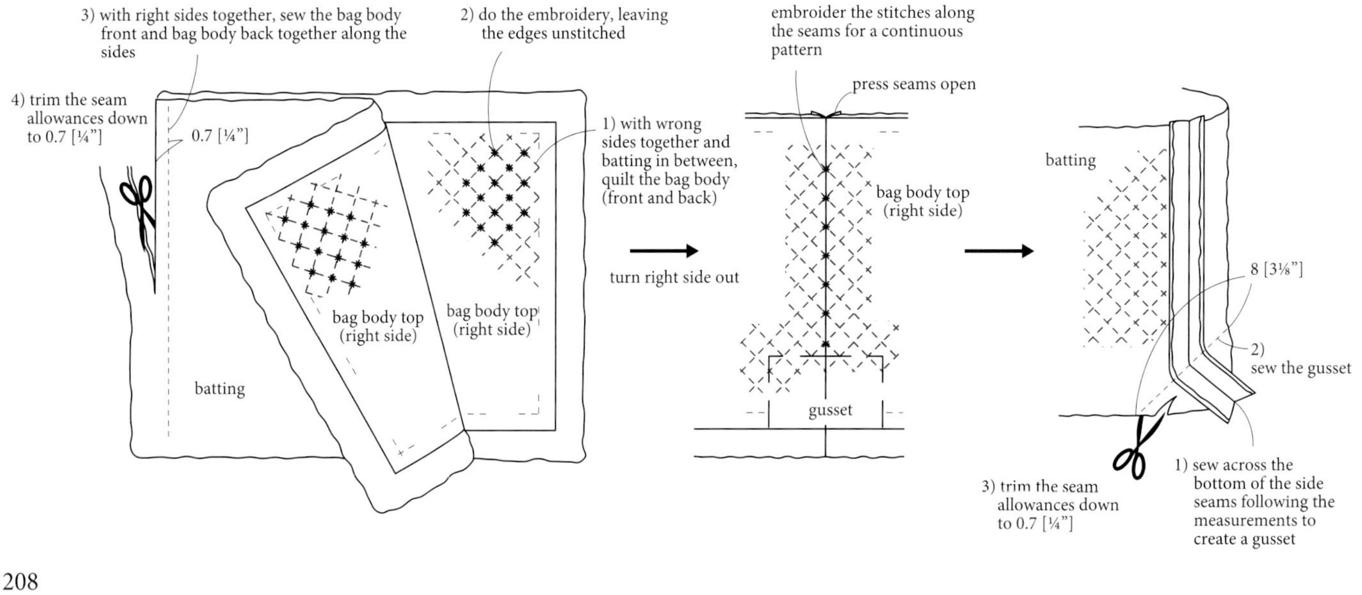
3) with right sides together, sew the bag body front and bag body back together along the sides
2) do the embroidery, leaving the edges unstitched
embroider the stitches along the seams for a continuous pattern
press seams open
4) trim the seam allowances down to 0.7 [¼"]
0.7 [¼"]
1) with wrong sides together and batting in between, quilt the bag body (front and back)
bag body top (right side)
bag body top (right side)
bag body top (right side)
batting
turn right side out
gusset
batting
8 [3⅛"]
2) sew the gusset
3) trim the seam allowances down to 0.7 [¼"]
1) sew across the bottom of the side seams following the measurements to create a gusset

Making the Bag Opening

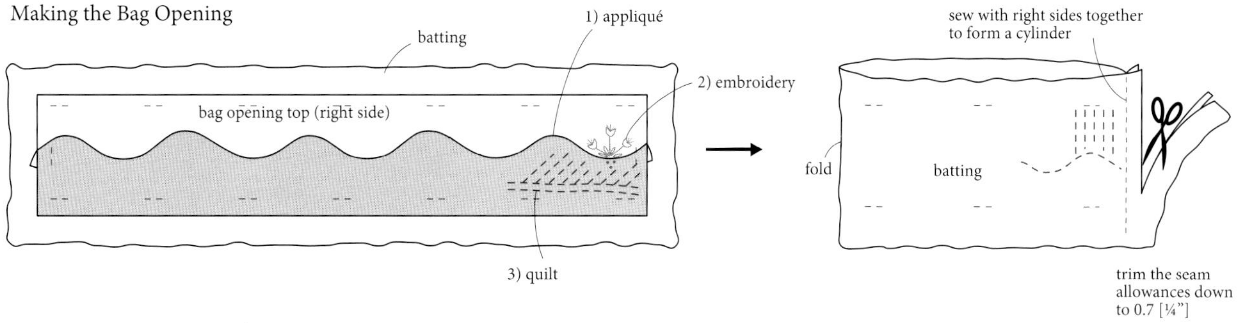
batting
1) appliqué
2) embroidery
bag opening top (right side)
3) quilt
sew with right sides together
to form a cylinder
fold
batting
trim the seam
allowances down
to 0.7 [¼"]

Making the Bag Facing

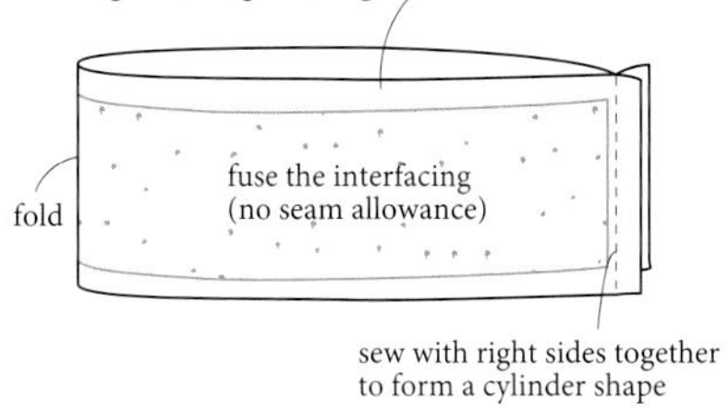
facing (wrong side)
fuse the interfacing
(no seam allowance)
fold
sew with right sides together
to form a cylinder shape

Making the Bag Lining

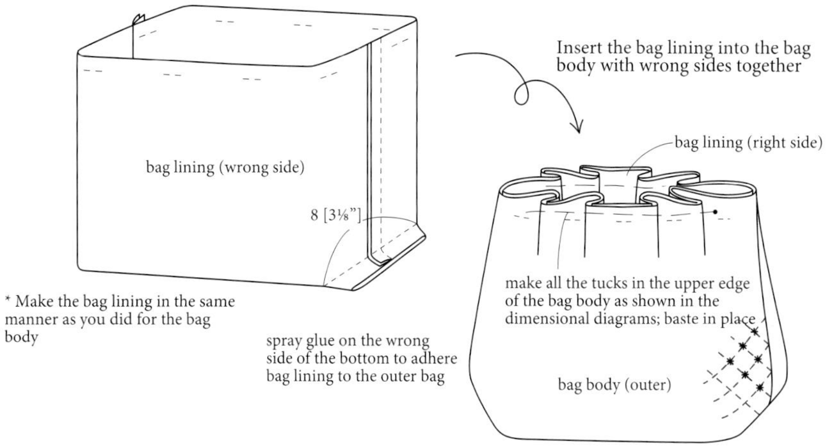
bag lining (wrong side)
8 [3⅛"]
* Make the bag lining in the same
manner as you did for the bag
body
spray glue on the wrong
side of the bottom to adhere
bag lining to the outer bag
Insert the bag lining into the bag
body with wrong sides together
bag lining (right side)
make all the tucks in the upper edge
of the bag body as shown in the
dimensional diagrams; baste in place
bag body (outer)

Sewing the Bag Together

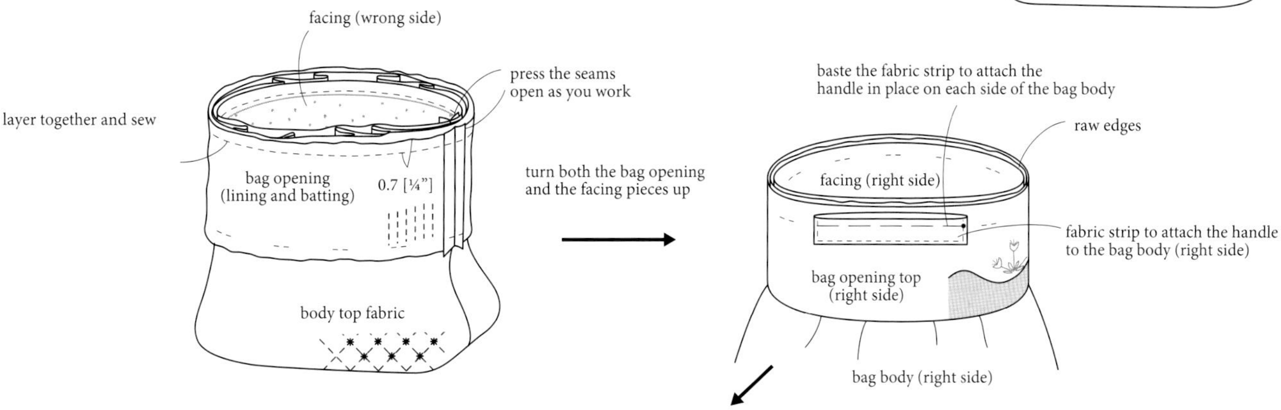
facing (wrong side)
press the seams
open as you work
layer together and sew
bag opening
(lining and batting)
0.7 [¼"]
body top fabric
turn both the bag opening
and the facing pieces up
baste the fabric strip to attach the
handle in place on each side of the bag body
raw edges
facing (right side)
fabric strip to attach the handle
to the bag body (right side)
bag opening top
(right side)
bag body (right side)

Binding the Raw Edges

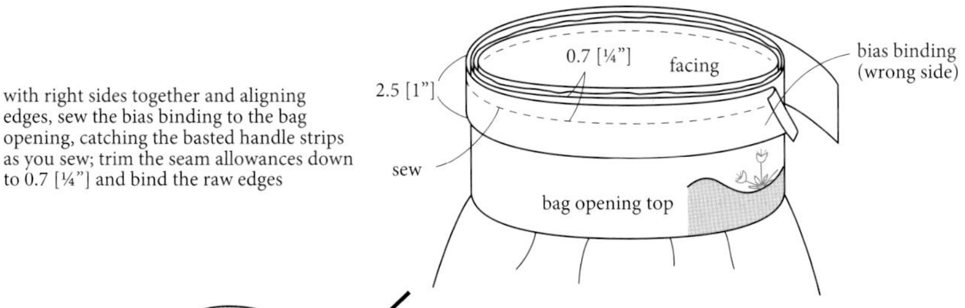
with right sides together and aligning
edges, sew the bias binding to the bag
opening, catching the basted handle strips
as you sew; trim the seam allowances down
to 0.7 [¼"] and bind the raw edges
2.5 [1"]
0.7 [¼"]
facing
bias binding
(wrong side)
sew
bag opening top

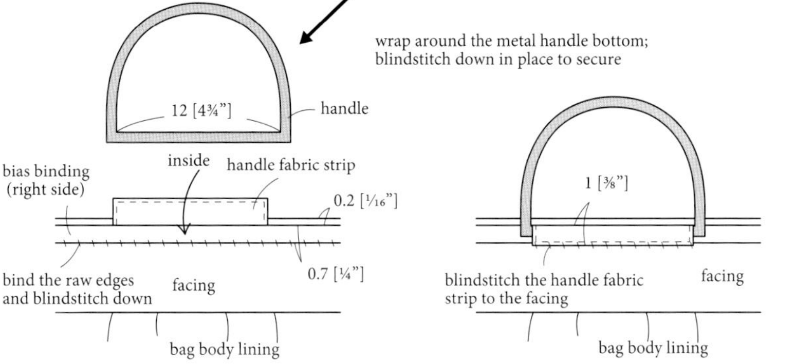
12 [4¾"]
handle
bias binding
(right side)
inside
handle fabric strip
0.2 [¹⁄₁₆"]
0.7 [¼"]
bind the raw edges
and blindstitch down
facing
bag body lining
wrap around the metal handle bottom;
blindstitch down in place to secure
1 [⅜"]
blindstitch the handle fabric
strip to the facing
facing
bag body lining

Finished Bag

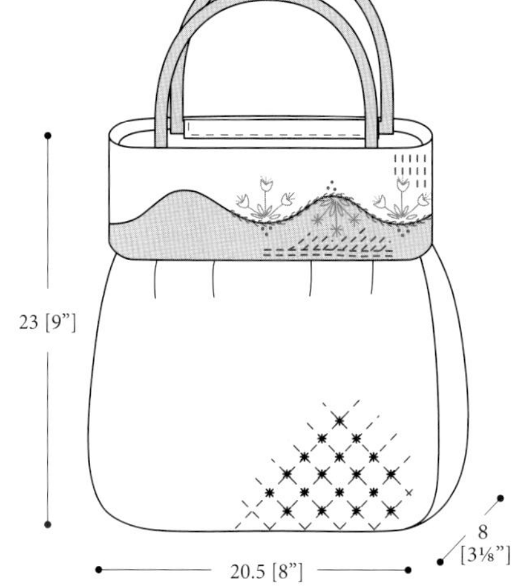
23 [9"]
20.5 [8"]
8
[3⅛"]

1 Pencil Case

Shown on p. 131

Pattern used 99

The full-size embroidery pattern is on p. 130.

► Materials Needed

Beige print (front background) - 15 × 25 cm [5⅞" × 9¾"]
Beige homespun (back background) - 15 × 25 cm [5⅞" × 9¾"]
Brown check (bottom) - 10 × 25 cm [4" × 9¾"]
Brown gingham check (gussets) - 10 × 15 cm [4" × 5⅞"]
Lining - 30 × 40 cm [11¾" × 15¾"]
Batting - 30 × 40 cm [11¾" × 15¾"]
Black plaid (bias binding) - 3.5 × 50 cm [1⅜" × 19¾"]
Scraps (zipper binding, zipper pull
1 zipper - 21.5 cm [8½"] long
1 Cat-shaped zipper decoration
Cord - 0.1 cm [1/16"] diameter
Embroidery floss

► Finished measurements

See the diagrams below.

► Instructions

1 Embroider the front background fabric; piece the front, back and bottom together to make the outside of the pencil case.
2 With right sides together and batting in between, sew the side seams.
3 Turn the piece right side out; baste and quilt the pencil case body.
4 Shape the piece into a cylinder with right sides out, sew in the zipper with the binding for each side.
5 Finish the end of the zipper with the scrap of fabric.
6 Make the gussets. With right sides together and batting against the top, sew around the edges, leaving the bottom open for turning. Turn right side out and quilt. Fold each in half with the right side facing inside and sew across the top to make a tuck.
7 With wrong sides together, sew the gussets to the ends of the zippered cylinder-shaped pencil case body; sew in an up/down motion while pinching the edges to sew the gussets on.
8 Attach the cat-shaped decoration to the zipper clasp with the cord, wrapping the cord with a scrap of fabric and blindstitching down to secure.

Pencil Case Top

Use 2 strands of floss unless otherwise specified.

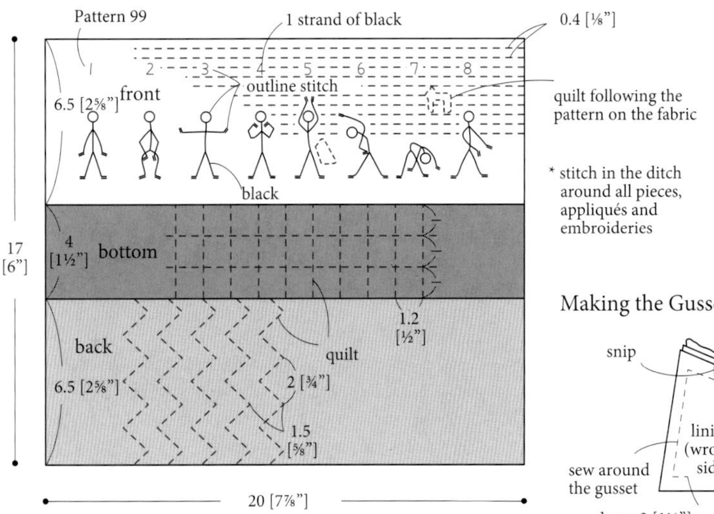

Gusset

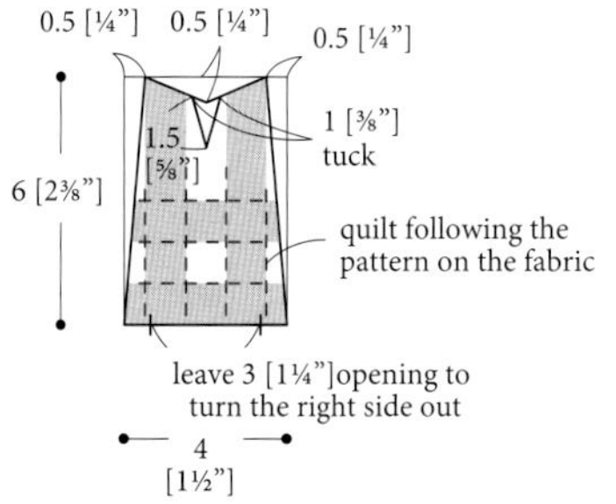

Making the Gusset - make 2

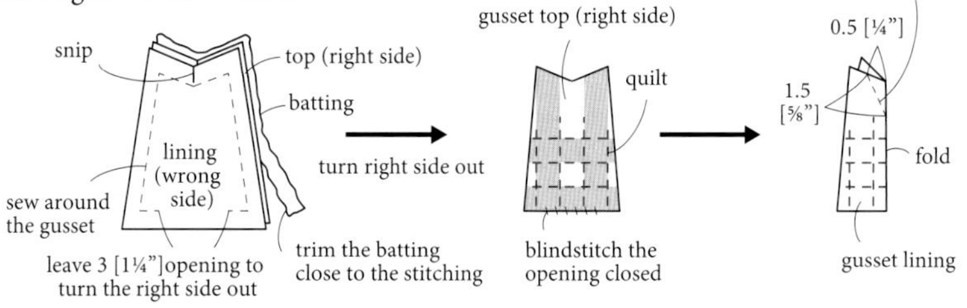

Sewing the Pencil Case Together

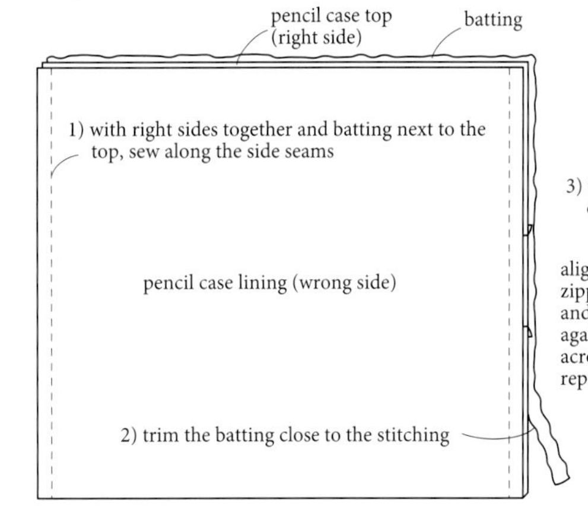

Sew in the Zipper and Bind Edges

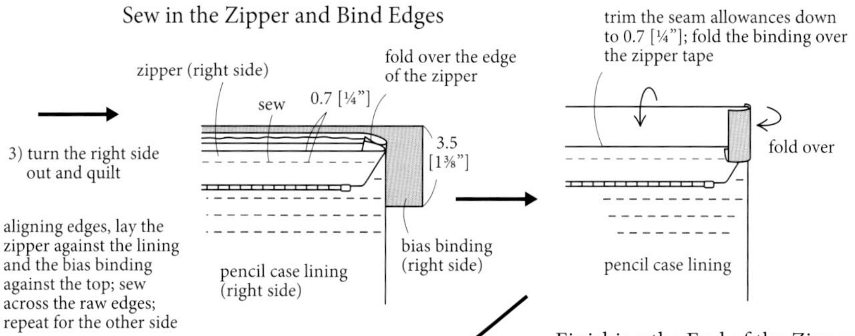

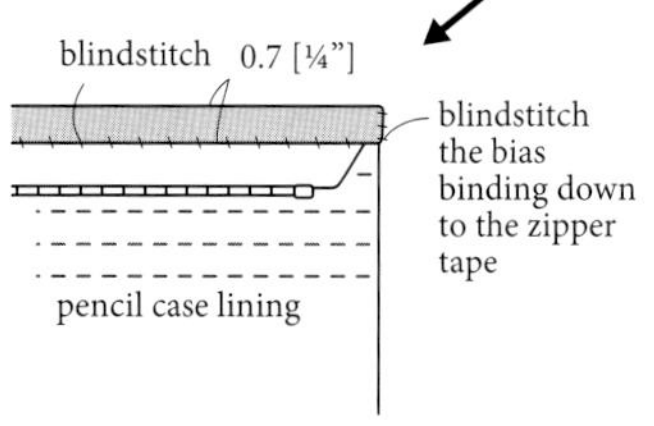

Finishing the End of the Zipper

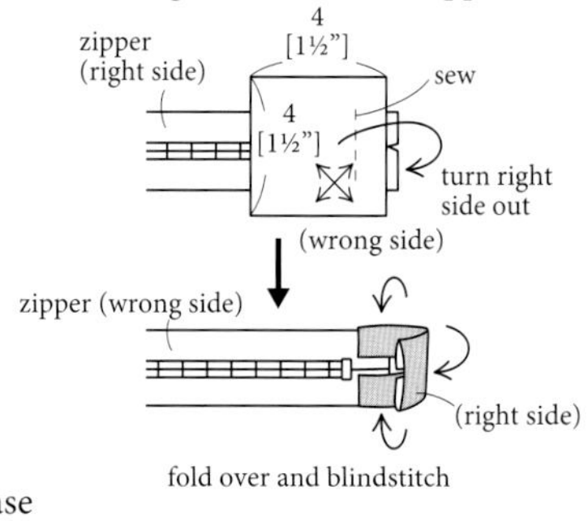

How to Sew Up/Down (Running Stitch)

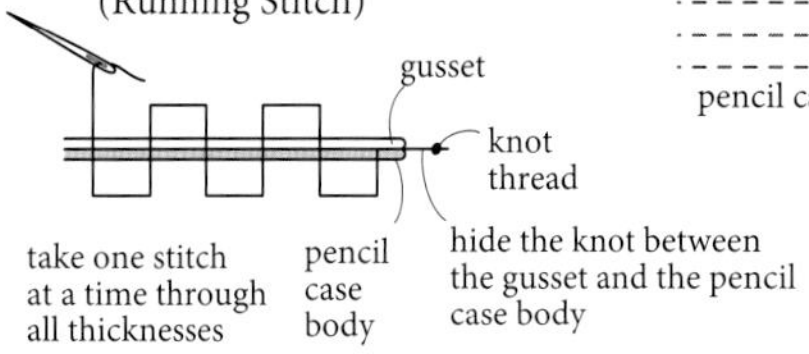

Sewing the Gusset to the Body

with lining sides together, sew in an up and down running stitch motion (take one stitch at a time to get through all thicknesses)

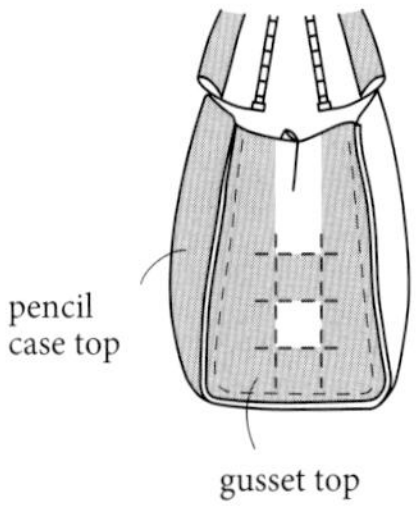

Zipper Pull

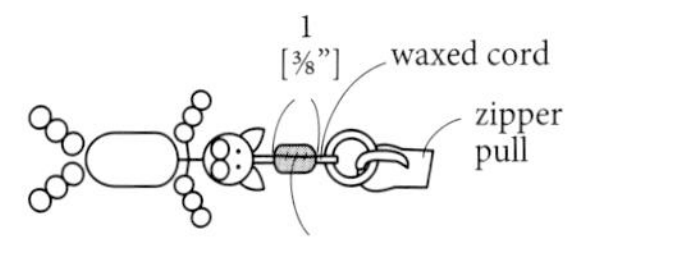

attach the cat decoration to the zipper clasp; wrap the waxed cord with fabric and blindstitch

Finished Pencil Case

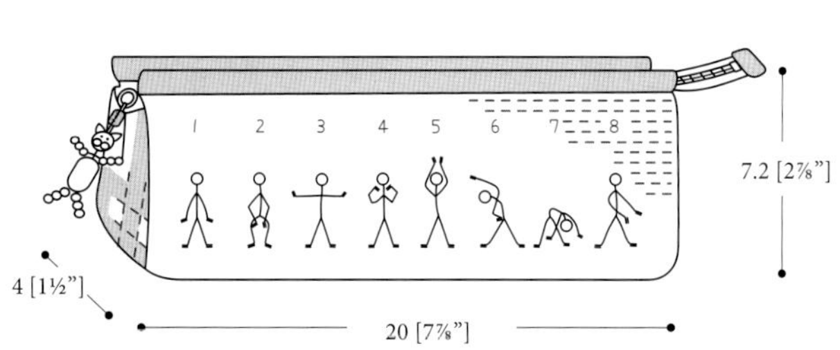

m Book Cover

Shown on p. 138

Pattern used 104

The full-size embroidery pattern is on p. 137.

► Materials Needed
Beige print (background top)
- 20 × 40 cm [7⅞" × 15¾"]
Beige homespun (book cover strap)
- 7 × 20 cm [2¾" × 7⅞"]
Lining
- 20 × 40 cm [7⅞" × 15¾"]
Lightweight interfacing
- 20 × 35 cm [7⅞" × 13¾"]
Brown homespun (bias binding)
- 3.5 × 20 cm [1⅜" × 7⅞"]
Embroidery floss - dk grey

► Finished measurements
See the diagrams below.

► Instructions
1 Embroider the background fabric to make the book cover top.
2 Fuse the interfacing to the wrong side of the top.
3 Make the strap. Fuse the interfacing to the lining; with right sides together, sew the top and lining along the long sides; turn right side out; topstitch.
4 With right sides together and book cover strap sandwiched in between in position, sew the top to the lining, leaving an opening for turning.
5 Turn right side out. Press the entire piece and bind the opening.
6 With the right side facing inside, fold the body on the pocket side at the fold line; whip stitch by passing the needle through the top fabric only.

► Tips
See the note below on making this book cover for western language books. *

Place a book cover over the book and turn the edge over and insert it in the strap according to the thickness of the book.

Dimensional Diagram*

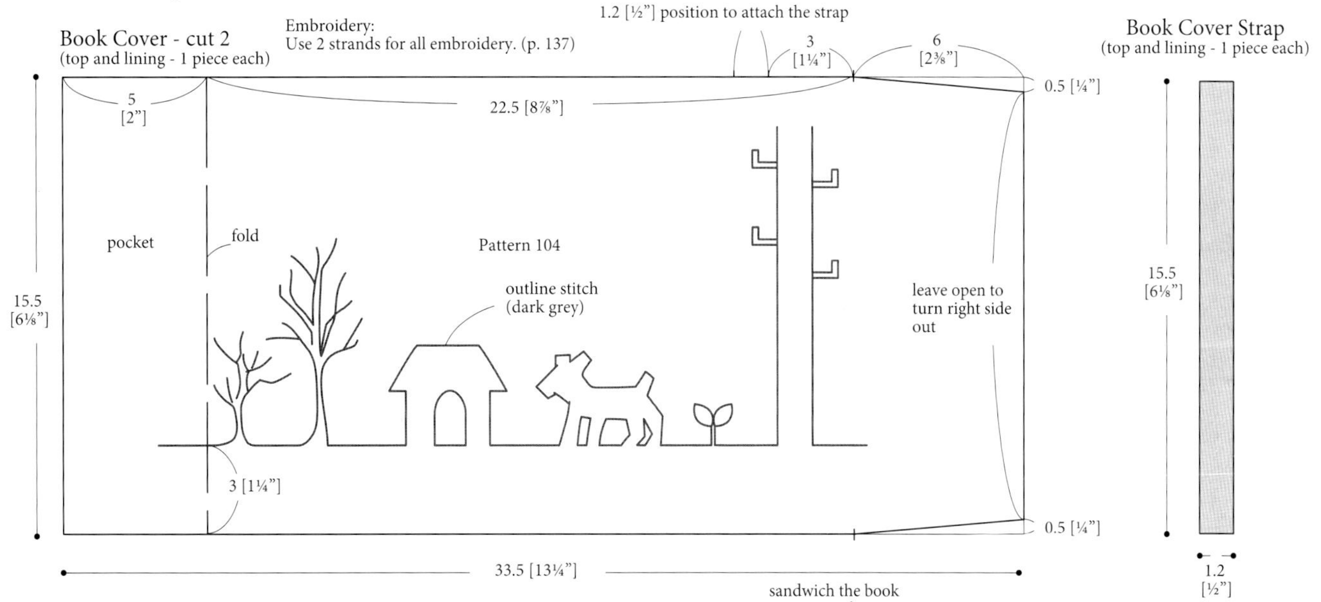

Making the Book Cover Strap

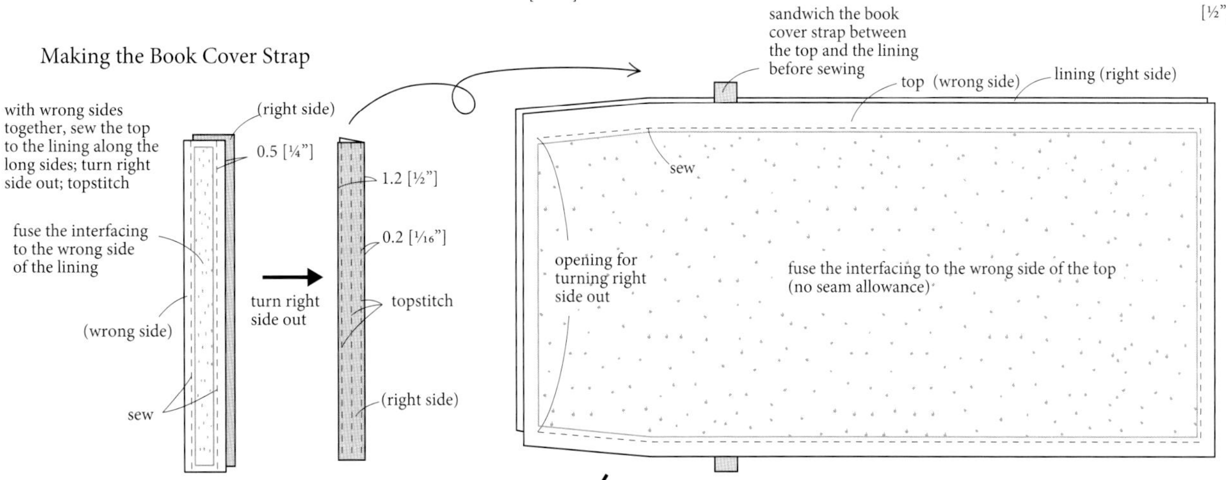

Binding the Opening

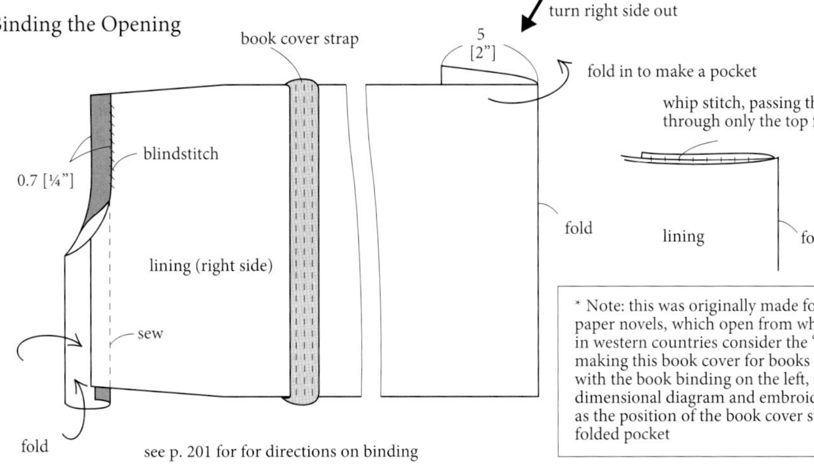

see p. 201 for for directions on binding

Finished Book Cover

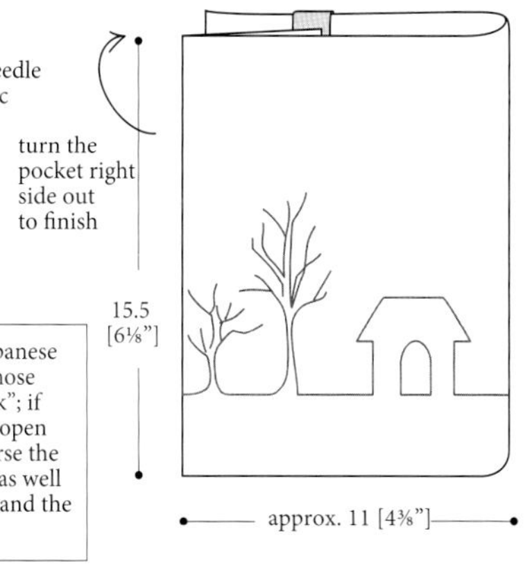

* Note: this was originally made for Japanese paper novels, which open from what those in western countries consider the "back"; if making this book cover for books that open with the book binding on the left, reverse the dimensional diagram and embroidery as well as the position of the book cover strap and the folded pocket

n Pouch

Shown on p. 139

Pattern used 105

The full-size embroidery pattern is on p. 141; the full-size templates for the pouch body can be found on pattern sheet insert A.

► Materials Needed
Beige print (front top)
- 20 × 35 cm [7⅞" × 13¾"]
Brown homespun (back top)
- 20 × 35 cm [7⅞" × 13¾"]
Brown plaid (top for strap)
- 10 × 30 cm [4" × 11¾"]
Scraps (patchwork and appliqué)
Navy print (strap top, lining)
- 15 × 20 cm [5⅞" × 7⅞"]
Scraps (zipper tab and zipper pull circle)
Lining- 40 × 50 cm [15¾" × 19¾"]
Batting - 40 × 50 cm [15¾" × 19¾"]
Bias strips (gusset)
- 2.5 × 15 cm [1" × 5⅞"]
Heavyweight interfacing (strap)
- 3 × 15 cm [1¼" × 5⅞"]
Interfacing (zipper tab)
- 3.5 × 20 cm [1⅜" × 7⅞"]
1 Zipper - 26 cm [10¼"] long
2 Buttons - 1.5 cm [⅝"] in diameter
1 Oval button - 2 cm [¾"] long
Cord - 0.1 cm [1/16"] in diameter
Embroidery floss

► Finished measurements
See the diagrams below.

► Instructions
1 Appliqué and embroider the pouch front background top.
2 With right sides together, sew the pouch front, back and bottom together to create the pouch body top.
3 With right sides together, layer the body top and lining with batting against the lining. Sew from the ◎ to the ★ on both the pouch front and back along the zipper opening edges.
4 Turn the pouch body right side out; baste and quilt.
5 With right sides together, fold in half and sew the side seams. Bind the side seams with the lining.
6 Sew the gusset. Bind the raw edges with the bias strips.
7 Make the zipper tab and strap.
8 Sew the zipper tab and zipper to the pouch.
9 Using a blindstitch, sew the strap to the pouch; sew the buttons on either side of the strap and sew all the way through to secure.
10 Attach the zipper pull to the zipper clasp to finish.

Pouch Body (Front, Back and Bottom)

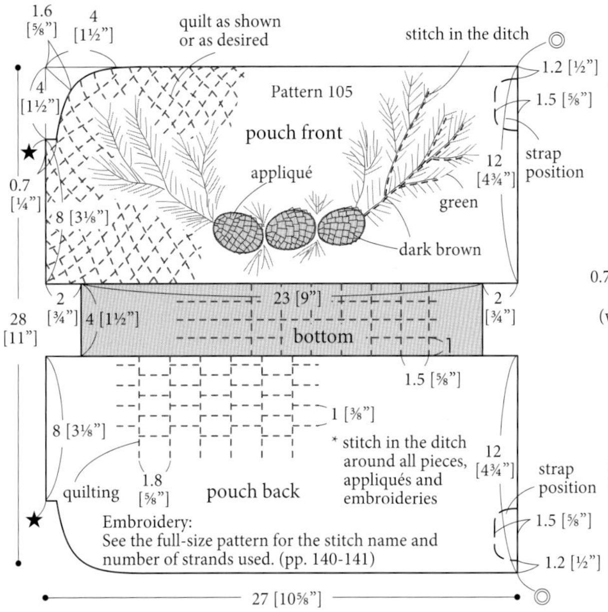

Strap - make 1
(top, appliqué top, lining, batting - cut 1 each)

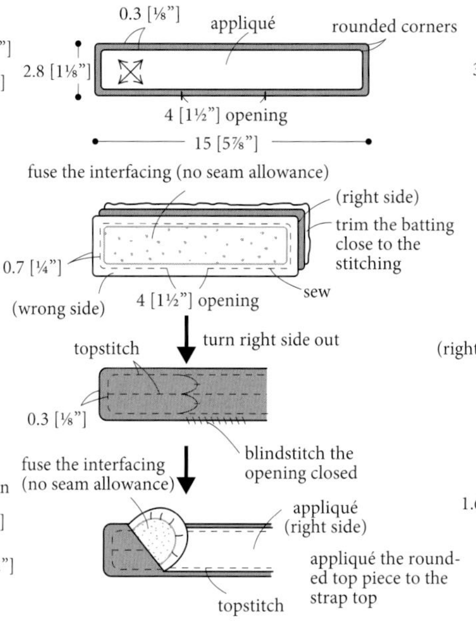

Zipper Tab - make 1

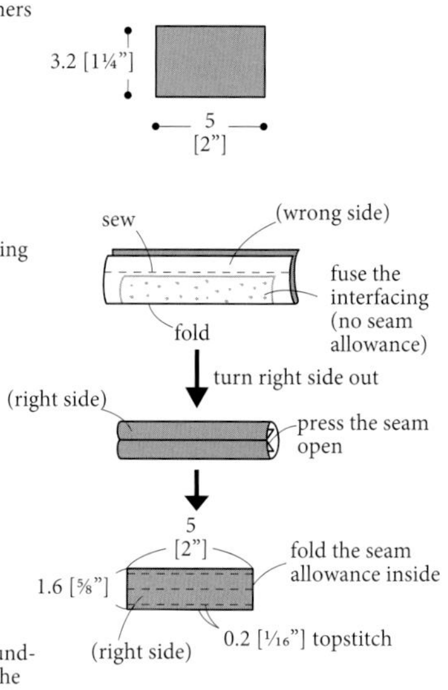

Sewing the Pouch Body Together

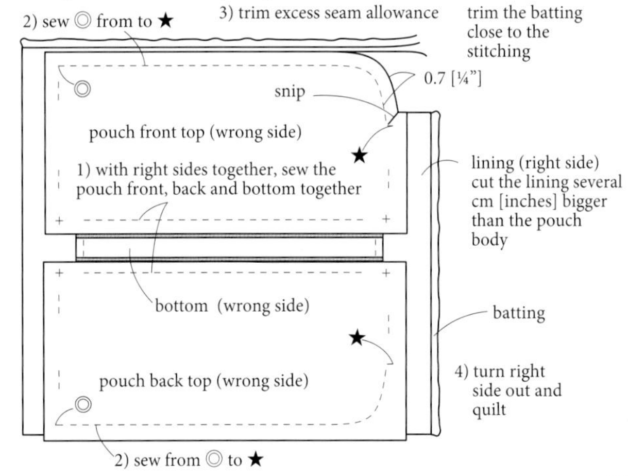

Sewing the Pouch Sides

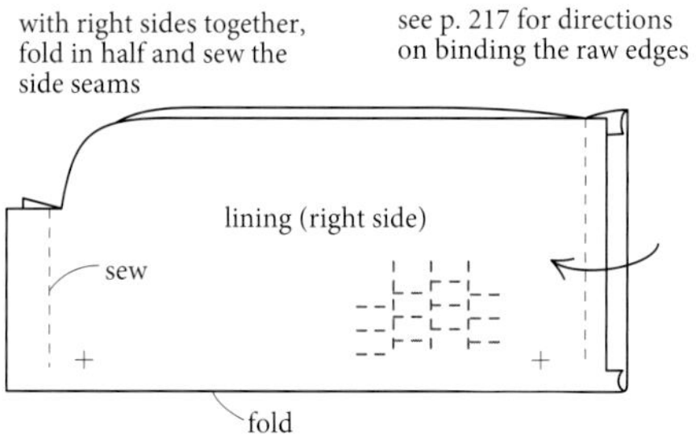

Sewing the Gusset

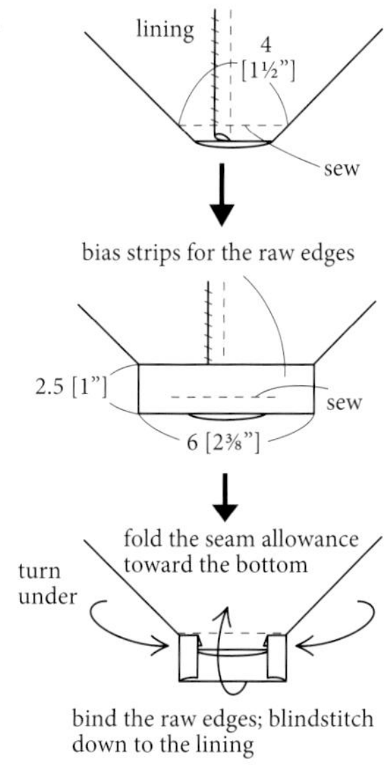

Attaching the Zipper Tab

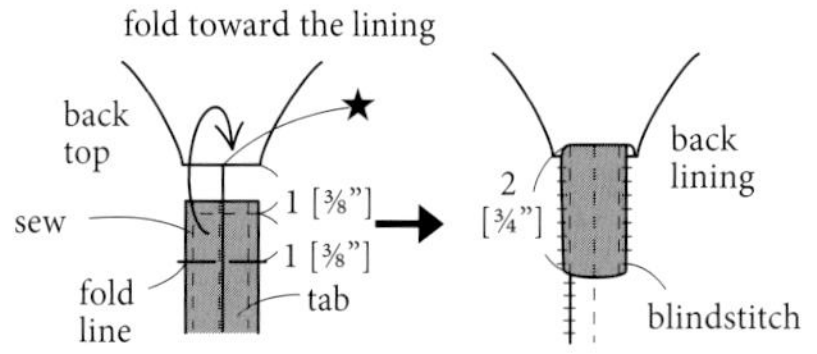

Sewing in the Zipper

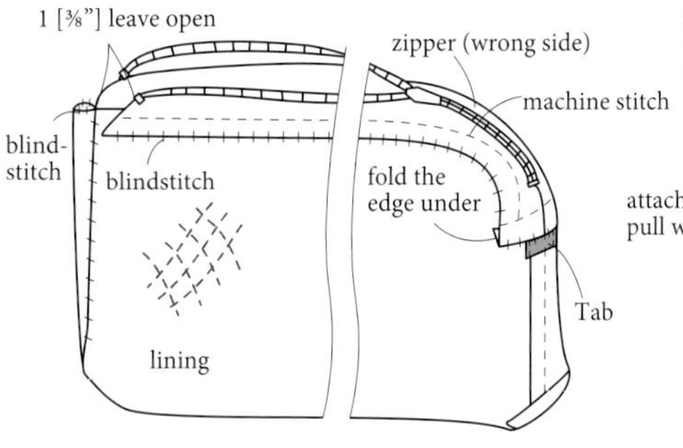

sew the zipper directly to the lining of the bag opening top of the pouch; machine stitch close to the teeth for both sides; blindstitch the zipper tape edges to the lining

Zipper Pull
(no seam allowance)

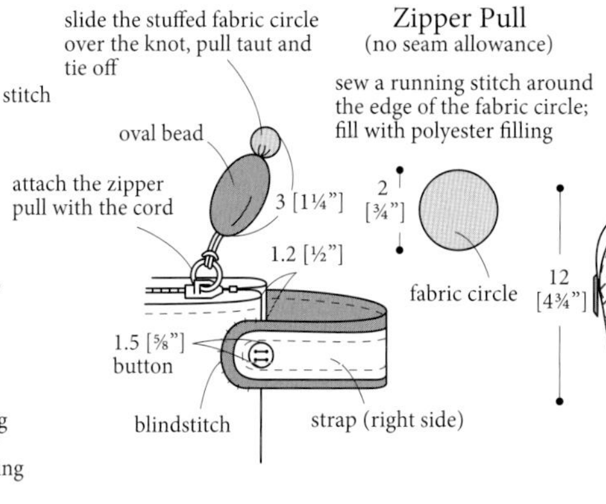

Finished Pouch

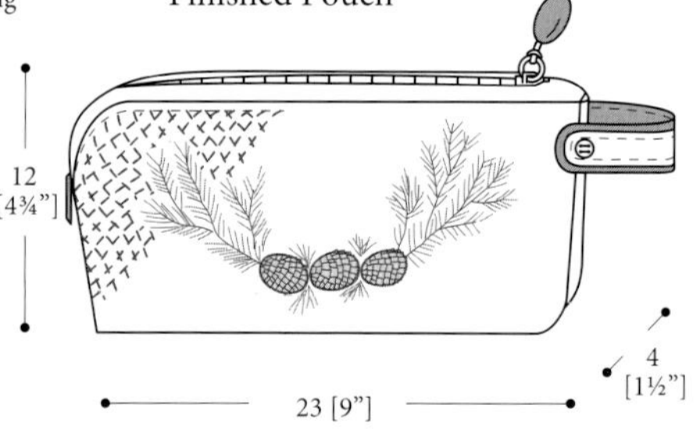

t Wall Hanging

Shown on p. 169

Patterns used 112~120

The full-size embroidery patterns are on pp. 161-167 and pp. 171-179.

► Materials Needed
Beige print (sashing)
- 90 × 110 cm [35⅜" × 43¼"]
Beige tree print (borders, block background)
- 110 × 230 cm [43¼" × 90½"]
Assorted fat quarters (piecing and appliqué)
Backing
- 110 × 130 cm [43¼" × 51¼"]
Batting
- 110 × 130 cm [43¼" × 51¼"]
Bias binding
- 2.5 × 440 cm [1" × 173⅛"]
Embroidery floss

► Finished measurements
97 × 118 cm [38⅛" × 46½"]

► Instructions
1 Piece, appliqué and embroider the house blocks for the quilt top.
2 Sew the house blocks together as shown in the dimensional diagram. Appliqué the inner border onto the outer border pieces; sew the border to the quilt center to complete the quilt top.
3 With wrong sides together and batting in between, baste, then quilt the top and backing.
3 Referring to the diagram below, bind the raw edges with the bias binding.

► Tips
Each house pattern is designed in such a way that when you follow the diagram, the ground appliqué lines up with the neighboring block across the three blocks in each row.

Quilt the "sky" background areas to appear as though there are wind currents blowing.

Stitch in the ditch around the embroideries of the tree trunks, branches and roofs of the houses.

Dimensional Diagram

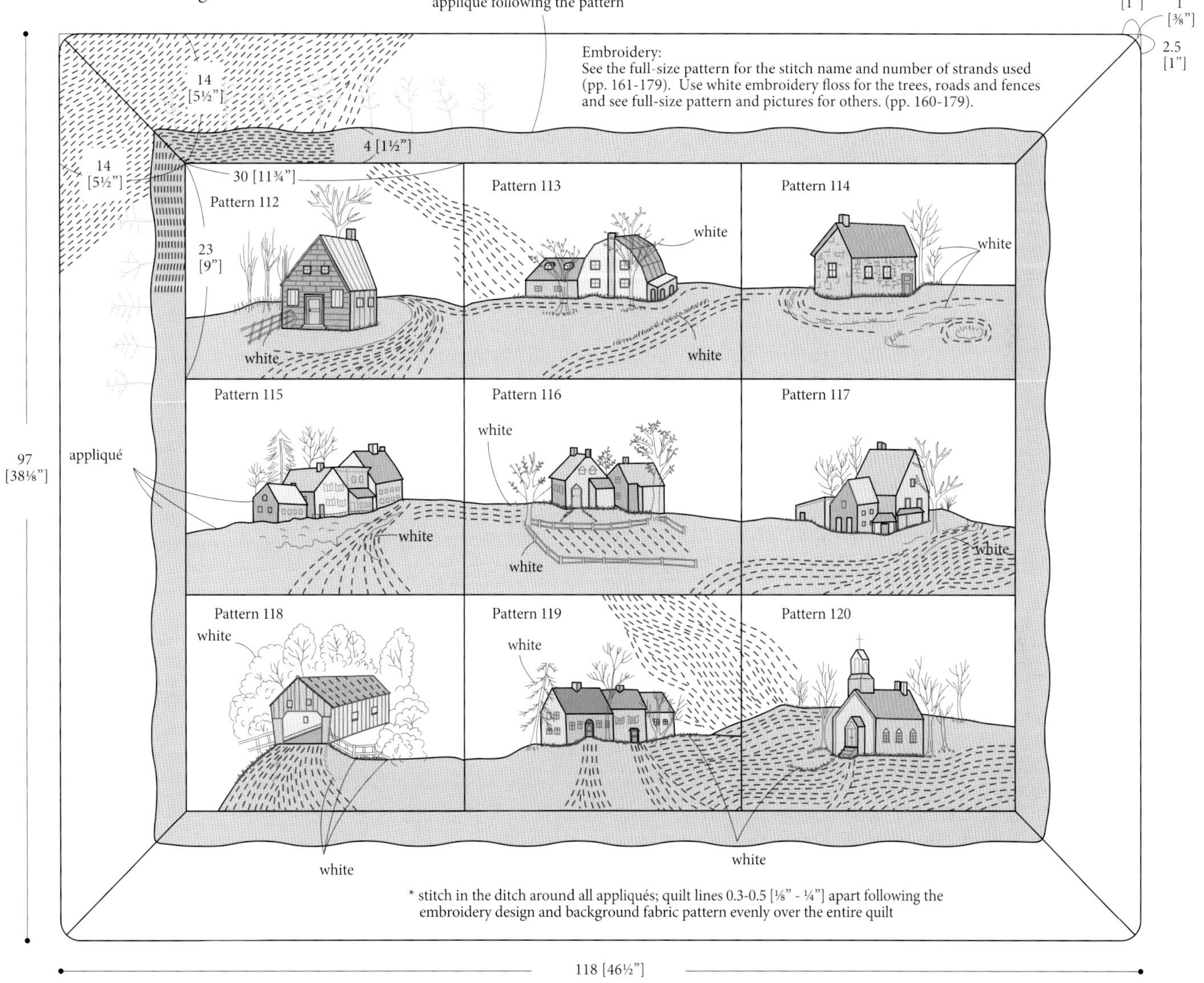

appliqué following the pattern
2.5 [1"]
1 [⅜"]
2.5 [1"]
Embroidery:
See the full-size pattern for the stitch name and number of strands used (pp. 161-179). Use white embroidery floss for the trees, roads and fences and see full-size pattern and pictures for others. (pp. 160-179).
14 [5½"]
4 [1½"]
14 [5½"]
30 [11¾"]
23 [9"]
Pattern 112
Pattern 113
Pattern 114
Pattern 115
Pattern 116
Pattern 117
Pattern 118
Pattern 119
Pattern 120
white
appliqué
97 [38⅛"]
* stitch in the ditch around all appliqués; quilt lines 0.3-0.5 [⅛" - ¼"] apart following the embroidery design and background fabric pattern evenly over the entire quilt
118 [46½"]

Binding the Quilt

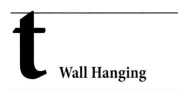

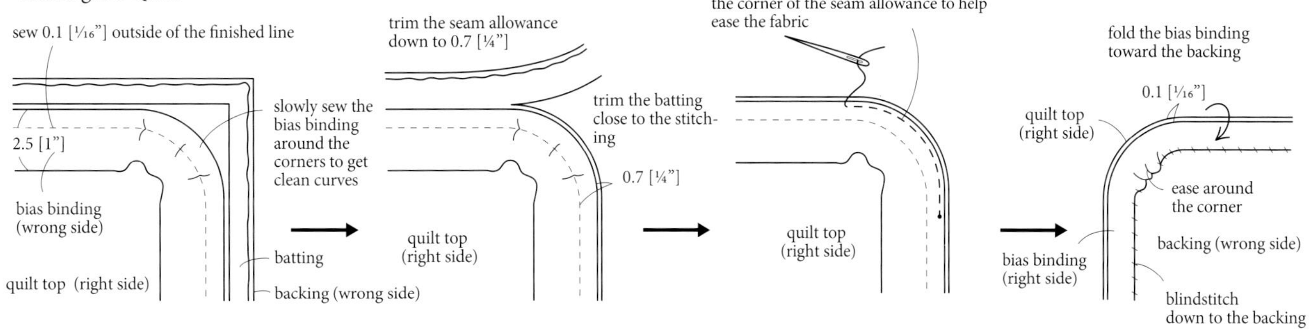

sew 0.1 [1/16"] outside of the finished line
2.5 [1"]
bias binding (wrong side)
quilt top (right side)
slowly sew the bias binding around the corners to get clean curves
batting
backing (wrong side)
trim the seam allowance down to 0.7 [¼"]
trim the batting close to the stitching
0.7 [¼"]
quilt top (right side)
sew a running stitch around the curves at the corner of the seam allowance to help ease the fabric
quilt top (right side)
fold the bias binding toward the backing
0.1 [1/16"]
quilt top (right side)
ease around the corner
backing (wrong side)
bias binding (right side)
blindstitch down to the backing

O Mini Bag

Shown on p. 146

Pattern used 107

The full-size embroidery pattern is on p. 145; the full-size templates for B (lower), the bag back and pocket can be found on pattern sheet insert A.

► Materials Needed
Beige print (bag front A top)
- 15×30 cm [5⅞" × 11¾"]
Lt brown print (pocket, bag back)
- 25×70 cm [9¾" × 27½"]
Brown homespun (zipper pull wrap, handle loops)
- 15×15 cm [5⅞" × 5⅞"]
Beige print (bag front B, lining)
- 55×70 cm, [21⅝" × 27½"]
Batting - 40×70 cm [15¾" × 27½"]
Bias binding
- 2.5×70 cm [1" × 27½"]
Interfacing
- 20×30 cm [7⅞" × 11¾"]
Double-sided fusible interfacing
- 15×30 cm [5⅞" × 11¾"]
1 Zipper - 16 cm [6¼"] long
1 Zipper - 24 cm [9½"] long
Lt grey suede tape
-1×68 cm [⅜" × 26¾"]
2 Wooden beads (zipper pull)
- 1.2 cm [½"] in diameter
Cord - 0.1 cm [1/16"] in diameter
Embroidery floss - green, dk brown

► Finished measurements
See the diagrams below.

► Instructions
1 With right sides together and batting against the lining, sew the pocket top and lining together along the top zipper edge only as shown. Turn right side out; baste and quilt. Sew in the pocket zipper and sew in the darts.
2 Fuse the two bag front B pieces with wrong sides together to each other using the double-sided fusible interfacing.
3 Embroider bag front A. With right sides together, sandwich the fused bag front lower B's in between the bag front upper A. With the batting on the top, and the lining A against the back; sew across the top area only; turn right side out; flip the pocket top upper A sections up with the batting in between; quilt
4 Fuse the interfacing to the wrong side of the bag back lining; with wrong sides together and batting in between, machine quilt the bag back; bind the top edge.
5 Bind the top edge of the bag front (with pocket) as in step 4. With right sides together, sew the bag back and front together, with the handle loops in position. Sew the binding on; sew in the zipper; finish blindstitching the binding down.
6 Attach the handle through the handle loops; make and attach the zipper pulls to both zipper clasps.

Mini Bag Front (upper and lower)

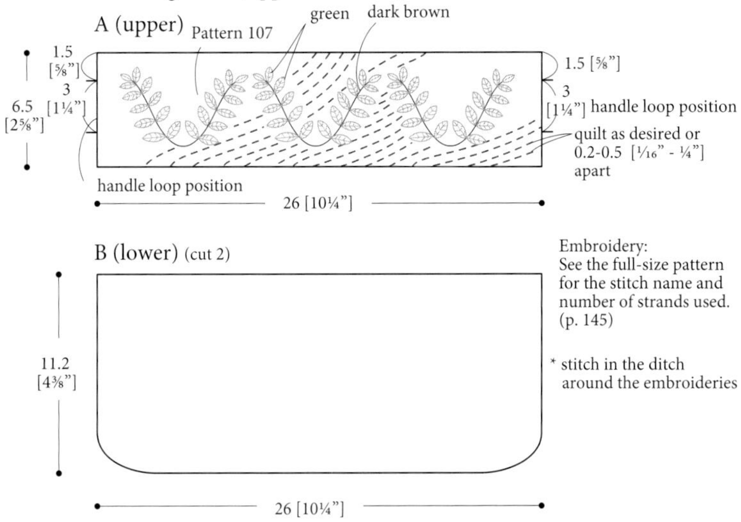

Mini Bag Back

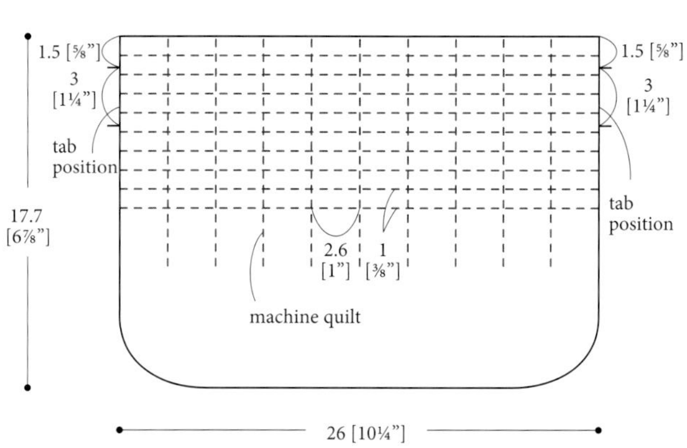

Pocket

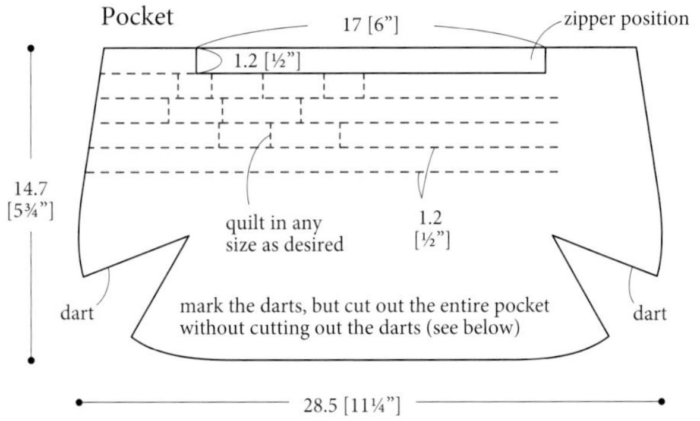

Handle Loops
(top and lining - cut 2 each)

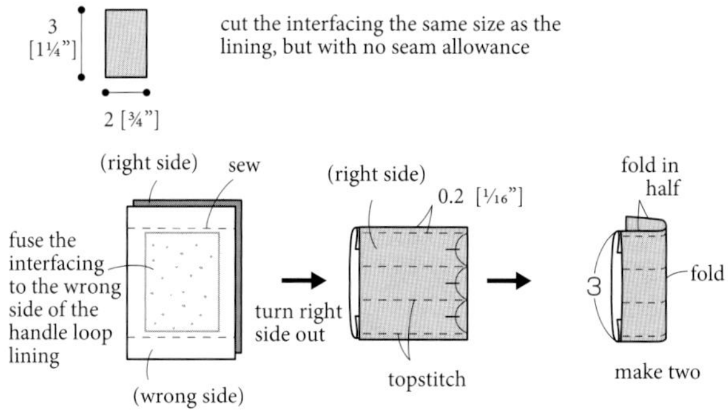

Making the Pocket

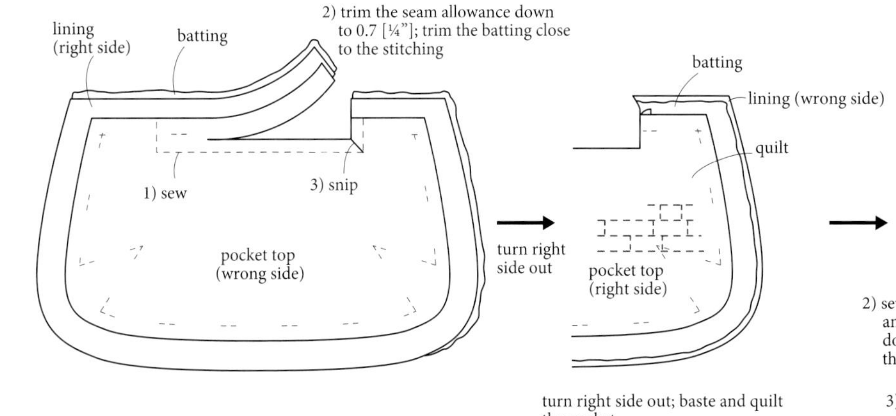

(1) with right sides together, lay the pocket top and lining together with batting against the lining; sew the zipper area as shown; (2) trim the seam allowance of the zipper area; (3) snip into the corners

turn right side out; baste and quilt the pocket

Sewing in the Pocket Zipper

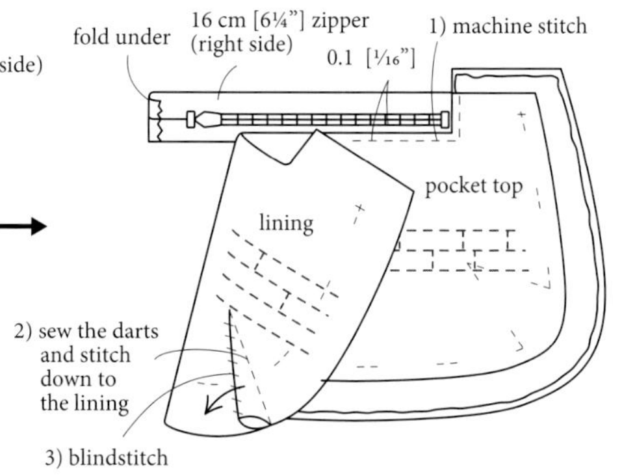

with the right side of the zipper against the pocket lining, sew the zipper to the pocket piece by machine; sew in the darts and stitch them down to the pocket lining toward the bag center

Making the Bag Front

fuse the two bag front B pieces wrong sides together using the double-sided fusible interfacing

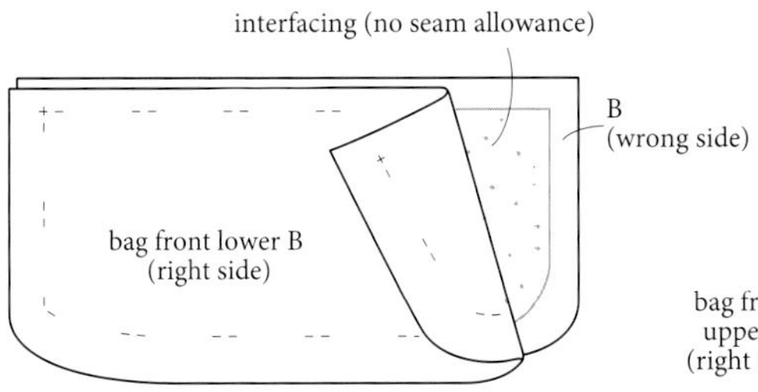

interfacing (no seam allowance)
B
(wrong side)
bag front lower B
(right side)

with right sides together, sandwich the fused bag front lower B's in between the bag front upper A with the batting on the top, and the lining A against the back; sew across the top area only; flip the pocket top upper A sections up with the batting in between; quilt

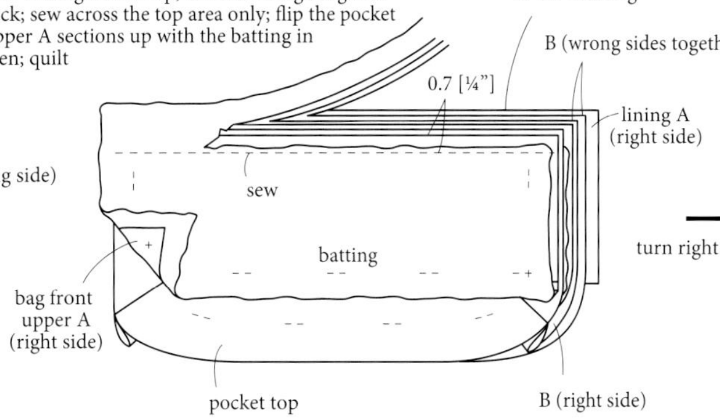

0.7 [¼"]
lining A
(right side)
sew
batting
bag front
upper A
(right side)
pocket top
B (right side)
turn right side out

trim the seam allowance down to 0.7 [¼"]; trim the batting close to the stitching

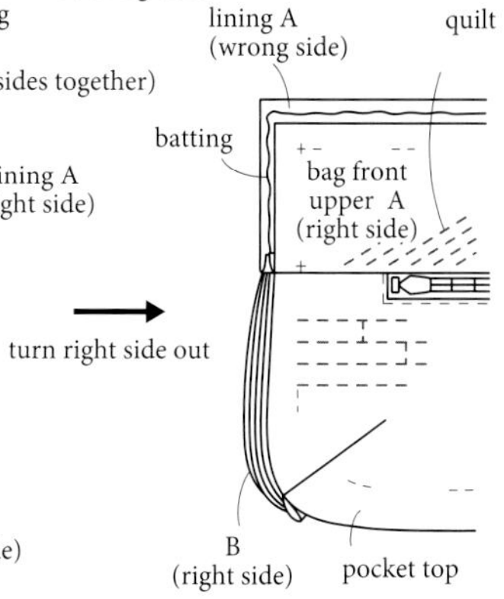

lining A
(wrong side)
quilt
B (wrong sides together)
batting
bag front
upper A
(right side)
B
(right side)
pocket top

Making the Bag Back

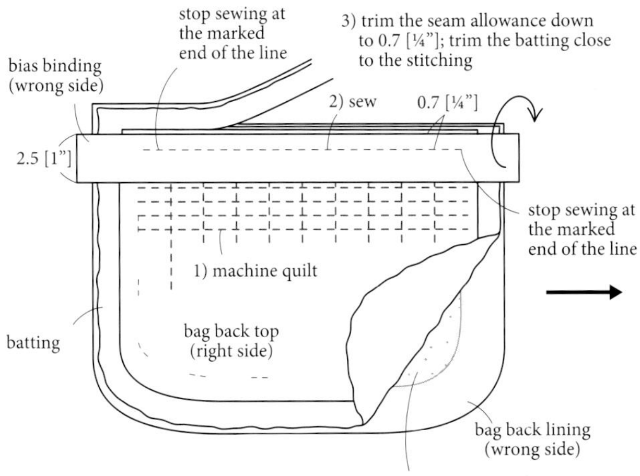

stop sewing at
the marked
end of the line
3) trim the seam allowance down
to 0.7 [¼"]; trim the batting close
to the stitching
bias binding
(wrong side)
2) sew
0.7 [¼"]
2.5 [1"]
stop sewing at
the marked
end of the line
1) machine quilt
batting
bag back top
(right side)
bag back lining
(wrong side)
fuse the interfacing (no seam allowance)

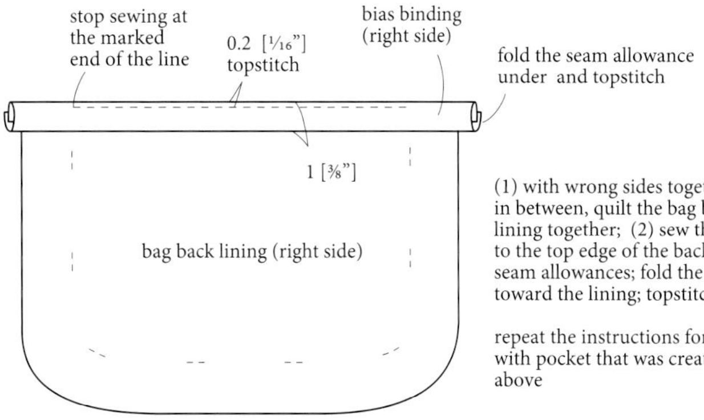

stop sewing at
the marked
end of the line
0.2 [1⁄16"]
topstitch
bias binding
(right side)
fold the seam allowance
under and topstitch
1 [⅜"]
bag back lining (right side)

(1) with wrong sides together and batting in between, quilt the bag back top and lining together; (2) sew the bias binding to the top edge of the back; (3) trim the seam allowances; fold the bias binding toward the lining; topstitch

repeat the instructions for the bag front with pocket that was created in the step above

Sewing the Bag Together

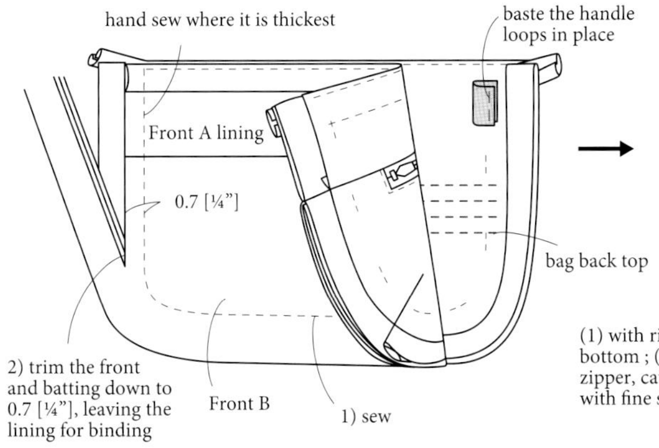

hand sew where it is thickest
baste the handle
loops in place
Front A lining
0.7 [¼"]
bag back top
2) trim the front
and batting down to
0.7 [¼"], leaving the
lining for binding
Front B
1) sew

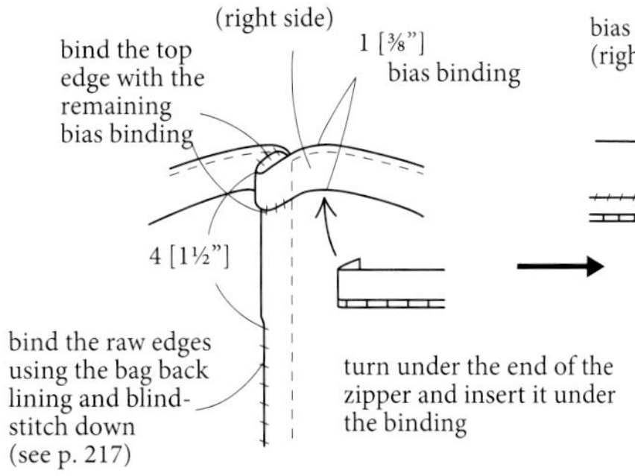

(right side)
bind the top
edge with the
remaining
bias binding
1 [⅜"]
bias binding
4 [1½"]
bind the raw edges
using the bag back
lining and blind-
stitch down
(see p. 217)
turn under the end of the
zipper and insert it under
the binding

Sewing in the Bag Zipper

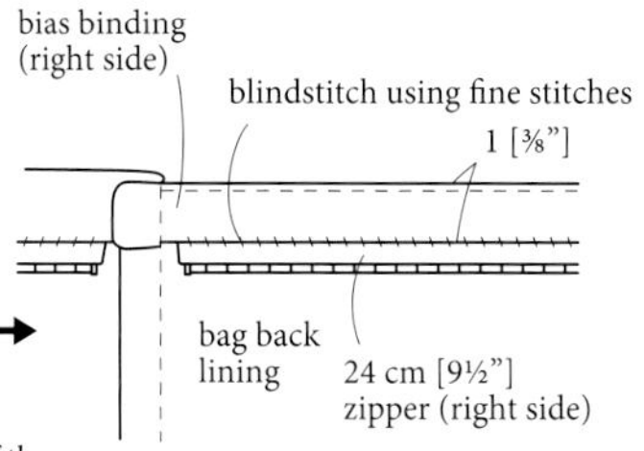

bias binding
(right side)
blindstitch using fine stitches
1 [⅜"]
bag back
lining
24 cm [9½"]
zipper (right side)

(1) with right sides together, sew the bag front (with pocket) and bag back together along the sides and bottom ; (2) trim the seam allowances; use the lining to bind the raw seam allowances; sew in the zipper, catching the edges of the zipper tape underneath the bias binding before blindstitching down with fine stitches

Making the Zipper Pulls

Pocket Zipper Pull

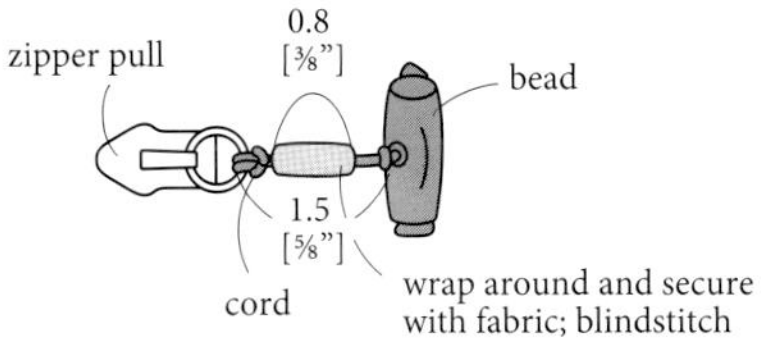

zipper pull
0.8
[⅜"]
bead
1.5
[⅝"]
cord
wrap around and secure
with fabric; blindstitch

Bag Opening Zipper

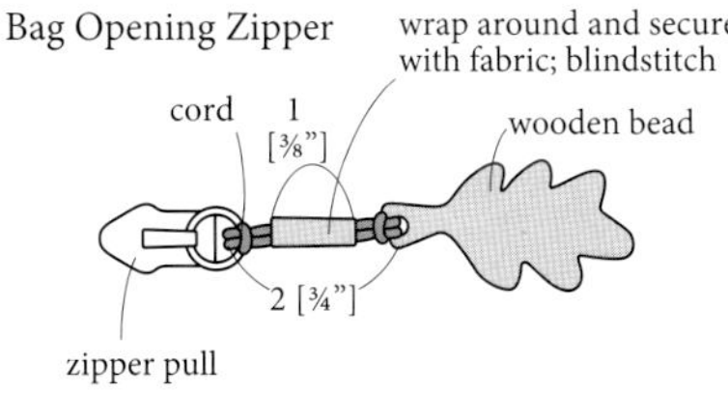

wrap around and secure
with fabric; blindstitch
cord
1
[⅜"]
wooden bead
2 [¾"]
zipper pull

Attaching the Handles

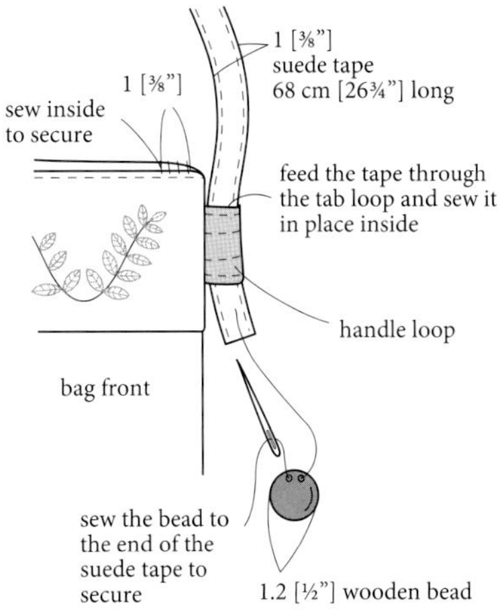

1 [⅜"]
suede tape
68 cm [26¾"] long
1 [⅜"]
sew inside
to secure
feed the tape through
the tab loop and sew it
in place inside
handle loop
bag front
sew the bead to
the end of the
suede tape to
secure
1.2 [½"] wooden bead

Finished Bag

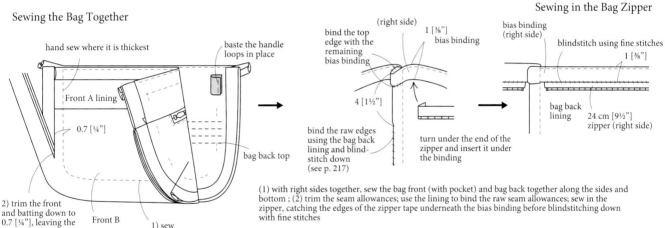

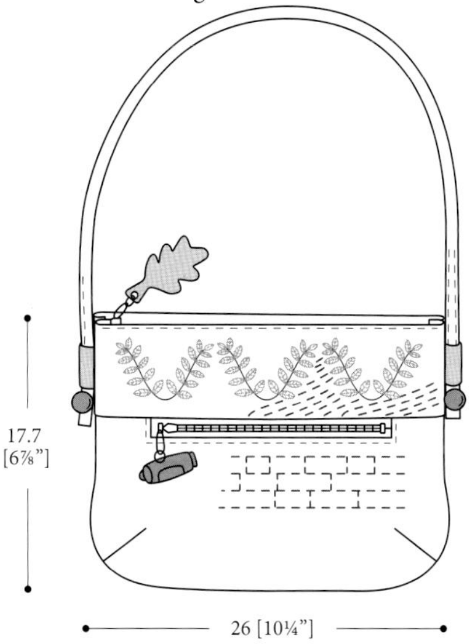

17.7
[6⅞"]
26 [10¼"]

p Drawstring Bag

Shown on p. 147

Pattern used 103

The full-size embroidery pattern is on p. 135.

► Materials Needed
Dk brown basket print (bag top)
- 15 × 40 cm [5⅞" × 15¾"]
Beige print (appliqué B)
- 15 × 40 cm [5⅞" × 15¾"]
Lt grey print (appliqué A)
- 10 × 40 cm [4" × 15¾"]
Brown homespun (drawstring tabs)
- 12 × 10 cm [4¾" × 4"]
Scraps (drawstring end wraps)
Lining - 30 × 45 cm [11¾" × 17¾"]
Batting - 30 × 45 cm [11¾" × 17¾"]
8 Wooden rings
- 1 [⅜"] in diameter
Grey and brown cord or woven tape
- 0.5 × 50 [¼" × 19¾"] long
2 Wooden beads
- 1 [⅜"] square
Embroidery floss

► Finished measurements
See the diagrams below.

► Instructions
1 Appliqué and embroider the bag top. (leave the embroideries on the sides unstitched).
2 Make the drawstring tabs with the wooden rings. Sandwich them between the layers and baste them in place.
3 Layer the pieces as shown below. Sew across the top only. Turn right side out and topstitch around the bag opening; baste and quilt.
4 Fold the bag body in half with the right side facing inside; sew the sides and bottom seams. Bind the raw edges with the remaining lining.
5 Press the side seams open. Finish the embroidery along seam for a seamless design.
6 Thread the woven tape or cords through wooden rings from each end; finish off the ends as shown.

► Tip
Embroider the design along the seam after sewing the sides so that the patterns flow seamlessly; then quilt in the ditch around them.

Dimensional Diagram

● = 0.8 [⅜"] wide positions to attach the tabs for the drawstring

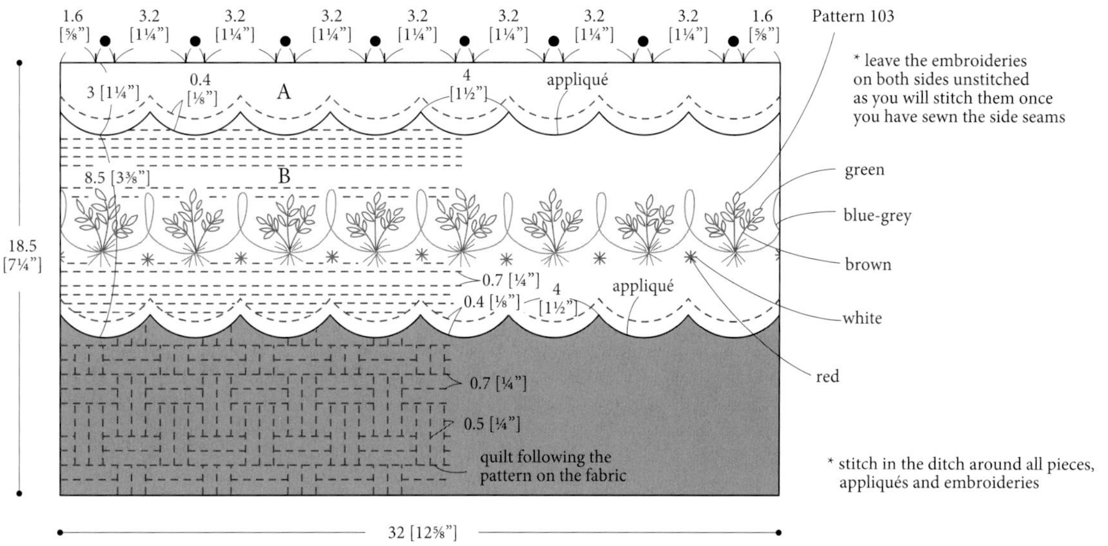

Embroidery:
See the full-size pattern for the stitch name and number of strands used. (p. 135)

Drawstring Tabs
(cut 8)

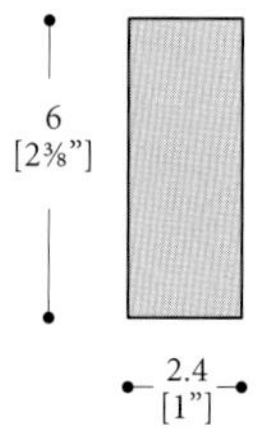

Making the Drawstring Tabs

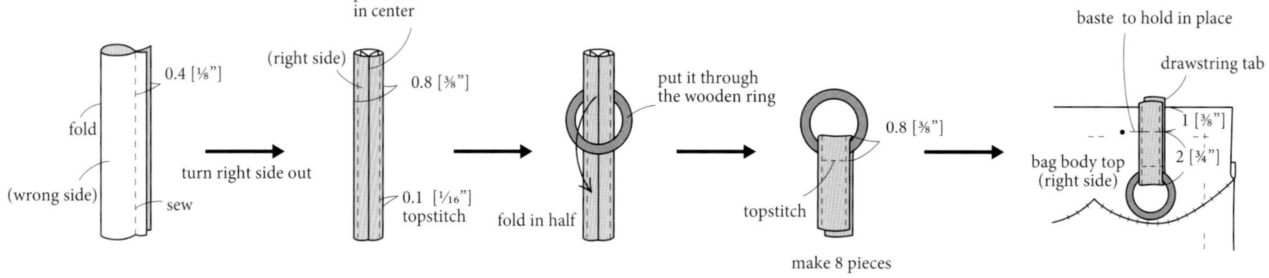

Basting the Tabs to the Bag Body

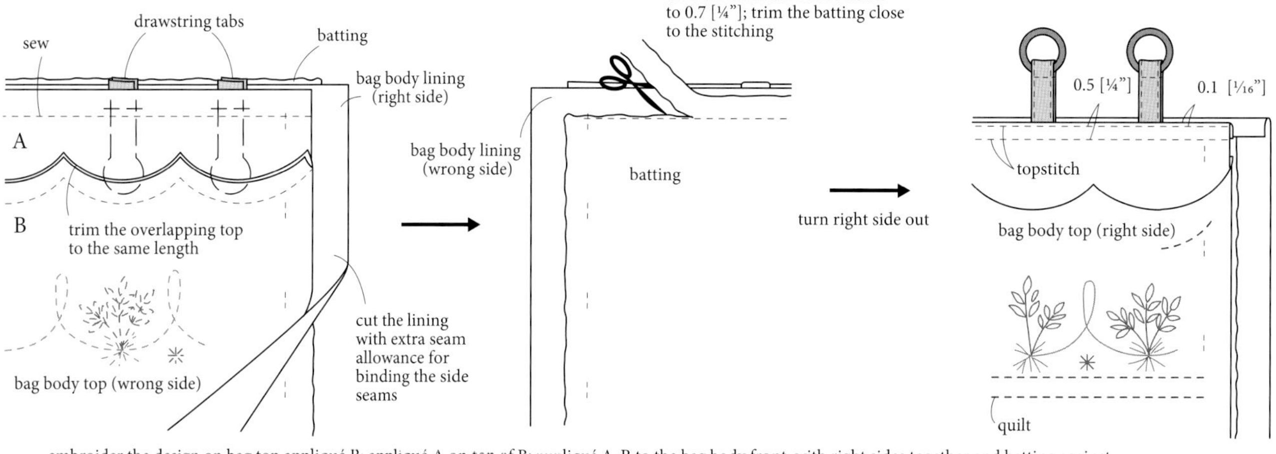

embroider the design on bag top appliqué B; appliqué A on top of B; appliqué A•B to the bag body front; with right sides together and batting against the lining, sandwich the drawstring tabs with rings between the top and lining; baste; sew only along the top edge; trim the seam allowances; turn right side out so that the tabs are sticking up; topstitch the top edge; quilt the bag body

Full-size Pattern for appliqué A (the scallop is the same for appliqué B)

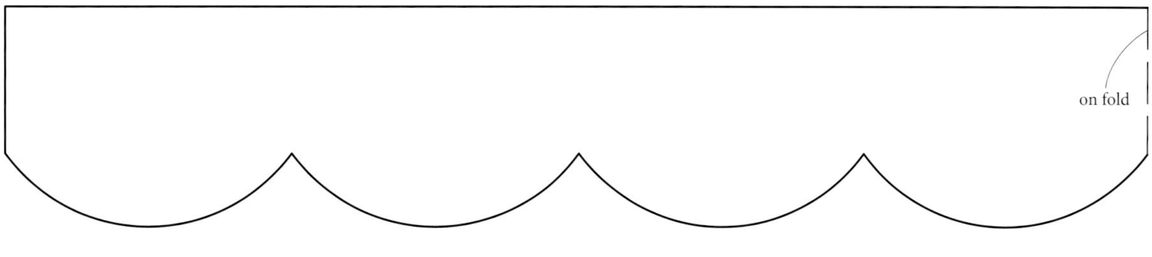
on fold

Sewing the Bag Together

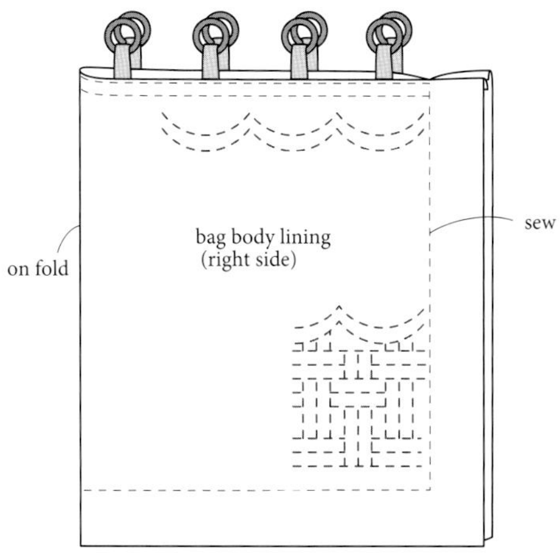
with right sides together, sew the side and bottom seams
on fold
bag body lining
(right side)
sew

Binding the Edges

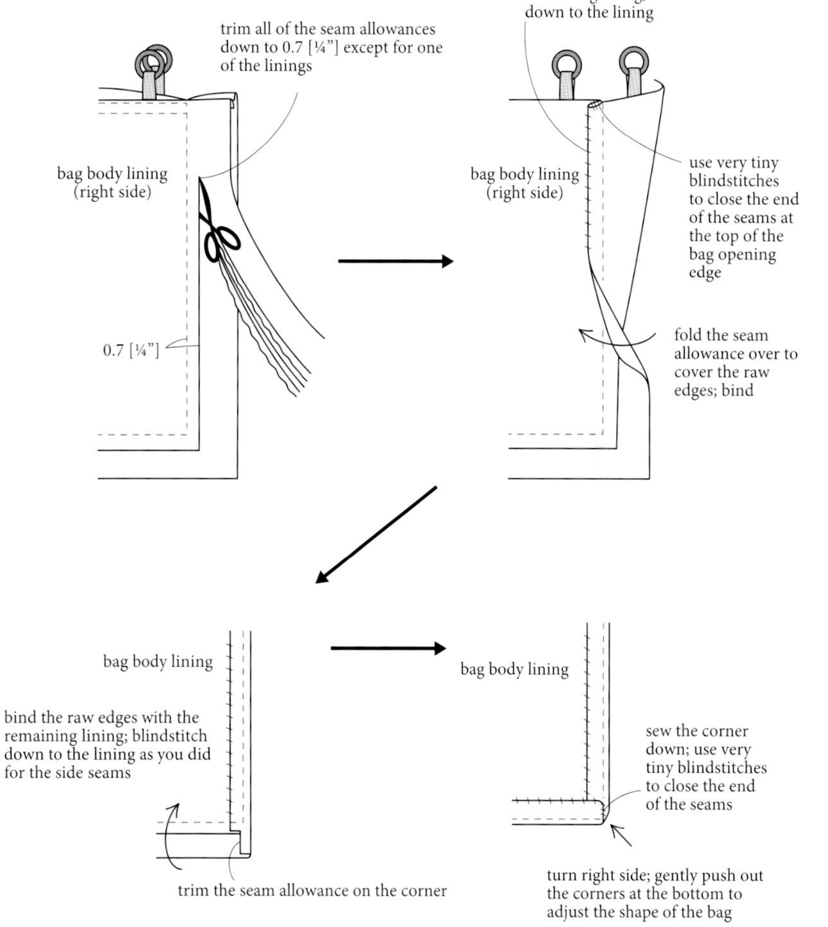
trim all of the seam allowances down to 0.7 [¼"] except for one of the linings
bag body lining
(right side)
0.7 [¼"]
bind the raw edges with the remaining lining; blindstitch down to the lining
bag body lining
(right side)
use very tiny blindstitches to close the end of the seams at the top of the bag opening edge
fold the seam allowance over to cover the raw edges; bind
bag body lining
bind the raw edges with the remaining lining; blindstitch down to the lining as you did for the side seams
trim the seam allowance on the corner
bag body lining
sew the corner down; use very tiny blindstitches to close the end of the seams
turn right side; gently push out the corners at the bottom to adjust the shape of the bag

Finishing the Embroidery on the Seams

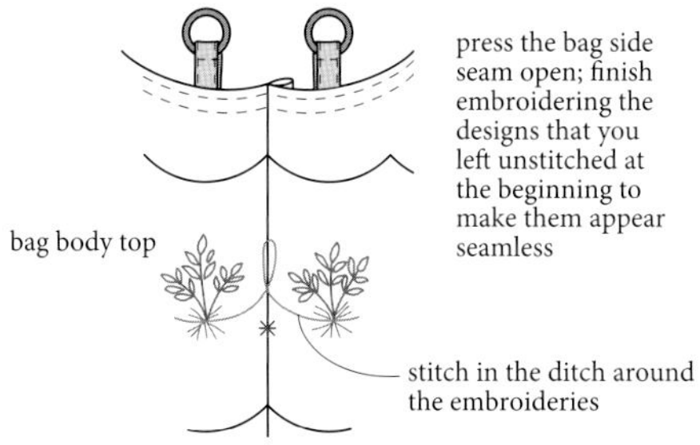
press the bag side seam open; finish embroidering the designs that you left unstitched at the beginning to make them appear seamless
bag body top
stitch in the ditch around the embroideries

Threading the Drawstring through the Tabs

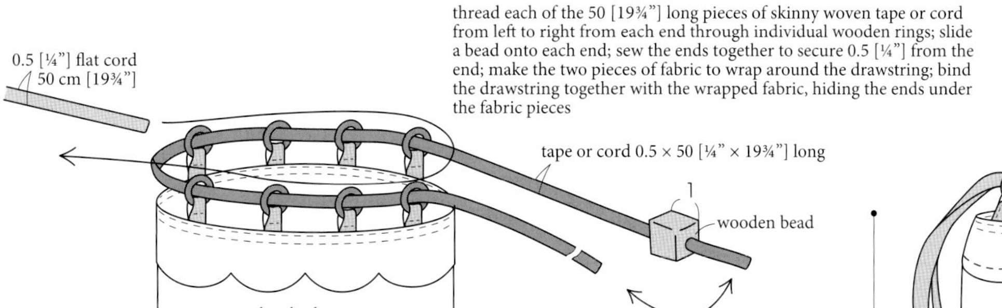
thread each of the 50 [19¾"] long pieces of skinny woven tape or cord from left to right from each end through individual wooden rings; slide a bead onto each end; sew the ends together to secure 0.5 [¼"] from the end; make the two pieces of fabric to wrap around the drawstring; bind the drawstring together with the wrapped fabric, hiding the ends under the fabric pieces
0.5 [¼"] flat cord
50 cm [19¾"]
tape or cord 0.5 × 50 [¼" × 19¾"] long
1
wooden bead
bag body top

Finished Pouch

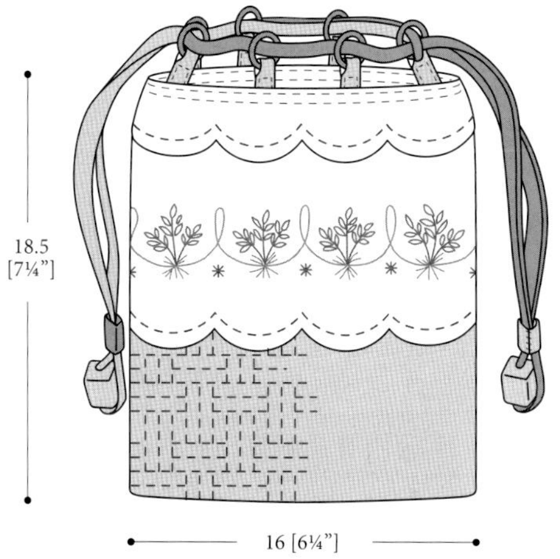
18.5
[7¼"]
16 [6¼"]

Drawstring End Wrap

(cut 2, no seam allowance)

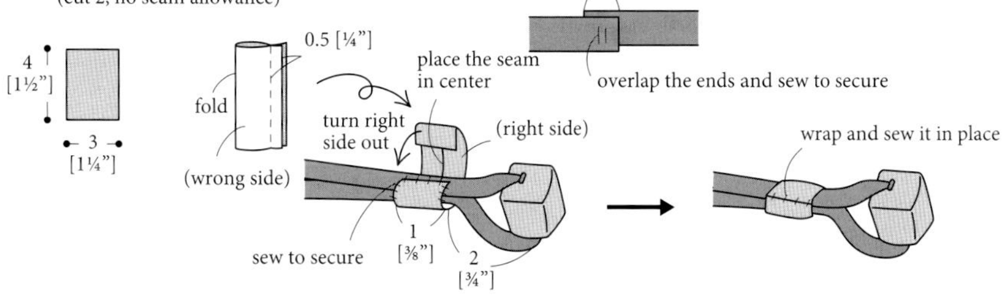
4
[1½"]
3
[1¼"]
fold
0.5 [¼"]
(wrong side)
place the seam in center
turn right side out
(right side)
sew to secure
1
[⅜"]
2
[¾"]
0.5 [¼"]
overlap the ends and sew to secure
wrap and sew it in place

q Mini Basket

Shown on p. 152

Pattern used 109

The full-size embroidery pattern is on p. 151; the full-size templates for the handle can be found on pattern sheet insert B.

► Materials Needed
Lt brown print (upper basket top)
- 13 × 40 cm [5⅛" × 15¾"]
Lt blue homespun (lower basket top)
- 10 × 40 cm [4" × 15¾"]
Assorted fat quarters or scraps (piecing and appliqué)
Brown homespun (bottom top)
- 15 × 15 cm [5⅞" × 5⅞"]
Beige homespun (handle top and lining A)
- 20 × 20 cm [7⅞" × 7⅞"]
Plaid homespun (handle top and lining B)
- 20 × 20 cm [7⅞" × 7⅞"]
Lining - 40 × 40 cm [15¾" × 15¾"]
Muslin (facing)
- 40 × 40 cm [15¾" × 15¾"]
Batting
- 40 × 40 cm [15¾" × 15¾"]
Interfacing
- 25 × 35 cm [9¾" × 13¾"]
Lt beige rickrack
- 1.5 × 40 cm [⅝" × 15¾"]
Clear template plastic
- 10 × 10 cm [4" × 4"]
Embroidery floss/Candlewicking thread in light beige

► Finished measurements
See the diagrams below.

► Instructions
1 Appliqué, embroider and piece the basket body top.
2 With wrong sides together and batting in between, baste and quilt the top and facing.
3 With right sides together and matching the designs, sew the side seams to create a cylinder shape. Turn right side out; sew the rickrack trim to the opening edge.
4 Fuse the interfacing to the body lining. With right sides together, sew the side seams. With right sides together, slip the lining over the basket body.
5 Make the basket bottom.
6 With right sides together, sew the bottom outer to the basket body.
7 Make the bottom lining and insert the template plastic between; blindstitch the bottom lining down.
8 Make the handle; sew it to the basket body. Pull the handle up.
9 Turn the seam allowance at the opening to the inside; blindstitch.

Dimensional Diagram

Basket Body Top
(top, batting and lining are the same dimensions; add seam allowance to the top and lining)

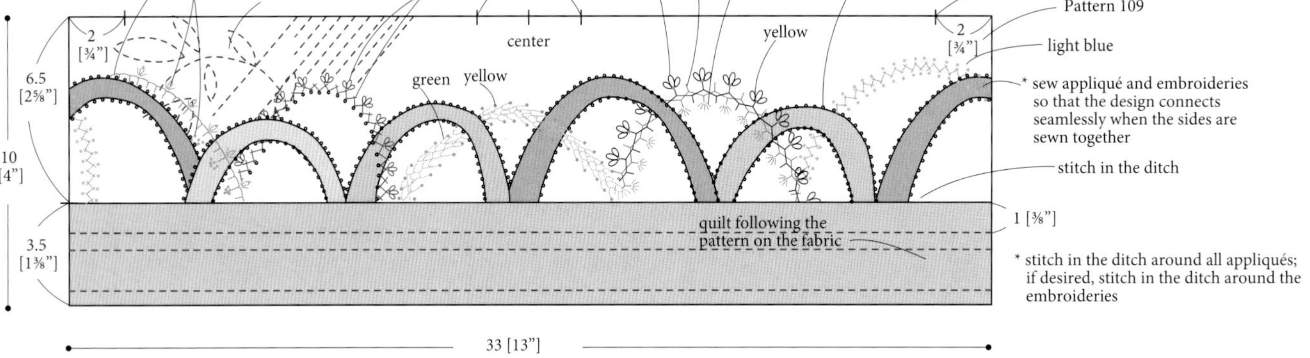

Embroidery:
See the full-size pattern for the stitch name and number of strands used. (p. 151)
white
grey
light blue
quilt following the pattern on the fabric
pink
4 [1½"] handle position
center
green
yellow
light blue
white
handle position
Pattern 109
light blue
2 [¾"]
6.5 [2⅝"]
10 [4"]
3.5 [1⅜"]
* sew appliqué and embroideries so that the design connects seamlessly when the sides are sewn together
stitch in the ditch
1 [⅜"]
quilt following the pattern on the fabric
* stitch in the ditch around all appliqués; if desired, stitch in the ditch around the embroideries
33 [13"]

Basket Bottom
(top, batting and lining are the same dimensions; add seam allowance to the top and lining)

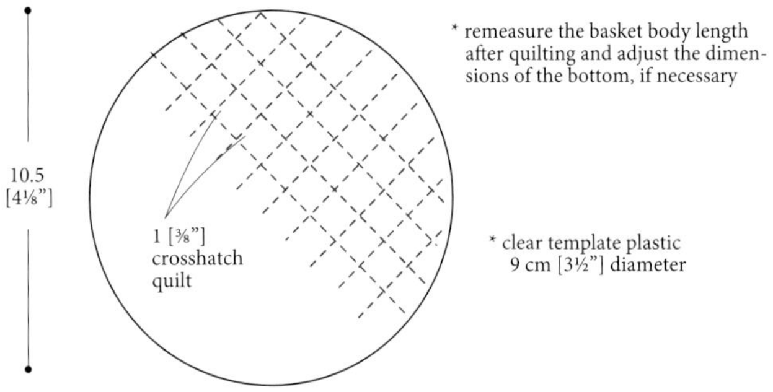

10.5 [4⅛"]
1 [⅜"] crosshatch quilt
* remeasure the basket body length after quilting and adjust the dimensions of the bottom, if necessary
* clear template plastic 9 cm [3½"] diameter

Handle
(top, batting and lining, cut 1 each)

handle top A

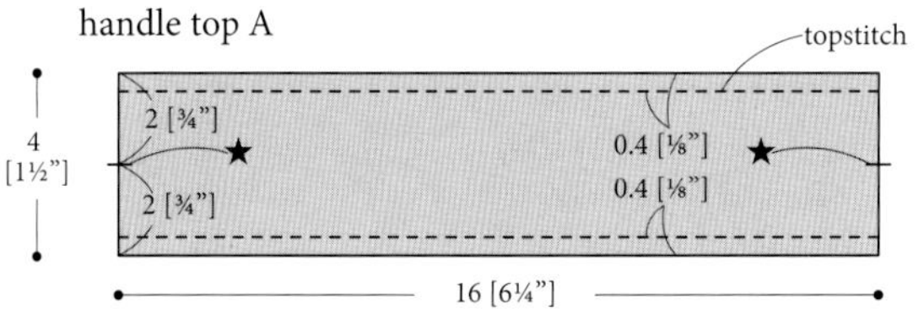

topstitch
4 [1½"]
2 [¾"]
0.4 [⅛"]
16 [6¼"]

handle top B

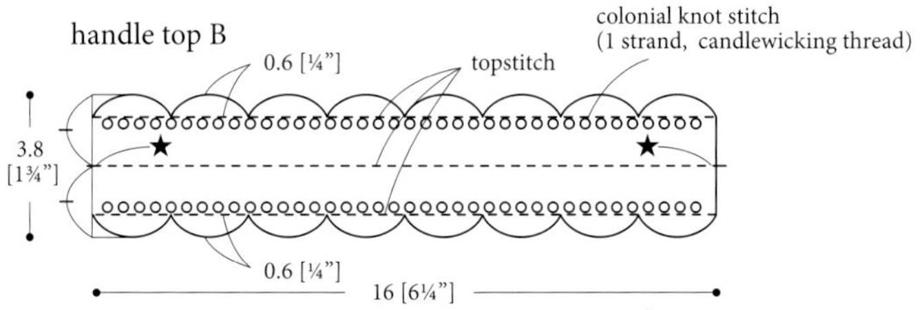

colonial knot stitch (1 strand, candlewicking thread)
0.6 [¼"]
topstitch
3.8 [1¾"]
16 [6¼"]

Making the Handle

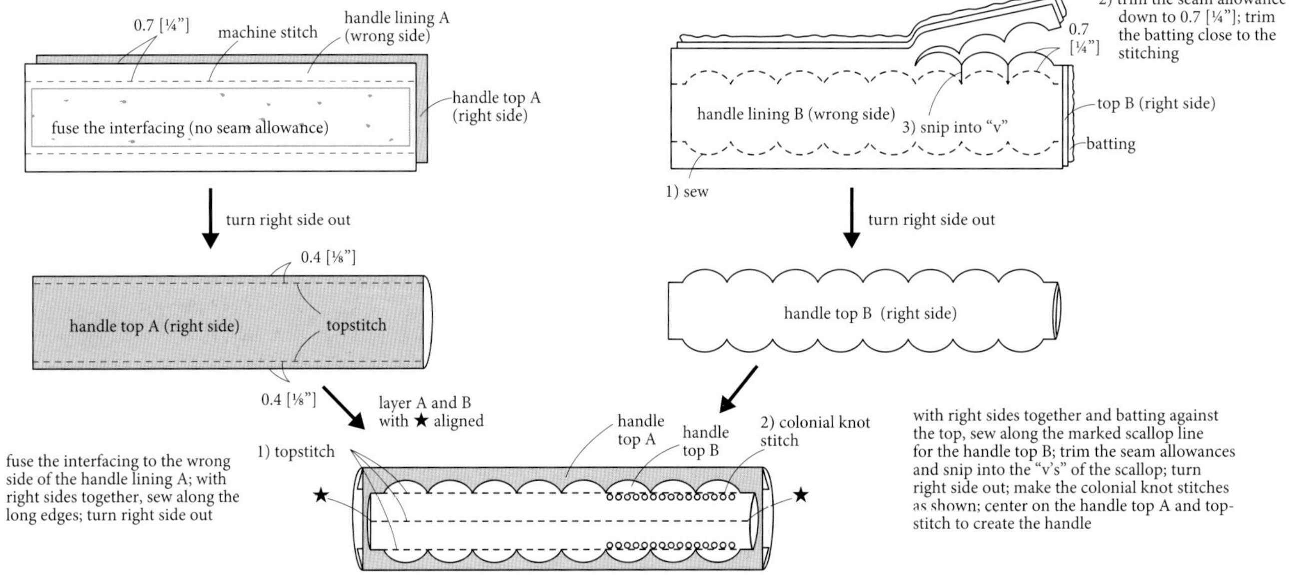

0.7 [¼"]
machine stitch
handle lining A (wrong side)
handle top A (right side)
fuse the interfacing (no seam allowance)
turn right side out
0.4 [⅛"]
handle top A (right side)
topstitch
layer A and B with ★ aligned
fuse the interfacing to the wrong side of the handle lining A; with right sides together, sew along the long edges; turn right side out
1) topstitch
handle top A
handle top B
2) colonial knot stitch
2) trim the seam allowance down to 0.7 [¼"]; trim the batting close to the stitching
top B (right side)
handle lining B (wrong side)
3) snip into "v"
batting
1) sew
turn right side out
handle top B (right side)
with right sides together and batting against the top, sew along the marked scallop line for the handle top B; trim the seam allowances and snip into the "v's" of the scallop; turn right side out; make the colonial knot stitches as shown; center on the handle top A and topstitch to create the handle

Making the Basket Body

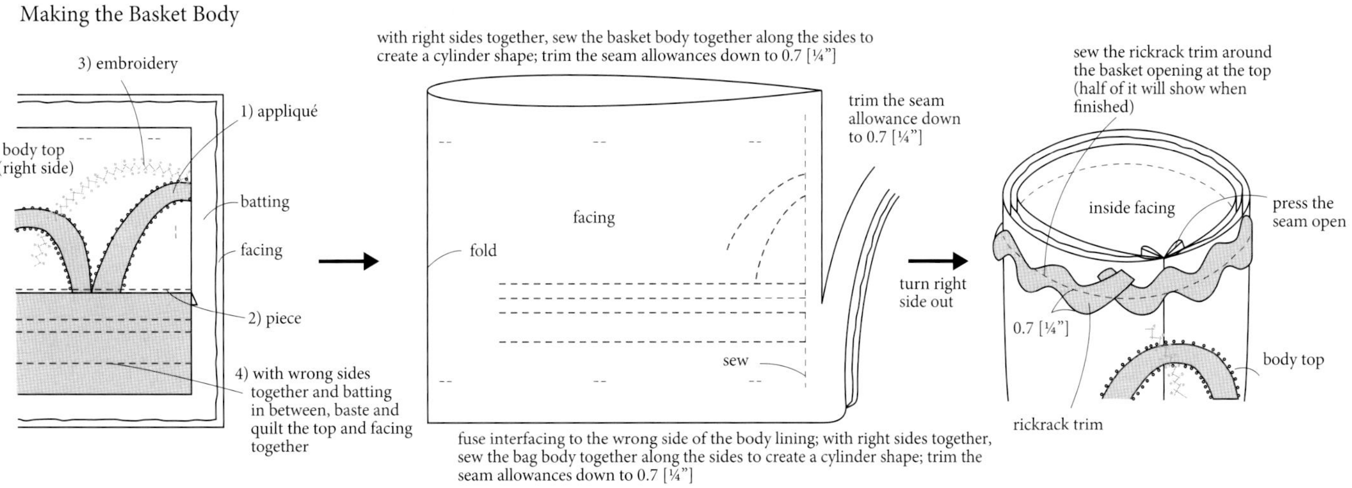

3) embroidery
1) appliqué
body top
(right side)
batting
facing
2) piece
4) with wrong sides together and batting in between, baste and quilt the top and facing together
with right sides together, sew the basket body together along the sides to create a cylinder shape; trim the seam allowances down to 0.7 [¼"]
facing
fold
sew
trim the seam allowance down to 0.7 [¼"]
fuse interfacing to the wrong side of the body lining; with right sides together, sew the bag body together along the sides to create a cylinder shape; trim the seam allowances down to 0.7 [¼"]
turn right side out
sew the rickrack trim around the basket opening at the top (half of it will show when finished)
inside facing
press the seam open
0.7 [¼"]
body top
rickrack trim

Making the Bottom

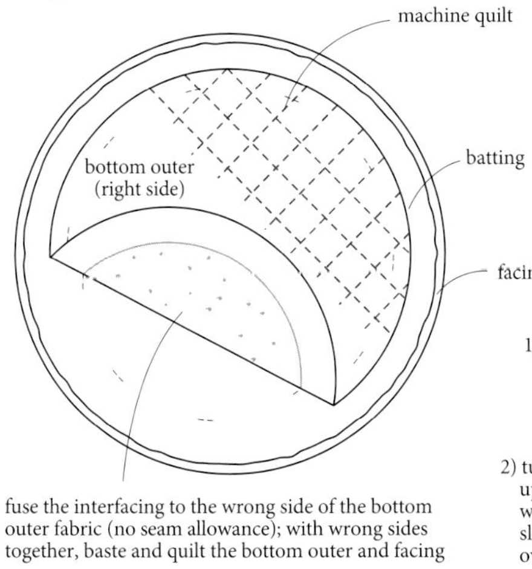

machine quilt
bottom outer
(right side)
batting
facing
fuse the interfacing to the wrong side of the bottom outer fabric (no seam allowance); with wrong sides together, baste and quilt the bottom outer and facing

Sewing the Basket Together

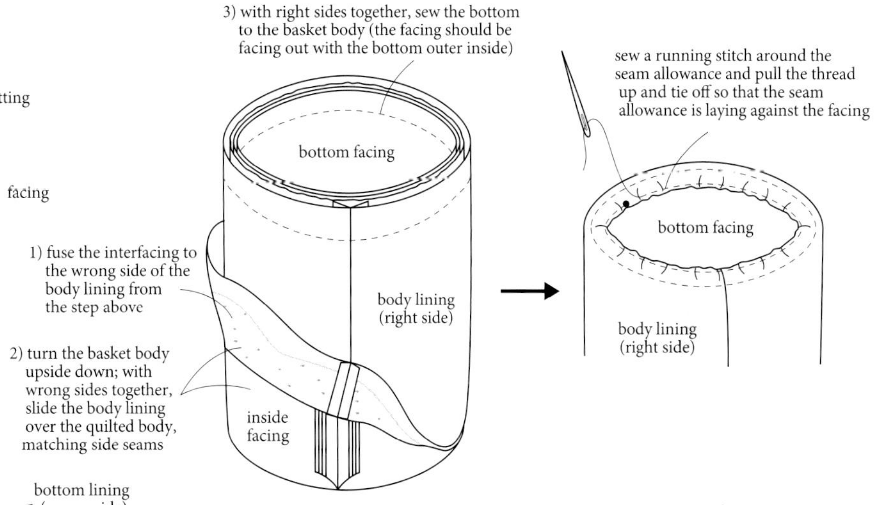

3) with right sides together, sew the bottom to the basket body (the facing should be facing out with the bottom outer inside)
bottom facing
1) fuse the interfacing to the wrong side of the body lining from the step above
body lining
(right side)
2) turn the basket body upside down; with wrong sides together, slide the body lining over the quilted body, matching side seams
inside facing
sew a running stitch around the seam allowance and pull the thread up and tie off so that the seam allowance is laying against the facing
bottom facing
body lining
(right side)

Finishing the Basket Bottom

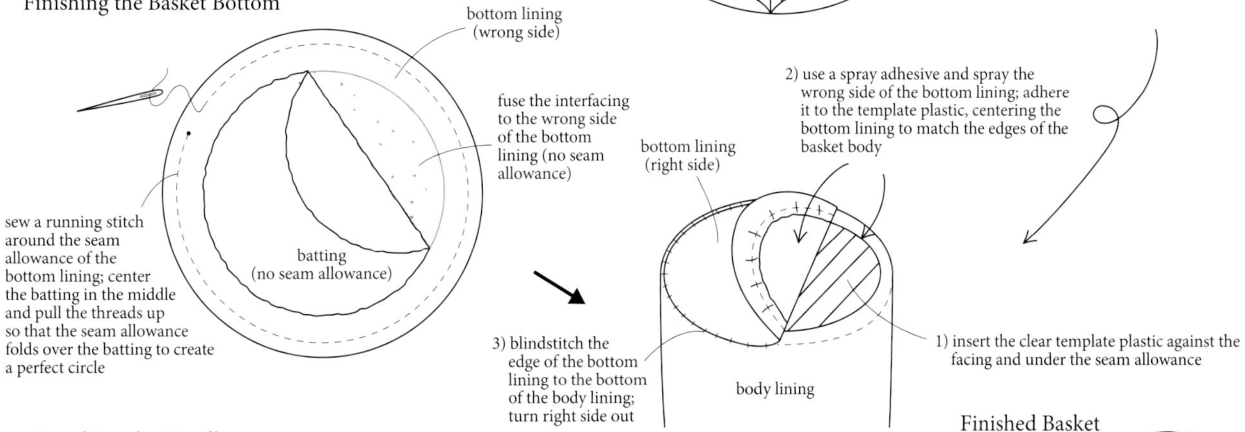

bottom lining
(wrong side)
fuse the interfacing to the wrong side of the bottom lining (no seam allowance)
sew a running stitch around the seam allowance of the bottom lining; center the batting in the middle and pull the threads up so that the seam allowance folds over the batting to create a perfect circle
batting
(no seam allowance)
2) use a spray adhesive and spray the wrong side of the bottom lining; adhere it to the template plastic, centering the bottom lining to match the edges of the basket body
bottom lining
(right side)
3) blindstitch the edge of the bottom lining to the bottom of the body lining; turn right side out
body lining
1) insert the clear template plastic against the facing and under the seam allowance

Attaching the Handle

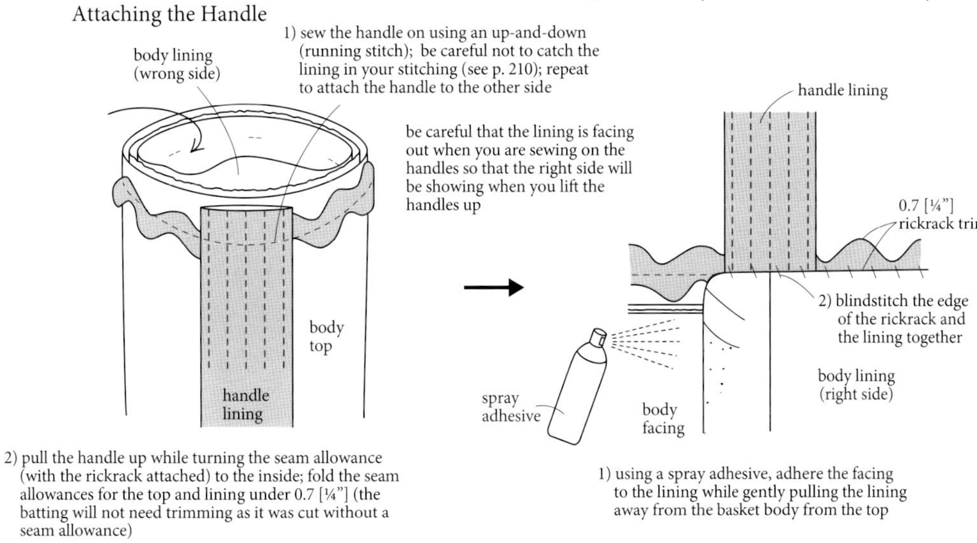

body lining
(wrong side)
1) sew the handle on using an up-and-down (running stitch); be careful not to catch the lining in your stitching (see p. 210); repeat to attach the handle to the other side
be careful that the lining is facing out when you are sewing on the handles so that the right side will be showing when you lift the handles up
body top
handle lining
2) pull the handle up while turning the seam allowance (with the rickrack attached) to the inside; fold the seam allowances for the top and lining under 0.7 [¼"] (the batting will not need trimming as it was cut without a seam allowance)
handle lining
0.7 [¼"]
rickrack trim
2) blindstitch the edge of the rickrack and the lining together
body lining
(right side)
spray adhesive
body facing
1) using a spray adhesive, adhere the facing to the lining while gently pulling the lining away from the basket body from the top

Finished Basket

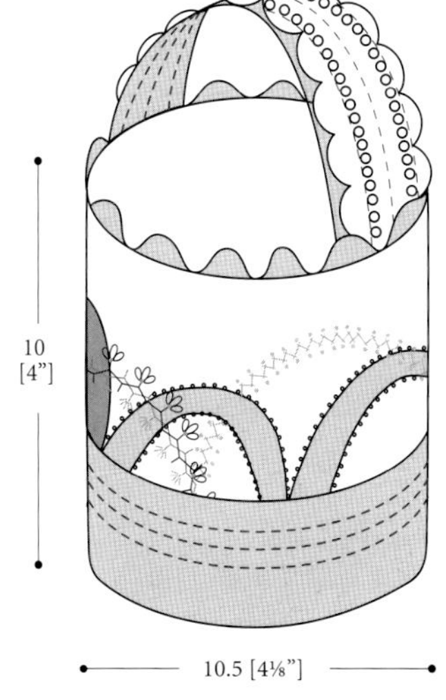

10
[4"]
10.5 [4⅛"]

r Handbag

Shown on p. 158

Pattern used 110

The full-size embroidery pattern is on p. 155; the full-size templates for the bag body can be found on pattern sheet insert B.

► Materials Needed
Brown homespun (bag front, bag back, gussets, handle loops)
- 110 × 55 cm [43¼" × 21⅝"]
Beige homespun (appliqué background)
- 40 × 25 cm [15¾" × 9¾"]
Assorted green prints (appliqué)
Lining
- 110 × 60 cm [43¼" × 23⅝"]
Batting
- 110 × 60 cm [43¼" × 23⅝"]
Green homespun (bias binding)
- 2.5 × 160 cm [1" × 63"]
Interfacing
- 25 × 50 cm [9¾" × 19¾"]
Wood handles (1 pair)
- 12 cm [4¾"] inside width
Embroidery floss

► Finished measurements
See the diagrams below.

► Instructions
1 Appliqué, embroider and piece the bag top.
2 With wrong sides together and batting in between, baste and quilt the bag front and lining.
3 Make the bag back following the directions in step 2.
4 Make the four handle loops. Thread them through the holes in the handle; baste in place in position on the bag front and bag back.
5 Make the bias binding for both the gusset and the bag opening.
6 With right sides together, sew the bias binding to the bag front and bag back at the bag opening edges. Sew the handle loops to the bag opening while you are binding the bag opening (see diagram below.)
7 With wrong sides together and batting in between, baste and quilt the gusset pieces.
8 Bind the top edges of the gussets with the short bias binding made from the bias strips. With right sides together, sew the gussets together at the bottom.
9 With right sides together, sew the bag front, bag back and gusset together to create the bag body; bind the raw edges. Turn right side out.

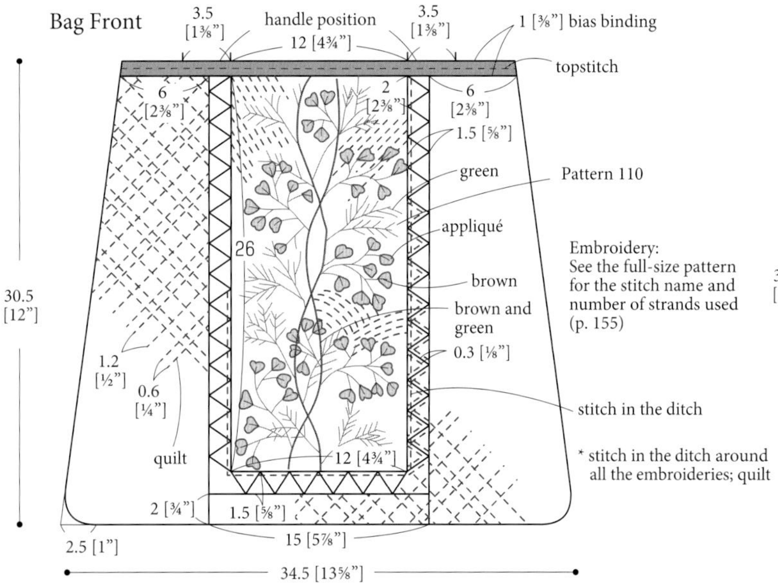

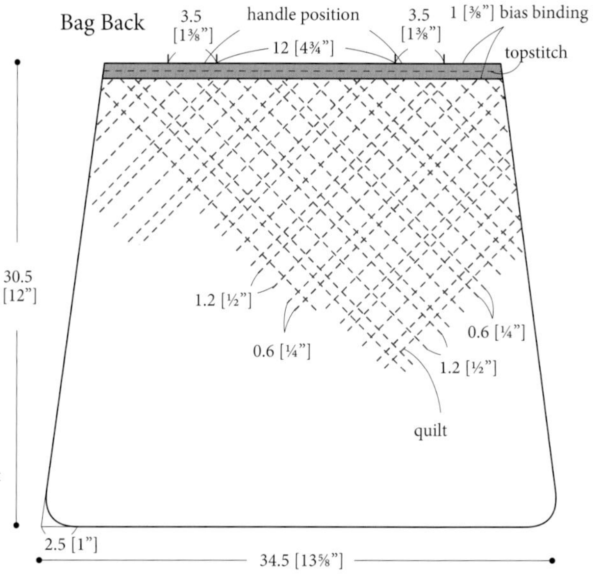

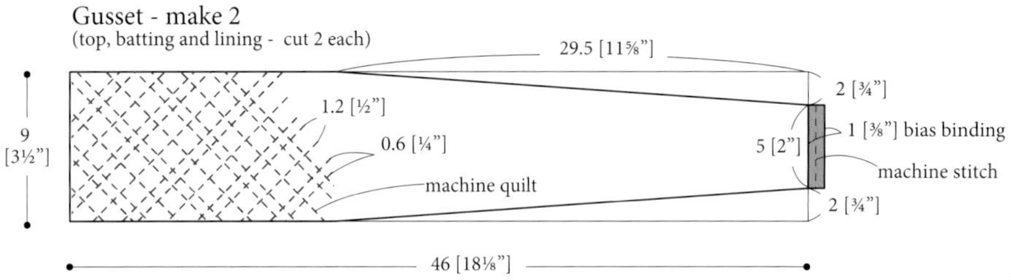

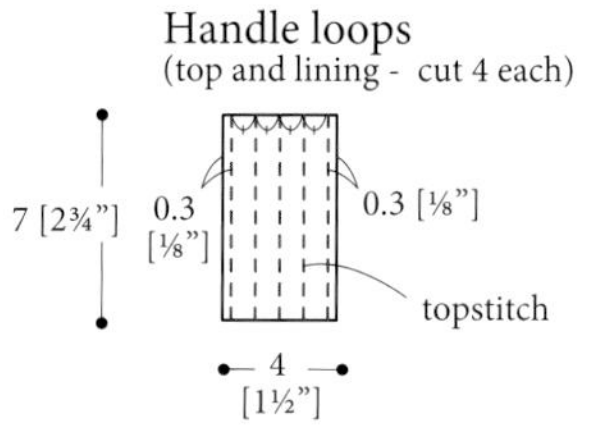

Making the Handle Loops

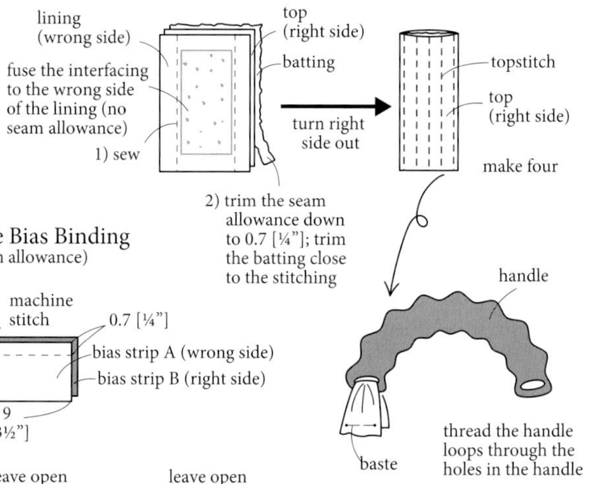

Making the Bag Front

with wrong sides together and batting in between, baste and qulit the bag front; repeat to make the bag back

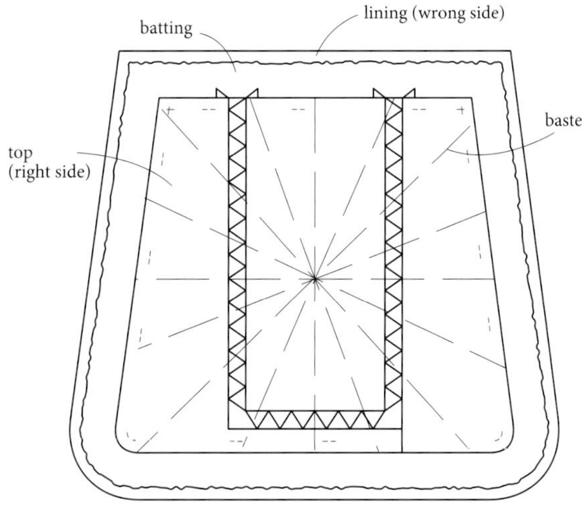

Making the Bias Binding

(no seam allowance)

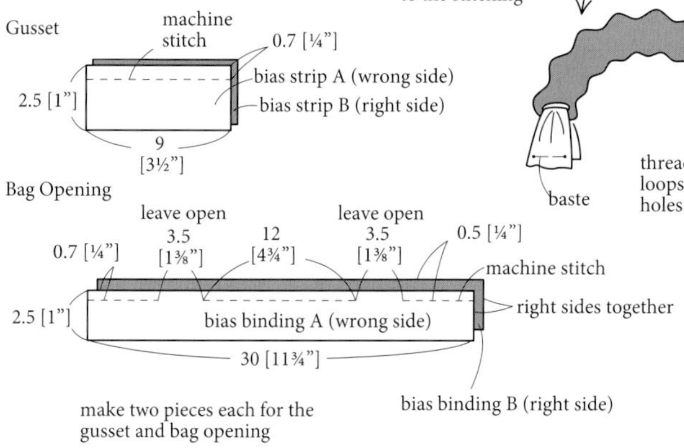

Attaching the Handles

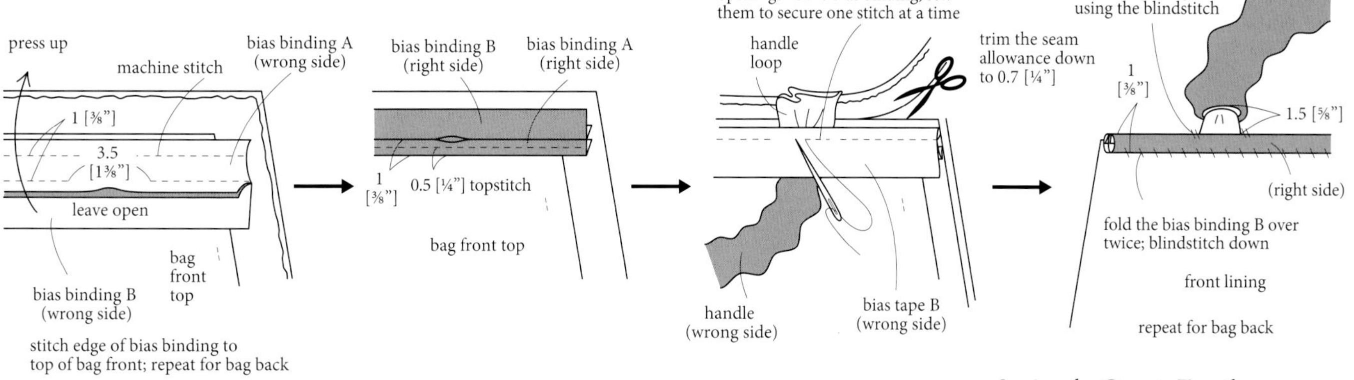
press up
machine stitch
bias binding A
(wrong side)
1 [⅜"]
3.5
[1⅜"]
leave open
bag
front
top
bias binding B
(wrong side)
stitch edge of bias binding to
top of bag front; repeat for bag back
bias binding B
(right side)
bias binding A
(right side)
1
[⅜"]
0.5 [¼"] topstitch
bag front top
insert the handle loops through the
openings in the bias binding; sew
them to secure one stitch at a time
handle
loop
trim the seam
allowance down
to 0.7 [¼"]
handle
(wrong side)
bias tape B
(wrong side)
sew the opening closed
using the blindstitch
1
[⅜"]
1.5 [⅝"]
(right side)
fold the bias binding B over
twice; blindstitch down
front lining
repeat for bag back

Sewing the Gussets Together

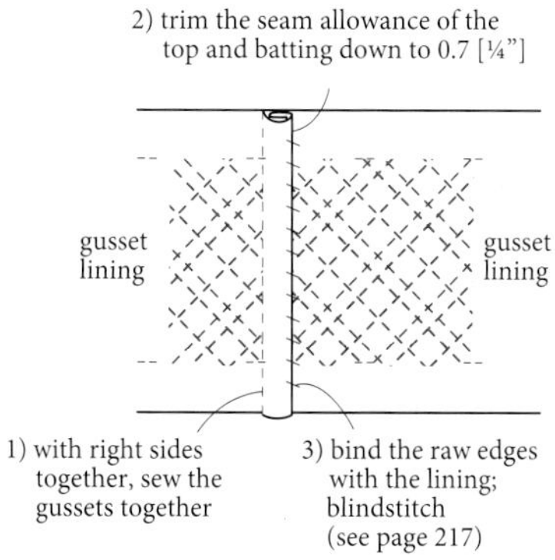
2) trim the seam allowance of the
top and batting down to 0.7 [¼"]
gusset
lining
gusset
lining
1) with right sides
together, sew the
gussets together
3) bind the raw edges
with the lining;
blindstitch
(see page 217)

Making the Gusset

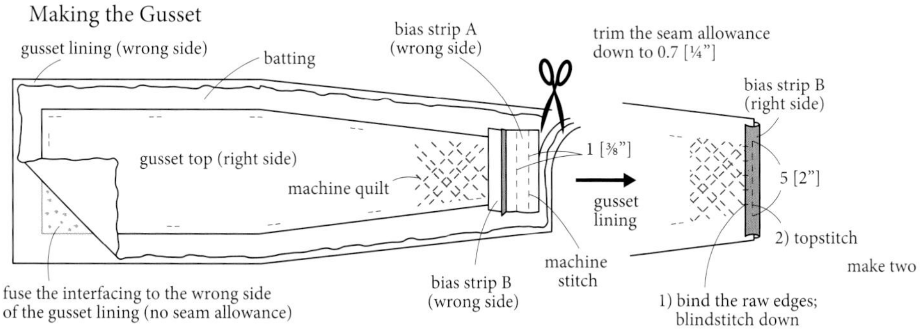
gusset lining (wrong side)
batting
bias strip A
(wrong side)
trim the seam allowance
down to 0.7 [¼"]
gusset top (right side)
machine quilt
1 [⅜"]
bias strip B
(right side)
5 [2"]
gusset
lining
2) topstitch
machine
stitch
make two
fuse the interfacing to the wrong side
of the gusset lining (no seam allowance)
bias strip B
(wrong side)
1) bind the raw edges;
blindstitch down

Sewing the Bag Body Together

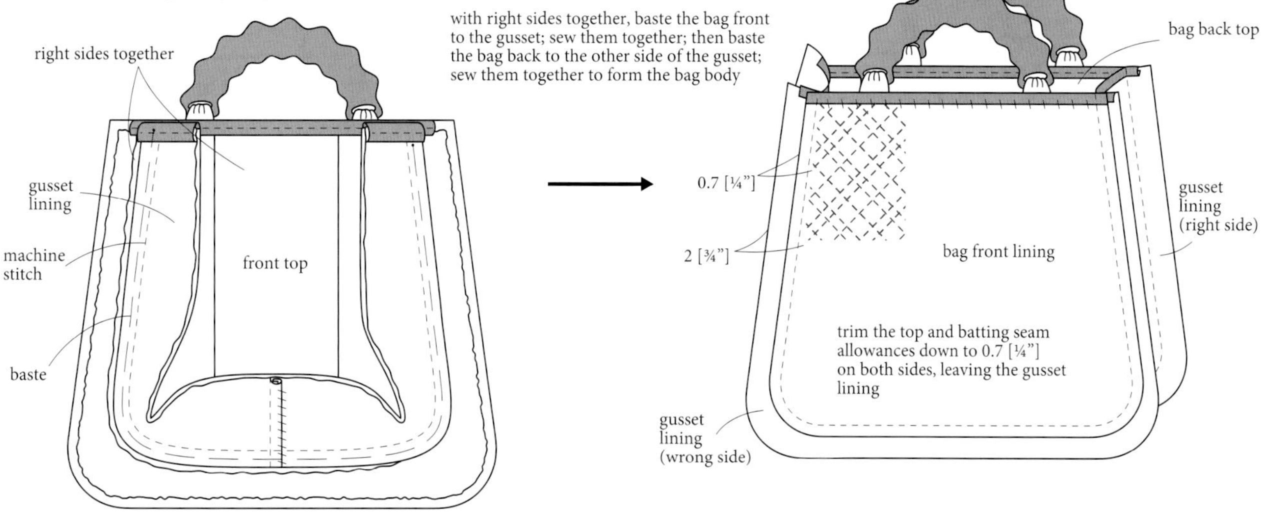
right sides together
with right sides together, baste the bag front
to the gusset; sew them together; then baste
the bag back to the other side of the gusset;
sew them together to form the bag body
gusset
lining
machine
stitch
front top
baste
bag back top
0.7 [¼"]
2 [¾"]
gusset
lining
(right side)
bag front lining
trim the top and batting seam
allowances down to 0.7 [¼"]
on both sides, leaving the gusset
lining
gusset
lining
(wrong side)

Binding the Edges

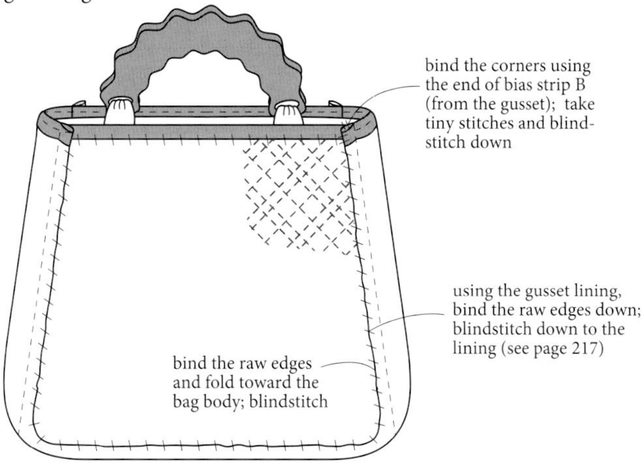
bind the corners using
the end of bias strip B
(from the gusset); take
tiny stitches and blind-
stitch down
using the gusset lining,
bind the raw edges down;
blindstitch down to the
lining (see page 217)
bind the raw edges
and fold toward the
bag body; blindstitch

Finished Bag

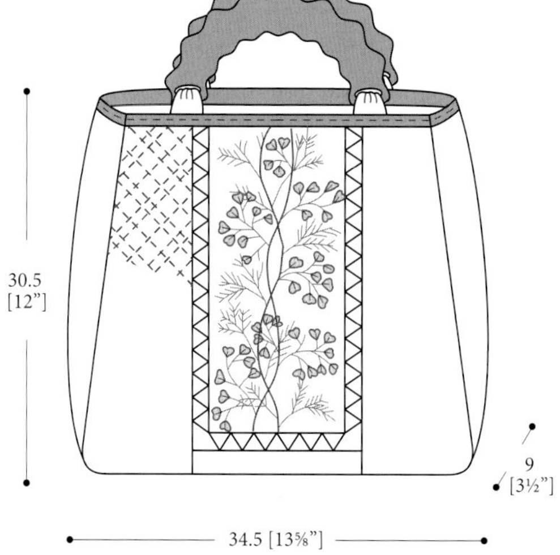
30.5
[12"]
9
[3½"]
34.5 [13⅝"]

S Handbag

Shown on p. 159

Pattern used 111

The full-size embroidery pattern is on p. 157; the full-size templates for the bag body, bag opening bias binding and zipper pull can be found on pattern sheet insert B.

► Materials Needed

Lt grey print (appliqué background) - 30×30 cm [11¾" × 11¾"]
Assorted fat quarters and scraps (piecing and appliqué)
Beige homespun (bag front, gusset/handle, gusset/handle lining, zipper opening (bias), zipper pull) - 70×100 cm [27½" × 39⅜"]
Beige homespun (bottom) - 15×30 cm [5⅞" × 11¾"]
Lining - 110×70 cm [43¼" × 27½"]
Batting - 110×70 cm [43¼" × 27½"]
Bias binding - 2.5×260 cm [1" × 102¼"]
Interfacing - 20×100 cm [7⅞" × 39⅜"]
1 Zipper - 28 cm [11"] long
5 Buttons
Embroidery floss
Candlewicking thread - lt beige

► Finished measurements

See the diagrams below.

► Instructions

1 Appliqué, embroider and piece the bag front top.
2 With right sides together and batting against the lining, sew the front top and lining together at the top edge only. Turn right side out; baste and quilt. Sew the darts.
3 Make the bag back following the directions in step 2.
4 With wrong sides together and batting in between, baste and machine quilt the bag bottom top and lining (with fused interfacing.)
5 Fuse the interfacing (no seam allowance) to the gusset and handle linings. Sew the gussets and handle top together; repeat for the lining. With wrong sides together and batting in between, baste and quilt the gusset/handle top and lining together.
6 With right sides together, sew the gusset/handle ends together to create a loop (note that the seams will align to the zipper opening).
7 Sew the zipper tabs to the zipper; sew the zipper to the zipper opening.
8 With right sides together, sew the bag front and bag back to the gusset/handle. With right sides together, sew the zipper opening to the bag body.
9 Do the remaining colonial knot stitches on the bag front to finish. Make the zipper pull and attach it to the zipper clasp.

Bag Front

Embroidery:
See the full-size pattern for the stitch name and number of strands used. (p. 157)

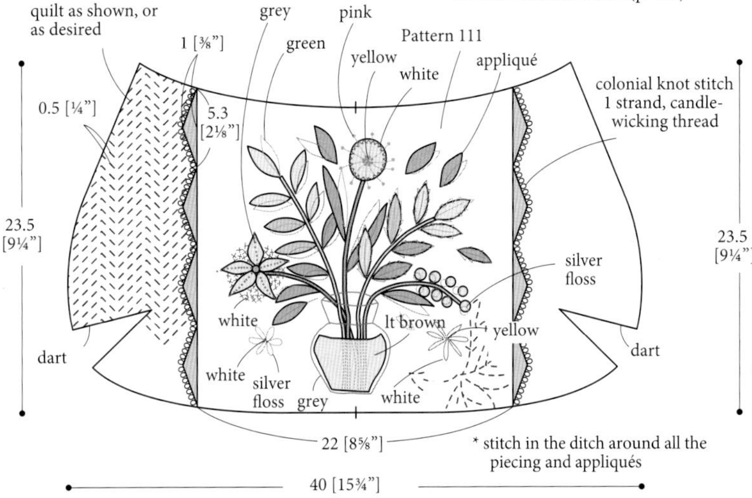
quilt as shown, or as desired
grey
pink
green
yellow
white
Pattern 111
appliqué
1 [⅜"]
0.5 [¼"]
5.3 [2⅛"]
colonial knot stitch 1 strand, candlewicking thread
23.5 [9¼"]
silver floss
white
lt brown
yellow
dart
white
silver floss
grey
white
22 [8⅝"]
* stitch in the ditch around all the piecing and appliqués
40 [15¾"]

Bag Back

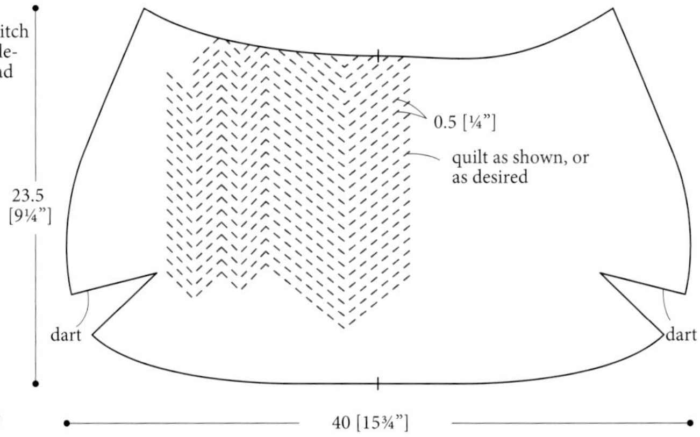
0.5 [¼"]
quilt as shown, or as desired
23.5 [9¼"]
dart
dart
40 [15¾"]

Bag Bottom

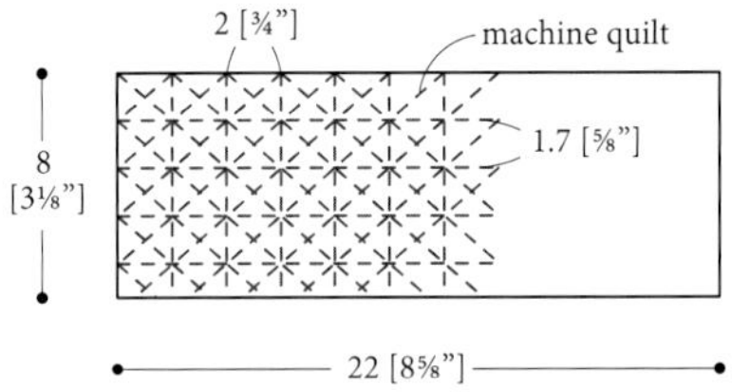
2 [¾"]
machine quilt
8 [3⅛"]
1.7 [⅝"]
22 [8⅝"]

Gusset/Handle (the top is a single piece of fabric; the gussets and handle are three pieces of lining)

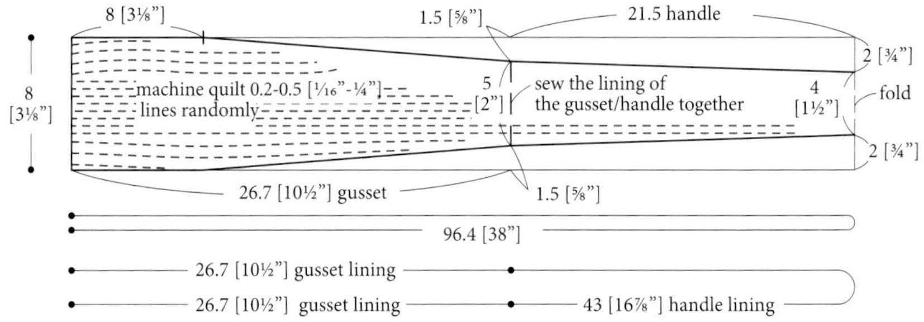
8 [3⅛"]
1.5 [⅝"]
21.5 handle
2 [¾"]
8 [3⅛"]
machine quilt 0.2-0.5 [⅟₁₆"-¼"] lines randomly
5 [2"]
sew the lining of the gusset/handle together
4 [1½"]
fold
2 [¾"]
26.7 [10½"] gusset
1.5 [⅝"]
96.4 [38"]
26.7 [10½"] gusset lining
26.7 [10½"] gusset lining
43 [16⅞"] handle lining

Zipper Opening

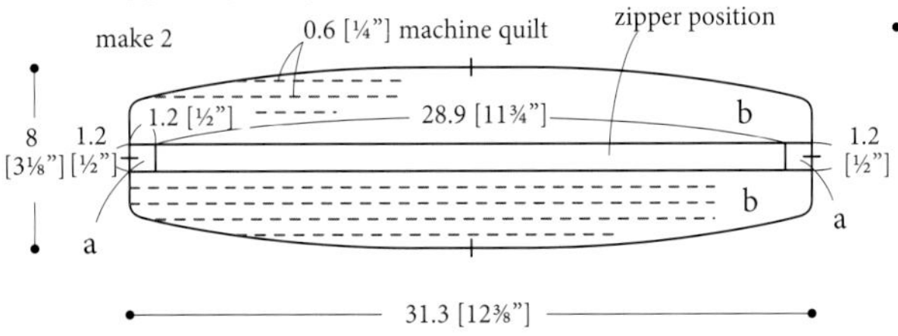
make 2
0.6 [¼"] machine quilt
zipper position
8 [3⅛"]
1.2 [½"]
1.2 [½"]
28.9 [11¾"]
b
1.2 [½"]
b
a
a
31.3 [12⅜"]

* Fuse the interfacing to the lining of the bottom, gusset, handle and zipper opening (no seam allowance).

Zipper Pull

Main Segment (top and lining - cut 1 each)

Loop (top and lining - cut 1 each)

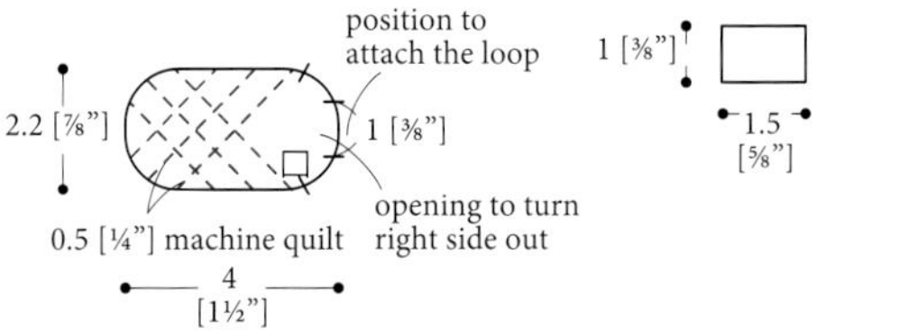
position to attach the loop
2.2 [⅞"]
1 [⅜"]
opening to turn right side out
0.5 [¼"] machine quilt
4 [1½"]
1 [⅜"]
1.5 [⅝"]

Making the Bag Front and Bag Back

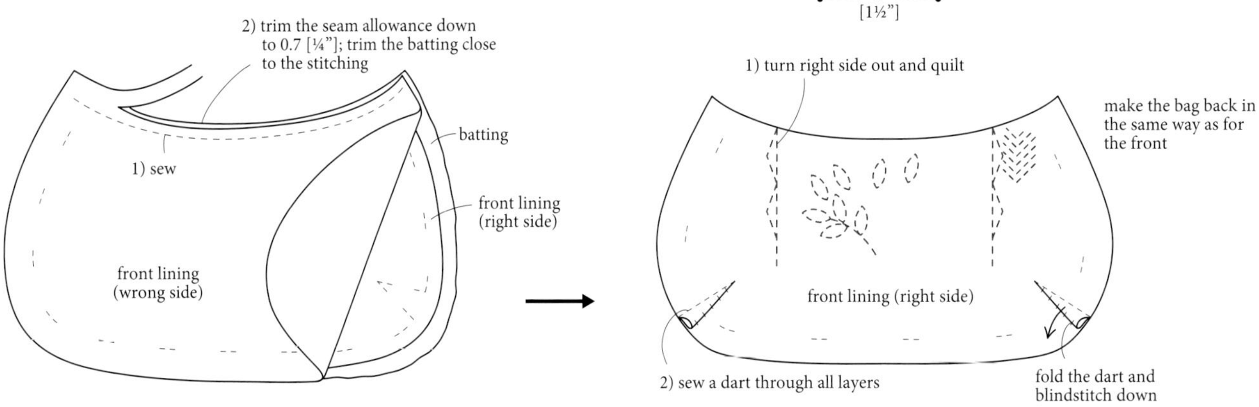
2) trim the seam allowance down to 0.7 [¼"]; trim the batting close to the stitching
1) sew
batting
front lining (right side)
front lining (wrong side)
1) turn right side out and quilt
make the bag back in the same way as for the front
front lining (right side)
2) sew a dart through all layers
fold the dart and blindstitch down

Sewing the Gusset, Handle and Bottom Together

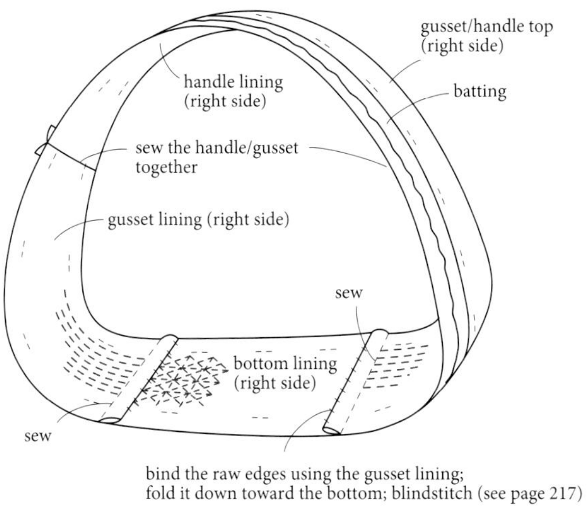
gusset/handle top
(right side)
handle lining
(right side)
batting
sew the handle/gusset
together
gusset lining (right side)
sew
bottom lining
(right side)
sew
bind the raw edges using the gusset lining;
fold it down toward the bottom; blindstitch (see page 217)

Sewing the Bag Front, Bag Back and Gusset Together

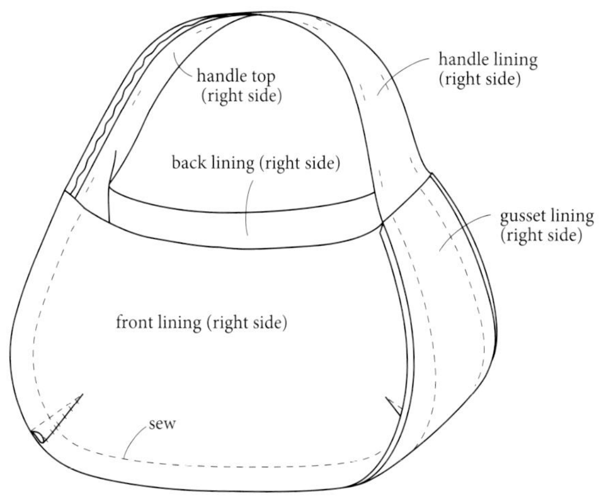
handle top
(right side)
handle lining
(right side)
back lining (right side)
gusset lining
(right side)
front lining (right side)
sew

Binding the Edges

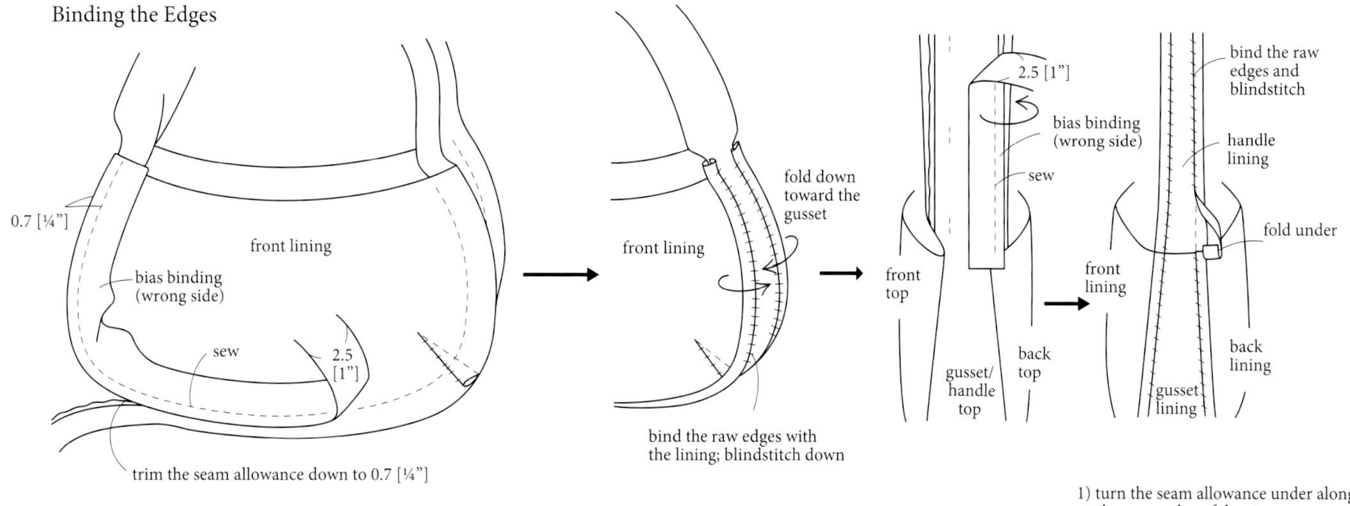
0.7 [¼"]
front lining
bias binding
(wrong side)
sew
2.5
[1"]
trim the seam allowance down to 0.7 [¼"]
front lining
fold down
toward the
gusset
bind the raw edges with
the lining; blindstitch down
2.5 [1"]
bias binding
(wrong side)
sew
front
top
gusset/
handle
top
back
top
bind the raw
edges and
blindstitch
handle
lining
fold under
front
lining
back
lining
gusset
lining

Making the Zipper Opening

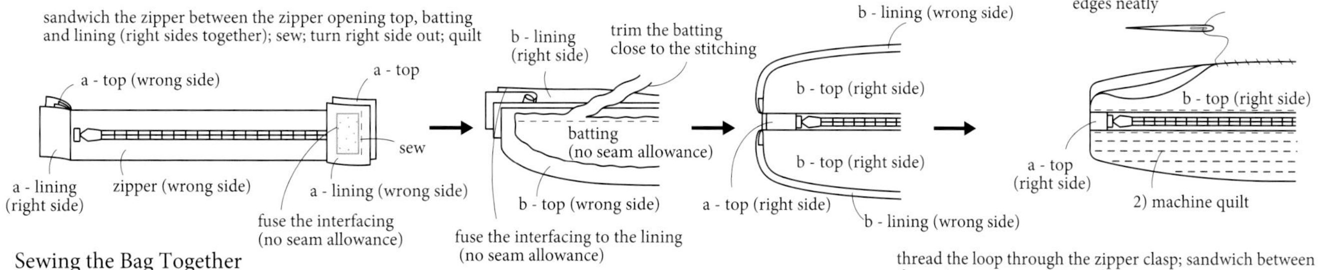
sandwich the zipper between the zipper opening top, batting
and lining (right sides together); sew; turn right side out; quilt
a - top (wrong side)
a - top
sew
a - lining
(right side)
zipper (wrong side)
a - lining (wrong side)
fuse the interfacing
(no seam allowance)
b - lining
(right side)
trim the batting
close to the stitching
batting
(no seam allowance)
b - top (wrong side)
fuse the interfacing to the lining
(no seam allowance)
b - lining (wrong side)
b - top (right side)
b - top (right side)
a - top (right side)
b - lining (wrong side)
1) turn the seam allowance under along
the outer edge of the zipper opening,
then blindstitch together to finish the
edges neatly
b - top (right side)
a - top
(right side)
2) machine quilt

Sewing the Bag Together

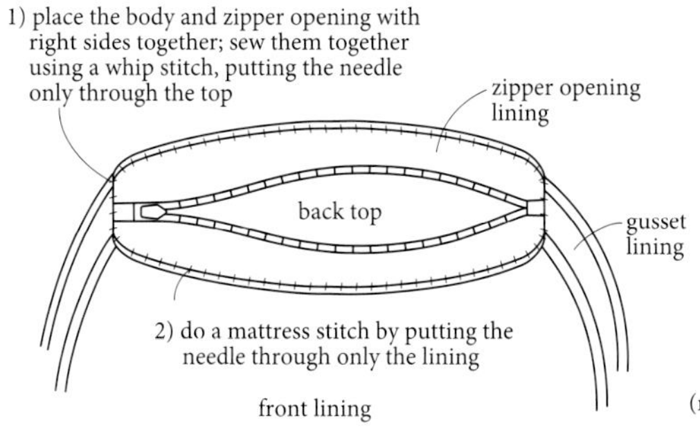
1) place the body and zipper opening with
right sides together; sew them together
using a whip stitch, putting the needle
only through the top
zipper opening
lining
back top
gusset
lining
2) do a mattress stitch by putting the
needle through only the lining
front lining

Making the Zipper Pull

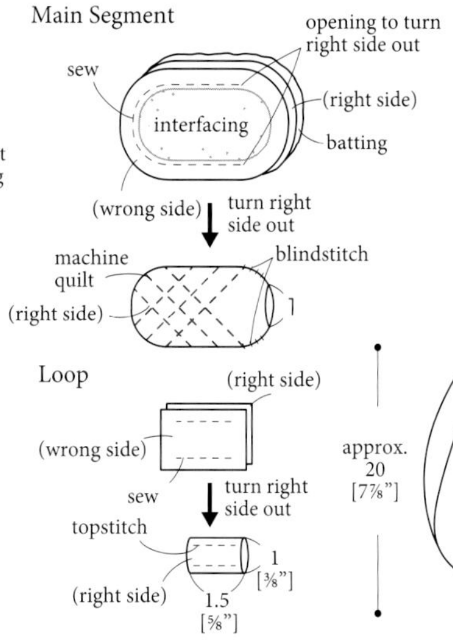
Main Segment
sew
opening to turn
right side out
(right side)
interfacing
batting
(wrong side)
turn right
side out
machine
quilt
blindstitch
(right side)
Loop
(right side)
(wrong side)
sew
turn right
side out
topstitch
1
[⅜"]
(right side)
1.5
[⅝"]

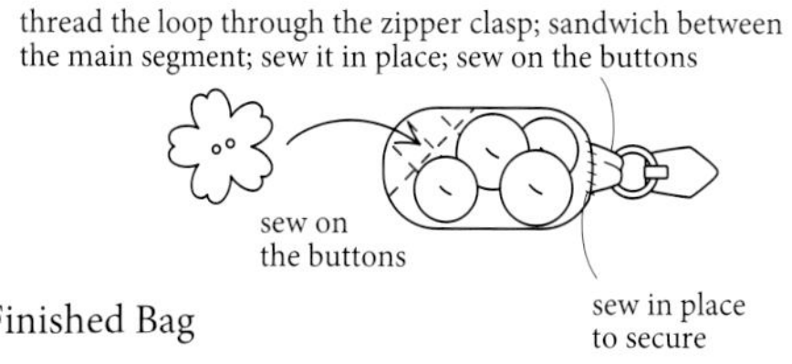
thread the loop through the zipper clasp; sandwich between
the main segment; sew it in place; sew on the buttons
sew on
the buttons
sew in place
to secure

Finished Bag

approx.
20
[7⅞"]
8
[3⅛"]
approx. 40 [15¾"]

Finishing the Bag

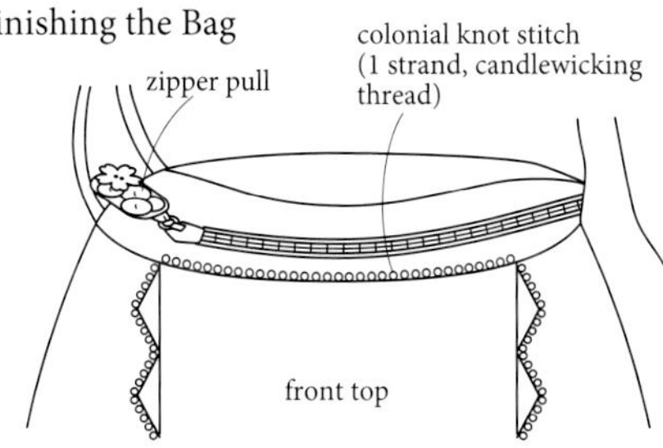
zipper pull
colonial knot stitch
(1 strand, candlewicking
thread)
front top

Yoko Saito

Originally from Ichikawa City in Chiba Prefecture in Japan, Yoko Saito established her quilting school and shop, Quilt Party, in 1985. She soon garnered a reputation for her masterful use and personal style of "taupe colors", as well as her beautifully precise needlework. In addition to her regular appearances on Japanese television and in magazines, she has published numerous books. In recent years, she has begun to branch out internationally, holding quilt exhibitions and workshops in countries as far as France, Italy and Taiwan. In 2008 she commemorated 30 years of her creative career with the Yoko Saito Quilt Exhibition at the Matsuya department store in Ginza, Tokyo.

Original Title	Saito Yoko no Patchwork wo Tanoshimu Shishu Patterns 120
Author	Yoko Saito
First Edition	Originally published in Japan in 2008
Copyright	©2008 Yoko Saito, ©2008 Nihon Vogue-Sha; All rights reserved.
Published by:	Nihon Vogue Co., Ltd. 3-23 Ichigaya Honmura-cho, Shinjuku-ku, Tokyo, Japan 162-8705 http://book.nihonvogue.co.jp

Translation	©2013 Stitch Publications, LLC
English Translation Rights	arranged with Stitch Publications, LLC through Tuttle-Mori Agency, Inc.
Published by:	Stitch Publications, LLC P.O. Box 16694 Seattle, WA 98116 http://www.stitchpublications.com
Printed & Bound	KHL Printing, Singapore
ISBN	978-0-9859746-5-7
PCN	Library of Congress Control Number: 2013948313

Staff

Book Design/Layout	Goji Morofuji
Photography	Akinori Miyashita Kana Watanabe (full-size patterns and step-by-step lessons)
Styling	Kumiko Uematsu
Illustrations	Factory Water
Pattern Illustrations	Nobuyuki Nagaoka
Editorial Assistant	Sakae Suzuki
Editor	Jun Sasaki

Quilt Party, Co., Ltd. (shop and school)

Quilt Party Co., Ltd.
Active Ichikawa 2F
1-23-2, Ichikawa, Ichikawa-shi,
Chiba-Ken, Japan 272-0034

http://www.quilt.co.jp (Japanese)
http://shop.quilt.co.jp/en/index.htm (English)

Production: Satomi Funamoto, Kazuko Yamada, Katsumi Mizusawa, Masue Sato, Keiko Nakajima, Yoko Nakamura, Tsuko Yamazaki

Photography Collaboration

LECIEN Corporation Art and Hobby Division
(No. 25 embroidery thread, Cosmo Multi Work Stitch Work and One-Touch embroidery hoop on p. 181)
Yotsubashi Grand Square
1-28-3 Shinmachi, Nishi-ku
Osaka, Japan 550-0013
http://www.lecien.co.jp/en/

Kinkame Shigyo Co., Ltd.
(Candlewicking thread and lap hoop on p. 181)
1-2-15 Higashi Nihonbashi, Chuo-ku, Tokyo, Japan 103-0004

This English edition is published by arrangement with Nihon Vogue Co., Ltd. in care of Tuttle-Mori Agency, Inc., Tokyo

COUNTRY HOMES

ISBN: 2-85018-832-8

Translated from French by Simon Pleasance and Fronza Woods
Edited by Jennifer Ladonne
Art Direction: Pascal Fromont

Printed in France by Imprimerie Clerc

JEAN DEMACHY

COUNTRY HOMES

Elegant weekend retreats from around the world

Text by Olivier de Vleeschouwer

ELLE DECOR

filipacchi publishing

CONTENTS

INTRODUCTION

No matter what the season, there is something amazingly seductive about the idea of getting away to a weekend house. The nonstop hustle and bustle of city life may be intoxicating during the week, but true pleasure is to be found in escaping to the country, near or far, whether for a couple of days or a proper restorative holiday. And not surprisingly, given the element of escapism involved, country houses are often packed with more character and feeling than their urban counterparts; a city apartment can be a refuge come six o'clock, but a weekend place is where you go to breathe, to relax, to recharge. In short, it's where you find yourself again. In "Country Homes: Elegant Weekend Retreats From Around the World," editor extraordinaire Jean Demachy skillfully culls the most intriguing and entrancing country houses from the pages of ELLE DECO magazines around the world. The characteristics they share? Smart design and dazzling style.

Demachy's selections—faithful to the ELLE DECO tradition of showcasing homes packed with ideas and inspiration—include the charming Sussex farmhouse of designer John Stefanidis, fashion powerhouse Pierre Bergé's breathtakingly chic retreat in Saint-Rémy-de-Provence, tastemaker Axel Vervoordt's eclectic Antwerp castle, and a striking Modernist glass pavilion by Thomas Phifer and Muriel Brandolini in New York's historic Hudson River Valley. The exquisite photographs of living rooms, bedrooms, kitchens, gardens, and swimming pools are tantalizing; you can practically catch the sweet scent of lavender in the breeze. From rustic cabins to stately manors to barefoot beach cottages, these are houses with emotional resonance. Their rooms have a bit of patina and heaps of personality. Best of all, they have been created with confidence by talented, stylish people as the backdrop to lives well lived—just like yours.

Margaret Russell
editor in chief, ELLE DECOR

OPPOSITE
The garden gives pride of place to flowers in white, Julie Prisca's favorites. In the midst of symmetrical, box-lined squares, aromatic herbs are within easy reach of the kitchen. The four buildings surrounding the garden lend it a much-appreciated privacy.

Cottages

THE DISCREET ALLURE OF ENGLISH-STYLE DECORATION

These singular homes do not harbor visions of grandeur. They are resolutely rustic, and have that good-natured simplicity that seems to put them on intimate terms with the birds, bees and, most of all, flowers. For some, you must duck your head a bit to get into the converted attic. Yet one happily complies; for these rural beauties aspire to nothing more than their own idiosyncratic style. Cottage owners cherish no illusions about their particular status. They're content to have finally found a quiet place where simplicity can flourish in the most surprising ways. Their personal vision — which never rules out originality or daring — insures homes of great originality that may also resemble the ideal of a happy household.

COUNTRYSIDE AT THE GATES OF PARIS

To summon the sun in Normandy, where she now lives all year round, home furnishings designer Julie Prisca painted the walls of her old post house with warm southern colors. In this bright and luminous atmosphere, Prisca finds many a source of inspiration through the large windows looking out over a delightful walled garden.

OPPOSITE
The only room in the house that features neutral shades, this large attic bedroom displays some of Julie's own creations, like the big zinc-and-glass lamp and amusing Medici-style vase made of chicken wire.

BELOW
Adjoining the bedroom, the attic bathroom is a showcase for natural materials. The basin surround is in beech wood. The mirror on its iron verdigris stand was also designed by the mistress of the house.

OPPOSITE
The provocative tones of the living room are a perfect antidote to Normandy's ever-changing skies. Saffron walls, green beams, cockscomb red sofa and steely blue armchairs all converge to form an optimistic whole that brightens at the least change of light.

BELOW
This symphony of colors begins in the entrance hall, where visitors are treated to an invigorating assortment of hues. The paneled stairway wall was painted lagoon green and the ceiling a deeper teal.

PAUL
ELUARD
poèmes
pour tous
ARBRES

A VILLAGE RESIDENCE DONE ON ENGLISH TIME

Because haste is not a typically British trait, the owner of this Elizabethan house preferred to live in it before plunging into all the restoration work that he nonetheless deemed vital. This was the only way, in his view, to make a successful renovation well in tune with the spirit of the place. The happy outcome supports this prudent theory.

OPPOSITE
In agreement with his architect Anthony Matthes, the owner Brian Godbold decided to add a small building on the garden side that now acts as greenhouse and shed. This Suffolk home has thus gained in both volume and character.

ABOVE
The master of the house has a special preference for low-ceilinged bedrooms, which guarantee intimacy. In this bedroom, the walls are covered with a classic blue-striped wallpaper (Colefax & Fowler). The twin 19th-century iron beds, picked up in a local antique shop, bring a sense of order and harmony to the room.

OPPOSITE
Everything in this bedroom is neatly matched at dignified right angles. The stately Empire bed has a bedside table from the same period. On the mahogany chest of drawers rest two fine copper oil lamps.

Suffolk, England

BELOW
Warm-hearted simplicity is the theme for this eat-in kitchen. A pleasing harmony prevails between the mellow pine furniture and the deeper tones of the earthenware dishes typical to the south of France. The master of the house evidently means to capture every last drop of warmth for this cheerful room.

OPPOSITE
A pedestal washbasin for each side of an elegant, wood-encased bathtub. To enhance the perfect symmetry of the decor, each basin has its own identical round mirror, intentionally diminutive to convey a feeling of intimacy. The armchair, covered in a muted striped fabric by Charles Hammond, and a soft-hued rug help give this room its comfortable, old-fashioned appeal.

FOLLOWING SPREAD
Hanging above the gas-fueled fireplace a pair of "forebears"—found in a secondhand store—keep stern watch over the living room, most likely approving of its very British atmosphere. A leather chesterfield is perfect for engulfing one luxuriously during long hours of reading and relaxation.

CLASSIC ROSES

PEACE AND QUIET ON A RIVERSIDE NEAR PARIS

The owners have made the very most of this large cottage-style house set alongside a riverbank. Its potential was obvious, but not without certain shortcomings. By adding extra windows, combining clear, bright colors, and marrying antique and contemporary furniture, the architect transformed this home into a lively symbol of Ile-de-France style.

OPPOSITE
On the garden side, walls were erected to create a pleasant area for relaxation, with a handsome graveled walk bisecting the close-cropped lawn. Because the façade was windowless, apertures were made to bring more light inside.

BELOW
In the inner courtyard, beneath a rebuilt roof, a large table welcomes friends who are always more than happy to make the most of this shady spot, cool even on hot summer days.

OPPOSITE
A series of low hedges designate the garden plots. In the kitchen garden, flowers and vegetables alternate inside box-hemmed rectangles. Waiting for the harvest season, old cloches and espaliered fruit trees create winningly charming scenes.

BELOW
Jars of jam, barbotine ware and a collection of antique pitchers: a pretty still life that truly transcends time.

OPPOSITE
All pink and petals, this bedroom is a celebration of feminine refinement, all the more lovely for its cozy sitting-room nook. Flowery chintz fabric, dressing table and an armchair with ruffled skirt come together with a subtle plaid-covered daybed to create an updated version of a beloved classic.

BELOW
In the hall, watering cans signify gardens—a central motif in this home. The console and pale wooden lamps were designed by the architect for the David Hicks Boutique.

AN AESTHETE'S ENCLAVE WITHIN RHAPSODIES OF GREEN

Under the Sussex sky, architect and decorator John Stefanidis cultivates his serious yet spontaneous love of gardening. His passion is such that in the space of just a few years, this modest farm has nearly vanished beneath an amazing profusion of spheres, pyramids and rectangles of green, giving his English retreat a continental flavor, half French, half Italian.

OPPOSITE
All around the house, John Stefanidis installed a series of small enclosures where flowers and shrubs extend a leafy invitation to meditate, read or just rest the eyes.

FOLLOWING SPREAD
The old stables were transformed into a large living room whose brick walls were painted matte white. The gentle lighting is the subtle result of screens filtering daylight through old windows. Here all the materials are natural, imparting an atmosphere of softness and comfort.

HINDUISM and BUDDHISM

Sussex, England

ABOVE
Over the years, trimmed hornbeam, box and yew have grown up to create dense and mysterious enclosures behind narrow painted gates. No nook in this garden has escaped the owner's magic touch.

OPPOSITE
In this cozy living room, everything harmonizes for a rose-colored view of comfort. Plain, floral and striped fabrics blend to give the room a poetic air.

OPPOSITE
Two facing stables were transformed into a wood-beamed greenhouse topped with a soaring pinnacle and housing lush, cascading vines. Here again, the space is demarcated by carefully manicured bushes and exuberant banks of roses.

FOLLOWING SPREAD
This part of the garden gives a clear glimpse of the ease with which the house seems to surrender to the voluptuous weight of blooms. John Stefanidis admits to an unbridled adoration for roses which, nonetheless, make room for stands of tentacled yellow mullein.

EARTH TONES AND FLOWERS FOR A GUEST HOUSE OF RARE DELIGHT

Surrounded by 300-year-old trees, the Norman abode that Pierre Brinon fell in love with is now a guest house in a league of its own, thanks to his keen eye and inimitable sense of hospitality. In this ample 19th-century building, constructed over the ruins of a castle, inventiveness is notable in each and every detail.

OPPOSITE
The owner's flair is not limited to decorating, his sizable kitchen puts forth fabulous feasts of his own devising. With its pink-brick walls, textured plaster ceiling and large slate floor tiles, this room makes cooking an inspired event enjoyed by one and all.

BELOW
Missing drawers in this seed cupboard were replaced by apples, which scent the entire room with the aroma of sunny orchards.

Normandy, France

OPPOSITE
The guest bedroom's high ceilings were cleverly accentuated by extending its white borders one-quarter down the wall. An unexpected stand-in for a headboard, equestrian enthusiasts will recognize a genuine saddle-rack.

BELOW
The inventiveness displayed in each nook and cranny is highlighted by the eclectic combinations that are its hallmark. Walls covered in raw linen go well with the hyacinth-blue woodwork. On an old offertory box, Pierre Brinon assembled a collection of zinc objects of all shapes and styles.

FOLLOWING SPREAD
The surprising corridor leading to the bedrooms on the second floor plays on an innovative juxtaposition of patterns, from floral to geometric. Not an experiment for the faint-hearted, but remarkably effective in its audaciousness. Brinon heightened the effect by painting all the woodwork purple.

OPPOSITE
In the dining room in the great tower of Axel Vervoordt's castle, lit by a carved wood and plaster chandelier (Jadis au Présent), the table has been set for an intimate dinner. Blue and white Chinese porcelain dishes and antique crystal glasses grace the table.

Stately Homes

OLD GRANDEUR MEETS NEW IDEAS

These are large houses—the kinds of homes where there are too many rooms to even consider using them all. And the windows are too old not to let in winter drafts, but what does it matter, since fireplaces abound, their flickering light casting deep shadows. In summer, when the hearths are cold, these same windows invite the sun inside to illuminate all the richness and grandeur enjoyed by ages past and generations to come. These handsomely proportioned homes have reassuringly thick walls. Walls that may creak and groan and echo yet always hold fast to their time-worn secrets. The history of a house does not progress at a human pace—it has its own way of changing the people who live within its graceful contours, under generous ceilings. A house with its own illustrious history is a character in its own right. Are we straying from decoration? Not as much as you might think. For decorating a home is perhaps above all an attempt to fathom the secrets of its soul.

AN ANTIQUARIAN'S RICH ABODE

In the Antwerp castle owned by Axel Vervoordt, the famous Belgian antiques dealer, all styles and all periods are welcome, provided that this man of taste has himself chosen the furniture and objects. Each piece is hand-picked and invites reminiscences from every corner of the world. The only criterion is an object's singular aspect, its grace and its rarity. And if the sales he organizes twice a year give him a chance to change decors, his fondness for eclecticism remains unperturbed, whatever is happening around him.

OPPOSITE
The magnificently proportioned swimming pool is fitted with an overflow system that allows the water to drain off at ground level over a wide border of large blue flagstones. The orangery windows were painted in bluish hues, no doubt to compensate for uncertain Belgian skies.

OPPOSITE
A beautifully preserved old tile floor and rustic country furniture adds up to a relaxed look for the guest-house kitchen, contrasting nicely with the more formal elegance of the main house. Impromptu family meals and dinners with close friends are served in this spacious room adjoining the orangery—much to the delight of all.

OPPOSITE
The far end of the orangery faces one of the estate's monumental gates while its front windows allow an unobstructed view of the swimming pool. An old red brick floor, wicker furniture from southeast Asia, and a profusion of plants all contribute to the light yet opulent atmosphere of the place.

ABOVE
Softly lit by the morning light, the small guest room is decorated with a majestic neoclassical Italian four-poster bed. Perfectly matching the colors of the walls, the Chinese vase fitted as a lamp sits on a painted Louis XVI console table.

OPPOSITE
From this corner of the orangery one can see the pool and the pool house. Arbors and trim lawns mark the careful upkeep of the 65-acre grounds.

OPPOSITE
Axel Vervoordt is famous for the variety (and rarity) of his collections. In this living room, whose walls were covered in whitewash mixed with iron oxide, precious ivory objects (Ming dynasty) decorate the corner of a coffee table made of bamboo matting (table designed by Axel Vervoordt). Behind a white-cotton slipcovered sofa, a collection of Sukhothai pottery.

AN OLD STONE FARM-HOUSE BECOMES A CHEERFUL FAMILY HOME

Both the main house and the former outbuildings of this 17th-century farm were restored by Yves Taralon to accommodate family and friends. Today it is a domicile at once open to all yet still fiercely respectful of its guests' privacy.

OPPOSITE
Set apart from the main house is a delightful little garden lodge, in the tradition of the potting shed or summer house. All around it a small garden designed by Alain Charles combines exotic grasses, herbs and flowers, mainly in pink.

BELOW
Yves Taralon turned what used to be a large square farmyard into a topiary garden. To do this the existing ground had to be carted away and good loam added. Box hedges and grass were planted to form an old 17th-century design. All around it, a gravel drive provides access to all the different buildings now transformed into living quarters.

OPPOSITE
The master bedroom opts for a warm, sophisticated atmosphere. A four-poster bed is framed by wine-colored curtains with thin stripes (Boussac) to match the bedding. The whites on the mantelpiece offset an eclectic collection of large plaster vases and a Roman style bust.

ABOVE
This huge yet comfortable living room-cum-library was installed in the attic.
There is no discord between the Louis XVI bed and a modern white-slipcovered sofa. The stairs leading to the upper level and the wrought-iron railings were made by a craftsman in Angers. Bookshelves of fir wood planks dramatically fill the entire wall up to the ceiling.

ABOVE
Upstairs, in a large painted cupboard with recycled wire-mesh doors, a collection of white earthenware has replaced rare books. The snug intimacy of this room makes it a very pleasant place for tea, and it is not unusual to find any one of several family members taking refuge up here to work or daydream.

OPPOSITE
A love of horses is apparent in the entrance hall, a vast room also used now and then for large mealtime gatherings. The blond softness of the formidable beech table by Carlos Scarpa (Forum Diffusion) is augmented by the Touraine light. Equestrian prints mounted in modern frames complete the theme and offset the neutral hues of the walls.

ABOVE
Situated between Toulouse and Carcassonne, the house combines a two-tone color scheme of blue and pink brightens its aspect whatever the season. The 19th-century winter garden invites sunshine all-year round.

OPPOSITE
Palms, clipped honeysuckle (Lonicera nitida) and lavender create an elegant cluster of greenery in front of the glass-paned winter garden.

AN ARTIST'S HOUSE NEAR TOULOUSE

To renovate this castle-sized villa, the painter Fabienne Villacreces gave full vent to her vivid imagination, unhesitatingly working wood, iron and zinc to create a home to match her dreams. The result conveys generosity and inventiveness, attesting to the owner's tremendous creativity and love of life.

FOLLOWING SPREAD
In the veranda, the antique garden furniture seems to have been there forever, between the yellow dazzle of an Abutilon Chinese lantern plant and a bright pink bougainvillea. An 18th-century Korean cupboard is a perfect addition to Géraldine Perrier-Dovon's textiles made specially for Fabienne Villacreces.

ABOVE
Comfort and light are the hallmarks of these two bathrooms. The high-ceilinged airiness of the upper bathroom contrasts with the artist's garret feel of the lower one. The modern tub in the smaller bathroom was designed by Philippe Starck and makes a perfect twosome with the glass cabinet, once owned by an early 20th-century dentist.

OPPOSITE
Cream walls, an old tiled floor and ultra-classical furnishings for the dining room. The repatinated draper's cupboard, converted into a buffet, houses its share of beautiful plates, old glasses and homemade jams. Around the table with its organdy cloth, a pretty set of 19th-century chairs.

A MAGICAL "PORT OF CALL" IN THE AUBRAC

In this erstwhile hotel set in the very heart of the Auvergne, the designer of the Tartine et Chocolat line of clothes set up a home filled with great ideas and true panache. Her goal? To create a generous and slightly crazy place to entertain in style. A habitat that, like its owner, is singularly difficult to tear yourself away from.

OPPOSITE
In the bathroom of the Crystal Room, twin tubs are set into a pile of volcanic rocks—ideal for two people to have a bath together without getting in each other's way. And the "outdoor" ambiance is sure to refresh.

BELOW
Under the inspired guidance of Catherine Painvin, the Aubrac Annex, a large and somewhat stern-looking house built with volcanic stone, was transformed into a magical hideaway so jaded visitors can leave charmed and renewed.

ABOVE
Nomadic souls are delighted when they come to rest in the Alexander Room, also known as the Traveler's Room, a handsome bedroom where one may find old pairs of skis nuzzling up to photos of elephants and fishing gear.

OPPOSITE
This flawless bedroom seems like the perfect place for falling in love all over again. White-silk sheets, curtains and a quilted bedspread (all made in Nepal) make for smooth nights and sunny awakenings.

FOLLOWING SPREAD

Between Auvergne and the Orient, the main living room mixes styles and makes colors come alive. On the parquet floors Afghan rugs add a vibrant splash of color, flannel-clad cushions gird low tables, while combination wool-and-cashmere curtains adorn the windows. On the far wall, shelves were improvised with cinder blocks and old doors.

A FORETASTE OF ETERNITY

The Gers is said to be the region of Europe where people live the longest. When Anne Gayet, a former Parisian antiques dealer set to work on the remains of a tumbledown post house left to a century of rack and ruin, she didn't just import the spirit of Gustavian style into the bucolic calm of these southerly climes, she quite simply succeeded in giving eternity a color.

OPPOSITE
The imposing building stands amid pines, turned golden in the evening light. Low walls encircling the house shelter several gardens planted with palm, olives and roses.

PRECEDING SPREAD, LEFT
In the hall, on beautiful square red tiles, the sideboard was left just as it was. The hefty chestnut staircase is also an original.

PRECEDING SPREAD, RIGHT
The azure-blue softness of the Gustavian style recurs in this large room where a c.1900 pool table takes pride of place. An old pharmacy wall unit serves as bookshelves.

OPPOSITE
Anne Gayet has a taste for beautiful materials and knows better than most how to play with the gentle harmonies of complicated color schemes. In the summer lounge, in front of a Regency fireplace, comfortable sofas (Maison de famille) and a coffee table (Flamant) were designed for convivial moments. In the foreground, a Directoire gaming table and a Louis XV chair.

OPPOSITE
All the floors in the house are outstandingly beautiful. The dining room is designed in the same tranquil spirit as the rest of the house. Beneath a late 19th-century bronze-and-crystal chandelier, the dining table is covered with a quilted cloth (Blanc d'Ivoire).

ABOVE
Looking out onto the swimming pool through elegant French windows, the summer living room is an ideal spot for savoring a cool moment. The Gustavian table and bench seat were two great finds in L'Isle-sur-la-Sorgue.

ABOVE

A stunning collection of silver-gilded mirrors brings a touch of opulence to balance the more rustic wood touches. Beneath a 17th-century pier glass, a handsome set of English terra-cotta terrines.

OPPOSITE

In one of the upstairs bedrooms, four late 19th-century chromatographs compare their faded hues. The obelisk doubling as a lamp base comes from L'Isle-sur-la-Sorgue (Quai des Lampes).

A FRENCH-STYLE RETREAT AT NEW YORK CITY'S DOORSTEP

The metamorphosis of these former stables into a small, delightful home reflects the vision of two interior designers who bring very contemporary sensibilities to their design without compromising their natural fondness for French style. All this with a good dose of daring, too.

OPPOSITE
Situated on the edge of a Connecticut forest, this retreat makes a wonderful weekend hideaway for Stephen Sills and his partner James Huniford. At ground level, a large living room and study share virtually the entire floor. Beneath the shingle roof, three bedrooms offer a lovely view over the surrounding trees.

TOP
The unusual gilded four-poster bed, covered in calico with an 18th-century paisley design becomes an almost sculptural centerpiece and offers the gilded motif echoed throughout the room.

BELOW
In the vestibule, two starfish mounted in hexagonal frames complement a shell-shaped ceiling light in white plaster. The naturalist theme extends to the cobbled floor in the form of three plumes of aloe, made of zinc, "sprouting" beneath the English table, which displays a Chinese design in the fashion of the early 19th century.

TOP
Shades of gray and white were used in this bedroom to create a soft and restful atmosphere. In front of the window, a small desk offers a view into the lush forest just outside.

BELOW
Rough white-marble paving stones cover the floor of the main room which opens straight onto the grounds through French doors. The decor here is wonderfully eclectic as illustrated by the Hiquely sculptures set between two pink-marble columns from Siena, Italy.

OPPOSITE
The unusual cobbled main floor is reminiscent of a winter garden. With an eye to symmetry, a second bull's-eye window was fitted to the left of the fireplace, where an 18th-century zinc aloe graces the mantelpiece. The same white-cotton slipcovers were used for both the Gustavian chairs and Regency sofas. The pedestal lamps are by Jean-Michel Frank.

OPPOSITE
The core of the house is formed by a huge 20-foot-high cylinder with large, cambered glass windows that look out over seven acres of awe-inspiring grounds. At the back, a small bridge seems to anchor the ship to shore.

Contemporary Style

LIVING WELL IN THE PRESENT

People who choose contemporary homes in the country may still harbor a soft spot for the lean, stark angles of the city, yet no other style brings one closer to nature, with plenty of windows for pure light, air and open space. If their glass-and-steel dwellings conjure up cathedrals of futuristic worship more than they do quaint little cottages, it is quite simply because this transparency, this openness, seems to them the best way of communing with the natural world that surrounds them. Following the sun's course across the sky, watching the wind toss the leaves, or dreaming under a canopy of blue are all pastimes made easy by spare unencumbered forms. To minimize the boundaries between inside and out and to bring in maximum light, these rural homeowners not only give shape to their modern aesthetic but boldly put forth a whole new notion of country living. When modernity meets the countryside, the result is unforgettable.

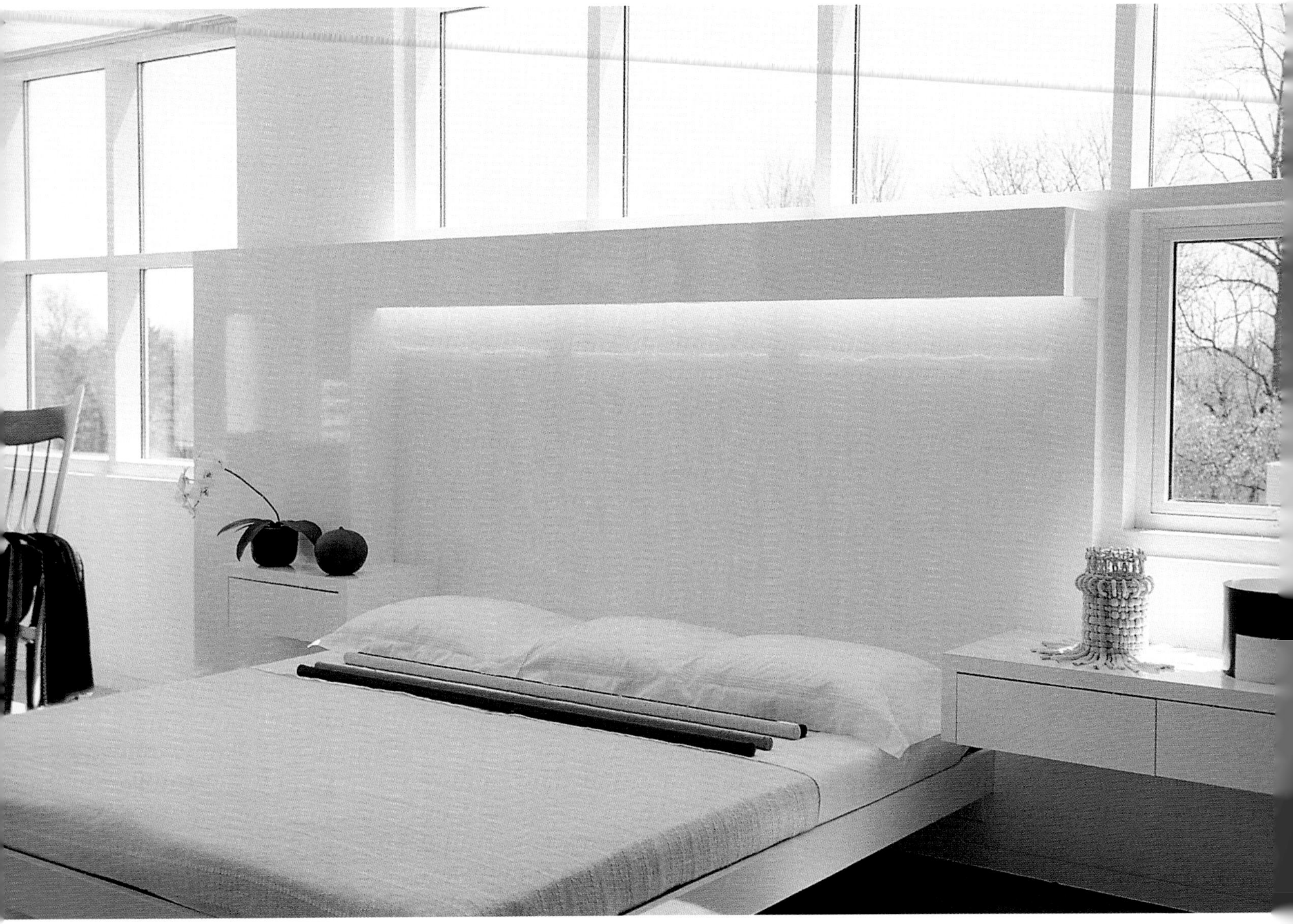

A HOUSE OF LIGHT

This house, built for a childhood friend by renowned architect Richard Meier, recalls the prow of a ship gallantly traversing one of the loveliest landscapes New Jersey has to offer. Designed to bring light to each and every corner, this structure matches magnificence with grandeur.

OPPOSITE
Austere without being monastic, the simplicity of this immaculate bedroom adds up to pure elegance. Between a Sam Maloof armchair and a Toshiko Takaezu sculpture, a single orchid becomes a work of art.

ABOVE
The kitchen is both luminous and functional. Its handsome proportions make for an even distribution of storage and appliances with room left over for colorful touches. The slightest ray of sunshine is enough to illumine the large terrace that functions as an extension of the kitchen.

New Jersey, U.S.

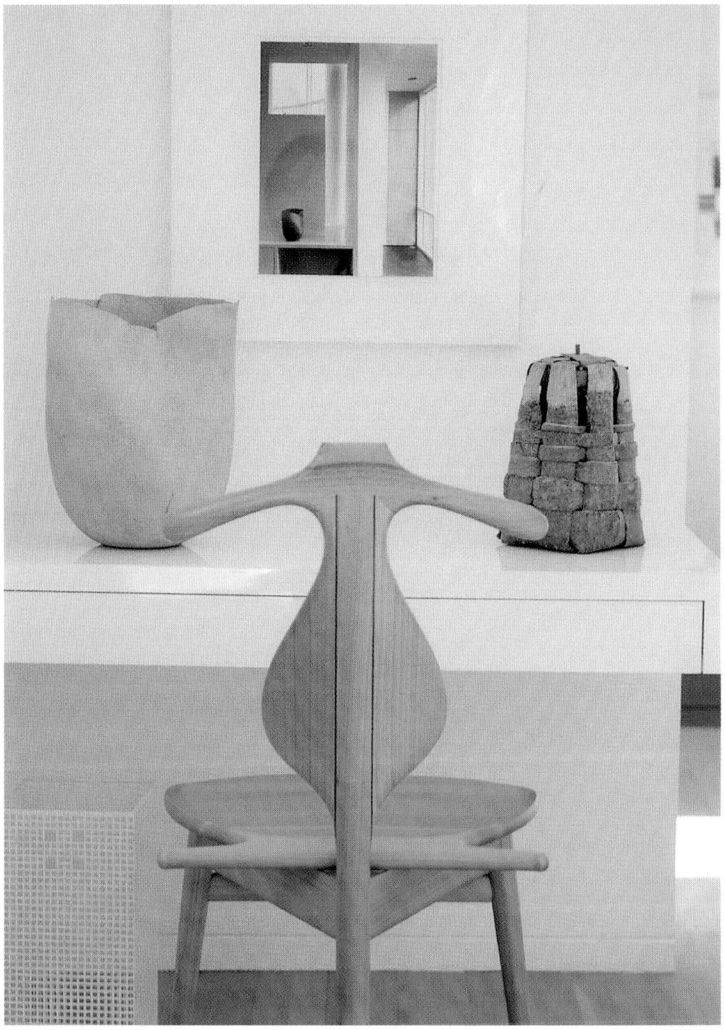

TOP, LEFT
Ceramic pyramid sculptures by William Wyman.

BOTTOM, LEFT
Within this thoroughly transparent construction, careful consideration went into the choice of each ornament. In this house, furniture and objects seem connected by mysterious bonds as powerful as they are invisible. Here, a Hans Wegner valet chair, a Dorothy Gill Barnes basket and a Scott Frances photograph.

TOP, RIGHT
With its cylinders and cubes, the design produced by Richard Meier for these door handles echoes his overall design.

BOTTOM, RIGHT
To reinforce the sense of continuous contact with the surrounding countryside, the architect designed this bathroom to open out onto the woods. The guiding principle of the house is to bring the outside closer for a sense of harmony with the world. The whiteness of the walls and materials, glass and mirrors, emanates the same purity that begins in the bedroom. The collection of pots is by Toshiko Takaezu.

TRANSPARENCY ON A LARGE SCALE

Designed by architect Thomas Phifer, in collaboration with Muriel Brandolini, this impressive "machine for living" is home to a family passionate about the natural world. Located near New York City, in the Hudson River Valley, this glass-and-steel construction offers a 360-degree view over fields of oak and maple forests that blaze with color each fall.

OPPOSITE
Suspended between earth and sky, the house creates a feeling of total symbiosis with the elements. Constantly changing, depending on the time of day and the season, the light here is an architectural component in its own right.

BELOW
The soaring ceilings of the living room are balanced by substantial large-scale furniture. Two sofas covered with Lulu DK's Icon linen and cotton fabric and a Floating Drinks cocktail table designed by Albrizzi succeed brilliantly; the rug is by A.M. Collections.

Upstate New York, U.S.

OPPOSITE
Over a two-year construction period, plans were constantly evolving. What was originally conceived of as a T-shape structure eventually grew into an H. This transformation was crucial for incorporating a screening room, a large office, fitness room and an indoor pool. An outdoor pool, built on the east side of the structure, is encircled by granite paving stones that interact with the lawn to create large geometric patterns. The house retains its human proportions since one cannot see the entire structure from any given angle.

ABOVE, LEFT AND RIGHT
The kitchen features stainless-steel cabinetry; the wood floor and furniture lend warmth to the space and underscore its connection with the outside. The Martin Szekely table in birch plywood with attached benches, from Galerie Kreo, is installed like a sculpture in the breakfast room.

ABOVE

The guest room offers sweeping views of the valley. The carpet, a grid of colored squares, was designed by Muriel Brandolini and makes the room both welcoming and cheerful. The Duplex brushed-steel floor lamp and W armchairs are by Andrée Putman for Ecart International.

OPPOSITE

More often than not, Muriel Brandolini works in an intuitive way. Here, she set about bringing the media room to life by using bright colors and furniture with round, generous shapes. In the screening room, Lloyd Schwan bookshelves and chaises longues by Pierre Charpin from Galerie Kreo.

NEW YORK

AN OLD STONE MILL BECOMES A CATHEDRAL OF GLASS

So as not to betray the spirit of an old mill, which was little more than a ruin, architect Jean-Paul Bonnemaison designed two very different façades. On the village side, stone walls match the church tower, while the other all-glass façade offers unobstructed views of Mont Ventoux and its snow-capped peaks.

OPPOSITE
This house has two distinct parts, one running along a village street and the other, higher side following the contours of the sloping ground. Interspersed with glass-paned walls, natural light pours in through all four living levels throughout the day.

FOLLOWING SPREAD
The interior furnishings were inspired both by Cistercian relics—with nearby Sénanque Abbey providing a magnificent example—and minimalist art. White, a symbol of purity, softens and unifies all the levels. The corner kitchen was installed beneath a wide arch.

AN ORIENTAL OASIS IN BORDEAUX

Two young travelers enthralled with Asia and the lifestyle of the Far East, were keen on reinterpreting an 18th-century Bordeaux mansion by imbuing it with an exotic mystique. The self-taught interior decorator Joanne de Lépinay, crazy about Vietnam and Indonesia, has thoroughly succeeded in meeting her desire for refinement with the flavor of faraway lands.

OPPOSITE
A definite change of scenery in the garden, where the gray cement pool reflects yucca, papyrus and bamboo. The feeling of stability and balance is enhanced by four large ceramic pots (Du Bout du Monde) and the symmetry of the plant beds in front of the stone windbreak.

BELOW
The box bushes atop large zinc pots (Domani) are periodically pruned in rounded contours. On the recliners, fabric from Djakarta.

PRECEDING SPREAD, LEFT
In the bedroom, oriental refinement and French elegance co-exist on the best of terms. Behind silk curtains (Jim Thompson), bamboo blinds conjure up Asia. The graceful Fortuny hanging lamps perfectly embody the play between opulent and spare.

PRECEDING SPREAD, RIGHT
In keeping with the house's general theme, the bathroom was rendered in soothing tones. The fittings are in Combrebrune stone from Gironde with a black-granite border.

OPPOSITE
The soft light in the living room is created by translucent blinds over each window, with the added purpose of insulating the room from the street. Most of the objects here have the Far East as their common motif. Framing the fireplace, surmounted by a large wheel on a stand (Asiatides), two elegant Thai urns symbolize perfection.

ON A FRENCH HILLSIDE LUXURY JAPAN-STYLE

The owner of this enchanting house brings his knowledge of the martial arts and meditation into play with his love of North American wood-frame houses. The two came together in the most congenial manner possible in this stunning yet modest home perched on a quiet, wooded hillside against a backdrop of the peaceful Le Perche region of northwest France.

OPPOSITE

Life is lived here Japanese-style. Meals are served at floor level on a cleverly conceived table with sliding leaves (Galerie Sentou). Parisian architect Sonia Cortese opted for an almost total absence of solid walls between rooms.

ABOVE

The bedroom aspires to achieve a Zen-like attitude. On the floor, rice-straw matting invites bare feet. Ottoman (Forum Diffusion), bamboo and paper lamp (Bô). The damask bedspread is from Caravane.

Le Perche, France

OPPOSITE
From the first designs to the last finishing touches, everything here grew out of the desire to blend with nature. Its beguiling simplicity was attained only with the utmost attention to the smallest of details. In summer, wide eaves protect the house inside from overheating in the ample sunlight.

FOLLOWING SPREAD, LEFT
Wood is the essential element here, its pliant warmth soothes and harmonizes. From the kitchen, a fine view over the Le Perche countryside.

FOLLOWING SPREAD, RIGHT
To heighten the impression of continuity between rooms, the walls never reach full ceiling height and always give way to glass or round apertures.

OPPOSITE
The living room and dining area adjoin the dojo, a small room dedicated to spiritual practices. Radiators are built into the floor and the masonry was designed to store heat during the day and release it at night. In such a minutely conceived structure, one can abandon oneself to the silence stretched out on the raised chaise longue by Christian Ghion (Forum Diffusion).

A RURAL REFUGE FOR TWO DIE-HARD NEW YORKERS

In this distinctly modern house, a museum director and her philosopher husband indulged all of their cherished notions for an ideal second home. The result is a streamlined place diametrically opposed to the let-your-hair down version of the usual country house. Here, the urban look blends seamlessly with the landscape and the functionality associated with city life gives way to an airy and relaxed (and completely elegant) simplicity.

OPPOSITE
The two-bedroom guest house is connected to the main house by a breezeway. A cleverly designed sloping roof dispenses with obtrusive gutters, while allowing rain water to be channeled to a pond at the bottom of the garden.

ABOVE
The ultra-functional master bathroom is floor-to-ceiling white, including flowers and furniture. The floor is paved in glass-mosaic ticle; chrome accents complete the look.

OPPOSITE
When architect Ali C. Hocek embarked on this project, he was well aware that his clients were city people, firmly rooted in a spare urban aesthetic. This greatly influenced his design of the single-level house. A Monica Armani table from Moss on the deck.

FOLLOWING SPREAD
Inside, most of the color comes by way of the artwork, all contemporary, and an integral part of the decor. A painting by Herman Cherry spans the far wall, the painting above the fireplace is by Charles Parness. The living area's sofas and lounge chair are by Poltrona Frau. Saarinen Executive chairs encircle a Mario Bellini table from Cassina.

OPPOSITE
Juan Montoya added a balcony and terrace to the preexisting sturdy granite house. As soon as fine weather arrives, it is here that Montoya spends his favorite moments, relaxing and reading under luxuriant shade trees.

Cabins

MAJESTY AMONG THE TREES

Cabins are some of the most elemental of structures. In any wooded area where mature trees are plentiful, homes hewn of wood have existed in some form throughout recorded history. Perhaps more than any other lodgings, these country dwellers are marked by their inherent relation to the elements, and as a result they harmonize to a far greater degree with the landscape from which they come. Wood, stone, metal and earth all collaborate to form homes of surprising warmth and stature. No longer simply rustic bumpkins, these sophisticated cousins to the old-fashioned cabin boast some of the more innovative techniques of home design, created by people who care about the quality of (and proximity to) the earth around them.

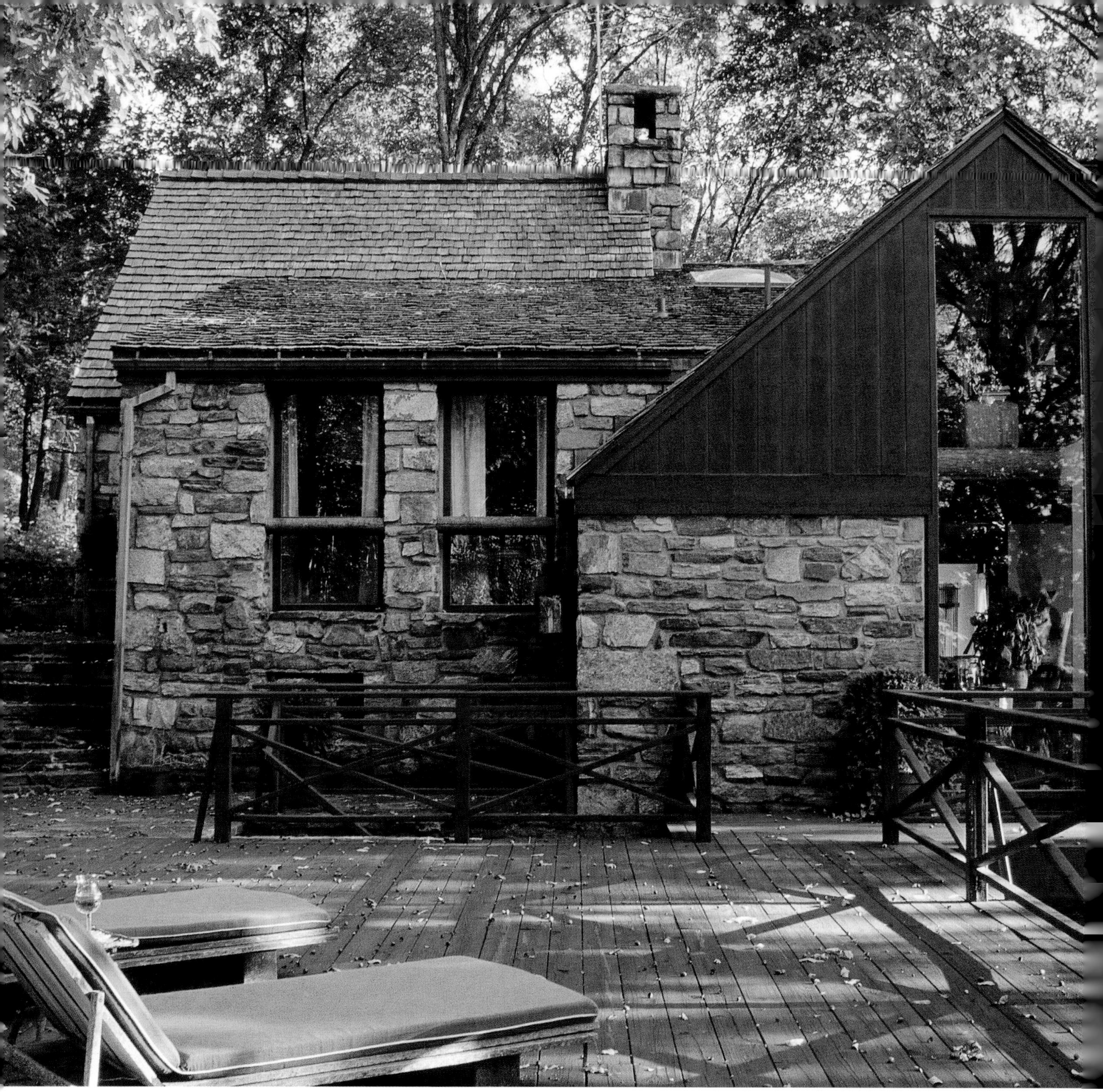

A DREAM HOUSE IN WOOD AND STONE

Decorator Juan Montoya unearthed a forlorn house deep in a forest near the Hudson River, a stone's throw from New York City. From that moment, he knew what he had to do. After major refurbishing work, which gave him a chance to redesign each and every room, the lonely house on the river turned into a wonderful secret retreat, full of books, paintings and antiques—all the trappings of a life well lived.

OPPOSITE AND BELOW
When Montoya discovered this house, it belonged to a hippie community that had constructed its own insular world on the 120-acre grounds. The fittings combine the use of wood, granite and glass, all local materials that help create a total harmony with the forest.

ABOVE

Books are the great passion of the master of this house. The armchairs in front of the desk designed by Montoya himself are from England and Holland.

An unusual collection of metal and gilded bronze objects go very well with the old flagstone floor and add a muscular character to the dining room. But pride of place goes to the lustrous dark-wood table, a country classic whose simple lines nevertheless impart elegance.

ABOVE
A 19th-century Florentine painting greets visitors in the hall. Near the sofa, also Italian of the same period, a small mahogany chair from Ireland holds interesting books.

On the shawl-covered 19th-century table, a miscellany of curious objects have many different origins. Whether brought back from travels or bought at yard sales, they create a very cozy atmosphere among books and candles.

FOLLOWING SPREAD
The furniture and lamps in the bedroom were all designed by Juan Montoya. The bamboo wall coverings bring an Eastern flair. An unusual large model sailboat evokes all the travels that helped create the wonderful eclecticism that is a signature of this house.

Upstate New York, U.S.

BELOW
In the well-equipped kitchen, natural materials are given primacy. Slate was used to cover both the floor and the birch-wood work surface. The ceilings of both the dining room and kitchen are made of bamboo.

OPPOSITE
While the black bathroom tiles add a little urban touch, the view over the woods leaves no doubt that you are in the country. A French vase from the 1920s stands out between stainless-steel basins.

BETWEEN LAKE AND FOREST, A PICTURE-PERFECT VIEW

It took no time at all for this matchless view across the wide expanse of Candlewood Lake, in Connecticut, to win over John Frieda, hairdresser to the stars. But the interior of the house wasn't at all to his liking. No matter, interior decorator Sharon Simonaire took things in hand, retaining just the skeleton of the house and, refurbishing all of the rooms.

OPPOSITE
Breakfast, a hallowed moment for city dwellers in the country, is taken on the pier, surveying the majestic sight of trees ablaze with color as Indian summer approaches.

BELOW
The many French windows on the all-wood façade guarantee complete communion with nature.

ABOVE

A loft-style kitchen opens onto the dining room and the living room with a wide walnut buffet that makes a fine serving area. Generous French windows lend the room a bright and friendly feel.

OPPOSITE

Exposed stonework and varnished wood bring a very cozy atmosphere to the living room, but a splash of color was needed to warm things up. A footrest covered in blue flannel seemed to fit the bill just right.

FOLLOWING SPREAD
John's bedroom is the largest in the house, and enjoys a 180-degree view of the property. His preference for blond and natural hues is evident in his choices for furnishings and bedding. The chest of drawers is flanked by a pair of leather and canvas bush chairs. At the foot of the bed, an old chest stands on a wide mat made of sea rushes.

THE LAKE HOUSE

New York publishing executive David Steinberger returned to his childhood summer home when he reclaimed this wood shingle house complete with stunning views over lake and woods. His wife, Dara Caponigro, an editor and designer, tackled the decoration. Her aim: inject the place with a feeling of modernity without trespassing on the cozy spirit dear to David's heart.

OPPOSITE
In warm, fine weather, much time is wiled away on the porch, where a view over the lake provides a refreshing change of scenery. The table and chairs are vintage Richard Schultz designs for Knoll. Dara Caponigro gave a place of honor to a 1960s molded-plastic armchair that came from her childhood home.

BELOW
With her preference for muted colors, Caponigro chose whites, grays and beiges for the indoor decoration. In the dining area, the Alzaia light is by Fontana Arte.

OPPOSITE
The floor and ceiling of the sunsplashed master bedroom are painted white. With a nod to the surrounding woodland, the ottomans are covered in a delicate fern-motif fabric by Old World Weavers.

FOLLOWING SPREAD
The large fireplace lets the family make the most of its lovely "cabin," summer and winter alike. Each season provides plenty of branches and flowers to complement the natural tones of the decor. The living room features a Cannes sofa by Crate & Barrel and a wicker ottoman by Bielecky Bros.

MODERN VARIATIONS IN NORMANDY

It began with the purchase of a typical Normandy cottage in the heart of the Auge region. But as the family grew, attempts to fit into the little house were in vain. Finally everyone agreed to build a modern all-wood dwelling in the style of Canadian far north. The cows still haven't got over it...

OPPOSITE
The earth tones of the kitchen-dining room, painted in shades of sienna and red ocher, lend it year-round warmth. The fireplace has been raised so the flames can be seen (and felt) at mealtimes.

BELOW
The wooden shutters open to give the guest bathroom a view to the front yard. Unique inside shutters can be closed for privacy.

ABOVE AND OPPOSITE
The house was designed by architect Gérard Colard and built in six months by local craftsmen. It resembles a self-contained hamlet made up of interlocking cells. To the north, the shingle roof extends very low toward the ground, keeping the house snug and warm in cold weather. Depending on its exposure, red cedar will fade gracefully as it ages, in shades varying from pale russet to dark gray.

FOLLOWING SPREAD
Originally built to minimize trips to the seaside, the pool is just about everyone's favorite room. Interior designer Martine Dufour had the bright idea of covering it with an industrial greenhouse to keep it light and airy while protecting it from the elements. The indoor temperature is adjusted automatically according to the outdoor conditions.

RE-CREATING NEW ENGLAND IN THE OLD WORLD

Faithful to the austere and symmetrical architectural spirit so prevalent on the East Coast of the United States, this ultra-functional house in the Brabant-Walloon region of Belgium was built in record time. Perfectly balanced forms and an abundance of indoor light are the main features of this structure with its combination of pine, cedar and oak.

OPPOSITE
Architects Pierre Hoet and Jean Massa make no secret of their admiration for New England homes. With a 65-foot-long veranda running the length of the façade, you would hardly think you were in the Belgian countryside. The roof of flat slate tiles look amazingly like shingles, a favorite roofing material on the other side of the Atlantic.

Brabant-Walloon, Belgium

BELOW
The wondrously bright dining room makes no excuses when it comes to whiteness. The Pausa seats (Flexform) and the glass-fronted Piroscafo cupboard (Molteni) stand on a bleached oak-parquet floor.

The same simplicity extends to the bedroom. Between the wall lights (Manufactor), a row of family photos. All the windows in the house are sash windows, New England-style.

OPPOSITE
Architect Pierre Hoet made the fireplace and coffee table himself, around which simple sofas (Padova) create a convivial atmosphere. The beautiful windows allow the natural surroundings to become an integral part of the decor.

FOLLOWING SPREAD
The huge kitchen is every bit a match for those spacious American kitchens. Planned for informal meals, it has all the functional features which make you want to roll up your sleeves and start cooking. Around the table lit by a Naviglio ceiling light, the upholstered Mixer seats (Flexform) are the only splash of color in the room.

OPPOSITE
Set in the midst of vineyards, Agnès Comar's house comes into view at the end of a drive lined by impressive plane trees. Depending on the time of day, the whitewashed walls reveal contrasting hues with ocher predominating.

Mediterranean Style

DECORATION WITH SOUTHERN ACCENTS

To escape the unrelenting gray of northern Europe, some people have opted for the south and its warm, sunny mornings. Living outdoors, forgetting all about rain, daydreaming by a pool amid lavender and rosemary, dining with friends beneath the arbor: who can resist the lure of these images of endless vacations? Leaving Normandy and Brittany to people who like changing skies, those whose eyes only truly come alive when they get south of the Loire don't do things by halves when it comes to creating their fantasy home in settings just this side of paradise. So many brightly colored regions in southern France full of homes with an infinite variety of styles—from farmhouses nestling beneath cypress trees or lost amid vines and olive boughs, to majestic villas exuding patrician exclusivity—each home celebrates a dolce vita with the sun as its witness.

AT HOME WITH FASHION DESIGNER AGNĒS COMAR

Agnès Comar has set up home in the Lubéron region of France in an old "tawery," a place where tallow for candles was once whitened. Dating from the 18th century, this noble dwelling favors light atmospheres for all its rooms, which are at once both simple and sophisticated.

OPPOSITE
Virginia creeper spreads over an arbor creating a sun-dappled shade, even at high noon. The setting is particularly pleasant and everyone enjoys this cool nook, be it over lunch or as the perfect spot to indulge in a long, quiet siesta.

ABOVE
In the middle of the kitchen-dining room, with its pale yellow walls, the centerpiece is a beautiful Bordeaux table (designed by Anne-Cécile Comar) surrounded by chairs that were stripped and repainted in country white.

The bathroom sinks and the surfaces surrounding the bathtub were created with "shrimp-pink" cement, a color that goes well with the fennel-green walls. The curtains are in light cotton terry. The kindly gaze of the caryatid, designed by Michel Biehn, surveys these rooms all dedicated to its inhabitants' well-being.

OPPOSITE
The bedroom is a celebration of white: a white four-poster bed, designed by Agnès Comar in painted beech wood; white bed linens, white bedspread trimmed with fennel-colored braid and white curtains in organdy. All add up to a sophisticated and peaceful refuge.

ALAÏA ETE 1992

COLOR FIRST AND FOREMOST...

Throughout their professional lives — one devoted to fashion, the other to film — Irène and Giorgio Silvagni have had a thousand and one opportunities to express their artistic temperaments and creative fantasies. A Bohemian spirit fills their Provençal farmhouse, a "ruin for sale" that had not been lived in for a hundred years, but which captured their hearts the moment they saw it.

OPPOSITE
A keen admirer of the Villa Medici, Giorgio painted the interiors himself, mixing pigments as the spirit moved him, or as the room's exposure dictated. The dark-hued wood of the Thonet chairs at the foot of the homemade bed bring an elegant contrast to the Matisse-blue walls.

OPPOSITE
It is hard to believe this garden was abandoned for so long. Olives, palms and various fruit trees have been planted around the pool nicknamed "The Unkind Pond" (La Désobligeante) because of its narrowness, best suited for solitary swims. In the height of summer, all this foliage guarantees a welcome coolness.

BELOW
Set amid prolific greenery, the farm partakes in a kind of hide-and-seek game of light and shade. The shutters were painted blue, a tribute to the blue of sea and sky.

FOLLOWING SPREAD
The antique curtains in the dining room beautifully complement the Roussillon ocher of the walls, while a quilted Provençal cloth brightens the table. On winter evenings, the candles in the candelabra and the lamps bring a romantic touch to dinner.

PIERRE BERGÉ'S PARADISE FOUND

Pierre Bergé discovered the village house of his dreams in Saint-Rémy-de-Provence where the inhabitants have remained true to their roots. Out of this 18th-century country home, with the talent for which he is well known, Bergé created a quiet refuge where he can surround himself with friends. Well removed from the hubbub of Paris, he comes here as often as possible to find new inspiration.

OPPOSITE
All around the ocher-stained pool house, large jardinières with olive trees cast their silvery reflection on the surface of the water. On either side of the pool, lined with lavender and cypress, recliners and parasols (Le Cèdre Rouge) beckon guests for an afternoon of pure relaxation. Instant magic.

OPPOSITE
Forming a double hedge along the walk linking the garden to the pool, hibiscus plants in terra-cotta pots provide a stunning display of flowers all summer long. For the patio, old flagstones and fine gravel.

BELOW
Even if Pierre Bergé had a pretty clear idea of what he wanted, he could not have done without the valuable help of landscape gardener Michel Semini and architect Hugues Bosc. Apart from the Chinese mulberry tree (on the right), that was there from the start, all the trees were planted as adult specimens to create the impression of an old garden.

OPPOSITE
The bedroom floor tiles (Didier Gruel) were cleverly laid to resemble a carpet. A painted metal bed (Estelle Garcin) and old wicker armchair (Xavier Nicod, L'Isle-sur-la-Sorgue) are in the same muted pastel tones. In the corridor, the star-shaped ceiling light made of painted paper was designed by Tom Dixon.

A DREAM HOUSE ON THE RIVER'S EDGE

A house as only children draw them: square, thoroughly symmetrical, with a door in the center, windows in neat lines, and a steep sloping roof. The day painter Bernard Dufour and his wife, interior designer Martine Dufour, glimpsed this house's silhouette in the midst of its luxuriant trees and gardens, they were both head over heels. Like a dream long nurtured, theirs finally came true on the banks of the Lot.

ABOVE

Siestas are oh so sweet in this "Miss Eliett" 19th-century beach chair made of Rubelli fabric and the imagination flows freely. A perfect spot for an artist nurturing new ideas.

OPPOSITE

The house, with its splendid roof of scaled slate tiles typical of the region comes into view at the end of a double raw of pruned box hedges. Thick stone walls keep the rooms delightfully cool, even on the hottest summer days.

ABOVE
This quintessential early 19th-century home has kept its authentic feel—one could almost be transported back in time. A large walnut table, opposite the huge dining room fireplace was designed by Bernard.

OPPOSITE
The owners of this house spent plenty of time choosing colors; all the rooms were whitewashed using local pigments. The billiard room features a Charles X billiard table with lion's heads and a painting by Bernard above the mantelpiece.

FOLLOWING SPREAD
Built in 1814, the old cowshed is so roomy that it can be used to store firewood and some of the painter's supplies. The old chesterfield may seem worn out, but it still surveys the canvases with a critical eye.

BETWEEN WARM STONE AND LAVENDER

Nestled at the foot of the Lubéron range in outstanding natural surroundings, this old farmhouse has found ways, down through the centuries, of turning its weekend guests into full-time residents. It's easy to see how this magnificent setting casts a spell on all who see it.

OPPOSITE
From one year to the next outbuildings were added to the original house to create its unique stepped contours. Amid ilex, pine, cypress, bay laurel, rosemary and olive, the house is now firmly anchored in the landscape.

BELOW
Landscape gardener Michel Semini had the bold idea of setting the swimming pool among 2,000 lavender bushes inventively pruned to form globes. The garden is deliberately devoid of flowers, instead paying tribute to the dryer more durable plants that surround it.

FOLLOWING SPREAD
Painted in straw tones, the bedroom is an impressive size—a huge loft, it comfortably serves as office and TV room as well. Large terra-cotta tiles were chosen for the floor accented with rattan matting.

ЗЕМЛЯ
ЗЕМЛЯ
ВОДА

ABOVE, LEFT AND RIGHT

The winter living room was designed by Michèle Belaiche, mistress of the house, who was keen to live all year round surrounded by pine trees. On the mantelpiece, Timorese drums. On either side of the fireplace, a pair of lovely old Provençal armchairs. To hide the radiator, Michèle designed the fanned oak screen herself. Large windows offer outstanding views over the trees.

THE EMBROIDERER'S ENCHANTED CASTLE

Edith Mézard lives and works in the Château de l'Ange — Castle of the Angel — in the small village of Lumières, on the edge of the Lubéron. Behind the fine pink-ocher façade, the famous embroiderer dedicates this bewitching place to the hues and textures of Italy. Dolce vita guaranteed....

ABOVE
Contrasting shades of red give the thick walls nobility and character. The cat, doubling as sentinel, assumes its duties with light-footed grace.

OPPOSITE
A path lined with cypress trees emphasizes the architecture of the façade and lends the air of a Tuscan villa. Climbing roses frame the front door on the garden side and suffuse the rooms with an irresistible aroma.

OPPOSITE
The summer dining room leads straight out into the garden. Around the large farmhouse table are old wood-slat garden chairs, their backs and seats covered with linen cushions for all-around comfort.

ABOVE
Hues of white and beige for the small library and sitting room. A coffee table by Jacqueline Morabito, lamp by Andrée Putman, and sofa by Yves Halard covered with a striped cotton ticking.

The kitchen, where family meals are served, is one of the house's central rooms. Designed by Michel Biehn, the storage units consist of built-in wicker drawers that match the dining chairs. Pots of aromatic plants ensure a constant supply of herbs.

FOLLOWING SPREAD
In the large living room with its classical elegance, a gilded wooden arrow, a decorative feature in the room, was unearthed in Michel Biehn's shop in L'Isle-sur-la-Sorgue. His shop also provided the little 19th-century Italian chair in gilded wood pictured in the foreground. The raw linen curtains are by Robert le Héros.

ACKNOWLEDGMENTS

The homeowners, designers and architects who welcomed ELLE DECOR
for the stories seen on these pages:

Michèle Belaiche, Pierre Bergé, Jean-Paul Bonnemaison, Muriel Brandolini, Pierre Brinon, Dara Caponigro, Anthony Collett, Agnès Comar, Sonia Cortesse, Bernard Dufour, John Frieda, Anne Gayet, Brian Godbold, Sandy and Lou Grotta, Ali C. Hocek, Pierre Hoet, James Huniford, Marin Karmitz, Alexandre, Bruno and Dominique Lafourcade, Edmund Leites, Joanne de Lépinay, Jean Massa, Mr. and Mrs. Mayer, Richard Meier, Edith Mézard, Mi Casa, Juan Montoya, Catherine Painvin, Thomas Phifer, Julie Prisca, Stephen Sills, Irène and Giorgio Silvagni, Rochelle Slovin, John Stefanidis, Yves Taralon, Axel Vervoordt, Fabienne Villacreces, Andrew Zarzycki.

And all those who wish to remain anonymous.

CREDITS

PHOTOGRAPHS BY

Fernando Bengoechea: pp. 126–131. **Gilles de Chabaneix**: pp. 184–189. **Vera Cruz**: pp. 190–195. **Jérôme Darblay**: pp. 70–75. **Jacques Dirand**: pp. 154–159, 208–213. **Scott Frances**: pp. 100, 102–103. **Patrice de Grandry**: back cover, bottom right; pp. 118–125. **Marianne Haas**: back cover, top right; pp. 28–37, 64–69, 132–141, 142–147, 166–171, 172–177, 178–183, 202–207. **Jean-Luc Laloux**: back cover, bottom left; pp. 160–165. **Guillaume de Laubier**: cover; back cover, top left, center left; pp. 4, 8–13, 14–21, 22–27, 38–43, 44–55, 56–63, 86–91, 92–99, 112–117, 196–201. **Nicolas Mathéus**: pp. 108–111. **Laura Resen**: pp. 148–153. **Gilles Trillard**: pp. 75–85. **William Waldron**: pp. 101, 104–107.

STORIES PRODUCED BY

François Baudot: back cover, top right; pp. 28–37, 86–91. **Marie-Claire Blanckaert**: cover; back cover, bottom right, center left; pp. 8–13, 14–21, 22–27, 44–55, 56–63, 70–75, 76–85, 92–99, 132–141, 142–147, 166–171, 172–177, 178–183, 190–195, 196–201, 202–207. **Michael Boodro**: pp. 100–107. **Franck Descombes**: back cover, bottom left; pp. 160–165. **Geneviève Dortignac**: pp. 112–117. **Laurence Dougier**: pp. 108–111. **Marie-Claude Dumoulin**: pp. 184–189. **Armel Ferroudj-Bégou**: pp. 118–125. **Alice Hanson**: pp. 4, 38–43. **Marie Kalt**: pp. 208–213. **Jesse Kornbluth**: pp. 126–131. **Françoise Labro**: pp. 154–159. **Mitchell Owens**: pp. 148–153. **Laure Verchère**: pp. 64–69.

ELLE DECOR (U.S.) and ELLE DECORATION (France) are both imprints of the Hachette Filipacchi Media group.
The content of this book was taken from ELLE DECOR and ELLE DECORATION.

PROVENCE, ENGLISH-STYLE

Reflecting the tastes of its British owners and the talents of a trio of architects, this country home built in the 1960s has matured beautifully in tune with the seasons. A stone's throw from St. Paul-de-Vence, this country hideout offers its inhabitants an incomparable lifestyle in the midst of nature.

OPPOSITE
Like all the houses in this area, this single-level country home was built entirely of stone. The garden was created by landscape designer Jean Mus in perfect harmony with the surrounding landscape.

ABOVE, LEFT AND RIGHT
More an outdoor living room than a terrace, this peaceful terrace acts as a link between house and pool. Furnished with white canvas cushions, the stone benches are deep enough to sit back in voluptuous repose. In summer, its shade delights readers or those seeking a cool place for drinks, and when evenings turn cooler, the fireplace makes autumn a welcome time. The lamps are Indian urns with iron shades made by a local craftsman.

ABOVE
The children's room is decorated to resemble a boat's cabin or fisherman's hut. Covered with wood-plank paneling painted in sky blue, the walls give the room a warm and welcoming feeling. The bunk beds are in hazel wood.

OPPOSITE
Done up with simple good taste, the bathtub allows a clear view to the forest (and a sun-drenched bath). Clean, symmetrical forms and a palette of mostly white help maximize the space. All add up to ultimate comfort in a small space.

TIME RECOVERED BENEATH PLANE TREES

Near St. Rémy-de-Provence, a family of stone enthusiasts turned this forgotten farmhouse into a garden of Eden skillfully divided between mineral and vegetable. While father and son plunged into impressive restoration projects, landscape gardener Dominique Lafourcade created a garden in tune with the surrounding landscape.

OPPOSITE
In the shade of two venerable plane trees, this impressive 18th-century bastide farmhouse left its heyday behind when all its shutters were closed and it sank into oblivion. Nowdays, family and friends come in droves to make new memories behind its welcoming threshold.

BELOW
In front of the fountain in the herb garden, a bed hemmed by pruned box contains basil, chives, parsley and tarragon. The garden's central theme is its many shades of silvery green. As for flowers, climbing roses, wisteria and oleander, are all seen to their best advantage in this setting.

ABOVE
Painted a dove gray that is as understated as it is elegant, the kitchen is both convivial and functional. Unearthed in local bric-a-brac shops, old pottery and bottles add to its earthy charm. The table is 19th-century oak, the chairs rattan.

OPPOSITE
Auction rooms and antique shops in Avignon, Arles and Nîmes are gold mines for bargain hunters. In this well-lit bedroom, an English brass bed and prints of the Greek philosophers create a classic atmosphere that is just right.

FOLLOWING SPREAD
The eclecticism that prevails in the living room decoration shows a confident eye and a mastery of harmonies. A tabletop was made-to-measure to bring new life to a pair of old joiner's trestles. Two olive pots were ingeniously transformed into lamps. On the left, a chest from an old sacristy, once used for storing cassocks.